D1751122

Development of Verb Inflection in First Language Acquisition

Studies on Language Acquisition
21

Editor
Peter Jordens

Mouton de Gruyter
Berlin · New York

Development of Verb Inflection in First Language Acquisition

A Cross-Linguistic Perspective

edited by

Dagmar Bittner
Wolfgang U. Dressler
Marianne Kilani-Schoch

Mouton de Gruyter
Berlin · New York 2003

Mouton de Gruyter (formerly Mouton, The Hague)
is a Division of Walter de Gruyter GmbH & Co. KG, Berlin.

♾ Printed on acid-free paper which falls within the guidelines
of the ANSI to ensure permanence and durability.

Library of Congress Cataloging-in-Publication Data

> Development of verb inflection in first language acquisition : a
> cross-linguistic perspective / edited by Dagmar Bittner, Wolfgang
> U. Dressler, Marianne Kilani-Schoch.
>   p.   cm. − (Studies on language acquisition ; 21)
>   Includes bibliographical references and index.
>   ISBN 3-11-017823-0 (cloth : alk. paper)
>   1. Language acquisition.   2. Grammar, Comparative and
> general − Verb.   3. Grammar, Comparative and general −
> Inflection.   I. Bittner, Dagmar.   II. Dressler, Wolfgang U.,
> 1939−   III. Kilani-Schoch, Marianne, 1953−   IV. Series.
>   P118.D465 2003
>   401'.93−dc21
>   2003007622

ISBN 3 11 017823 0

Bibliographic information published by Die Deutsche Bibliothek

Die Deutsche Bibliothek lists this publication in the Deutsche Nationalbibliografie;
detailed bibliographic data is available in the Internet at <http://dnb.ddb.de>.

© Copyright 2003 by Walter de Gruyter GmbH & Co. KG, D-10785 Berlin.
All rights reserved, including those of translation into foreign languages. No part of this book
may be reproduced in any form or by any means, electronic or mechanical, including photocopy,
recording, or any information storage and retrieval system, without permission in writing from
the publisher.
Cover design: Sigurd Wendland, Berlin.
Printed in Germany.

Contents

Introduction Dagmar Bittner, Wolfgang U. Dressler, and Marianne Kilani-Schoch	vii
Specific terms used in common by the contributors to the present volume	xxxix
Early verb development in one Spanish-speaking child Carmen Aguirre	1
Early verbal morphology in Turkish: Emergence of inflections Ayhan Aksu-Koç and F. Nihan Ketrez	27
The emergence of verb inflection in two German-speaking children Dagmar Bittner	53
Early phases in the development of Greek verb inflection Anastasia Christofidou and Ursula Stephany	89
The early verb development and demarcation of stages in three Russian-speaking children Natalia Gagarina	131
A case study of the early acquisition of verbs in Dutch Steven Gillis	171
Early development of verbal morphology in an English-speaking child Insa Gülzow	205
Early verb development in one Croatian-speaking child Antigone Katičić	239

Early verb inflection in French: An investigation of two corpora Marianne Kilani-Schoch	269
Emergence of verb paradigms in one Austrian child Sabine Klampfer	297
Early verb development in Finnish: A preliminary approach to miniparadigms Klaus Laalo	323
Acquisition of verb morphology in Italian: A case study Sabrina Noccetti	351
Early acquisition of the verbal complex in Yucatec Maya Barbara Pfeiler	379
Early verb inflection in Lithuanian Paweł Wójcik	401
Subject index	421

Introduction

*Dagmar Bittner, Wolfgang U. Dressler, and
Marianne Kilani-Schoch*

1. Pertinent issues in recent studies on child language acquisition

Two related controversies have been hotly debated in the field of language acquisition: How do children acquire grammar? When do children acquire grammar? Positions in this ongoing discussion do not only depend on basic assumptions on the nature of grammar, of language, of acquisition, etc. but also on how emergence of grammar is identified. Does it take place with the emergence of word-class distinctions or functional elements such as function words and affixes or with the appearance of certain word-order patterns or of spontaneous use of specific constructions?

The approach of the contributions to this volume concurs with most other contemporaneous approaches in assuming that grammar comes into existence with relevant generalisations over individual words and word forms. But, again, there is controversy about when and how we may identify generalisations in a child's linguistic output. Probably all models of acquisition take for granted that acquisition starts with item-based learning.[1] The transition from such item-based rote learning to pattern- or rule-based learning is then generally connected to the accumulation of some critical mass of relevant structures (cf. Marchman and Bates 1994; Caselli, Casadio, and Bates 1999; Elsen 2002). But there is much controversy on how this happens in detail and on how quantitative spurts and qualitative changes are best accounted for: how is the way paved for them, how do they proceed and how are they accomplished? All of these questions as to how and when this transition occurs are closely interconnected.

The contributors to this volume share the assumption that the acquisition of grammar is not determined by the existence of innate grammatical (or at least morphological) parameters which are set at a certain point in maturation or by critical-mass accumulation. However, one has to explicate the relevant steps in the child's process of generalising and abstracting over the input and intake and of extracting abstract patterns or rules. Recently, Tomasello (1992, 2001) has insisted on a long duration of item-based learning and has argued against the postulation of early generalisations. Particularly in regard to syntactic and morphological alternations, Tomasello assumes a protracted, imitative accumulation of item-based structures which not earlier than at the age of four years may give way to a dominant generalising learning mechanism.

For early phases of acquisition, Bowerman (1976), Langacker (1988), Bybee (1985, 1995), Tomasello (2000a) and others propose a usage-based model of grammar. This model is also meant to account better for language-specific differences in early acquisition than models which focus on rule acquisition and early grammatical generalisations. Slobin (1997, 2001) follows these proposals at least partially and assigns greater relevance to early language-specific diversity than in his earlier model of the language-making capacity (Slobin 1985). In Slobin (2001), he modifies his thesis of a universal set of early grammatical concepts and of the dominant role of semantic bootstrapping in the process of form-function mapping by assuming a "combination of thinking for speaking and typological bootstrapping...which seems to guarantee that language-specific form-function patterns will be established and maintained by the learner" (Slobin 2001: 285).

Usage-based models proceed from the assumption that "the units of language with which people operate are not presupposed or prejudged" (Tomasello 2000a: 78). Thus, in language acquisition, grammar does not start necessarily with establishing target-like categories. This is a decisive difference to most generative approaches. It is rather assumed that grammar or target grammatical categories and structures can be constructed or reconstructed in a stepwise way. This implies that unexpected and non-target-like forms may emerge as results of a child's abstractions and hypotheses (cf. below on blind alleys). Furthermore, this does not preclude the possibility that hypotheses on form-function mapping may be of a universal or, at least, very general nature. For linguistic capacities develop in connection with joint attentional skills of child and care-taker. These skills are apt to establish interaction-encompassing background frames (Tomasello 1988) and are linked to reasoning from the very beginning.

The grammatical domain which develops very early and first approaches target-like structures in linguistic categorisation is phonology. Development of syntax and morphology, at least after the one-word (or one-element) phase, presupposes a decomposition of the sound chain into units from sentences (or utterances) over words to syllables and phonemes (or even other phonological units, cf. Dziubalska-Kołaczyk 2002). All these units, however a theory defines them, and a sufficient number of their representatives and properties must be categorised for morphology and syntax to develop. Moreover, it is assumed that children very early start to differentiate word classes (cf. section 4 and e.g. Lieven 1998; Vihman 1999; Behrens 2001; Tomasello 2001). Consequently, early learning, which is primarily imitative of course, does not preclude abstractions and generalisations over the input and the child's own repertoire.

An acquisition model which explicitly assumes children's reanalysis of their own output as the main driving force of linguistic development is Elbers (2000) with its "output as input hypothesis". Another acquisition model which integrates item-based learning and processes of generalisation is Karmiloff-Smith's (1992) model of "representational redescription". The central point and process type of this model is a cyclic reiterative process of successive abstraction over acquired linguistic representations in each domain and beyond single domains. This process of redescription applies both to item-based representations and to representations abstracted from them. This model is constructivist and thus similar to the equally constructivist model of "self-organisation", as developed, inter alia, by Karpf (1991), Dressler and Karpf (1995). Children, in their intake and uptake interact selectively with their linguistic environment, based on their present repertoire and the properties of the input, in particular the parameters of saliency and naturalness. This interaction leads to pattern selection both on the paradigmatic axis (i.e. selection among competing structures) and on the syntagmatic axis (selection within the sound chain). The more children advance, the more actively they may engage in the construction of their patterns (self-organisation in the strict sense), including the formation of non-target-like hypotheses, when they construct so-called blind alleys which lead away from the adult targets and which children have to give up soon afterwards. It has been shown that children may start to engage in such "wrong" hypotheses very early on (e.g. reduplicative structures in Greek, Lithuanian and Russian verb inflection; cf. Dressler 1997a, Kilani-Schoch et al. 1997).

All of these conceptions deliver good arguments for looking for processes of grammaticisation from the earliest acquisition phases onwards. Despite the seemingly great variation in acquisition, especially in its constructivist interpretation, results of research in grammar since Edward Sapir and Roman Jakobson, followed by Dan Slobin's arguments on "thinking for speaking" (Slobin 1997) encourage acquisitionists not to abandon the thesis of universal points of departure in the acquisition of language and grammar. On the one hand, different grammars represent in their essential components different solutions for the same problems of language production and receptive processing (cf. Seiler's both universalist and typological work on linguistic operations as problem solving devices 1978; 1986, 2000). The same speech act and its semantic and syntactic structuring can be materialised by different means and structural elements cross-linguistically and even within each language. For example, Krifka (1989, 1992) demonstrated such variations with complementary means of coding cumulativity and quantification of events (ongoing vs. completed events in final analysis) within verb- vs. noun-phrases. Or for instance Gil (1991) showed how number of nominal referents may be symbolised even outside nouns and noun phrases (cf. also Dressler 1968). On the other hand, particularly early phases of language acquisition are characterised by species-specific conditions that guide perception of the world and its verbal rendering. The above-mentioned joint attentional skills and the establishment of frames for communicative interaction and for first grammaticisable notions (cf. Slobin 1985) are in part subject to universal conditions. Therefore, at first, language-specific differences in language acquisition might regard primarily and predominantly formal means rather than the construction of functional grammatic distinctions. As a consequence we do not assume that the acquisition of grammar starts with the establishment of target-like language-specific categories. Rather we think of successive processes of differentiation and of constructive dissociation of universal base conditions into language-specific categories.

One aim of the research presented in this volume is to look for possible universal points of departure in language acquisition in the realms of verb inflection and for how language-specific structures emerge. Morphology and particularly verb inflection offer a promising area for such investigations, because both emerge later than phonology, and the acquisition of its core is achieved by the age of three years of age, even for languages with relatively poor morphology on the one hand and for languages with very rich morphology on the other. This relatively short period facilitates longitudinal research as compared to syntactic processes, as they have been investigated so far in item- or usage-based approaches. Even more than previous studies which appear to assume the same learning mechanism for syntax and morphology (cf. Akhtar and Tomasello 1997; Pine, Lieven, and

Rowland 1998), we will differentiate between morphological and syntactic generalisations, and focus on the first.

2. Studies on the acquisition of verb inflection

Due to the importance of the verb and its relevance for clause structure, the acquisition of the inflectional properties of the verb is a traditional object of investigation in child language research. However, most work has been done on the acquisition of aspect-tense inflection (for an actual overlook cf. Weist 2002) and correlations of semantic classes of verbs and inflectional types (cf. Bloom, Lifter, and Hafitz 1980; Slobin 1985; Shirai and Anderson 1995; Wittek 2002) as well as on word order properties of inflectional types (cf. Jordens 1990; Meisel 1992; Poeppel and Wexler 1993; Wijnen 1998). The emergence of paradigmatic relations between inflectional forms and the order of inflectional contrasts has been much less studied as a topic of its own in the past decades. Only a comparatively small sample of languages, most of them belonging to the traditionally investigated language families, has been considered.[2] However, it is fair to say that a cross-linguistic perspective on the early emergence of verb inflection and paradigm construction is still lacking and that our insights in the processes of paradigm and category (re)construction are still only preliminary.

Considering models dealing with the acquisition of inflection and paradigm construction in detail, mainly three concepts can be distinguished: the dual-mechanism model of Pinker, Marcus and colleagues, the connectionist models established by Marchman, Plunkett, and others, and the net-work model of Bybee which is closely related to usage-based models (cf. Langacker 1988; Tomasello 2000a).

The dual-mechanism model (Pinker and Prince 1992; Clahsen 1999), establishes two qualitatively different structural levels for the processing of regular vs. irregular inflecting forms. Regular forms are generated from a base form via the operation of a symbolic rule, whereas all irregular forms are stored in the lexicon. The strong distinction between the two domains raises the question how (over)regularizing of irregular forms in child and adult language can be explained. Bybee (1995) also criticises the central role the model assigns to token frequency in establishing productive patterns or default rules. Marcus et al (1992), Clahsen (1997), Clahsen, Aveledo, and Roca (2002) have discussed these critiques. One of the results has been to reduce reliance on token frequency. However, several critiques against the model have not been answered satisfactorily. First of all, these are the adequacy of two qualitatively different levels in the lexicon and in morphological processing, second, the specific claims on defaults made in the model, cf. the panel discussions on Clahsen (1999).

The notion of "miniparadigm", which is central for the investigations of this volume, has been first used by Pinker (1984) within the framework of Lexical Functional Grammar. He proposed a progression from word-specific to general paradigms as "a process whereby the child first creates word-specific miniparadigms and only later abstracts the pattern of inflection contained within them to create general inflectional paradigms" (1984: 180). This process is assumed to be guided by innate learning devices including the stepwise enrichment of paradigm complexity by adding new values and new dimensions. In Pinker's view miniparadigms are sets of hypothesised feature equations entered into the grammar and appended to entire words. However, Pinker leaves it unclear how and when the child arrives at creating equations, i.e. by which steps and processes the child extracts the right hypotheses, and what the first miniparadigms exactly mean in the development of morphology.

Bybee's net-work model (1988) takes type frequency as the main criterion for the emergence and productivity of a pattern. Patterns emerge by net-work connection of semantical and phonological properties of single word forms. Productivity is further dependent on the restrictedness of a pattern. On the contrary, lexical strength, i.e. token frequency of a certain form, is responsible for the power of the net-work connections the form exhibits. The higher the lexical strength of a certain form, the more it tends to be stored separately, with only less or no involvement in net-work patterns, and the higher is the potentiality of separate semantic/functional developments. Bybee argues that forms with high token frequency will be learned early and by rote-learning. It follows from the model that general inflectional patterns emerge through accumulation of types of certain connections. In contrast to the dual-mechanism model, in the network model all morphological properties and processes are part of the lexicon, no separate rule component nor any different levels of processing are assumed. The model proposes two types of schemas serving morphological structure. Source-oriented schemas "are generalisations over pairs of basic and derived forms", i.e. they determine which patterns are applicable to a certain (base) form. Product-oriented schemas "are generalisations over sets of complex or 'derived' forms" (Bybee 1995: 430), i.e. they describe the prototypical formal properties which express a certain grammatical function. It follows from these twofold schemas that the production of a certain form is determined by the properties of the base form and by the expected formal properties of the output form.

Also the connectionist models reject the assumption of a separate or specific component of abstract rules. Formal generalisations emerge from the accumulation of individual lexical patterns. Various connectionist models simulate acquisition processes of the learning of certain inflectional contrasts quite well, based simply on weights of frequency and distribution of input features and their connections (cf. Plunkett and Juola 1999). However, morphosemantics, i.e. the meaning of inflectional categories, and the relation of inflection to syntax have been nearly completely neglected so far (with the exceptions of Cottrell and Plunkett 1994; Plaut and Gonnerman 2000). This lacuna is paradoxical, because there exist many connectionist studies on the acquisition of word meaning (e.g. Dorffner 1992; cf. MacWhinney 2000), and because acquisition of morphology is considered to be a special instance of lexical learning. Moreover, most connectionist models lack the notions of lexical entry (but see MacWhinney 2000) and paradigm, which the authors of this volume, like all morphologists, consider to be indispensable.

Far from denying their important findings on the acquisition of inflectional morphology, we find in the recent usage-based and connectionist approaches a rather restricted focus on inflectional development. All of them primarily deal with single inflectional contrasts and are merely form-oriented in their analyses. The construction of paradigms in form and meaning has not been investigated so far. The grammatical concepts represented by the forms acquired, their internal hierarchy, their correlation with cognitive principles, and their impact on the order of acquisition are still open questions. There is only little knowledge on the grammatical distinctions the child assigns to contrasting inflectional forms. The first steps into grammar, i.e. the beginning of its detection, is even less known up to now.

In section 1, we already criticised that, in our view, within usage-based models the emphasis on language-specific and item-specific aspects in the acquisitional process tends to restrict attempts towards finding out common or universal conditions of language acquisition. The proponents of this model not only negate innate modules but apparently any innate and specifically linguistic predispositions which even emergentists accept, e.g. Karmiloff-Smith (1992). Their assumption of an excessively long period of rote-learning of verb-specific inflectional forms (cf. Tomasello's 1992 verb-island hypothesis), in our view, undervalues young children's capacity for morphological generalizations. However, we agree with Tomasello (2001: 183–184) that it belongs to the outstanding questions of child language research "how do children select what they need from all the language they hear", "on what basis do children make analogies or form schemas", and we would add: what are the universal steps and operations on the way from pragmatic to grammatical and finally adult-like interpretation of the input. Cross-linguistic evidence from typologically similar and different languages promises to advance our knowledge about the emergence and development of grammatical categories, on their interplay, and of possible conditioning factors. This volume is meant to contribute to this goal.

3. The pre-/protomorphological approach to the emergence of verb inflection

The present volume provides the fruits of a long-term cooperation of the authors on this topic. The theoretical and organisational core of this research has been the "Crosslinguistic Project on Pre- and Protomorphology in Language Acquisition" coordinated by Wolfgang U. Dressler in behalf of the Austrian Academy of Sciences. The project intends to answer basic questions such as:

A) How can we explain that young children appear to acquire very different morphological systems in similar ways but with great time lags in the emergence of morphological patterns (e.g. Turkish vs. English children)?
B) How can we explain not only the similarity of development but also of structural principles of target morphologies without assuming a sizable number of innate morphological principles of universal grammar?
C) But why is then hypothetically innate grammatical morphology (as opposed to extragrammatical morphology, see below) nearly absent in certain isolating languages as well as in early stages of language acquisition?

The project aims at a theory-guided comparative analysis of longitudinal data sampled from about the age of 1;2 to 3;0. It encompasses nearly two dozen, predominantly morphology-rich languages among the Indo-European, Finno-Ugric and Semitic language families, plus Turkish, and the Meso-American languages Yucateco Maya and Huichol. The perspective is more typological than crosslinguistic in that its agenda is to set up comparative schemes which allow to distinguish between similarities in typologically distinct languages and differences in typologically similar languages. Furthermore we strive for differentiating between typological dependency and system-specific (Wurzel 1984; Dressler et al. 1987) adequacy in morphological development.

The epistemological approach of the project is characterised by the use of functional explanation (cf. Dressler 1995). The linguistic approach is either based on, or at least compatible with, the model of Natural Morphology and the model of self-organisation of developing systems (cf. Kilani-Schoch 1988; Dressler et al. 1987; Dressler 1997b, 1999; Dressler and Karpf 1995). Moreover, this model distinguishes gradually prototypical vs. non-prototypical morphology (cf. Dressler and Merlini Barbaresi 1994): prototypical verbal categories are person, number, tense, mood and voice, whereas most of the non-finite categories are non-prototypical. On the level of universal preferences, the parameters of iconicity, morphotactic and morphosemantic transparency, indexicality, and (bi)uniqueness are the most relevant.

In studying language acquisition, we make a distinction between grammatical morphological rules vs. extragrammatical operations (of "expressive" morphology), as represented by young children's onomatopoetic reduplications, truncations and fillers. We assume (cf. Dressler 2001) that typologically relevant morphological distinctions concern only morphological grammar and not extragrammatical operations, such as onomatopoetic reduplication in premorphology (cf. in this volume Russian, Finnish, French, German, Lithuanian[3]). According to the concept of language types as ideal constructs which are more or less approached by actual languages (cf. Skalička 1979; Dressler et al. 1987; Kilani-Schoch 1988), we can provisionally assign the languages of this volume to a gradual continuum between two ideal language types, as far as verb morphology is concerned:[4]

1) inflecting-fusional type <---> isolating type: Lithuanian – Greek – Russian – Croatian – Italian – Spanish – Yucateco Maya – German – Dutch – French – English.
2) agglutinating type <---> inflecting-fusional type: Turkish – Finnish – Yucateco Maya – the other languages

The acquisition of verb inflection is in focus since 1998. Since 2000 there exists a close cooperation with the project "Syntactic Consequences of the

Acquisition of Morphology" at the Zentrum für Allgemeine Sprachwissenschaft, Typologie und Universalienforschung in Berlin (ZAS = 'Research Centre for General Linguistics, Typology and Universals'). In this project, the investigation of the emergence of verb inflection in Russian, German and English is the starting point for a comparative study of simultaneous syntactic acquisition processes. In September 2000, a workshop at ZAS in Berlin allowed to elaborate a first review of joint work done within both projects on verb inflection and to prepublish the results in the ZAS Papers in Linguistics (ZAS-PiL 18). For the present volume, the contributions to the ZAS volume have been thoroughly reworked and enriched, and completely new chapters on Dutch, Greek, Italian and Turkish have been added. This volume presents the state of research of both projects on the emergence of miniparadigms in thirteen languages (with two varieties of German) and its relevance for the acquisition of verb morphology.

We define a true miniparadigm as corresponding to a non-isolated set of minimally three phonologically unambiguous and distinct inflectional forms of the same lemma produced spontaneously in contrasting syntactic or situative contexts in the same month of recordings (cf. Kilani-Schoch and Dressler 2002, Kilani-Schoch this volume). We expect children to abide by these criteria progressively in their development. In other words we hypothesise several successive steps or paths to miniparadigms during which the children evolve towards an ever less partial and vague detection of morphological alternations. The papers of the volume show that the building of miniparadigms can be described as a slow extension and development of verb forms up to a point where some qualitative change may occur. It is as if the children tried successive approximations until they had enough experience for starting to actively construct morphology. This process appears to be related to a lexical growth although not directly derivable from it.

Among typological differences in the early emergence of verb forms and of verb morphology, the following appear to bear on the relative approximation of verb systems to the morphology-rich ideal inflecting vs. the ideal agglutinating vs. the ideal isolating type, which is devoid of inflectional morphology and, a fortiori, of morphological grammar.

1. Morphological richness (as defined by the amount of productive morphology), characteristic of languages approaching the ideal agglutinating and inflecting types, should make children more aware of the importance of morphology. Thus, they should detect morphology earlier than children acquiring languages poorer in morphology (cf. Slobin 1985).

2. Due to the greater quantity of paradigm members in languages with richer morphology, in strongly agglutinating and stronger inflecting languages miniparadigms as a result of paradigm construction should emerge earlier and occur more frequently than in weaker inflecting languages.
3. Morphological richness, thus heterogeneity, might induce children to be more selective in the forms they produce, by paying more attention to the functional context of the forms they take up and produce. In contrast, morphological poverty might render them less sensitive to morphological heterogeneity. Thus children acquiring a strongly agglutinating or a strongly inflecting language should confuse forms less often than children acquiring a weakly inflecting language. However, selectivity is also subject to interindividual variation.
4. Agglutinating languages have a greater preference for a) constructional iconicity, b) morphotactic transparency, c) biuniqueness than (at least strongly) inflecting languages. Therefore, agglutinating Turkish a) has no modifications such as ablaut and umlaut (Germanic languages), gradation (Finnish), palatalisations (Slavic and Romance languages), which all decrease the degree of constructional iconicity, b) has nearly no morphonological rules which make inflection less transparent in inflecting languages and also in Finnish, c) has no allomorphy or cumulative morphology, as they are rampant in inflecting languages. For example, Turkish has just one suffix for each case and for plural, which are signalled separately, e.g. nom.sg. *ev* 'house', loc.sg. *ev-de*, nom.pl. *ev-ler*, loc.pl. *ev-ler-de*, whereas in Russian, case, number, and gender are signalled simultaneously and with different allomorphs in different inflection classes, e.g. nom./acc.sg.msc. *dom*, dat./loc.sg.msc. *dom-u* vs. nom.sg.fem. *kniga*, acc.sg.fem *knig-u*, gen.sg.fem. *knig-i*, dat.sg.fem. *knig-e*. These are further properties which should facilitate acquisition of morphology, including the establishment of miniparadigms, in Turkish as opposed to less agglutinating Finnish and to inflecting languages.
5. In a seemingly paradoxical contrast, homophony (as opposed to biuniqueness, see Kilani-Schoch and Dresssler 2000, 2001) has been proposed as a possible factor for favouring the emergence of verb forms in early phases of the acquisition of inflecting languages. The reasoning goes as follows: if there is ambiguity (instead of biuniqueness or, at least, uniqueness), much opacity (instead of morphotactic transparency), and less constructional iconicity, then homophonous forms (including syncretisms) are easier to handle in the earliest phases of mor-

phology acquisition, because they occur in more environments than heterogeneous forms and are thus more usable. (Note that homophony plays a bigger role in weaker than in stronger inflecting languages.) This would predict that infinitives emerge earlier when they are homophonous with other verb forms, as in English, French, German, than in other languages. Furthermore, this would explain the presence of a root-infinitive stage in the three above-mentioned languages (Pierce 1992; Wexler 1994) vs. the absence in other languages (cf. Phillips 1995).

Our developmental approach does not assume an innate morphological module but is constructivist (cf. section 1), i.e. based on the model of self-organising processes (autopoiesis, cf. Karmiloff-Smith 1992; Karpf 1991; Dressler and Karpf 1995). Children interact selectively with the environment, their selection of data from the environment (first intake, next uptake, then output) is carried out on the basis of the criteria available in each phase.

Important constructivist principles are those of pattern selection and of self-organisation: pattern selection means that the child selects some forms in some contexts due to token frequency and saliency (cf. Bates and MacWhinney 1987). Self-organisation means that children do not merely imitate input elements, but construct themselves their patterns in reaction to the intake, i.e. in uptake and production. This constructive character of acquisition becomes evident in overgeneralisation and particularly when children enter blind alleys (s. above section 1). Self-organisation also means that increasing complexity of the inventory leads to successive dissociations of more global systems into more specific, complementary systems, which gives rise to modularity or at least compartmentalisation (as division of labour).

According to Dressler and Karpf (1995), we divide morphological development into the three main phases of premorphology, protomorphology, and morphology proper (or modularised morphology).[5] The three phases assumed here are based on the following theoretical claims:

a) We can consider the premorphological phase of language acquisition as the phase before the detection of grammatical morphology. Extragrammatical (or "expressive") morphological operations and precursors of later grammatical rules consisting only of rote-learned forms occur. The selection of grammatical precursors is based on principles of naturalness and constructivism. In the premorphological phase, no system of

grammatical morphology has yet become dissociated from a general cognitive system that handles, inter alia, words of whatever form. This global system becomes dysfunctional, when children are in growing need of a rapid expansion of their lexical inventories and when (in many languages) expanding syntax needs morphological marking of syntactic categories.
b) During the protomorphological phase of language acquisition, children detect and reconstruct or construct creatively morphological patterns of analogies or of first rules. In order to handle the increasing morphological complexity, a primitive system of morphology dissociates from phonology, syntax and the lexicon. In this period also most interindividual variation is to be expected.
c) In the first phases of morphology proper (also called "modularised morphology" by those who believe in a modular compartmentalisation of adult language), the child's systems approach qualitatively, if not quantitatively, the adult models. In passing over to this stage, the two main functions of word formation, namely lexical enrichment and motivation need to be served. This leads to ever greater complexity, paralleled and even more increased by the accumulation of inflectional devices. In order to serve the different functions of inflection and word formation, the primitive morphological system must dissociate, giving rise to separate submodules of inflection and word formation. In this way morphology becomes modularised. Hence morphology proper initiates when the basic language-specific properties of target morphology are acquired and structurally differentiated (i.e. compartmentalised) into verbal vs. nominal inflection vs. word formation.

4. From pre- to protomorphology in verb inflection

Verb inflection does not emerge at once but in many steps. As we argue in this volume, the most relevant ones are the steps towards inflectional contrasts and miniparadigms. In agreement with many psycholinguistic studies (see section 1.), we take for granted that some sort of accumulation process is necessary for the emergence of (proto)morphology and that this process progressively renders other learning mechanisms mandatory, i.e. both mechanisms which are already at work in other domains or which are new.[6] Recall, however, that we argue for pattern selection and not merely for item storage already at the beginning of language development (see section 1. and 3.).

What we try to do in this volume is to look further into some more controversial aspects of this general learning mechanisms. The first aspect encompasses the link between morphology and other components on the one hand, between the emergence of verb morphology and other morphological subsystems, on the other. The problem is to find out what is the driving force in the development of morphological processing. What are the interconnections between morphological, lexical and syntactic development and what depends on what? Within morphology, where processing seems to emerge simultaneously in several areas, we ask whether this emergence represents a switch from absence to presence of morphology rather than a gradual, continuous process.

Another problem is how to measure the accumulation process, i.e. what kind of categories should be analysed and which comparisons should be undertaken. This is dealt with in detail by Gillis (Dutch) and by Klampfer (German) in this volume. Cumulative overviews of the child's verb lexicon (especially new verb-lemmas vs. new verb-forms) by Gillis allow a quantitative delineation of phases without any real verb spurt. Klampfer focusses on lexical diversity and demonstrates that the emergence of verb morphology is related also to an increase rather than to a spurt in lexical diversity. Also the other contributions take the modelling of growth and the critical mass hypothesis as basic questions and provide relevant data. A lexical verb spurt is presented for the German (Bittner), Spanish (Aguirre), Russian (Gagarina), Croatian (Katičić), Italian (Noccetti), and Turkish (Aksu-Koç and Ketrez) children. In Greek (Christofidou and Stephany), Finnish (Laalo), Lithuanian (Wójcik), Yucatec Maya (Pfeiler), French (Kilani-Schoch), and English (Gülzow) children, it is rather a steady accumulation of verb lemmas which has been found.

This leads us to the role of the input for acquisition and to the nature of the input dependency (Gallaway and Richards 1994, Richards 1994). Current research is still far from solving this complex question which now extends to what the source of input for analysis actually is, either production or comprehension (Elbers 2000). The results obtained in this volume are modest but relevant in that they concord with the findings of previous studies (Gillis and De Houwer 1998; Wijnen, Kempen, and Gillis 2001) which provided evidence against a straightforward correlation between input frequency and order of development.

Finally, it appears throughout the volume that the transition from lexical processing to morphological patterning is not an automatic consequence of lexical learning but results from an active construction by the child (cf. Karmiloff-Smith 1992). Instead of a continuous quantitative build-up of rote-learnt inflectional forms, some sort of detection mechanism of the morphological principles of form-meaning distinctions and of morphological segmentation seems to take place at one particular point of development, after a period of successive attempts and approximations. In other words, we are induced to assume a turning-point between premorphology and protomorphology.

If this assumption is correct, it entails that the detection mechanism is sufficiently general to apply wherever possible, i.e. in every domain or area of morphology. To that extent pre- and protomorphology have to be considered as local and global, i.e. they can be, and actually should be, limited first to microdomains, but more or less rapidly, depending on target-morphology and on individual factors, changes in one domain lead to changes in other domains. As to the problem where morphological processing is likely to emerge first, we propose that detection of morphology starts in the morphologically richest domain.

In the Natural Morphology approach of language acquisition, following MacWhinney (1978), we distinguish between pattern extraction (not to be confused with pattern selection in premorphology), illustrated by examples of surface analogies, i.e. analogies based on concrete forms, and more abstract rule extraction, e.g. in the establishment of verbal classes. In this volume, focussed on the detection of verb inflection, we are concerned with pattern extraction only, whereas rule extraction is a matter beyond our scope.

One of the central issues in the contributions to this volume are the acquisitional processes of the transition between premorphology and protomorphology. Our previous research and the contributions to this volume support the following assumptions on main developmental steps:

In premorphology, we typically observe one rote-learnt form per verb lemma (cf. Tomasello 1992; Vihmann 1999), which may be a base-form, e.g. infinitive (basic inflected form) or 3.Sg.Pres. in languages where this is the base form, either inflected with a person marker (e.g. Dutch, German) or just with the stem vowel (e.g. Lithuanian, Croatian, often in Spanish and Italian) or totally uninflected (e.g. Turkish, French). Alternatively, these first verb forms may be child-specific: either due to phonological change, i.e. prosodic reduction to a monosyllabic or bisyllabic form or segmental simplification or substitution, incl. reduplication (e.g. Finnish). The present contributions support the hypothesis that input frequency of a certain word form is a crucial parameter for early rote-learning (see Bybee 1995; Gillis this volume, also on the co-occurrence of further parameters). But no knowledge of morphological categories can yet be attributed to these forms. Furthermore, it is very likely that even word class distinctions are not yet present in this early phase. Verbs, verbal prefixes, abverbials, and nouns can equally be used in order to refer to the same situation, request or desire (cf. Aksu-Koç and Ketrez; Gillis; Gülzow; Laalo; Pfeiler; Bittner this volume; Tomasello 1992).

Particularly in the earliest phases predicative functions may be expressed by extragrammatical means, as, for instance, by sound imitations and traditional or creative onomatopoeia, including onomatopoetic reduplications. Thus young children have a rich repertoire of means for expressing predication, before they dispose of appropriate verb forms. But even when they have such forms of specific verbs expressing a specific pragmatic or morphosemantic sense, they may use simultaneously for the same sense non-verbs instead of verb forms with other verb lemmas. However, a more systematic investigation of such asymmetries among verb lemmas would be required in order to think of avoidance strategies and have evidence for the precedence of morphosemantics over morphotactics in the emergence of miniparadigms.

We consider such predecessors of verbs as non-verbs, which serve the predicative function in a format which is exceptional or even absent in adult speech. Trivially these forms emerge in the one-element phase where, usually polyfunctional, holophrastic protowords (cf. Gillis and De Schutter 1986) have (also) a predicative function. Most of the contributions to this volume give specimina of such early predecessors (cf. Aksu-Koç and Ketrez; Gagarina; Gillis; Gülzow; Laalo; Wojcik this volume). Without any attempt at exhaustiveness, the occurrence of the following types of predecessors can be stated:

a) adverbs such as "away", often difficult to distinguish from verbal particles (separable verb prefixes in Dutch and German),
b) deictics or other attention getting/directing forms,
c) onomatopeia, which can replace verbs or nouns,
d) fillers for monosyllabic verbs,
e) fillers, reduplications and other self-created items which all do not exist in the target language, and which preserve the prosodic pattern of the target verb structure. Finally, and most frequently,

f) nouns, which are at first often difficult to differentiate from verbs (see Gillis; Pfeiler this volume), parallel to the difficulty of disentangling predicative and nominative functions. These predicative nouns may be base forms, e.g. in existential sentences, or case forms representing, e.g., the direct object of not-expressed transitive verbs or the indirect object of verbs of giving (cf. Aksu-Koç and Ketrez; Gagarina this volume). Later there occur more complex structures where the verb is missing alongside verbal constructions.

The development towards morphological analysis and pattern recognition seems to be undissociable from a quantitative enrichment of lexical, syntactic and morphological structures. The mostly reported processes which can be regarded as general features of a period of transition towards protomorphology are the following:

Syntactic development: although syntactic processes have not been investigated in detail, most of the authors hint at a remarkable correlation between the onset of morphological development and the evolution of syntactic processes. First of all, overcoming the one-word stage seems to be a prerequisite for morphological development. Even in the morphologically rich languages such as Finnish, Turkish, Russian and Lithuanian, the enrichment of syntactic complexity precedes or parallels qualitative changes in verb inflection. Emergence and regular use of overt subjects appears to be a syntactic precondition. Gillis (for Dutch) emphasises a spurt in the use of (the suppletive) auxiliaries at the onset of the development of personnumber inflection with regular inflecting verbs. The latter is confirmed by the studies on Yucatec Maya (Pfeiler), English (Gülzow), Standard German (Bittner, see also Bittner 2002), and Spanish (Aguirre). Furthermore, als already mentioned above, some authors register an increase in lexical diversity with respect to word classes in general, insofar as different types of nouns, verbs, and also functional words (or fillers instead) enter the child's lexicon (cf. Klampfer, Noccetti, Gillis, Aksu-Koç and Ketrez).

Morphological development: all authors report an increase in inflectional types within a relatively short period. At the same time, many of the investigated children extend the use of one of the inflectional types they had already used in premorphology (cf. Aksu-Koç and Ketrez, Klampfer, Katičić, Gillis, Bittner, Christofidou and Stephany, Aguirre, Pfeiler). Thus, an increase and/or a change in the type of errors or overgeneralizations appear. Some authors concur in considering this to imply the selection of a default form of the verb itself, i.e. an early form-function generalisation (Aguirre; Bittner; Christofidou and Stephany; Gülzow; Katičić). Accompanied by the syntactic developments described above, finite verb forms replace erroneous non-finite ones. With some of the investigated children, target finite forms occur for the first time (cf. Klampfer on Austrian German; Gillis on Dutch, where this seems to be child-specific; Gülzow on English, where this is explained by typological conditions). A second (sometimes a third) inflectional type of the same lemma is going to be used regularly for a small group of verbs. These first contrasting inflectional pairs still probably consist of rote-learned forms, mainly a non-finite or base form vs. a finite form. When certain types of inflectional contrasts become numerous with different verbs, precursors of two- and three-member miniparadigms emerge. For Dutch, a different syntactic use of finite and non-finite forms is proposed and discussed (Gillis). Where they exist in the target language, the emergence or increasing use of auxiliaries result in first productions of analytical verb constructions.

As Kilani-Schoch, Noccetti, and Gagarina emphasise, the transitional period is determined by the presence of features of both the pre- and the protomorphological phase. Its main characteristics are the quantitative enrichment of morphological diversity by rote-learning and the emergence of very first generalisations on morphological structures. Some children accompany the transition from pre- to protomorphology with a spurt in the verbal lexicon (reported for the Lithuanian, Italian, and Spanish child, both of the French children, the Berlin German child, two of the Russian children). With other children, a more continuous enrichment in verb lemmas and new inflectional structures has been reported (cf. for the Dutch, Croatian, Turkish, and Yucatec child, the Munich German child (Bittner), and the Russian children). Obviously, the occurrence or non-occurrence of a lexical verb spurt is a child-specific aspect of development. Both types of development are compatible with a critical-mass account of the detection of morphology. Klampfer invented a way to measure the amount of miniparadigms per attested lemmas. Although not all authors employed this calculation, it can be hypothesised that the critical-mass of verb lemmas (necessary for allowing the detection of morphological patterns) varies in relation to the criteria: morphological richness, uniformity and transparency of the target inflectional system. The children acquiring Turkish, Russian, Finnish and also Spanish exhibit comparatively lower amounts of verb lemmas at the onset of protomorphology than the children acquiring German and English for instance.

The transition period ends by a turn from mere quantitative enrichment of the child's actively used morphological structures towards a new quality characterized by grammaticisation (Stephany 1985) and the onset of pattern recognition.

Protomorphology starts when the first target-like inflectional contrasts become regular and when the respective forms are employed with (the majority of the) new lexemes. Furthermore, at this turning point, the verb and the subject phrase are going to be established as obligatory parts of the utterance. On the one hand, the grammatical system is now dissociated into a noun and a verb domain (or at least a predicate and an argument domain) enclosing specific types of grammatical structures. On the other hand, a morphological and a syntactic component or module with morphological forms and syntactic positions starts to develop. All authors of this volume agree that both emergence of inflectional contrasts (at the noun or the verb level) and of morphology-determined substitutions are the overt and relevant morphological features for the onset of protomorphology.

In some of the corpora investigated for the volume (cf. Croatian, Spanish, German, French (one child), Yucatec-Maya), the emergence of "true" miniparadigms, i.e. paradigms fulfilling the above-mentioned criteria (cf. section 3.), is simultaneous with the onset of protomorphology, whereas in others it occurs either before (e.g. in the morphology-rich languages Finnish and Lithuanian but also in Dutch and in one German child), or after this onset (Turkish, Greek, Russian, Italian, one French child and English). We do not know yet what these differences exactly mean and why it takes more time for some children, e.g. in one and the same language, to reach this point. More research on more children will help to answer this question. But these preliminary findings indicate relative mutual independence of our two notions of protomorphology and miniparadigm and highlight the methodological reliability of the 3-member miniparadigm criterion, i.e. that the children in fact dispose over a sufficiently large number of stored miniparadigms as they can be expected to appear within limited corpora. Analogies, which are another evidence for the detection of morphology, typically emerge in parallel to, or after, the emergence of true miniparadigms.

All authors agree that the demarcation of pre- and protomorphology should hold for morphology at large, thus not separately for verbs vs. nouns, etc. This is what we expect in a model of subsequent modularisation of morphology first and of its submodules later. Of course, this cannot imply that miniparadigms emerge everywhere at the same time, be it in productive vs. unproductive classes or in verbs vs. nouns (particularly if one subsystem is much richer than the other one). The assumption is just that once children detect the morphological principles of segmentation and recurrence of form and meaning, they can apply them everywhere in morphology. As a consequence, other factors such as typological parameters, productivity, iconicity, or transparency, etc. must be made responsible for early vs. late emergence of different morphological patterns. Although only single children are studied in the present papers and child-specific developments cannot be excluded, the importance of those parameters can be easily grasped by a comparison of the time intervall between the emergence of the first verbs and of the first true miniparadigms. Detecting and (re)constructing true miniparadigms takes only two to four months for the children who acquire the languages which possess the morphology-richest and at the same time most transparently organised verb systems, i.e. Turkish, Finnish, Russian and Croatian. The same process takes the children who acquire Yucatec Maya, Italian, French (one of the two), Dutch, German, and English double time or even more. Not surprisingly, among the latter are the languages with less transparently organised verb inflection, especially with a high amount of syncretisms or homophonies in basic morphological categories (most in French, least in Italian).[7]

The evidence that the languages of this volume provide for the relevance of the criterion of miniparadigms for the acquisition of morphology, is not only cross-linguistic. We hope to get hold of both general, if not universal, characteristics of the acquisition of verb morphology, and of typological ones, insofar as there is pertinent diversity in our sample among languages which approach the inflecting-fusional, the agglutinating and isolating language type.

Notes

1. Cf. MacWhinney (1978); Slobin (1985); Pinker (1984); Bybee (1991); Tomasello (1992); Karmiloff-Smith (1992); Dressler and Karpf (1995); Dressler et al. (to appear).
2. E.g. Pinker (1984); Bybee (1991); Marcus et al. (1992); Behrens (1993); Clahsen and Rothweiler (1993); Caselli et al. (1993); Pizutto and Caselli (1994); Mueller Gathercole, Sebastián, and Soto (1999); Ragnarsdóttir, Simonsen, and Plunkett (1999); for languages of other language families see e.g. Stephany (1985); Smoczyńska (1985); Toivainen (1997); Berman and Armon-Lotem (1997); Allen (1998).
3. Filler-like reduplications in Greek and Lithuanian are a later phenomenon.

4. Note that the nominal and the verb system may behave very differently in typological variation, e.g. French is very isolating in the noun (even more so than English), but weakly inflecting in the verb (here English is more isolating).
5. For other tripartite models see MacWhinney (1978), Gentner and Markmann (1997) and Tomasello (2000b), and for the discussion of phases Berman (1986)
6. Cf. Pinker (1984); Marcus et al. (1992); Bates, Dale, and Thal (1995); Behrens (1999); Elman et al. (1996); Maratsos (1999); Mueller Gathercole, Sebastián, and Soto (1999); Elbers (2000); MacWhinney (2000); Tomasello (1992, 2001).
7. A middle duration of time has been found for the children acquiring Spanish, French (one of the two), and Greek. No time calculation is possible for the Lithuanian child, because the onset of verb use is not attested in the data and miniparadigms are present shortly after the onset of recording.

References

Akhtar, Nameera, and Michael Tomasello
    1997   Young children's productivity with word order and verb morphology. *Developmental Psychology* 33: 952–965

Allen, Shanley
    1998   Categories within the verb category: Learning the causative in Inuktitut. *Linguistics* 36: 633–677.

Bates, Elisabeth, and Brian MacWhinney
    1987   Competition, variation, and language learning. In: Brian MacWhinney (ed.), *Mechanisms of Language Acquisition*, 157–193. Hillsdale New Jersey/London: Lawrence Erlbaum.

Bates, Elizabeth, Philip S. Dale, and Donna Thal
    1995   Individual differences and their implications for theories of language development. In: Paul Fletcher, and Brian MacWhinney (eds.), *The Handbook of Child Language*, 96–151. Oxford: Blackwell.

Behrens, Heike
    1993   Temporal reference in German child language: Form and function of early verb use. Ph.D. thesis, Universiteit van Amsterdam.

Behrens, Heike
   1999   Was macht Verben zu einer besonderen Kategorie im Spracherwerb? In: Jörg Meibauer, and Monika Rothweiler (eds.), *Das Lexikon im Spracherwerb*, 32–50. Tübingen: Francke.

Behrens, Heike
   2001   Cognitive-conceptual development and the acquisition of grammatical morphemes: The development of time concepts and verb tense. In: Melissa Bowerman, and Stephen C. Levinson (eds.), *Language Acquisition and Conceptual Development*, 450–474. Cambridge: Cambridge University Press.

Berman, Ruth
   1986   A step-by-step model of language acquisition. In Iris Levin (ed.), *Stage and Structure: Reopening the Debate*, 191–219. Norwood, New Jersey: Ablex.

Berman, Ruth, and Sharon Armon-Lotem
   1997   How grammatical are early verbs? *Annales littéraires de l'Université de Franche-Comté 631*: 17–56.

Bittner, Dagmar
   2002   Emergence of grammatical complexity and markedness in the acquisition of verb and noun phrases in German. In: Katarzyna Dziubalska-Kołaczyk, and Jarek Weckwerth (eds.), *Future Challenges for Natural Linguistics*, 25–56. München: Lincom.

Bloom, Lois, Karin Lifter, and Jeremie Hafitz
   1980   Semantics of verbs and the development of verb inflection in child language. *Language* 56: 386–412.

Bowerman, Melissa
   1976   Semantic factors in the acquisition of rules for word use and sentence construction. In: Donald M. Morehead, and Ann E. Morehead (eds.), *Normal and Deficient Child Language*, 89–179. Baltimore: University Park Press.

Bybee, Joan
   1985   *Morphology: A Study of the Relation between Meaning and Form*. Amsterdam/Philadelphia: John Benjamins.

Bybee, Joan
   1988   Morphology as lexical organization. In: Michael Hammond, and Michael Noonan (eds.), *Theoretical Morphology*, 119–141. New York: Academic Press.

Bybee, Joan
1991 Natural morphology: The organization of paradigms and language acquisition. In: Thom Huebner, and Charles Ferguson (eds.), *Crosscurrents in Second Language Acquisition and Linguistic Theories*, 67–91. Amsterdam: John Benjamins.

Bybee, Joan
1995 Regular morphology and the lexicon. *Language and Cognitive Processes* 10: 425–455.

Caselli, Maria C., Laurence B. Leonard, Virginia Volterra, and M. Grazia Campagnoli
1993 Toward mastery of Italian morphology: A cross-sectional study. *Journal of Child Language* 20: 377–393.

Caselli, Maria C., Paola Casadio, and Elisabeth Bates
1999 A comparison of the transition from first words to grammar in English and Italian. *Journal of Child Language* 26: 69–111.

Clahsen, Harald
1997 The representation of German participles in the German mental lexicon: Evidence for the dual-mechanism model. *Yearbook of Morphology* 1996: 73–96.

Clahsen, Harald
1999 Lexical entries and rules of language: A multidisciplinary study of German inflection. *Behavioral and Brain Sciences* 22: 991–1013.

Clahsen, Harald, Fraibet Aveledo, and Iggy Roca
2002 The development of regular and irregular verb inflection in Spanish child language. *Journal of Child Language* 29: 591–622.

Clahsen, Harald, and Monika Rothweiler
1993 Inflectional rules in children's grammars: Evidence from the development of participles in German. *Yearbook of Morphology* 1992: 1–34.

Cottrell, Garrison W., and Kim Plunkett
1994 Acquiring the mapping from meaning to sounds. *Cognitive Science* 16: 379–412.

Dorffner, Georg
1992 Taxonomies and part-whole hierarchies in the acquisition of word meaning – a connectionist model. *Proceedings of the 14th Annual*

Conference of the Cognitive Science Society, 803–808. New Haven: Erlbaum.

Dressler, Wolfgang U.
1968   Studien zur verbalen Pluralität. Wien: Böhlau.

Dressler, Wolfgang U.
1995   Wealth and poverty of functional analyses with special reference to functional deficiencies. In: Sharon Millar, and Jacob Mey (eds.), *Form and Function in Language*, 11–39. Odense: Odense University Press.

Dressler, Wolfgang U. (ed.)
1997a   *Studies in Pre- and Protomorphology*. Wien: Verlag der Oesterreichischen Akademie der Wissenschaften.

Dressler, Wolfgang U.
1997b   Universals, typology, and modularity in Natural Morphology. In: Raymond Hickey, and Stanisław Puppel (eds.), *Language History and Linguistic Modelling*, 1399–1421. Berlin/New York: de Gruyter.

Dressler, Wolfgang U.
1999   What is natural in Natural Morphology? *Travaux du Cercle Linguistique de Prague/Prague Linguistic Circle Papers* 3: 135–144.

Dressler, Wolfgang U.
2001   Extragrammatical vs. marginal morphology. In: Ursula Doleschal, and Anna M. Thornton (eds.), *Extragrammatical and Marginal Morphology*, 1–10. München: Lincom.

Dressler, Wolfgang U., and Annemarie Karpf
1995   The theoretical relevance of pre- and protomorphology in language acquisition. *Yearbook of Morphology* 1994: 99–122.

Dressler, Wolfgang U., and Lavinia Merlini Barbaresi
1994   *Morphopragmatics*. Berlin/New York: Mouton de Gruyter.

Dressler, Wolfgang U., Willi Mayerthaler, Oswald Panagl, and Wolfgang U. Wurzel
1987   *Leitmotifs in Natural Morphology*. Amsterdam/Philadelphia: John Benjamins.

Dziubalska-Kołaczyk, Katarzyna
2002   *Beats-and-binding Phonology*. Frankfurt: Lang.

Elbers, Loekie
2000   An output-as-input-hypothesis on language acquisition. In: Peter Broeder, and Jaap Murre (eds.), *Models of Language Acquisition*, 244–271. Oxford: Oxford University Press.

Elman, Jeffrey L., Elisabeth Bates, Mark H. Johnson, Annette Karmiloff-Smith, Domenico Parisi, and Kim Plunkett
1996   *Rethinking Innateness: A Connectionist Perspective on Development*. Cambridge Mass./London: MIT Press.

Elsen, Hilke
2002   The acquisition of German plurals. In: Sabrina Bendjaballah, Wolfgang U. Dressler, Oskar E. Pfeiffer, and Maria D. Voeikova (eds.), *Morphology 2000*, 117–127. Amsterdam: John Benjamins.

Gallaway, Clare, and Brian J. Richards
1994   *Input and Interaction in Language Acquisition*. Cambridge: Cambridge University Press.

Gentner, Dedre, and Arthur Markman
1997   Structure mapping in analogy and similarity. *American Psychologist* 52: 45–56.

Gil, David
1991   *Universal Quantifiers: A Typological Study*. Konstanz. (Eurotyp/Working paper 12.)

Gillis, Steven, and Annick De Houwer
1998   *The Acquisition of Dutch*. Amsterdam: John Benjamins.

Gillis, Steven, and Georges De Schutter
1986   Transitional phenomena revisited: Insights into the nominal 'insight'. In: Bjoern Lindblom, and Rolf Zetterstroem (eds.), *Precursors of Early Speech*, 127–142. New York: Stockton Press.

Jordens, Peter
1990   The acquisition of verb placement in Dutch and German. *Linguistics* 28: 1407–1448.

Karmiloff-Smith, Annette
1992   *Beyond Modularity: A Developmental Perspective on Cognitive Science*. Cambridge, Mass./London: MIT Press.

Karpf, Annemarie
1991   Universal grammar needs organization. *Folia Linguistica* 25: 329–360.

Kilani-Schoch, Marianne
1988 *Introduction à la morphologie naturelle.* Bern: Lang.

Kilani-Schoch, Marianne, Anna De Marco, Anastasia Christofidou, Maria Vassilakou, Ralph Vollmann, and Wolfgang U. Dressler
1997 On the demarcation of phases in early morphology acquisition in four languages. In: Katarzyna Dziubalska-Kołaczyk (ed.), *Pre- and Protomorphology in Language Acquisition*, 15–32. (Papers and Studies in Contrastive Linguistics 33.) Poznań: Adam Mickiewicz University.

Kilani-Schoch, Marianne, and Wolfgang U. Dressler
2000 Are fillers as precursors of morphemes relevant for morphological theory? In: Wolfgang U. Dressler, Oskar E. Pfeiffer, Markus Poechtraeger, and John R. Rennison (eds.), *Morphological Analysis in Comparison*, 89–111. Amsterdam: John Benjamins.

Kilani-Schoch, Marianne, and Wolfgang U. Dressler
2001 On the possible rise and inevitable fall of fillers. *Journal of Child Language* 28: 250–253.

Kilani-Schoch, Marianne, and Wolfgang U. Dressler
2002 The emergence of verb paradigms in two French corpora as an illustration of general problems of pre- and protomorphology. In: Maria D. Voeikova, and Wolfgang U. Dressler (eds.), *Pre- and Protomorphology: Early Phases of Morphological Development in Nouns and Verbs*, 45–59. München: Lincom.

Krifka, Manfred
1989 *Nominalreferenz und Zeitkonstitution: Zur Semantik von Massentermen, Pluraltermen und Aspektklassen.* München: Fink.

Krifka, Manfred
1992 Thematic relations as link between nominal reference and temporal constitution. In: Ivan Sag, and Anna Szabolcsi (eds.), *Lexical Matters*, 29–53. Stanford, California: Leland Stanford Junior University, Center for the Study of Language and Information.

Langacker, Ronald
1988 A usage-based model. In: Brygida Rudzka-Ostyn (ed.), *Topics in Cognitive Linguistics*. Amsterdam: John Benjamins.

Lieven, Elena V.M. (ed.)
1998 *Developing a Verb Category: Cross-linguistic Perspectives. Linguistics* 36, 4. Berlin: Mouton de Gruyter.

MacWhinney, Brian
  1978   *The Acquisition of Morphophonology.* (Monographs of the Society for Research in Child Development 43, 1/2.) Chicago: University of Chicago Press.

MacWhinney, Brian
  2000   Lexicalist connectionism. In: Peter Broeder, and Jaap Murre (eds.), *Models of Language Acquisition*, 9–31. Oxford: Oxford University Press.

Maratsos, Michael
  1999   Some aspects of innateness and complexity in grammatical acquisition. In: Martyn Barrett (ed.), *The Development of Language*, 191–228. Hove: Psychology Press.

Marchman, Virginia, and Elisabeth Bates
  1994   Continuity in lexical and morphological developmennt: A test of the critical mass hypothesis. *Journal of Child Language* 21: 339–366.

Marcus, Gary F., Steven Pinker, Michael Ullman, Michelle Hollander, T. John Rosen, and Fei Xu
  1992   Overregularization in language acquisition. *Monographs of the Society for Research in Child Development* 57.

Meisel, Jürgen M. (ed.)
  1992   *The Acquisition of Verb Placement.* Dordrecht: Kluwer.

Mueller Gathercole, Virginia C., Eugenia Sebastián, and Pilar Soto
  1999   The early acquisition of Spanish verbal morphology: Across-the-board or piecemeal knowledge? *The International Journal of Bilingualism* 3: 133–182.

Phillips, Colin
  1995   Syntax at age 2: Crosslinguistic differences. *MIT Working Papers in Linguistics* 26: 325–382.

Pierce, Amy
  1992   *Language Acquisition and Syntactic Theory: A Comparative Analysis of French and English Child Grammars.* Dordrecht: Kluwer.

Pine, Julian, Elena V. M. Lieven, and Caroline F. Rowland
  1998   Comparing different models of the development of the English verb category. *Linguistics* 36: 807–830.

Pinker, Steven
 1984   *Language Learnability and Language Development.* Cambridge: Harvard University Press.

Pinker, Steven, and Alan Prince
 1992   Regular and irregular morphology and the psychological status of rules of grammar. *Proceedings of the 17th Annual Meeting of the Berkeley Linguistics Society*, 230–251. Berkeley, CA.

Pizzuto, Elena, and Maria C. Caselli
 1994   The acquisition of Italian verb morphology in a cross-linguistic perspective. In: Yonata Levy (ed.), *Other Children, Other Languages*, 137–187. Hillsdale, New Jersey: Lawrence Erlbaum.

Plaut, David C., and Laura M. Gonnerman
 2000   Are non-semantic morphological effects incompatible with a distributed connectionist approach to lexical processing? *Language and Cognitive Processes* 15: 445–485.

Plunkett, Kim, and Patrick Juola
 1999   A connectionist model of English past tense and plural morphology. *Cognitive Science* 23: 463–490.

Poeppel, David, and Ken Wexler
 1993   The full competence hypothesis of clause structure in early German. *Language* 69: 1–33.

Ragnarsdóttir, Hrafnhildur, Hanne-Gram Simonsen, and Kim Plunkett
 1999   The acquisition of past tense in Icelandic and Norwegian children: An experimental study. *Journal of Child Language* 26: 577–618.

Richards, Brian J.
 1994   Child-directed speech and influences on language acquisition: methodology and interpretation. In: Clare Gallaway, and Brian J. Richards (eds.), *Input and Interaction in Language Acquisition*, 74–106. Cambridge: Cambridge University Press.

Seiler, Hansjakob (ed.)
 1978   *Language Universals.* Tübingen: Narr.

Seiler, Hansjakob
 1986   *Apprehension: Language, Object and Order.* Teil III: The universal dimension of apprehension. (Language Universal Series 1/III.) Tübingen: Narr

Seiler, Hansjakob
  2000   *Language Universals Research: A Synthesis.* Tübingen: Narr.

Shirai, Yasuhiro, and Roger W. Anderson
  1995   The acquisition of tense aspect morphology: A prototype account. *Language* 71:743–762.

Skalička, Vladimir
  1979   *Typologische Studien.* Braunschweig: Vieweg.

Slobin, Dan I.
  1985   Crosslinguistic evidence of the language-making capacity. In: Dan I. Slobin (ed.), *The Crosslinguistic Study of Language Acquisition,* 1157–1256. Vol. 2. Hillsdale, New Jersey: Lawrence Erlbaum.

Slobin, Dan I.
  1997   From "Thought and Language" to "Thinking for speaking". In: John J. Gumperz, and Steven C. Levinson (eds.), *Rethinking Linguistic Relativity,* 70–96. Cambridge: Cambridge University Press.

Slobin, Dan I.
  2001   Form/function relations: How do children find out what they are? In: Michael Tomasello, and Elizabeth Bates (eds.), *Language Development: The Essential Readings,* 267–290. Malden, Mass./Oxford: Blackwell.

Smoczyńska, Magdalena
  1985   The acquisition of Polish. In: Dan I. Slobin (ed.), *The Crosslinguistic Study of Language Acquisition,* 595–686. Vol. I. Hillsdale, New Jersey: Lawrence Erlbaum.

Stephany, Ursula
  1985   *Aspekt, Tempus und Modalität: Zur Entwicklung der Verbalgrammatik in der neugriechischen Kindersprache.* Tübingen: Gunter Narr.

Toivainen, Jorma
  1997   The acquisition of Finnish. In: Dan I. Slobin (ed.), *The Crosslinguistic Study of Language Acquisition.* Vol. 4, 87–182. Mahwah, New Jersey: Lawrence Erlbaum.

Tomasello, Michael
    1988   The role of joint attentional processes in early language development. *Language Sciences* 1: 69–88.

Tomasello, Michael
    1992   *First Verbs: A Case Study of Early Grammatical Development.* Cambridge: Cambridge University Press.

Tomasello, Michael
    2000a   First steps towards a usage based theory of language acquisition. *Cognitive Linguistics* 11: 61–82.

Tomasello, Michael
    2000b   Acquiring syntax is not what you think. In: Dorothy Bishop, and Laurence B. Leonard (eds.), *Speech and Language Impairments in Children: Cause, Characteristics, Intervention and Outcome*, 1–15. Hove: Psychology Press.

Tomasello, Michael
    2001   The item-based nature of children's early syntactic development. In: Michael Tomasello, and Elizabeth Bates (eds.), *Language Development: The Essential Readings*, 169–186. Malden, Mass./Oxford: Blackwell.

Vihman, Marilyn V. (ed.)
    1999   First steps in morphological and syntactic development: Cross-linguistic evidence. *International Journal of Bilingualism* 3.

Weist, Richard
    2002   The first language acquisition of tense and aspect: A review. In: Rafael Salaberry, and Yasuhiro Shirai (eds.), *The L2 Acquisition of Tense-aspect Morphology*, 21–78. Amsterdam: John Benjamins.

Wexler, Ken
    1994   Optional infinitives, head movement, and the economy of derivations. In: David Lightfoot, and Norbert Hornstein (eds.), *Verb Movement*, 305–350. London: Cambridge University Press.

Wijnen, Frank
    1998   The temporal interpretation of Dutch children's root infinitivals: The effect of eventivity. *First Language* 18: 379–402.

Wijnen, Frank, Masja Kempen, and Steven Gillis
    2001   Root infinitives in Dutch early child language: An effect of input. *Journal of Child Language* 28: 629–660.

Wittek, Angelika
    2002   *Learning the Meaning of Change-of-state verbs: A Case Study of German Child Language*. Berlin/New York: Mouton de Gruyter.

Wurzel, Wolfgang U.
    1984   *Flexionsmorphologie und Natürlichkeit*. Berlin: Akademie Verlag.

Specific terms used in common by the contributors to the present volume

Extragrammatical operations are operations which resemble morphological rules but whose only unifying property is that some principle of morphological grammar is violated.

Frozen forms or *formulaic forms* are a subset of rote-learnt, contextually/situationally bound, morphologically non-distinctive forms.

Isolated paradigm: an isolated paradigm is a paradigm which differs morphologically or morphonologically from all other paradigms.

Lemma: we assign the term lemma to the abstract base of a lexical entry (often called lexeme), i.e. to the correlation of (specific) lexical meaning with (specific) phonological material, which creates the lexical sign.

Macroclass: a macroclass is the highest, most general type of inflectional class, which comprises several classes or (sub)classes and microclasses and whose nucleus is prototypically a productive microclass.

Microclass: a microclass is a set of those paradigms which share exactly the same morphological and morphonological generalisations.

Miniparadigm: a miniparadigm is a non-isolated set of minimally three phonologically unambiguous and distinct inflectional forms of the same lemma produced spontaneously in contrasting syntactic or situative contexts in the same month of recordings.

Modularised morphology: Morphology proper (also called "modularised morphology" by those who believe in a modular compartmentalisation of adult language) initiates when the basic language-specific properties of the target morphology are acquired and structurally differentiated (i.e. compartmentalised) into verbal vs. nominal inflection vs. word formation.

Morphological productivity: We make a sharp differentiation between morphological productivity and recurrence, frequency or generality of a form (as "productive" is often used in acquisition studies). Productivity, as the core of morphology, is the capability of a morphological pattern or rule to apply freely to new forms. Hence it is not relevant in the earliest phases of morphological development.

Paradigm: a paradigm comprises all inflectional forms (types) of one lemma.

Premorphology: The premorphological phase of language acquisition is the phase where morphological operations occur - both extragrammatical (or "expressive") ones and precursors of later grammatical rules. These precursors consist of rote-learned forms whose selection is assumed to be based on principles of naturalness and constructivism.

Protomorphology: The protomorphological phase of language acquisition is the phase where children start to construct creatively morphological patterns of analogies and of first rules. In this period also most interindividual variation is to be expected.

Rote-learned forms: early inflectional forms which do not show recurrent inflectional contrasts with other forms of the same lemma are regarded as rote learned.

Steps: the term steps is used here to refer to successive sequences of development within one grammatical (sub)system as opposed to phases which hold for several systems.

Token: every occurence of any form of a lemma is counted as a single token.

Type: a type is a grammatical form of a lemma, i.e. an inflectional form in our investigation.

Early verb development in one Spanish-speaking child

Carmen Aguirre

0. Introduction

This paper studies the acquisition process of Spanish verbal morphology in a monolingual child. The study examines the first 50 verb lemmas and covers the period from age 1;7 to 1;10. During this period the child enters the proto-morphological stage and builds the first mini-paradigms.

The data shows that this Spanish child follows two main stages during the verb acquisition process:

1. A pre-morphological stage in which verbs are only acquired as lexical elements.They are treated as structureless words and become the main element in the development of thematic and semantic relations. Grammatical features and meaning linked to verbal morphology are still absent. This pre-morphological stage lasts until 1;8 in our data.
2. A morphological stage in which verb suffixes begin to be analyzed as separate units. At this stage, the relationship between form and meaning begins to be established and the categories linked to the verb (tense, aspect, agreement, mood etc.) begin to be acquired. At this moment, the first mini-paradigms appear, which suggests that the acquisition process of verb morphology has started. At 1;9, the child enters the proto-morphological stage.

1. Description of Spanish verbal morphology
1.1. Productive categories

- Non-finite forms: infinitive, gerund and past participle.
- Finite forms represent five verbal categories: Tense: present, past and future.
- Mood: indicative, subjunctive, conditional and imperative.

- Aspect: perfect and imperfect.
- Person: 1, 2 and 3.
- Number: singular (s) and plural (p).

Indicative mood patterns with four simple tense categories: one present, one future and two past tenses: perfect and imperfect. Subjunctive has one tense category for the present, one for the past and one for the future (unproductive). Imperative has two forms: one for the second person singular and one for the second person plural. There are also two grammatical periphrases commonly used: the continuous present (*estoy comiendo* 'I am eating') and the periphrastic future, which is used much more than the synthetic one, *voy a comer* 'I am going to eat').

1.2. Spanish base and verbal suffixes

Normally, the base of a Spanish verbal form is a stem (the root plus the thematic vowels: *a*, *e* or *i*). Therefore, verbal forms consist of:

$$[ROOT + THEMATIC\ VOWEL]_{STEM} + SUFFIX_1 + SUFFIX_2$$

The first suffix ($suff_1$) carries tense, mood and aspect information. The second suffix ($suff_2$), the agreement suffix, refers to person and number. Changes in the thematic vowel also have a morphosemantic value.

1.3. Verb macroclasses

There are two macroclasses, signaled by the thematic vowels (*a* vs. *e / i*):

1st macroclass *cantar* 'to sing'
2nd macroclass *temer* 'to be afraid' / *partir* 'to leave'.

The first macroclass (*-ar* verbs) has the highest type frequency (more than 90% of verbs). It is the only productive class.

The degree of congruity of the different classes is very high: the *er/ir* macroclass does not differ much from the dominant macroclass *ar*. Most of the tense, aspect, mood markers ($suff_1$) and the agreement markers ($suff_2$) are superstable markers (Dressler et al. 1987) because they hold throughout the conjugation.

Microclassses are mainly formed by alterations in the root. There are only some cases of alterations in suffixes in the case of verbs like *dar* 'give', *estar* 'be' (1s *doy, estoy* instead of *do, *esto), in the strong perfects (*anduvo, supo* instead of *andó, *sabió) and participle (*hecho, abierto* instead of *hacido, *abrido) and in the short imperatives (*sal, ven, di* instead of *sale, *vene, *dice)

Spanish verbal morphology is highly iconic (Dressler et al. 1987), firstly because the most frequent and semantically least marked categories are encoded featureless (pres, 3s, and imp) and secondly because suffixes are more or less the only markers. There is almost no syncretism; homophony is rare (e.g. 3s.pres.ind and 2s.imp are homophonous).

1.4. Model paradigms (*cantar* 'to sing', *temer* 'to be afraid' and *partir* 'to leave')

Present
SG	1	canto	temo	parto
	2	cantas	temes	partes
	3	canta	teme	parte
PL	1	cantamos	tememos	partimos
	2	cantáis	teméis	partís
	3	cantan	cantaron	parten

Simple perfect past
SG	1	canté	temí	partí
	2	cantaste	temiste	partiste
	3	cantó	temió	partió
PL	1	cantamos	temimos	partimos
	2	cantasteis	temisteis	partisteis
	3	cantaron	temieron	partieron

Imperative
SG	2	canta	teme	parte
PL	2	cantad	temed	partid

Analytic past perfect (auxiliary + participle)
SG	1	he	cantado / temido / partido
	2	has	cantado / temido / partido
	3	ha	cantado / temido / partido
PL	1	hemos	cantado / temido / partido
	2	habéis	cantado / temido / partido
	3	han	cantado / temido / partido

Suppletives
Ser 'be': soy, eres, es, somos, sois, son.
Ir 'go': voy, vas, va, vamos, vais, van.

2. Data base
2.1. General data base

This study is based on the longitudinal spontaneous speech data of one Spanish boy, Magín.[1] This boy is the third and youngest child of a couple living in Madrid. The mother, who was the researcher, recorded him regularly in everyday situations. Data collection started at 1;7, when he was beginning to build up two-word utterances and it ended when the child was 2;7. Table 1 shows the period under study.

Table 1. Investigated data of Magín

Age	MLU (in words)	Time of recordings (in minutes)	Number of analyzable utterances
1;7	1.2	30	182
1;8	1.4	60	392
1;8.15	1.4	45	234
1;9	1.8	30	105
1;9.15	1.7	60	310
1;9.27	1.7	60	477
1;10	1.8	90	748
1;10.16	2.0	60	350
1;10.20	2.0	45	278
1;10.27	2.3	60	366

3. Magín's verbal production
3.1. Quantitative data of verbal production

Table 2. Number of verb lemmas, types and tokens from 1;7 to 1;10 (without repetitions and frozen forms, percentages with respect to the number of analyzed utterances)[2]

Age	Lemma	New Lemma	Types	Tokens	Tokens %	Morph. Errors	Errors %	Analyzed Utter.
1;7	8	8	13	81	44	21	26	182
1;8	25	19	33	206	33	57	28	626
1;9	35	12	57	278	31	49	18	892
1;10	58	24	108	677	38	90	13	1742

The phases during this period are:

Pre-morphology: 1;7 – 1;8
Proto-morphology: 1;9 – 1;10

Proto-morphology begins with the emergence of the first verbal mini-paradigms.

3.2. The pre-morphological stage
3.2.1. Emergence of the first verbal forms

As shown in the table above, Magín uses a high percentage of verbs from the very beginning. As he enters the two-word stage at 1;7, we find that almost 40% of the utterances produced include a verb and a lot of these utterances consist of just a verb. At this moment Magín's MLU is only 1.2 and most of the expressions are one-word utterances.

Before the first tape was recorded, there were diary notes made of the first words acquired by Magín in the one word-stage. At the very beginning he uses only a few words. Some of them are verbs. At 1;4 he employs *ma* for *quema* 'it burns' in any dangerous situation or *apapa*, for *apaga* 'switch off!', when he wants to switch the light on or off. One month later, at 1;5, he begins to use the imperative *abre* 'open' and a formulaic utterance *be abá* instead of *quiero beber agua* 'I want to drink water'. He seems to have amalgamated the verb *beber,* which he has truncated to *be*, with *agua,* possibly taken from the frequent adult question addressed to the child: *¿quieres beber agua?* 'do you want to drink water?'. At 1;6 he employs *quere* and *quero* (3s and 1s, respectively of 'want') and the imperative *quita* 'keep away'.

The high number of verbs documented in the data from the very beginning (see table 2) shows that predication is essential in Magín's first verbal communication and he does not have any problem in using verbs to make these predications.[3] This characteristic of Magín's early acquisition of verbs explains why we find almost no precursors of verbs made with onomatopoeic elements or with nouns. Only one onomatopoeic element, created by the child, is found: *ufu*. He employs it like an imperative when he wants to blow up a balloon; but it appears at 1;9, when the child is already in the proto-morphological stage.

Word combinations and context adequacy indicate that Magín knows about the meaning of the verbs. At the same time, the syntax begins to develop and the child uses the small set of verbs that he has in his repertory in thematic relations with the appropriate nouns in the appropriate context. The following examples show some multi-word utterances where the verb appears in thematic relations with nominal phrases:

Verb + Object
(1) *Nariz moja.*   'nose wet'   (1;8.15)
(2) *Zapato toma.*   'shoe take'   (1;8.15)

Subject + Verb
(3) *Agua quema.*   'water burns'   (1;7)
(4) *Mamá cae.*   'mummy falls down'   (1;7)

3.2.2. Emergence of verbal categories

Table 3. Emergence of verbal categories (number of tokens)

Age	Pres. Ind.	Imp.	Inf.	Past Part.	Ger-und	Synth. Perfect Past	Anal. Perfect Past	Pres. Subj.	Pres. Progr.	Imperf. Past
1;7	28	13	23					7		
1;8	94	56	24	25		1		8		
1;9	199	12	16	29		7	14	1		1
1;10	414	101	97	29	5		20	11	2	

Repetitions and frozen forms have been excluded from the analysis in all the tables.

Table 4. Development in the use of grammatical persons (number of tokens per month)

Age	Utter.	Present forms (tokens)						Past forms (tokens)					
		Singular			Plural			Singular			Plural		
		1st	2nd	3rd	1st	2nd	3rd	1st	2nd	3rd	1st	2nd	3rd
1;7	182	1		25		2							
1;8	626	4		62		28							
1;9	892	27		113	15	45				8/14			
1;10	1742	45	1	299	24	32				–/17			

In the 3s column, the first number corresponds to the synthetic past and the second number to the analytic past. In the 3p column, almost all the occurrences correspond to the forms *no (es)tán* and *se van*. Most of them are agreement errors. Not taking these forms into account, we only have a single 3p form at 1;8, seven at 1;9, and nine at 1;10.

At the pre-morphological stage (1;7 and 1;8), Magín uses mainly three verbal forms: 3s.pres.ind, 2p.imp and infinitives (see tables 3 and 4). The verbal form most often employed is the 3s.pres.ind. Twelve verb lemmas appear in this form (q*uema* 'it burns', *cae* 'it falls down', *pincha* 'it pricks', *moja* 'it wets', *sabe* 'he knows'). Imperatives are also very much employed. We find eight verb lemmas in imperative form (*abre* 'open', *echa* 'throw', *quita* 'take away'). Magín uses also six verb lemmas in infinitive form. They appear very often with the preposition *a*, as it normally appears in adult speech when addressing the child to give an imperative meaning (*a mir* – instead of adult *a dormir* – 'to sleep', *abrir* 'to open', *ver* 'to see').

Magín also uses:

First singular present forms with 3 verb lemma: *quito* 'take off' and *pongo* 'I put it', but they are always used with imperative value and *quemo* 'I burn'.[4]

3s.pres of subjunctive forms: *abra* 'open (subjunctive)' and *eche* 'throw (subjunctive)', that are always employed instead of the imperative, and one correct use of the subjunctive *de* 'give' in the imperative negation (*no de*[5] 'give not').

Two verbs in the 3p.pres form[6], *no tan*, instead of the adult form *no están*, (*no tan e pipi*. 'Are not the bird'), and *be van,* instead of the adult form *se van* (*be van, avión* 'leave, the plane'). These two forms are used to express non-existence.

And finally, we find at 1;8 two change-of-state verbs in participle form. These verbs are *asustar* 'frighten' and *romper* 'break'. They are only produced in these perfect forms and the auxiliary is always absent:

(5) *Tutado avón* (*asustado avión*) 'frightened plane'
(6) *Tutado po allí* (*asustado por allí*) 'frightened there'
(7) *Ta toto* (*está roto*) '(it) is broken'

The lack of productivity suggests that these participle forms are still unanalyzed (morphologically and syntactically) and that this kind of predication is very close to adjectival predication.

As we have seen, different verbal forms have been used, but morphological rules are not operative at this stage and the verbal forms produced are rote-learned. Consequently most of the verbs are used in only one form. This gives rise to a lot of agreement errors. The rate of agreement errors is 26 % and 28% at 1;7 and 1;8 respectively.

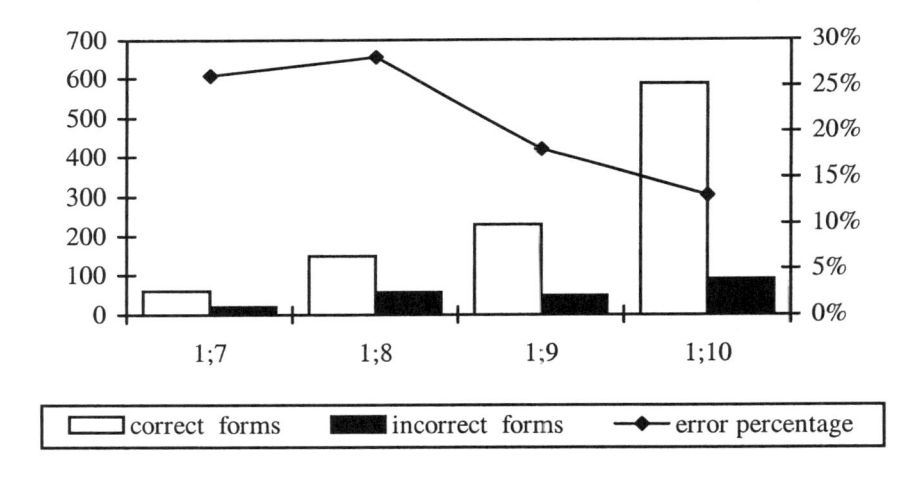

Figure 1. Magín: Development of agreement errors

Some of these errors are produced in question-answer structures, where it is easy to see that the child is not able to change the person that he has heard in the question in order to arrive at the correct form in the answer:

(8) *MOT: ¿*Te lo abro*? 'Shall I open it?'
    *CHI: *Abro.* 'I open' (instead of imperative)
(9) *MOT: ¿*Que lo eche*? 'Shall I throw (3s.subj)it?'
    *CHI: *Eche.* 'Throw (3s.subj)'

Absence of productivity in the use of the verb forms is observed in the difference between lemmas and types presented in table 2 and 3. At 1;7 the number of verb lemmas used by the child is 8 while the number of verb types is 13. The same difference is found at 1;8, where we find 25 verb lemmas and 33 verb types.

Mueller Gathercole, Sebastián, and Soto (1999) examine verb-by-verb the Maldonado-Vidal's corpus reporting on a similar acquisition process. These authors find that their two subjects produce several verbal forms very early on, but only a single form per verb. Similarly, they observe a relatively high frequency of errors in both children before the contrastive use of verbal forms is acquired. These authors claim that each error involves the use of a single or earlier-acquired form instead of the necessary construction (Mueller Gathercole, Sebastián, and Soto 1999: 145, 148).

Magín sometimes appears to have stored just the most frequent input form; for instance, he uses the verb *dormir* 'sleep' in the infinitive because his mother says often *a dormir* when she wants the baby to go to sleep. In some cases the child may pick up a less frequent form and may overgeneralize its usage by chance. This seems to be the case with the 3p *no (es)tán* 'they are not', a form that he uses to express non-existence. He has picked up this verbal form while looking at, and playing with, a drawing book together with his mother. This book was especially designed for learning the numbers, so it had many balloons, dolls, etc.[7]

Nevertheless, as we have seen at the beginning of this section, most of the verbs are used in 3s.pres.ind or in the homophonous 2s.imp. These forms are the simplest because they are morphologically featureless. They are only built with the stem (root + thematic vowel), without any suffix. 3s.pres.ind can also be seen as the semantically least marked form and the most frequent. In this respect it will be the best candidate in Spanish to be taken as a default form in verbal morphology acquisition. A very similar situation is found in Finnish, Lithuanian and Croatian (see Laalo; Wójcik; Katičić this volume).

In tables 3 and 4, we see that the development in the use of verbal forms shows a great increase in the 3s.pres.ind and a progressive decrease of the other forms. The child uses the old verbs that he already knows in their rote-learned forms, but the new lemmas are mostly acquired in 3s.pres.ind which begins to be a default form. The initial phase of proto-morphology is characterized by a considerable overuse of this form. We will return to this in the next section.

3.2.3. Emergence of mini-paradigms – pre-paradigm step[8]

Table 5. Magín's variation in inflectional forms at 1;7 and 1;8

Age	Lemma		Infl. class	Form	Category
1;7	abrir	'open'	class 3	abrir*	inf.
				abre	imp.
				abra*	1/3s.pres.sub.
	estar	'be'	class 1	(es)tá	3s.pres.ind.
				(es)tán*	3p.pres.ind.
	quemar	'burn'	class 1	quemo	1s.pres.ind.
				quema	3s.pres.ind.
1;8	abrir	'open'	class 3	abrir*	inf.
				abre	imp.
				abren*	3p.pres.ind.
	estar	'be'	class 1	(es)tá	3s.pres.ind.
				(es)tán*	3p.pres.ind.
	echar	'throw'	class 1	echa	imp.
				eche*	1/3s.pres.sub.
	ver	'see'	class 2	ver	inf
				ve	3s.pres.ind.
	caer	'fall down'	class 2	cae	3s.pres.ind.
				caía	3s.imp. past.ind.
	ir	'go'	suppletive	va	3s.pres.ind.
				van*	3p.pres.ind.

The asterisk means that there is an agreement, tense or mood error.

The verb *abrir* 'open' is the only one that appears in different verbal forms. Judged from the adult targets, it appears with a lot of agreement and mood mistakes. This shows that the child is only aware of the fact that some words have different endings. Accordingly, we find a very interesting sequence of words in the first recording session, in which Magín wants his mother to open a bag, but she does not open it. The child gets increasingly anxious and, instead of repeating the imperative form *abre* (also 3s.pres) he tries to reach his objective by using various forms that he is hearing, at this moment, from his mother. One of them is an immediate repetition (*abro* 1s.pres.). All the others (*abra*[9] with imperative tone, *abrir* infinitive) cannot be considered repetitions. The child has picked them up during the conversation and he uses them incorrectly.

At the end of the pre-morphological period (1;8) some two-member paradigms develop but not enough correct morphological variety is available yet for the child to engage in morphological analysis.

We claim that all these different forms are rote-learned and therefore, part of his lexicon. Magín does not identify the suffixes as morphological elements that semantically and syntactically encode distinct categories linked to the verb (person, tense, mood etc.). The use of these endings in verbal forms does not reveal any procedure based on processing. That is to say any procedure in which the child is applying morphological rules. As a result, these different ending forms are not productive, yet. For this reason we cannot consider this case a real mini-paradigm.

Two main reasons lead us to this conclusion. The first one is quantitative. At this stage the child still has too few examples of different verb forms for one single verb. Most of the verbs are used in only one grammatical person and one single tense. However, a sufficient number of elements are needed for developing morphology. The second reason is qualitative. The high level of agreement and mood errors produced leads us to conclude that these different verbal suffixes are still unanalyzed, they are different variants of one single form and one single meaning. Nevertheless, these inflectional forms can be considered as precursors of the development of verbal morphology.

3.3. The proto-morphological stage

At this stage, the child begins to go beyond the lexical verb meaning and he acquires the categories agreement and tense.

For the first time, we find evidence that Magín analyzes the verbal suffixes as verb elements that convey information about tense and person (subject of the predication). This discovery is triggered by the lexical acquisition of the first different verb forms. Once it is produced, it also triggers the quick acquisition of the agreement morphology of Spanish and, thus, initializes proto-morphology with the emergence of the first mini-paradigms.[10]

3.3.1. Emergence of mini-paradigms in proto-morphology

Table 6. Magín's true mini-paradigms and two-member mini-paradigms at 1;9

Lemma		Infl. class	Form	Category
ir	'go'	suppletive	va	3s.pres.ind
			van	3p.pres.ind
			vamos	1p.pres.ind
			ido	past.part
caer	'fall down'	class 2	cae	3s.pres.ind
			caía	3s.past.imperf.ind
			cayó	3s.synt.past.perf
quitar	'take off'	class 1	quita	3s.pres.ind./imp
			quito	1s.pres.ind
estar	'be'	class 1	(es)tá	3s.pres.ind
			(es)tán*	3p.pres.ind
asustar	'frighten'	class 1	asusto	1s.pres.ind
			asustado	past.part
pinchar	'prick'	class 1	pincha	3s.pres.ind
			pinchan	3p.pres.ind
querer	'want'	class 2	quiere*	3s.pres.ind
			quiero	1s.pres.ind
romper	'break'	class 2	rompe	3s.pres.ind
			roto	past.part

Table 7. Magín's true mini-paradigms and two-member mini-paradigms at 1;10

Lemma		Infl. class	Form	Category
ir	'go'	suppletive	va	3s.pres.ind
			vamos	1p.pres.ind
			ido	past.part
			ve	imp.
hacer	'make'	class 2	hace	3s.res.ind
			haces	2s.pres.ind
			haga	3s.pres.sub
			hagas	2s.pres.sub
estar	'be'	class 1	(es)tá	3s.pres.ind
			(es)tán	3p.pres.ind
			estoy	1s.pres.ind
asustar	'frighten'	class 1	asusta	3s.pres.ind
			asuste*	3s.pres.sub
			asustado	past.part

Table 7. continued

Lemma		Infl. class	Form	Category
mojar	'wet'	class 1	moja	3s.pres.ind
			mojan	3p.pres.ind
			mojado	past.part
quitar	'take off'	class 1	quito	1s.pres.ind
			quite	3s.pres.sub
			quita	imp
abrir	'open'	class 3	abrir	inf
			abre	imp
			abro	1s.pres.ind
venir	'come'	class 3	viene	3s.pres.ind
			venir	inf
			ven	imp
pasar	'pass'	class 1	pasa	3s.pres.ind/imp
			pasado	past.part
picar	'bite'	class 1	pica	3s.pres.ind
			picado	past.part
pillar	'catch'	class 1	pilla	3s.pres.ind
			pillar	inf
pinchar	'prick'	class 1	pincha	3s.pres.ind
			pinchan	3p.pres.ind
quemar	'burn'	class 1	quema	3s.pres.ind
			quemamos	1p.pres.ind
caer	'fall down'	class 2	cae	3s.pres.ind
			cayó	3s.synt.past.perf
coger	'take'	class 2	cojo	1s.pres.ind
			cogiendo	gerund
poder	'take'	class 2	puedo	1s.pres.ind
			puede*	3s.pres.ind
querer	'want'	class 2	quiere	3s.pres.ind
			quiero	1s.pres.ind
ser	'be'	class 2	es	3s.pres.ind
			son	3p.pres.ind

The mini-paradigms formed as a result of unmotivated phonological variations have not been considered in the table. Since the number of mini-paradigms attested in a corpus depends on sample size, we propose two sample-size independent values for investigating the development of the paradigm formation capacity in a child. The first value, P (utter.), is calculated by dividing the number of mini-paradigms by the number of analyzed utterances per month. The second value, P (lem.), which serves as an index for the paradigm formation capacity of the child in relation to his verb lexicon: it is calculated by dividing the number of mini-paradigms by the number of verb lemmas per month. The paradigm values P (utter.) and P (lem.) are intended to provide an objective base for the comparison of mini-paradigms across corpora and languages (see also Klampfer and Katičić this volume).

Table 8. Emergence of mini-paradigms

Age	True mini-paradigms all/new parad.	2-member mini-paradigms all/new parad.	Mini-paradigms per month	Paradigm values P(utter.)	Paradigm values P(lem.)
1;7	–/–	1/1	1	0.5%	12.5%
1;8	–/–	5/4	5	0.9%	20%
1;9	2/2	7/6	9	1,0%	25%
1;10	8/8	10/6	18	1,0%	32,7%

The strongest evidence showing that Magín has entered the protomorphological stage is the emergence of mini-paradigms in verb acquisition. But also, at the same time, the first auxiliary verbs appear with the first periphrastic verb constructions: analytic past perfect, at 1;9 and, later on, at 1;10, the first present progressive forms (*estar* 'to be' + *gerund*). At 1;10, we can also find the first modal verb *poder* 'can'. We do not find any plural variation in names yet, subject pronouns are not documented in the data and articles are very often replaced by fillers. Therefore, we can conclude that the acquisition of verbal morphology is the first step for morphological development in Spanish.

Our data shows a real spurt in the mini-paradigms' emergence (see tables 5, 6, 7 and 8). Magín reaches the barrier of three true mini-paradigms (Kilani-Schoch and Dressler 2000) at the onset of proto-morphology (1;9), and one month later, Magín has already built 2 four-member mini-paradigms, 6 three-member mini-paradigms and 10 two-member paradigms.

This stage is also very important for the acquisition of verb vocabulary (see table 3). The increase in the number of verbs used is dramatic. The number of verb lemmas in Magín's vocabulary is only about 27 when he is 1;8, 39 at 1;9 and it reaches 63 at 1;10.[11] We are justified in saying that a verb spurt takes place at this stage. The MLU, which reveals the syntactic development, increases in the same striking way (see table 1), from 1.4 at

1;8.15 to 1.7 at 1;9.27 and to 2.3 at 1;10.27. The moment of identification of verbal categories, when verb morphology starts to develop and the child enters the proto-morphological stage, is also a key moment in the acquisition of verb vocabulary and syntax.

It seems that a sufficient number of lexical verbs must be stored so that the child begins to build up the first mini-paradigms. This "sufficient number" seems relatively low in the case of Spanish if we compare it with other languages under study, like German (Klampfer 2000, this volume; Bittner this volume), English (Gülzow this volume) and French (Kilani-Schoch this volume)

As we have seen, we find the first three-member mini-paradigms in Magín's data at 1;9 when he has only about 40 verbs in his lexicon. When a sufficient number of different verb forms for the same lemma are acquired, the child begins to discover morphological regularities and the verbal suffixes begin to be analyzed as separate elements that encode related, though independent, meanings. Suffixes are now linked to the verb in order to add new semantic and grammatical information. They can be seen as independent meaningful elements. This discovery accelerates the acquisition process of the Spanish verb morphology.

At this stage, the development of morphology is initiated with the emergence of the first mini-paradigms. Nevertheless, we claim that they are still stored in the lexicon, element by element and together with the verb. The child must have stored an important number of verbs, each of them in different forms, in order to begin to build a system. The development of morphological rules presupposes a high number of verbal forms. It should be mentioned that the first overgeneralizations, a proof of the presence of morphological rules, will appear one month later.

López Ornat (1994) also reports on the delay in Spanish acquisition overgeneralizations. This author establishes four phases for verbal morphology acquisition and overgeneralizations take place at phase 3, the "rigid rules" phase. In the same line, Mueller Gathercole, Sebastián, and Soto (1999) consider that over-regularized forms do not emerge until well after the relevant forms become contrastive.

As mentioned above, the development of mini-paradigms is the strongest argument in support of the claim that the child is entering the proto-morphological stage. Another argument that supports this claim has to do with the mistakes concerning the development of agreement errors. During this period the child begins to use the verbal forms more accurately and the rate of errors decreases in this period (see figure 1), from 28% at 1;8 to

18% and 13% at 1;9 and 1;10 respectively. We can also see an interesting change of error type. Before proto-morphology, most of the errors were produced because the verbs were used in a single form or, when we found more than one form, they were unmotivated phonological variations. In the proto-morphology stage, however, the overuse of the 3s.pres.ind provokes most of the mistakes. The old errors appear as a consequence of the lack of morphology, but the new ones show that the child has taken a form as default form.

3.3.2. Verb categories in proto-morphology

Magín's entry into the proto-morphological stage shows an interesting increase of the 3s.pres.ind forms (see tables 4, 5, 6 and 7). 30% of the verb tokens belonged to this form in pre-morphology and they reach 43% at this stage. It should be remembered that this is the morphologically simplest form (the root + thematic vowel) and the only homophonous one (3s.pres = 2s.imp).

Most of the new lemmas appear for the first time in this form and many agreement errors are produced because the 3s is used instead of any other person.[12] 2s.ind (the marker is an -s) is absent and the child uses a 3s in its place. In this period, 1s of indicative begins to appear properly sometimes, but very often is replaced for 3s. Finally, we find some occurrences of 3s instead of 3p. The overuse of this verbal form leads us to maintain that it has been taken as a default form that the child uses when he does not master the target form. Mueller Gathercole, Sebastián, and Soto also report a clear overabundance of 3s for one of their two subjects. They affirm that this form acts as the unmarked form and appears to be a "default" form for this subject (1999: 152)

The entrance into the proto-morphological period is also characterized by the productive use of past participle in analytical past perfect constructions. This new form causes the emergence of some new mini-paradigms at 1;9 and 1;10 (see tables 9 and 10).

At 1;10, the infinitive also starts to be used as a complement to modal verbs (*querer* 'want' and *poder* 'can'); the first gerund forms appear with the first uses of the present progressive (*estar* 'be' + gerund) and the pres. subj. is now correctly used in negative orders (*no haga(s)* don't make, *no toque(s)* don't touch). At the same time, new verbs (not only *estar* 'be', *ir* 'go' and *pinchar* 'prick') can be seen in 3p.pres.ind.

According to Magín's data until 1;10, the order of acquisition of verbal categories in Spanish is the following: 3s.pres.ind > imp > inf > past participle > 1s.pres.ind > 3s.pres.subj > 3p.pres.ind > gerund.[13] All of these verbal categories are present in the mini-paradigms (tables 8, 9, and 10).

3.4. Tense-aspect and agreement distinction in the same verb lemma

Looking at the first mini-paradigms we can observe that there is not just one pattern. Regarding morphology acquisition, the child seems to be acquiring the tense-aspect distinction first and, a little bit later, agreement, as well as some other distinctions that do not fit these two main groups, namely infinitive – present, imperative – present and indicative – subjunctive (only for prohibitive at this stage).

Tense-aspect distinction:
Present / Past Perfect
ir 'go':	3s.pres	*va*	– 3s.past perfect		*se ha ido*
romper 'break':	3s.pres	*rompe*	– 3s.past perfect		*se ha roto*
caer 'fall':	3s.pres	*cae*	– 3s.synthetic past perf.		*cayó*
			– 3s.past imperf		*caía*
asustar 'frighten':	1s.pres	*asusto*	– past participle		*asustado*
			(the auxiliary is absent)		

Present / Gerund
coger 'take':	1s.pres	*cojo*	– gerund		*cogiendo*

Agreement distinction:
Singular – Plural
ir 'go':	3s.pres	*va*	– 3p.pres	*van*	– 1p.pres	*vamos*
pinchar 'prick':	3s.pres	*pincha*	– 3p.pres	*pinchan*		
ser 'to be':	3s.pres	*es*	– 3p.pres	*son*		

1st – 3rd person singular
querer 'want':	3s.pres	*quiere*	– 1p.pres	*quiero*
poder 'can':	3s.pres	*puede**	– 1s.pres	*puedo*
estar 'be':	3s.pres	*está*	– 1s.pres	*estoy*

3rd – 2nd person singular
hacer 'do':	3s.pres	*hace*	– 2s.pres	*haces*
hacer 'do':	3s.pres.sub	*haga**	– 2s.pres.sub	*hagas*

Similar findings are reported by Mueller Gathercole, Sebastián, and Soto (1999). With regard to person, tense and number, they argue that it is impossible to say that one of these categories emerges or is acquired before the others. In this respect, they support that the child gains a command of aspects of the paradigm in a piecemeal fashion (Mueller Gathercole, Sebastián, and Soto 1999: 146).

Other researchers on Spanish verb morphology acquisition defend the earlier acquisition of agreement vs tense-aspect. Grinstead (2000) examines Linaza's corpus and considers that person agreement, but not number or tense, is used contrastively in the early stage. However, Linaza's corpus is relatively poor on data as not enough verbs are documented to be able to make such a generalization. Also, a contrastive use of the same lemma is not presented in Grinstead's analysis either. Fernández (1994) analyzes López Ornat's corpus and finds that this subject make the first verb contrast in person (1s.pres – 3s.pres) but this contrast cannot be regarded as fully productive because it only occurs with a couple of verbs.

3.5. Inflectional classes

The mini-paradigms show that there is no preference for the first macroclass in the first verbs acquired by the child. During the pre-morphological stage, there is a predominance of verbs from the *er* class. This fact is not striking: there may be few verbs in the second macroclass, but some of them are among the most token-frequent in Spanish. At this stage, the verb is only a lexical element and the class system has not begun to develop, thus token frequency is of paramount importance.

At the proto-morphological stage, the tendency is reversed and most of the new verbs learned belong to the first macroclass. It is likely that, once class formation has started, the verbs belonging to the first macroclass are easier to acquire.

4. Conclusions
4.1. Developmental stages

In Magín's data, the acquisition of Spanish verbal morphology shows two main stages. A pre-morphological stage that lasts till 1;8 and a proto-morphological one that begins at 1;9. During the pre-morphological stage the verbs are learned as structureless lexical elements. At 1;7 verbs begin to be the main component in predication structures in which thematic relations are involved. At 1;9, the child enters the proto-morphological stage and the verb endings begin to be identified as meaningful elements. At that moment the morphological component starts to develop and the first mini-paradigms emerge.

4.1.1. The pre-morphological stage

During this period, when using verbs, the child pays attention only to their lexical meaning. He uses inflected forms, but they are still unanalyzed. That means that it is rote-learned. The only category present is the verb itself, other categories linked to the verb (tense, person, mood etc.) do not yet appear to be identified.

We have seen in our data that, at this stage, different verbal forms of the same verb are not normal and if they appear, they are context-bound or unmotivated phonological variants. This situation results in a lot of mistakes since the used form is not adequate to most contexts.

The most frequently chosen verbal form in Spanish is the 3s.pres. ind or the homophonous 2s.imp. form. They are the morphologically simplest (only the stem), the most frequent and the semantically least marked forms. The number of verbal items that appear for the first time in this form increases gradually when we approach proto-morphology.

Some other verbs are only used in infinitive, past participle, 1s.pres.ind. and 3p.pres.ind. These are normally cases in which the child has fixed the most frequent form for a particular verb in adult speech when addressing the child (infinitives like *dormir* 'sleep' or past participles like *roto* 'broken') or not very frequent verbal forms "captured" by the child in a given context. That is the case with the 3p.pres.ind. forms *no (es)tán* 'are not' *y se van* 'they go' that appear only in negative contexts, when something disappears. Preferences for certain phonological patterns are also important for a given form to be fixed.

4.1.2. The proto-morphological stage

During this period the verbal suffixes start to be analyzed as meaningful elements and paradigms are gradually constructed. That can be seen as an intermediate stage in which morphology begins to develop, but morphological rules are absent and verbal forms are still rote-learned.

The use of the 3s.pres.ind increases dramatically. It is found in most of the mini-paradigms and it begins to be a default form. Most of the agreement errors involve its overuse. At 1;9 the first true mini-paradigms appear. One month later we can find a real mini-paradigm spurt. Overgeneralizations are not yet found.

The proto-morphological stage can be said to coincide with an intensive development in verb lemma acquisition and in syntax.

4.2. Concluding remarks

During the pre-morphological stage, the child does not analyze the end of the verb as a suffix at all. This is because the acquisition of verbal morphology has not yet taken place.

An economy consideration, one form – one meaning, corresponding to the preference for an invariant relation between form and meaning, predicts the tendency that the child will choose one form and only one for every verb. Normally the form will be context-bound, in the first uses. This main assumption helps to explain why Magín normally has, in this first period, only one form for every verb.

An interesting problem is why the child chooses one form from the set of potential paradigmatic forms rather than another. In general, Magín chooses a given form because:

a) it is the simplest morphological form (the base form if it is a standard form in the target language);

b) it is the most frequent morphological form;

c) it is the most frequent form for a particular verb in child-directed speech;

d) it is perceptually the most salient form for any child and the easiest to produce.

e) it is the form "captured" by the child in a given context; after which he fixes it.

We claim that at the pre-morphological stage, one of these factors or a combination of them can explain the first verbal forms used by the child. Simplicity and frequency underlie all these conditions. Frequency is important in the morphological verbal system (b) and in the specific verbal forms (c). Simplicity predicts in the morphological level (a) that stem forms will appear earlier than inflected forms. On the phonological level, saliency is understood as phonological simplicity (d). The easier the form is to perceive and to produce, the more salient it is.

Considerations (a), (b), and (d) explain why 3s.pres.ind (the most frequent form) is the first to appear when it is a stem. It is morphologically simplest because there is no suffix, and easy to perceive and to produce because it ends in a vowel.[14] In this respect, it is noteworthy that this form is the first to be acquired, not only in Spanish but also in the other languages discussed in this volume in which we find this particular fact; namely Finnish, Lithuanian and Croatian.

2s.imp. is among the first forms to appear when it is also a stem form. That is the case in Spanish in which 3s.pres.ind is homophonous with the 2s.imp. In Magín's data, 2s.imp. is also a very frequently used form. A similar situation is documented in Finnish (see Laalo this volume).

Homophony, related to frequency (homophonous forms are more frequent than not homophonous ones), has been an argument to explain the overuse of infinitives in German and French (see Klampfer; Kilani-Schoch this volume). This can also be a further argument to explain the early emergence of these two verbal forms in Spanish.

Point (c) predicts that we will find also some diversity of verb-forms in first verb-vocabulary. This assertion is corroborated by Magín's data (e.g. *dormir* 'sleep' infinitive, *asustado* 'frightened' past participle).

Consideration (d) helps also to predict that we will find differences between languages. For example, 3s.pres.ind is very salient in Spanish because it ends in an open syllable, but not in German because it ends in a stop [*t*]. This difficulty of perceiving and producing this last consonant explains why this very frequent form appears so late in some German speaking children, although German is a relatively rich inflected language (cf. Klampfer this volume).[15]

The final point (e) predicts that we will find differences between the children that acquire the same language. We have taken into consideration the data of only one child, but we find some verb forms used, like the already discussed 3p.pres.ind of verb *estar* 'to be', *están*, that should not be expected in other children because it is not frequent in input data and it is morphologically marked.

In summary, this period should generally be characterized by diversity among acquisition processes of different languages (inter-lingual diversity) as well as diversity among children learning the same language (intralingual diversity). At the proto-morphological stage, the child discovers morphology. Verbal suffixes are understood as meaningful elements and the verbal paradigms begin to develop. We hold that the entrance into this stage will be triggered and guided by the morphological characteristics of the language the child is exposed to and, hence, naturalness considerations and typological constraints may predict the acquisition process of verb morphology across languages. We expect that a language with rich verbal inflection, like Spanish, will favour the discovery of verbal morphology. The high diversity of verbal forms with which the child is confronted will make morphological structure much more evident. That is borne out in Magín's data. Proto-morphology begins very early on and paradigm construction shows an early and clear spurt.

The high degree of universal naturalness of Spanish verbal inflection leads us also to predict that the proto-morphological stage will begin early in the process of acquisition compared to other languages. Neither the number of errors in the same process nor the number of overgeneralizations will be very high. This prediction is corroborated by our data where the proto-morphological stage develops early on, the number of errors is not high at this stage, and overgeneralizations are sparse and occur relatively late.

Naturalness considerations predict that the child will start with the least marked form: the 3s.pres.ind, in Spanish, as we have already discussed. Therefore we expect that this form will be the first one to appear. This prediction, in fact, is borne out in our data. As we have seen that 3s.pres.ind can be regarded as a default form in Magín's data and that this form is one of the components in almost all mini-paradigms.

Notes

1. The data presented in this study are included in Aguirre's Ph.D. dissertation (Aguirre 1995).
2. To qualify as an utterance, a production has to include at least one meaningful unit resembling a Spanish word in form and meaning. Babbling, vocalizations and completely incomprehensible strings were not considered utterances. Citations (e.g. nursery rhymes and songs) and direct imitations were excluded from the analysis.
3. We find in the data an apparently strange decrease in the use of verbs (from 39% utterances with verb at 1;7 to 28% at 1;8). The development of syntax,

during the two-word stage, may cause a paradoxical phenomenon. It may be the case that limitations in processing capacity make it very difficult to form utterances with more than two words. This leads the child to omit the verb when two other elements take part in the thematic relations. That is the case with the utterances involving locative relations that we find at 1;8: *(Es)t(r)ella arriba* 'star up'. *Avión po(r) ahí* 'plane there'. *Aba tacita* 'water little cup'.

4. We find also *quiero* (*quiero aba*. 'I want water'), in diary notations.
5. There is an agreement error: 3s instead of 2s.
6. Nearly all of these occurrences of 3p are agreement errors. The subject normally appears in singular. At that moment the child is not able to use the plural in nouns.
7. This generalized use of the third person plural can also be due to a phonological preference. Magín likes to pronounce words finishing in a stressed vowel plus an *n*, especially after a dental. He always pronounces this final *n* in nouns (*avión* 'plane', *tatón* for *ratón* 'mouse' and for *caracol* 'snail') with strength and he often uses this phonological sequence babbling when he plays with sounds.
8. Cf. Kilani-Schoch and Dressler (2000).
9. In this case the child either added, erroneously, the thematic vowel *a* of the first conjugation, instead of using the appropriate thematic vowel *e*, or he selected the prohibitive form of subjunctive *no abras*.
10. A similar proposal has been made in syntax to explain the acquisition of functional categories: the Lexical Learning Hypothesis (Clahsen and Penke 1992; Meisel and Müller 1992). Under this assumption, it is only when the child learns the lexical elements that new projections are added to existing phrase-structure representations. Clahsen, Eisenbeiß, and Penke (1996) defend "Morphological Bootstrapping". Their idea is that functional categories such as IP, AGRP, etc. or syntactic features may come into the child's phrase structure as a consequence of the child's learning a regular inflectional paradigm.
11. Although the number of analyzed utterances is much higher in the last recordings there are some diary notations that show that Magin's verb vocabulary is not higher during the time of the first recordings.
12. Only the old agreement mistake, already discussed in 3.2.3., *(es)tán* 'are' for *(es)tá* 'is', is still abundant.
13. For some categories the proposed order of acquisition may need refinement because they can be acquired rather simultaneously (see tables 3, 4, 8–10).
14. In the first stages, syllables finishing in a vowel (CV) are preferred over syllables finishing in a consonant (CVC, VC). Final consonant elisions are frequent in early child speech in all kinds of words (Bernhardt and Stemberg 1998).
15. We find also cases in which this final *t* is produced very early. Anna, the German child studied by Bittner, produced very early 3s.ind. In these cases we can consider that input frequency is more powerful than saliency.

References

Aguirre, Carmen
1995   La Adquisición de las Categorías Gramaticales en Español. Ph.D. dissertation, University Autónoma of Madrid.

Bernhardt, Barbara H., and Joseph P. Stemberg
1998   *Handbook of Phonological Development: From the Perspective of Constraint-based Nonlinear Phonology*. San Diego/London: Academic Press.

Clahsen, Harald, and Martina Penke
1992   The acquisition of agreement morphology and its syntactic consequences: New evidence on German child language from the Simone-corpus. In: Jürgen M. Meisel (ed.), *The Acquisition of Verb Placement*, 181–223. Dordrecht: Kluwer.

Clahsen, Harald, Sonja Eisenbeiß, and Martina Penke
1996   Lexical learning in early syntactic development. In: Harald Clahsen (ed.), *Generative Perspectives on Language Acquisition: Empirical Findings, Theoretical Considerations, Crosslinguistic Comparisons*, 129–159. Amsterdam: John Benjamins.

Dressler, Wolfgang U., Willi Mayerthaler, Oswald Panagl, and Wolfgang U. Wurzel
1987   *Leitmotifs in Natural Morphology*. Amsterdam/Philadelphia: John Benjamins.

Fernández, Almudena
1994   El aprendizaje de los morfemas verbales: Datos de un estudio longitudinal. In: López Ornat, Susana (ed.), *La adquisición de la lengua española*, 29-47. Madrid: Siglo XXI.

Grinstead, John
2000   Case, inflection and subject licensing in child Catalan and Spanish. *Journal of Child Language* 27: 119–155.

Kilani-Schoch, Marianne, and Wolfgang U. Dressler
2000   The emergence of verb paradigms in two French corpora as an illustration of general problems of pre- and protomorphology. Poster presented at the 9th International Morphology Meeting, Vienna, February 2000.

Klampfer, Sabine
    2000   Early verb development in one Austrian child. In: Dagmar Bittner, Wolfgang U. Dressler, and Marianne Kilani-Schoch (eds.), *First Verbs: On the Way to Mini-paradigms*, 7–21. (ZAS Papers in Linguistics 18.) Berlin: Zentrum für Allgemeine Sprachwissenschaft, Typologie und Universalienforschung (ZAS).

López Ornat, Susana (ed.)
    1994   *La adquisición de la lengua española*. Madrid: Siglo XXI.

Meisel, Jürgen, and Natascha Müller
    1992   Finiteness and verb placement in early child grammar. In: Jürgen M. Meisel (ed.), *The Acquisition of Verb Placement*, 109–138. Dordrecht: Kluwer.

Mueller Gathercole, Virginia C., Eugenia Sebastián, and Pilar Soto
    1999   The early acquisition of Spanish verbal morphology: Across-the-board or piecemeal knowledge? *International Journal of Bilingualism* 3: 133–182.

Early verbal morphology in Turkish: Emergence of inflections*

Ayhan Aksu-Koç and F. Nihan Ketrez

0. Introduction

Turkish inflectional morphology is very regular and emerges quite early (Aksu-Koç and Slobin 1985; Baykoç-Dönmez and Arı 1992; Ekmekçi 1979). Children produce single word utterances constituted of inflected nouns or verbs even before they produce word combinations. In this paper, we focus on the emergence of verbal morphology in a Turkish child's speech between the ages 1;3 and 2;0. We look for evidence of productivity in the contrastive use of inflected versus non-inflected forms. We analyze the observed developments in terms of two stages and complete our analysis when our subject begins to display competence in the use of basic inflectional paradigms. Finally, we discuss the acquisition strategies that might be operative during this early period.

1. Verbs in Turkish
1.1. Syntactic and morphological properties

Turkish is an agglutinative language in which both inflection and word formation are mainly realized by means of suffixation. Most words undergo allophonic variation subject to rules of vowel and/or consonant harmony. Each morpheme is syllabic and stress is typically word final.

The inflectional verbal affixes mark negation, tense/aspect, modality, number and person. Voice particles (such as the causative or the passive), when present, are interposed between the verb and the tense/aspect morphemes. Alternative orderings in the combination of some of these morphemes (tense/aspect/modality, person/number and question) are possible within the bounds of semantic plausibility.[1] Since there is overt agreement marking on the predicate, subject nouns are typically omitted. Object nouns may also be omitted depending on the context of utterance.

Verbs assign structural and inherent cases that are marked through overt affixation in the case of accusative, dative, ablative, locative and instrumental. Nominative case and singular are unmarked base forms that have no phonological realization. Nouns are also marked for plurality and possession but there is no gender. Verbs in embedded structures may also have case and possessive morphology in addition to the nominalization suffixes. Nouns, when they are in predicate position, take agreement and/or tense marking just like verbs. The tense and agreement markers for nouns and verbs are homophones, but their stress pattern is different: for example, in *aç-tı* open-PAST 'he opened' stress is on the final syllable, whereas in *aç-tı* hungry-PAST 'he was hungry', stress is on the initial syllable.

Word order is flexible and subject to pragmatic rules (Erguvanlı 1984), however the canonical order is SOV. Morpheme order within the word is only relatively fixed, being subject to semantic restrictions, as noted above. Examples (1) and (2) illustrate morpheme order and case marking in Turkish.

(1) *(Ben) (o-nu) (Istanbul-da) gör-me-di-m.*
     I   s/he-ACC Istanbul-LOC see-NEG-PAST-1S
     'I did not see him/her in Istanbul.'

(2) *(O) (Ankara-dan) (Izmir-e) (tren-le) git-mi-yor.*
     s/he Ankara-ABL   Izmir-DAT train-INS git-NEG-PROG
     'S/he is not going to Izmir from Ankara by train'

1.2. Inflectional morphology

The verbal affixes for tense-aspect-modality (TAM) are multifunctional. The tense/aspect affixes are the definite past (*-DI*), the progressive (*-Iyor*), the habitual/possibility marker (*-Ir*) (the so called 'aorist'), the inferential/reported past (*-mIş*), and the future (*-(y)AcAK*) that are applied to the verb root/stem with proper phonological variants determined by vowel harmony rules.[2] These inflections assume aspectual functions depending on context: the progressive (*gel-iyor* 'is coming') and habitual (*gel-ir* 'comes') mark types of imperfectivity; the definite past (*gel-di* 'came') and the inferential (*gel-miş* 'has come') may indicate perfectivity or the perfect depending on context, however their main opposition is in terms of evidential modality. These affixes may be stringed together to create complex meanings (*gel-iyor-du* 'was coming', *gel-iyor-muş* 'was evidently coming'). Other modal distinctions are expressed with the necessitative (*-mAlI*), abilitative/potential (*-(y)AbIl*), optative (*-yA*), and conditional (*-sA*) suffixes (Aksu-Koç 1988: 17). Person/number suffixes mark subject-verb agreement and have four paradigms as shown in table 1.

Table 1. The four agreement paradigms in Turkish

	I. (*-Iyor, -mIş, -AcAk, -Ir, mAlI, Ø*)	II. (*-dI* & *-sA*)	III. (*-yA*)	IV. Imperative
1S	*-(y)Im*	*-m*	*-(y)Im*	-
2S	*-sIn*	*-n*	*-sIn*	Ø
3S	Ø	Ø	(*-sIn*)	*-sIn*
1P	*-Iz*	*-k*	*-AlIm*	-
2P	*-sInIz*	*-nIz*	*-sInIz*	*-In(Iz)*
3P	*-lAr*	*-lAr*	*-lAr(sInlAr)*	*sInlAr*

The first agreement paradigm is applied after the present/progressive (*-Iyor*), the habitual/possible (*-Ir*), the inferential/reported past (*-mIş*), the future (*-yAcAK*), the necessitative (*-mAlI*), and the copula (Ø). The second is limited to the definite past tense (*-DI*) and to the conditional mood (*-sA*). The third agreement paradigm is restricted to the optative (*-yA*). The third person form of the optative is usually replaced with the third person form of the fourth agreement paradigm, which is restricted for the imperative.

The negative marker (*-mA*) is always after the verb stem: it follows the derivational suffixes that mark voice (passive (*-Il/-In*), causative (*-DIr*), reciprocal (*-Iş*) and reflexive (*-In*) and precedes the other inflectional markers as in (3a) and (3b).

(3) a. *aç-mı-yor-um*
open-NEG-PROG-1S
'I am not opening (it)'

b. *aç-tır-mı-yor-um*
open-CAUS-NEG-PROG-1S
'I am not letting (him) open (it)'

The question particle (*mI*) appears in two different positions with respect to the agreement marker. It precedes the first agreement paradigm and appears between the TAM markers and the agreement marker, and follows the other agreement paradigms, occurring at the end of the word, as in (4a) and (4b).

(4) a. *aç-ıyor-mu-sun ?*   b. *aç-tı-n   mı?*
    open-PROG-QUES-2S   open-PAST-2S QUES?
    'Are you opening (it) ?' 'Did you open (it)?'

Turkish derivational morphology is also very rich. However, since in the period of development analyzed here derivational processes on the verb are not fully observed, derivational morphology will not be discussed further.[3]

2. Methodology

The data used for the present purpose consists of the spontaneous speech samples of a Turkish monolingual child Deniz, daughter of university educated parents living in Istanbul. Recordings, each of which is about 20 minutes long, were made by one of the parents, at home, with intervals of about 20 days. The data were transcribed, coded morphologically, and entered the computer following CHAT transcribing conventions of the CHILDES project (MacWhinney 1995). Our analyses cover the period between 1;3.3 and 1;9.19 during which inflectional paradigms emerge and show significant development. Table 2 gives overall information about this database.

Table 2. Age, MLU, total number of morphemes and utterances/session for Deniz

Session	Age	MLU in morphemes	Total number of morphemes	Total number of utterances
1	1;3.3	1.26	117	98
2	1;3.12	1.34	101	75
3	1;3.27	1.24	96	77
4	1;5.9	1.20	105	87
5	1;5.28	1.58	217	137
6	1;6.9	1.73	192	111
7	1;7.3	2.53	639	252
8	1;7.8	1.95	317	162
9	1;7.23	2.74	548	200
10	1;8.11	2.93	838	286

Table 2. continued

Session	Age	MLU in morphemes	Total number of morphemes	Total number of utterances
11	1;8.14	3.03	570	188
12	1;8.27	3.42	938	274
13	1;9.1	3.28	627	191
14	1;9.19	2.01	517	148
15	1;10.3	3.81	1339	351
16	1;10.19	3.52	448	127
17	1;11.10	3.64	1414	388
18	1;11.23	3.17	1306	412
19	2;0.4	4.06	1076	265

Each verb or the relevant context was targeted for analysis. All utterances consisting of frozen forms, imitations, incomprehensible strings, songs and interjections were excluded. The quantitative analyses were carried out with the use of CLAN programs.

We look at the emergence and productivity of inflectional morphology, which includes tense-aspect-modality markers, the negative marker, and agreement paradigms for verbs.[4] The aim is to trace the emergence pattern of each morpheme and to investigate its productivity, which requires use with different verbs and/or in different verb-inflection combinations. Another criterion for productivity is the presence of the inflection in the subsequent sample. Similarly, a verb that is used with different tense/aspect and modality markers and/or different person markers is considered to be productive.

3. Results

3.1. Demarcation of the stages

We analyze early morpho-syntactic development in Deniz's speech in terms of two stages (Aksu-Koç 1997, 1998; Ketrez 1999; Aksu-Koç and Ketrez 1999). Stage I is represented by the sessions between 1;3.3–1;5.9 and is the pre-morphological stage where no verbal or nominal inflection is observed. Stage II, between 1;5.28–1;9.19 corresponds to the proto-morphological period where inflectional morphology for the verb (TAM and agreement marking) and the noun (case and number) categories become productive. We take the emergence of derivational processes evidenced by the productive use of causative and passive inflections at 1;19.9 to mark the end of this early phase. Table 3 summarizes the lexical developments across stages I and II.

It is observed that there is a notable increase in the number of items in all lexical categories. In stage I, one or two new verbs enter the child's lexicon in each sample, resulting in a 100% increase in the number of verbs across samples. However, there is no sign of inflectional morphology, either on verbs or nouns.[5] More typical is the use of onomatopoeic forms and extra-grammatical processes such as repetition and analogy.

Table 3. Type (lemma)/ Token frequencies for lexical classes in stages I and II

Stage I	MLU $_{(in\ morphemes)}$ [lowest – highest] : 1.20–1.34		
Lexical Class	Types	Tokens	Utterances
Nouns	46	272	337
Proper Nouns	8	32	337
Verbs	*7*	*8*	*337*
Pronouns	2	6	337
Stage II	MLU $_{(in\ morphemes)}$ [lowest – highest] : 1.58–3.42		
Lexical Class	Types	Tokens	Utterances
Nouns	197	847	1949
Proper Nouns	32	145	1949
Verbs	*80*	*1224*	*1949*
Pronouns	12	173	1949

In stage II, the proportion of new verbs added per sample shows a relative decrease (70%), while there is increasing evidence for inflectional modification. Within this stage we consider the first two samples, 1;5.28–1;6.9, to be transitional to proto-morphology since productivity, evidenced by the increase in the proportion of inflected verb types and tokens (6% and 12%, respectively), is limited to a single form (cf. section 4.3, table 4). In proto-morphology proper between 1;7.3 and 1;9.19, both the variety of inflections and the proportion of inflected verb types (19%) and tokens (33%) increase. Onomatopoeic forms are replaced by adult words, and the use of repetitive processes decreases. Case marking which shows that nouns are being used as arguments of verbs, and responses to adult queries with the appropriate questioned element, provide evidence for developments in syntax (Aksu-Koç and Ketrez 1999). These changes constitute the basis for the demarcation between pre- and proto-morphological stages.

3.2. Predecessors of verb forms

In stage I between (1;3.3–1;5.9) there is no evidence for the verb category since we have only one word utterances without inflections or a few rote-learned forms. Majority of these words are monosyllabic nouns that are phonological variants of adult forms (such as *da-at* = kağıt 'paper', *maa-am* = maymun 'monkey'), as well as forms created by reduplication (such as *mi mi* = kedi 'cat') or onomatopoeia. When used to refer to the action that can be carried out with the object named, such nouns function as extragrammatical predecessors of verbs, as in (5a) and (5b) from (1;3.3). The child's response in (5a) could be interpreted either as 'a picture' or as 'draw', whereas in (5b) the mother's response questioning the agent of the action 'you', shows that she is presupposing the activity 'make (a picture)', having interpreted Deniz's utterance *da:at da:at da:at* as the statement of an intention for action.

(5)   a. MOT: ben   ne   *yap-ı-yım?*
                   I   what   do-OPT-1S
                   'what shall I make?'
          DEN: *da:at (:kağıt)*
                   'paper (= picture /let's draw)'

   b. %sit: takes the paper from her mother
      DEN: *da:at da:at da:at (=kağıt)*
                 paper paper paper
      MOT: sen   mi   *yap-acak-sın?*
                  you   QUE   do-Fut-2S
                  'are you going to make (it)?'

There are singular instances of unmarked verb forms such as *al* 'take' and *gel* 'come', however, onomatopoeic and repetitive strategies such as in (6) from (1;3.12) are more pervasive.

(6) %sit: Deniz and her mother are looking at a picture book.
    MOT: *bisiklet-i-ne   bin-miş   göl-ün*
         bicycle-POSS&3S-DAT get+on-MIŞ lake-GEN&3S
         kenar-ı-na   gel-miş
         side-POSS&3S-DAT come-MIŞ
         'he got on his bicycle and came to the lake side'
    DEN: *bamm:@o bamm:@o*
    MOT: *bam@o diye düştü*
         'it fell going bamm'

Other constructions that function as predecessors of verbs are frozen or partially analyzed forms which consist of an inflectional segment that starts with a stressed syllable plus a 'filler' syllable, formed by analogy to adult inflected verbs. Such analogical formations (e.g. child form: *&ın-m-az* &-PASS-NEG-AORIST; adult form: *kaşı-n-m-az* scratch-PASS-NEG-AORIST 'one does not scratch', or the frozen form *oyna-ya* modeled after *oyna-ma* 'play-NEG' from a song) suggest that the child has extracted a relatively invariant segment of high frequency from adult speech and assimilated it to the bisyllabic word pattern representative of her productions at this stage. Use of such inflectional complexes without a verb, or of verbs with meaningless extra syllables (e.g. *gel-bi-xxx-yiz* come-xxx-AOR:1PL?) reflects sensitivity to patterns of the input, but lack of a full analysis of words into combinable units as yet (Aksu-Koç 1997). During this period, Deniz can only be credited with 'partial knowledge of a morpheme' or some knowledge of a phonological frame extracted from the input. In producing these incomplete forms she is attempting "to supply something" while "that knowledge of what needs to be supplied and how to supply it develops considerably later" (Peters and Menn 1993: 745–750). Thus the morphological replacement of phonologically empty shapes appears to be a gradual process.

3.3. Emergence of verb forms: Overview of development

During the period between 1;3.3–1;9.9 total number of different verbs recorded in Deniz's speech is 80. This number is just seven during stage I, and increases steadily with about 10 verbs per three weeks, to reach 33 at 1;7.3 when she starts using several inflections and has the first 3-member paradigm. When the ratio of all utterances with verbs to total number of analyzed utterances is considered, it is observed that 63% of her utterances has a verb in stage II whereas almost none (2%) did in stage I.

Table 4 presents the distribution across sessions of number of verbs per sample, number and proportion of new verbs added, number of inflectional types and tokens, and their respective proportions in the total number of utterances analyzed. It is observed that inflections appear at 1;5.28, there is a spurt in development both in correct and incorrect inflectional modification at 1;7.3, and then a gradual increase in their correct, and decrease in their erroneous use. It is also observed that the proportion of utterances containing an inflected verb increases steadily with age. We discuss the nature of these developments in the following sections.

Table 4. Number of verbs (lemmas), inflectional types (incorrect types*), tokens (incorrect tokens*), and their proportion in the total number of analyzed utterances [a]

Age	No. of verbs	No. of new verbs added	% of new verbs added	No. of inflectional types	No. of inflectional tokens	prop. of types in total no. of utters.	prop. of tokens in total no. of utters.
1;3.3	3	3	1.0	3	3	.03	.03
1;3.12	1	1	1.0	1	1	.01	.01
1;3.27	1	1	1.0	1	1	.01	.01
1;5.9	2	2	1.0	2 (1*)	2 (1*)	.02	.02
1;5.28	10	6	.60	8 (4*)	18 (4*)	.06	.13
1;6.9	15	9	.60	7 (1*)	11 (1*)	.06	.10
1;7.3	26	11	.42	27(16*)	47 (22*)	.11	.19
1;7.8	17	7	.41	15	19	.09	.12
1;7.23	29	7	.24	34 (4*)	59 (4*)	.17	.27
1;8.11	25	4	.16	41 (6*)	91 (6*)	.14	.32
1;8.14	22	7	.32	33 (1*)	64 (1*)	.18	.34
1;8.27	44	7	.16	79 (5*)	137 (5*)	.29	.50
1;9.1	25	7	.28	45 (5*)	74 (5*)	.24	.39
1;9.19	26	8	.31	48	69	.32	.47

[a] values for total number of analyzed utterances/session is given in table 2.

3.3.1. The verb category in stage I (pre-morphology): (1;3.3–1;5.9)

In stage I we observe only a few instances of what belongs to the verb category in the adult language and these are in bare root form. An example is seen in (7) where *bak* 'look' is considered as a word that lacks categorical properties.

(7) MOT: *bak-ıca-n mı?* (1;3.3)
look-fut-2sg QUE
'Will you look?'

DEN: *bak   bak.*
look look

The first TAM inflection (*-DI*) appears once in the first session and once in the third session, but there is no evidence for productivity. Its use with more than one verb is observed at 1;5.9 when Deniz has seven different verbs in her speech.

(8) MOT: *düş-tü* (1;3.3)
fall-PAST
'it fell'

DEN: *ma:mu: [:maymun]*
monkey
'monkey'

DEN: *düt-tü [:düştü].*
fall-PAST
'it fell'

We find occasional instances of another inflection which, however, can be identified neither as (*-Iyor*) nor as (*-Ir*), and remains to be an unanalyzed imitative formation as in (9).

(9) MOT: *yok, orası elle-n-mez* (1;3.12)
no   there touch-PASS-NEG:AOR
'no, one does not touch there'

DEN: *elle-n-me-ye*
touch-PASS-NEG:?
'not touch?'

During this stage Deniz produces only two instances of agreement marking, again in the last session. This data is presented in table 5 below.

In summary, the earliest verbs are not productively used but are associated with limited contexts. They occur either in uninflected form or as frozen units. There are no verbs that occur in more than one form, thus no mini-paradigms.

3.3.2. Stage II: (proto-morphology): (1;5.28–1;9.19)

In the substage transitional to proto-morphology (1;5.28–1;6.9), productive inflectional marking begins and the first two-member paradigms appear. In example (10) we see a verb that bears various inflections in successive utterances.

(10) DEN: *anne* **ga:k** *[kalk] anne* (1;5.28)
　　　　　Mother　get-up　　　mother
　　　　　'Mother, get up, mother.'

　　　DEN: **ka:k-ti** *[kalktim]*
　　　　　Get-up-past-*01sg.

　　　DEN: **ga:-di-m** *[kalktim]*
　　　　　Get-up-past-1sg.

The second substage of the proto-morphological period is marked by the entry of new inflections and appearance of the first three-member paradigms at 1;7.3. Table 5 presents the total number of different verbs types (lemmas) and tokens produced with particular TAM inflections and the negation marker in Deniz's speech during stages I and II.

a. Tense-aspect-modality and negation marking:

The figures in table 5 show the gradual nature of development during the proto-morphological period. Between 1;5.28–1;6.9, by which time Deniz is using 13 different verbs, only the definite past marker (*-DI*) is used productively. Two new TAM inflections associated with two new agreement paradigms emerge in the subsequent sessions; the optative (*-yA*) at 1;7.3 and the progressive (*-Iyor*) at 1;7.8. At this time she has about 33 verbs in her repertoire. About a month later we have evidence for the use of the inferential (*-mIş*) and the habitual/possible (*-Ir*). Example (11) shows the use of a verb with all obligatory inflections in a multi-word utterance.

(11) MOT: *Deni::z, n-a:p-iyo-sun?* (1;7.23)
Deniz, what-do-prog-2sg
'Deniz, what are you doing?'
DEN: ben badi *[pazil]* **yap-iyo-m**
I puzzle make-prog-1sg
'I am making a puzzle.'

Table 5. Number of verb types 'lemmas' & (tokens) used with different types of TAM inflections and the negative marker in stages I and II (the numbers in bold represent the proto-morphological stage)

Age	-DI	-Iyor	-mIs	-(y)AcAK	-Ir	-(y)A	-mA
1;3.3	1(1)	–	–	–	–	–	–
1;3.12	–	–	–	–	–	–	–
1;3.27	1(1)	–	–	–	–	–	–
1;5.9	2(3)	–	–	–	–	–	–
1;5.28	**8(17)**	2(2)	–	–	–	–	–
1;6.9	**4(9)**	–	–	–	–	–	1(1)
1;7.3	**20(59)**	1(1)	–	–	–	2(7)	**3(8)**
1;7.8	**6(7)**	8(11)	–	–	–	2(4)	–
1;7.23	10(18)	14(25)	–	2(7)	–	3(4)	3(4)
1;8.11	11(35)	9(16)	4(9)	–	2(4)	10(14)	6(7)
1;8.14	11(21)	7(14)	1(1)	2(6)	2(4)	4(7)	5(13)
1;8.27	19(41)	7(14)	1(1)	4(4)	5(17)	13(21)	–
1;9.1	10(10)	14(21)	4(6)	8(10)	1(2)	4(9)	9(11)
1;9.19	15(18)	15(24)	–	4(6)	2(2)	7(7)	11(17)

By the end of the proto-morphological stage, our subject is using the six inflections that require four different agreement paradigms productively with more than half of the 80 different verbs in her vocabulary. These data suggest that learning about the nature of inflectional marking in the input waits upon the acquisition of a minimum number of verbs and a single inflection in the context of which principles of segmentation can be discovered and generalizations to new inflections becomes possible, thus lending support to the critical mass hypothesis which proposes that developments in morpho-syntax are related to changes in the size of vocabulary (Marchman and Bates 1994).

In table 5 we also observe the emergence of the negative marker *-mA* which is around 1;6.9. We do not have any instances of omission in Deniz's speech although we have records of such errors as well as errors of substitution in the early speech of other children (Ketrez 1999). Such errors typically involve the overgeneralization of one of the lexical negatives of the paradigm of nonverbal predicates (*yok* 'nonexistant' for negating existential predicates, and *değil* 'is not' for negating substantive predicates) to verbal predicates, consistent with an early tendency in child speech for sentence external negation (Aksu-Koç and Slobin 1985: 849–850).

b. Agreement and question marking:

The emergence of agreement markers is presented in table 6. Verbs with a command function (imperatives) and those that have 3rd person subjects have been excluded from the analysis because they do not mark person overtly and thus cannot provide evidence for the emergence of agreement markers. These verbs are presented in table 6 to give a complete picture. The last two columns display the number of verbs that lack an obligatory agreement marker and those that have an agreement marker. It is observed that there is an increase in overt agreement marking and a decrease in the omission of agreement as Deniz goes through the two stages.

Table 6. Number of verb types used with and without agreement markers in stages I & II

Age	3S subject	Command (2nd Sing.)	Omission of Agreement	Overt Agreement
1;3.3	1	1	1	–
1;3.12	–	1	–	–
1;3.27	1	–	–	–
1;5.9	–	–	1	2
1;5.28	4	5	3	5
1;6.9	2	12	–	2
1;7.3	8	16	5	22
1;7.8	12	5	–	3
1;7.23	8	13	3	16
1;8.11	17	5	1	17
1;8.14	7	10	–	15
1;8.27	38	–	3	43
1;9.1	25	–	2	20
1;9.19	21	–	–	32

The distribution of the agreement marker across the paradigms is shown in table 7. The *z-agreements* of paradigm I are the set of markers attached to

(-mIş), (-Iyor), (-Ir) and the future (-AcAK). The *k-agreements* of paradigm II are those that are attached to (-DI). Finally, *agreement* paradigms III and IV, the *sIn-agreements,* are particularly relevant to the optative (-yA). The emergence of the individual agreement paradigms is closely related to the emergence of the TAM markers. We do not observe any delay in any of the agreement paradigms independent of the emergence of TAM.

Agreement errors consist predominantly of omissions (in favour of the unmarked base forms of imperative or 3rd person singular) rather than substitutions (see also section 4.4.2. table 10). This fits the structure of Turkish where semantically unmarked base forms (also nominative and singular in nouns) are also formally unmarked.

Table 7. Number of verb types used with and without agreement markers across the four agreement paradigms in stages I and II

Age	Par I	Omission of I	Par II	Omission of II	Par III & IV	Omission of III & IV
1;3.3	0	0	0	1	0	0
1;3.12	0	0	0	0	0	0
1;3.7	0	0	0	0	0	0
1;5.9	0	0	2	1	0	0
1;5.28	0	0	5	2	0	0
1;6.9	0	0	2	0	0	0
1;7.3	1	0	22	4	2	1
1;7.8	0	0	2	0	2	0
1;7.23	9	1	8	0	2	2
1;8.11	4	1	5	0	10	1
1;8.14	5	0	10	0	7	0
1;8.27	19	1	11	1	13	1
1;9.1	11	0	5	1	4	0
1;9.19	19	0	6	0	7	0

The question particle (*mI*) appears at 1;5.28 with (*-DI*) in the unmarked form for 3rd person singular, in the utterances *ol-du mu?* 'has it fit?' and *al-dı mı?* 'has he taken?'. By 1;8.11, it is used with the 1st person singular of agreement paradigms II, and III, following (*-DI*) and (*-yA*) in utterances *al-dı-m mı?* 'have I taken?' and *oynı-yı-m mı?* 'shall I play?' and *oku-yı-m mı* 'shall I read?'. Use with the Ist agreement paradigm is observed at 1;8.14: *yer mi-sin?* 'would you (like to) eat?'. There is no error in the use of the question marker throughout the period analyzed despite the fact that its placement varies depending on the agreement paradigm. In both agreement paradigms II and III (*mI*) follows the verb inflected for TAM and agreement, whereas in paradigm I it has to be inserted before the agreement markers. It is not surprising that (*mI*) appears later in agreement paradigm I in view of Slobin's (1973) operating principle 'avoid interruptions' of morphological sequences.

3.4. Emergence of mini-paradigms

To determine productivity we looked at the total number of verbs that occur in only one form versus those that appear in more than one form. In the first stage there are seven verbs recorded and they all occur in single form, whereas in the second stage, 45 verbs (57%) appear in various forms while 35 verbs (43%) are produced without any variation in morpho-syntactic form. Among the verbs appearing in a single form, seven are always in the base form whereas 28 are morphologically marked (8.9% and 35% of the total, respectively). We consider this as evidence for productive use in the second stage and the lack of it in the first stage.

3.4.1. Two and three member mini-paradigms

The appearance of mini-paradigms mark the beginning of the proto-morphological period (see table 8). In the transitional stage between 1;5.28–1;6.9 only 2-member mini-paradigms that involve contrasts between an unmarked verb and its form inflected with the past (*-DI*) (either in unmarked 3rd person singular or 1st person singular) are observed. At 1;7.3 additional contrasts with the 1st plural for (*-DI*) and the negative marker as well as the first 3-member mini-paradigms emerge. The latter provide evidence for the productive use of the progressive (*-Iyor*), the optative (*-yA*) and their associated 1st singular and plural markers. These developments lead to an increase in errors. While errors of omission involve TAM and agreement markers (from paradigms I and III), errors of substitution involve the misuse of the 2nd person singular of agreement paradigm II instead of the 1st singular. This error seen in children acquiring other languages as well (Wojcik and Smoczyńska 1997), may be due to the fact that in speech directed to her the child hears verbs in second person singular and perceives this marker as a morpheme that marks herself.

Table 8. First 2- and 3-member mini-paradigms in Deniz stage II

age	lemma	translation	form	category
1;5.28 (2-member)	kalk	get up	kalk	Imp.
			kalk-tı-m	PAST-1S
	ol	be	ol-du	PAST
			ol-du mu ?	PAST QUE
	otur	sit	otur	Imp.
			otur-du	PAST
1;6.9	gel	come	gel	Imp.
			gel-di-m	PAST-1S
1;7.3*	git	go	git-ti-m	PAST-1S
			git-ti-k	PAST-1P
	ye	eat	ye-di-m	PAST-1S
			ye-me	(Imp)-NEG
1;7.3 (3-member)	boya	paint	boya-yı-m	OPT-1S
			boya-dı	PAST
			boya-dı-m	PAST-1S
	gel	come	gel	Imp.
			gel-me	(Imp)-NEG
			gel-di-m	PAST-1S
	kapat	close	kapat	Imp.
			kapat-tı	PAST
			kapat-tı-m	PAST-1S
1;7.8	gel	come	gel	Imp.
			gel-iyor	PROG
			gel-di-m	PAST-1S
1;7.23	al	take	al	Imp.
			al-dı-m	PAST-1S
			al-dı mı?	PAST QUE
	gel	come	gel-di-m	PAST-1S
			gel-iyor-um	PROG-1S
			gel-di-k	PAST-1P

* Only examples displaying new contrasts are presented

An inspection of table 8 shows that some verbs appear in successive sessions as bearers of new inflection types. For example, the progressive (*-Iyor*) and thus the agreement markers of paradigm I appear first on the verb *gel* 'come' which is first productive at 1;6.9 and appears in different inflectional forms in successive sessions (6 different forms between 1;6.9–

1;7.23). Such a pattern suggests that new forms first appear on verbs that have achieved productivity with other inflections, already having been analyzed into root/stem vs. inflectional segments.

Starting with the session at 1;7.23 multi-member paradigms are observed in Deniz's speech. Table 9 displays examples of increasing complexity at their first age of appearance.

3.4.2. Multi-member mini-paradigms

Table 9. First multi-member mini-paradigms in Deniz stage II between 1;7.23–1;8.27

Age	lemma	translation	form	category
1;7.23 (4-member)	git	go	git	Imp.
			git-ti-m	PAST- 1S
			gid-iyor-um	PROG-1S
			gid-eceğ-im	FUT-1S
(5-member)	yap	do/make	yap	Imp.
			yap-ma	(Imp.)-NEG
			yap-ma-m	NEG.AORIST-1S
			yap-ıyor-um	PROG-1S
			yap-acağ-ım	FUT-1S
1;8.11 (6-member)	oku	read	oku	Imp.
			oku-ma	(Imp.)-NEG
			oku-yor-um	PROG-1S
			oku-yı-m mı?	OPT-1S QUE
			oku-ya-lım	OPT-1P
			oku-sun-lar	OPT-3P
1;8.27 (9-member)	yap	do / make	yap	Imp.
			yap-ma	(Imp.)-NEG
			yap-ıyor	PROG
			yap-ıyor-um	PROG-1S
			yap-ıyor-sun	PROG-2S
			Yap-mı-yı-m	NEG-OPT-1S
			Yap-tı	PAST
			Yap-tı-n	PAST-2S
			Yap-mış	EV

The habitual/possible (*-Ir*), the future (*-AcAk*) and the evidential (*-mIş*) are the new TAM inflections, and the 1st and 3rd person plural of agreement-paradigm III are the new agreement contrasts. The early emergence of multi-member paradigms is not surprising given the structure of the input; rich productive morphology appears to induce the child to focus on acquiring inflections early on (Aksu-Koç and Slobin 1985).

Table 10 gives an overall view of the developments observed in paradigm building in stage II. The first column gives the number of different verbs the child tried to produce in more than one form during that session. The second column shows the number of verbs she failed to produce in more than one form due to an error of substitution and/or omission in TAM and/or agreement marking, as shown in the last two columns. The other columns give the frequency of mini-paradigms with 2-or-more members produced without any error.

Table 10. Frequency of mini-paradigms with 2-, 3-, 4-, 5-, 6- or more-members in stage II.

age	no. of verbs	failed attempts	2-member	3-member	4-member	5-member	6- or more member	errors of substitution	errors of omission
1;5.28	4	(1)	3	–	–	–	–	2	2
1;6.9	2	(1)	1	–	–	–	–	–	2
1;7.3	13	(6)	4	3	–	–	–	8	11
1;7.8	4	(0)	3	1	–	–	–	–	–
1;7.23	18	(2)	9	3	3	1	–	–	6
1;8.11	15	(1)	8	2	2	1	1	–	5
1;8.14	9	(1)	2	2	3	–	1	–	1
1;8.27	21	(1)	7	3	7	1	2	–	4
1;9.1	15	(0)	8	2	2	2	–	1	3
1;9.19	16	(0)	8	2	3	–	2	–	–

It is observed that both the number of verbs that get to be used in more than one form and the number of forms that a given verb gets to be used in, increase steadily over the span of the few months under consideration. The verbal complex gets constructed, at first, in a piecemeal fashion, by the addition of morphemes almost one at a time. Deniz starts with the past inflection (*-DI*), adding the agreement markers only in the next session. About a month and a half later, two new inflections (*-Iyor*) and (*-yA*), and the associated agreement markers of paradigms I and III enter her speech. After a time lag of two weeks, (*-Ir*) and (*-mIş*), two inflections that also belong to agreement-paradigm I are observed. The decreasing time period between these successive new acquisitions suggests that while the initial learning of agreement-paradigms I and III posed a difficult task, once mastered, patterns of agreement-paradigm I could easily be generalized to (-*Ir*) and (-*mIş*). The higher frequency of errors observed in producing the optative (-*yA*), on the other hand, could be due to the low level of phonological salience of the 1st person singular and therefore a difficulty in parsing it as a separate morpheme.

3.5. Development of paradigm formation capacity and the role of input

These developments surveyed in the speech of one subject have shown that the acquisition of verbal morphology in Turkish is an early but nevertheless gradual process. The factors that affect the course of this process are the learning mechanisms the child brings to the task (processing strategies and conceptual categories), the structural characteristics of the input, and the nature of social interactional patterns.

The fit between the structural characteristics of Turkish and children's various learning strategies were discussed in detail in Aksu-Koç and Slobin (1985: 871–872). Let us recapitulate those points particularly relevant to the learning of inflectional morphology. The inflectional paradigms (both nouns and verbs) are extremely regular, and morphemes are attached to the roots with minimal modifications required by vowel harmony. The syllabic and generally stressed TAM markers suffixed to the verb root constitute perceptually salient data available to immediate memory. The typically monosyllabic verb root plus its grammatical marker constitute a short unit that can be easily stored for later analysis, once a critical mass is reached. In short, characteristics of the inflectional system make it highly accessible for the child's processing and memory capacities, and can account for the precocity of the developments observed.

Another important factor is frequency in the input. In line with Slobin's (1987) principle of 'frequency reflects function', we find that grammatical markers that are obligatory are acquired earlier than those that are optional. A comparison of number marking on verbs and nouns illustrates the point. Our data shows that person-number marking on verbs appears before number marking on nouns, and number marking on nouns is late relative to case marking. In Turkish, both agreement and case marking express syntactic relations, whereas number marking on nouns has no such role, and is, therefore, not a high-frequency characteristic of the input. The singular form of the noun is numerically neutral: it is not marked for plural after numerals, and it can denote a plurality of objects depending on context (Lewis 1967: 25). Consequently, the frequency of plural in the input depends on the frequency and the semantics of the stem, i.e. whether the entity referred to occurs as one or many. The 3rd person plural agreement marker is similarly subject to a number of constraints. It is ungrammatical with (–) animate and optional with (+) animate subjects, preferred only in case of (+) definites. Children appear sensitive to the feature of optionality since overmarking is not observed, and the obligatory 1st person plural emerges both before the optional 3rd person plural and before nominal number.

The gradualness of development, on the other hand, appears to be more a function of the child's learning strategies operative in the discovery of an abstract general principle that involves inflectional marking. The data suggest that this principle is discovered in the context of the direct past marker (-*DI*) which is the 'best exemplar' of its set because it is semantically the least complex and the least specific, and is transferred to other TAM (and agreement) inflections only after some time. Ninio (1999: 113) who observes a similar initial temporal lag followed by fast generalization in the learning of intransitive verbs, proposes a mechanism of 'prototype' or 'model learning', noting that "the time it takes to apply the new rule to yet another verb is much longer at the beginning of acquisition of that rule; the more verbs the children have already learned to produce in the relevant pattern the shorter it becomes". Another example of this general acquisition strategy that underscores the gradual nature of development manifests itself when the child is at the threshold of discovering derivational morphology. Towards the end of the proto-morphological period, our subject is observed to use novel verbs – most of which are marked for changes in valency (such as causative, passive, reflexive) – as unanalyzed complex units. Such use in appropriate contexts probably facilitates the analysis of the verbs in terms of argument structure and the discovery of the principles of derivational morphology.

Mechanisms of prototype or model learning can also be invoked to account for the progressive changes in the early semantics of the TAM markers. In a previous analysis of the role of input in the development of TAM morphology, we looked at the frequency of occurrence of (-*DI*), (-*Iyor*), (-*mIş*) and (-*Ir*) with different verbs in Deniz's speech, and her mother's child directed speech (Aksu-Koç 1998). Each verb in the mother's and the child's speech was coded in terms of their lexical aspect following Vendler's (1967) classification. We found a tendency to use a given inflection with a specific class of verbs in the mother's speech and a corresponding bias in the child's speech, an observation also made for English by Shirai and Anderson (1995). This distributional bias is particularly strong in the initial phase of the acquisition of each inflection, and particularly for those inflections that are acquired first: the child's use is restricted almost exclusively to the aspectual class of verbs the inflection occurs most frequently with in the mother's speech. For example, when it first appears between 1;5.9–1;6.9, the definite past (-*DI*) is used only with achievement verbs (e.g. *ol-* 'become', *bit-* 'finish'; 67% in mother's and 100% in child's speech), whereas it's use gets extended to accomplishment (e.g. *boya-* 'paint') and activity verbs (e.g. *ye-* 'eat') a month later.[6] The second inflection (-*Iyor*), first restricted to activity (e.g. *gel-* 'come', *de-* 'say'; 79% in mother's and 78% in child's speech) and stative[7] (e.g. *yat-* 'lie down'; 11% in mother's and 22% in child's speech) verbs, however, is generalized to achievements and accomplishments only two weeks later. This distributional bias is weaker and lasts for a shorter period for the habitual-generic (-*Ir*) first used with activity verbs (e.g. *çiz-* 'make scratches'; 57% in mother's and 83% in child's speech), and the inferential (-*mIş*) most frequently used with inherently stative nonverbal predicates (e.g. *burday-mış*, here-EV 'it is here'; 50% in mother's and 52% in child's speech). The data suggest that the child has assigned the core meanings of 'completion' to (-*DI*), 'ongoingness' to (-*Iyor*), normative or potential behavior to (-*Ir*), and stativity to (-*mIş*). The source of these definitions is the lexical aspect of the verbs the inflections occur with highest frequency in the input, filtered through the child's cognitive-perceptual preferences that allow for the abstraction of prototypical event structures from contexts of use. This correspondence between the mother's and the child's use of inflections reflects a sensitivity on the part of the child to the statistical regularities in the input, and shows that she is paying attention to morpho-semantic patterns in addition to morpho-syntactic regularities (Aksu-Koç 1998).

Patterns in the input are not static however, and change in response to the child's level of competence. The fine-tuning in CDS to match the learner's level is revealed by a comparison of the complexity of speech directed by three mothers – including Deniz's – to their children at two different points in development, once at 1;3 and once at 2;0 years (Ketrez 2000). The speech of the mothers is found to be morpho-syntactically less complex when the child is 1;3 than when the child is 2;0. The percentage of increase in the MLU of the mothers is not the same as that in the children's speech, however, there is a parallelism in the increase in the number of morphemes per utterance. Furthermore, MLU's based on morphemes increase more than MLU's based on words, both in the speech of children and mothers, indicating that it is the complexity within words that brings about variation.

Another study that shows how CDS presents a rich database to the language learner by revealing the structural characteristics of the input is Küntay and Slobin's (1999) analysis of a Turkish mother's speech to a 1;8 to 2;3 years old. Given the pragmatically motivated variations in word order, the same intention is expressed in alternative ways in a series of consecutive utterances, thereby providing the child with multiple contrasts to help solve the segmentation problems while maintaining the invariance in the order of morphemes within a word. Küntay & Slobin (1999: 2–3) identify sequences of utterances where the same intention is repeated, however with lexical substitution and rephrasing, reordering of elements, and/or addition and deletion of specific reference. They find that about 53% of the verbs are repeated in such sequences, and that, when repeated, about 41% of the verbs change their form, while the rest retain the same morphological form. These findings suggest that the child is faced with a level of variability that is at the same time constrained by consistency, clarity and pervasiveness of marking, yielding a balance between 'variation' which facilitates segmentation and 'frequency' which facilitates the abstraction of regularities.

4. Concluding remarks

In summary, in stage I, our subject produces verbs as lexical units. However, these words do not exhibit adult-like morphological and syntactic properties. In stage II, verbs emerge and provide evidence for the development of an adult-like verb category. Morpho-syntactic evidence is found in the productive use of the different TAM and agreement markers with different verbs, as well as case marking on nouns. The developments show that the child has grasped the basic patterns of verb inflection by the end of this period, around 20 months of age. Although the level of competence she has achieved at this point may seem precocious, it is not surprising since there are no inflectional subclasses of verbs in Turkish and the TAM and agreement morphology is extremely regular. Furthermore, the canonical SOV order, and the high frequency of verb-only utterances in the input favor the phonological saliency of verbs and inflectional suffixes.

Our findings provide evidence for the view that Turkish children go through a "pre-morphological" (Dressler and Karpf 1995) stage throughout which they hardly provide any evidence for syntactic categories in their grammars, and a "proto-morphological stage" throughout which they gradually build the verbal and the nominal categories of their language with their associated morphology. Our data, as we have argued elsewhere (Aksu-Koç 1997; Ketrez 1999; Aksu-Koç and Ketrez 1999), thus support the claims for gradual development favoured by views advocating social-cognitive processes for the building up of categories such as the noun and the verb (Tomasello 1992), or learning mechanisms sensitive to the statistical properties of the input (Braine 1994; Pine, Lieven, and Rowland 1998).

Notes

* The data reported in this paper is part of the project "A longitudinal study of the acquisition of Turkish" that was supported by grants from the Boğaziçi University Research Fund, Project Numbers 94 SO 064, 96 S 0017.
1. For example, past + conditional expresses 'past conditional' (e.g. *gör-dü-yse* 'see-PAST-COND' = 'if he saw') while conditional + past expresses 'counterfactual' (e.g. *gör-se-ydi* 'see-COND-PAST' = 'if he had seen'. Thus, ordering of particles is crucial for resultant meanings, and when only one meaning is possible, ordering is fixed (Aksu-Koç and Slobin 1985: 842). See Sebüktekin (1974) for a detailed exposition of alternative morpheme orders in the Turkish verb complex.
2. Capital letters indicate vowel/consonant alternations due to rules of harmony.
3. During the period analyzed we find evidence in our subject's speech for diminutive marking on nominals but not on any verbal form. Our impression is that diminutive marking is not a pervasive phenomenon at least in the speech of this mother-child pair.
4. Substantive predicates (nominal and adjectival) are not included in the analysis.
5. Both the Accusative and the Dative are observed once, but are found to be missing in several obligatory contexts.
6. Data representing the more flexible, differentiated use of the inflections with verbs of other types of lexical aspect is presented in Aksu-Koç 1998.
7. *-Iyor*, which is not strictly a progressisve but rather an imperfective marker in Turkish, can be used with statives.

References

Aksu-Koç, Ayhan
    1998   The role of input vs. universal predispositions in the emergence of tense aspect morphology: Evidence from Turkish. *First Language* 18: 255–280.

Aksu-Koç, Ayhan
    1997   Verb inflections in Turkish: A preliminary analysis of the early stage. In: Wolfgang U. Dressler (ed.), *Studies in Pre- and Protomorphology*, 127–139. Wien: Verlag der Österreichischen Akademie der Wissenschaften.

Aksu-Koç, Ayhan
    1988   *The Acquisition of Aspect and Modality: The Case of Past Reference in Turkish.* Cambridge: Cambridge University Press.

Aksu Koç, Ayhan, and F. Nihan Ketrez
    1999   Once there was (not) a verb. Paper presented at the VIIIth International Congress on the Study of Child Language (IASCL), University of the Basque Country, San Sebastian-Donostia, Spain, July 12–14, 1999.

Aksu Koç, Ayhan, and Dan I. Slobin
    1985   The acquisition of Turkish. In: Dan I. Slobin (ed), *Crosslinguistic Study of Language Acquisition*. Vol. 1, 839–878. New Jersey: Lawrence Erlbaum.

Baykoç-Dönmez, Necate, and Meziyet Arı
    1992   12–30 Aylık Türk çocuklarında dilin kazanılması [Acquisition of language in 12–30 month old Turkish children]. *Gazi Üniversitesi Gazi Eğitim Fakültesi Dergisi [Gazi University Journal of the Faculty of Education]* 8 (3): 115–161.

Braine, Martin D. S.
    1994   Is nativism sufficient? *Journal of Child Language* 21: 9–31.

Dressler, Wolfgang U., and Annemarie Karpf
    1995   The theoretical relevance of pre- and proto-morphology in language acquisition. *Yearbook of Morphology* 1994: 99–122.

Ekmekçi, Özden
    1979   Acquisition of Turkish: A longitudinal study on the early language development of a Turkish child. Unpublished Doctoral Dissertation, University of Texas, Austin.

Erguvanlı, Eser E.
1984   *The Function of Word Order in Turkish Grammar.* Berkeley: University of California Press.

Ketrez, F. Nihan
1999   Early verbs and the acquisition of Turkish argument structure. Unpublished M. A. Dissertation, Boğaziçi University, İstanbul, Turkey.

Ketrez, F. Nihan
2000   Variation in Turkish mothers's style. Paper presented at the 10th International Conference on Turkish Linguistics (ICTL), Boğaziçi University, İstanbul, Turkey, August 16–18, 2000.

Küntay, Aylin, and Dan I. Slobin
1999   Discourse behavior of lexical categories in Turkish child directed speech. Paper presented at the VIIIth International Congress on the Study of Child Language (IASCL), University of the Basque Country, San Sebastian-Donostia, Spain, July 12–14, 1999.

Lewis, Geoffrey
1967   *Turkish Grammar.* Oxford: Oxford University Press.

MacWhinney, Brian
1995   *The CHILDES Project: Tools for Analysing Tal.* New Jersey: Lawrence Erlbaum.

Marchman, Virginia, and Eliabeth Bates
1994   Continuity in lexical and morphological development: A test of the critical mass hypothesis. *Journal of Child Language* 21: 339–366.

Ninio, Anat
1999   Model learning in syntactic development: Intransitive verbs. *International Journal of Bilingualism* 3: 111–131.

Pine, Julian M., Elena V. M. Lieven, and Caroline F. Rowland
1998   Comparing different models of the development of the English verb category. *Linguistics* 36: 807–830.

Peters, Ann M., and Lise Menn
1993   False starts and filler syllables: Ways to learn grammatical morphemes. *Language* 69: 742–762.

Sebüktekin, Hikmet
    1974   Morphotactics of Turkish verb suffixation. *Boğaziçi Üniversitesi Dergisi* 2: 87–116.

Shirai, Yasuhiro, and Roger W. Andersen
    1995   The acquisition of tense-aspect morphology: A prototype account. *Language* 71: 743–762.

Slobin, Dan I.
    1987   Frequency reflects function. Paper presented at the Conference on the Interaction of Form and Function in language, University of California at Davis, January 17–18, 1987.

Slobin, Dan I.
    1973   Cognitive prerequisites for the development of grammar. In: Charles A. Ferguson, and Dan I. Slobin (eds.), *Studies of Child Language Development*, 175–208. New York: Holt, Rinehart and Winston.

Tomasello, Michael
    1992   *First Verbs: A Case Study of Early Grammatical Development.* Cambridge: Cambridge University Press.

Vendler, Zeno
    1967   Verbs and times. In: Zeno Vendler (ed.), *Linguistics in Philosophy*, 97–121. Ithaca, New Jersey: Cornell University Press.

Wojcik, Pawel, and Magdalena Smoczyńska
    1997   Acquisition of Lithuanian verb morphology. In: Wolfgang U. Dressler (ed.), *Studies in Pre- and Proto-morphlogy*, 83–100. Wien: Verlag der Österreichischen Akademie der Wissenschaften.

The emergence of verb inflection in two German-speaking children*

Dagmar Bittner

0. Introduction

This paper discusses the emergence of verb morphology in two German-speaking children. It is focused on the role of protomorphology as a transitional period between rote-learning and the productive use of morphological distinctions.

1. Verb morphology in Standard German

German has comparatively rich verb morphology. One of the central features is subject/verb agreement in person and number. Since there are some syncretisms in agreement symbolization, pro-drop constructions are restricted to special contexts. In addition to person and number, the categories tense, mood, and voice are realised by verb inflection either analytically or synthetically. The complexity of verb inflection is greatly reduced by syncretism and by fusional inflection (*sag-te* 'say-' 1/3s.pret.ind.act). Analytical constructions can consist of two to four elements (*habe gefragt* '(I) have asked' 1s.pret.ind. act.; *wird gefragt worden sein* 'will have been asked' 3s.fut.pf.ind.pass/3s.pret.conj.pass). With respect to inflectional behaviour, two classes of verbs are to be distinguished: so-called weak verbs vs. so-called strong verbs. Weak verbs build one inflectional class and show regular inflection. Strong verbs can be divided into a number of sub- or microclasses, according to their patterns of stem vowel alternation and the distribution of strong and weak forms in their paradigms, cf. A. Bittner (1996).[1] However, because the two children analysed in this study are not producing forms of strong verbs in other than the present tense or perfect forms, it is not necessary to go into more detail here. The only feature of strong verbs appearing in the analysed data, is the stem vowel alternation in the present singular.[2]

In the following, only those verb structures are described which are relevant to the acquisition processes in the pre- and protomorphological phase of the observed children:

- person/number with lexical verbs, cf. a),
- *sein*-auxiliary in the present and past tense, cf. b),
- modal verbs in the present tense, cf. c), and
- past participles and analytical perfect, cf. d).

a) Nearly all verbs take the person/number suffixes given in table 1. These suffixes occur in all tenses. However, only the present tense, which has no special tense inflection, is used in the data.

Table 1. Person/number-inflection of lexical verbs (example: machen 'to do')

	singular	plural
1. person	mach-e	mach-en
2. person	mach-st	mach-t
3. person	mach-t	mach-en

Most strong verbs show stem vowel alternation in present singular, cf.

(1) inf: *fahren* 'to drive' 1s: *fahre*   2s: *fährst* 3s: *fährt*
     sehen 'to see'   *sehe*   *siehst*   *sieht*
     geben 'to give'   *gebe*   *gibst*   *gibt*

b) The present and past forms of the auxiliary *sein* 'to be' are more or less suppletive, cf. table 2 and 3.

Table 2. Person/number forms of sein-auxiliary in the present tense

	singular	plural
1. person	**bin**	**sind**
2. person	**bist**	**seid**
3. person	**ist**	**sind**

Table 3. Person/number forms of sein-auxiliary in the past tense

	singular	plural
1. person	**war**	**war-en**
2. person	**war-st**	**war-t**
3. person	**war**	**war-en**

c) Modal verbs behave differently from main verbs in the singular paradigm, cf. table 4.

Table 4. Person/number forms of modal verbs (example: können 'can')

	singular	plural
1. person	kann	könn-**en**
2. person	kann-**st**	könn-**t**
3. person	kann	könn-**en**

d) The past participle is formed with the prefix *ge-* + verb stem + suffix *-t*. Past participles of strong verbs show stem vowel alternation and/or take suffix *-en* instead of *-t*, cf.:

(2) weak verbs
 machen 'to do' – ***ge**-mach-**t*** 'done'
 kaufen 'to buy' – ***ge**-kauf-**t*** 'bought'

 strong verbs
 bringen 'to bring' – ***ge**-brach-**t*** 'brought'
 gehen 'to go' – ***ge**-gang-**en*** 'gone'

The analytical perfect (perfect tense) is formed with the present tense form of the verb *sein* 'to be' or *haben* 'to have' + past participle.

(3) *er ist gekommen* 'he has come'
 sie sind gerannt 'they have run'

 er hat geglaubt 'he has thought'
 sie haben geschlafen 'they have slept'

With respect to the productivity of inflectional classes, we can restrict our description to the fact that the inflectional pattern of weak verbs is the most frequent and the only productive one.

2. Data description

For the present study, longitudinal data of two girls, Anna and Caroline, has been analysed. In the case of Anna, these are 10 recordings (each approximately one hour long) in the age range of 1;8 – 2;1 (table 5). In the case of Caroline, a larger number of recordings in the age range of 1;6 – 2;2 have been analysed (lasting from a few minutes up to one hour). For the purposes of the present analyses, they have been arranged into two data sets per month (table 6).³ Recordings of both girls mainly took place at the girl's home, where Anna would play with the interviewer and Caroline would play with her mother. Occasionally kitchen work, dinner and other home situations were included.

Table 5. Data of Anna

age	analysed utterances[4]	utterances with verbs:	
		numbers	%
1;8.10	293	52	17,7
1;8.29	218	76	34,8
1;9.14	237	65	27,4
1;10.0	266	86	32,3
1;11.6	313	165	52,7
1;11.20	284	147	51,8
1;11.30	248	132	53,2
2;0.5	292	150	51,4
2;0.29	525	288	54,9
2;1.13	345	209	60,6

Table 6. Data of Caroline

age	analysed utterances	utterances with verbs:	
		numbers	%
1;6	150	11	7,3
1;8	195	24	12,3
1;9a	192	25	13,0
1;9b	348	60	17,2
1;10a	268	45	16,8
1;10b	368	64	17,4
1;11a	386	111	28,8
1;11b	320	55	17,2
2;0a	398	83	20,9
2;0b	197	35	17,8
2;1a	514	118	23,0
2;1b	711	255	35,9
2;2a	607	224	36,9

Both girls are first born children. Anna is growing up in Berlin, Caroline in Munich. Anna can be described as an early talker and a rather segmental child. Formulaics, frozen forms and imitations are less attested in her data.

Caroline can be characterised a rather (but not extremely) formulaic child. Songs, nursery rhymes, and some special play routines as well as frozen forms are numerous in her data.

3. Predecessors of verbs in predicative function

A detailed investigation into the predecessors of verb utterances and the emergence of tense-aspect meaning in German-speaking children is given in Behrens (1993). In case of the two children under investigation, only the following shall be mentioned: Anna already uses a considerable number of verbs at the beginning of the recordings (table 7). Extragrammatical predecessors of verbs are not (any more?) documented in her data. Nevertheless, a remarkable amount of verbal prefixes and adverbs replacing lexical verbs is attested (34 > 21 > 24 instances in the first three recordings), cf. *ab* 'from/off', *putt* 'broken/smashed', *auf* 'open/up', *weg* 'away/off'. Caroline frequently uses deictic elements (cf. *da* 'there', *das/die* 'this/that') as well as child specific forms when she wants initiating a certain action of the adult (looking, giving, drawing, repairing etc.). Verbal prefixes are rare in her recordings at age 1;6 and 1;8.[5]

4. The emergence of verbs

The present analyses will concentrate on verb forms that could be regarded as spontaneous productions, in the sense that they are not frozen or citation forms[6] or immediate imitations of verb forms of the adult interlocutor. Table 7 and 8 give the remaining number of lemmas[7], types, and tokens.

Table 7. Anna – numbers of verb lemmas, types, and tokens

age	lemmas/new	types	tokens
1;8.10	25	28	45
1;8.29	22 / 15	23	47
1;9.14	32 / 21	42	53
1;10.0	28 / 11	36	67
1;11.6	66 / 35	83	144
1;11.20	52 / 19	68	116
1;11.30	45 / 22	57	92
2;0.5	40 / 15	54	111
2;0.29	100 / 43	134	277
2;1.13	67 / 26	97	201

58 Dagmar Bittner

Table 8. Caroline – numbers of verb lemmas, types, and tokens

age	lemmas/new	types	tokens
1;6	9	11	12
1;8	13 / 12	16	22
1;9a	11 / 4	17	23
1;9b	23 / 11	27	59
1,10a	24 / 14	32	44
1;10b	39 / 25	44	65
1;11a	41 / 22	49	108
1;11b	27 / 8	33	54
2;0a	40 / 13	57	77
2;0b	25 / 8	29	33
2;1a	54 / 19	70	114
2;1b	76 / 31	113	235
2;2a	75 / 18	105	222

Tables 5 and 6 given in the previous chapter showed that verb usage increases earlier with Anna than with Caroline. Even in her first recordings, Anna uses verbs in more than 30% of her utterances. Since the age of 1;11, more than 50% of her utterances consistently contain a verb. With Caroline, verbs are attested in 30% of her utterances only at the end of the observed period, i.e. at age 2;1b and 2;2a.[3] Comparable differences appear in the number of documented verb lemmas. At the end of the observed period, 232 verb lemmas are counted for Anna and 194 for Caroline. However, with respect to morphological diversity (i.e. average of types per lemma, extractable from tables 7 and 8), Anna is only slightly more advanced in the beginning: 1,3 vs. 1,2 types per lemma. Both children reach a value of 1,4 types per lemma at the age of 2;1.

It will be argued here that the transition from pre- to protomorphology (cf. the introduction to this volume) takes place after the age of 1;10 with Anna and after the age of 1;11 with Caroline. Various changes in speech production can be observed in the following month. In verb usage these are: a) stable occurrence of more than the initially two or three verb types, b) development of prototypical intra-verbal form contrasts, c) emergence/ regular use of modal verbs, d) emergence/increase of analytical verb constructions. Additionally, there are changes in syntax as: a) increase of multi-word utterances, b) emergence/increase of/in overt subject candidates, c) emergence/increase of/in determiners and pronouns.

In the following, the development towards the first productive inflectional contrasts will be discussed.

5. The premorphological phase
5.1. Emergence of verb forms

With respect to the emergence of verbs and verb inflection we do find different morphological forms from the onset (of observation) with both children.[9] Table 9 and table 10 give a summery of the documented verb forms in premorphology according to the morphological ending. Suppletive verb forms are not counted in these tables.

Table 9. Anna – formal analysis of non-suppletive verb forms (lemmas/tokens)

age	-en	-t	-∅	-e	past part.[10]
1;8.10	13/23	9/15	6/6		1/1
1;8.29	10/30	11/13			2/2
1;9.14	20/25	16/23	2/2	2/2	1/1
1;10.0	15/33	9/15	9/16	1/1	2/2

Table 10. Caroline – formal analysis of non-suppletive verb forms (lemmas/tokens)

age	-en	-t	-∅	-e	past part.	-st
1;6	1/1		5/5		1/1	
1;8	6/8	2/3	5/8			
1;9a	8/12	4/4	3/3	1/2		
1;9b	17/44	1/1	6/6	2/2		1/1
1;10a	13/26	2/2	7/8	2/2	1/1	
1;10b	29/44	5/11	4/5	1/1		1/1
1;11a	28/80	4/6	4/9	1/1	4/4	
1;11b	18/36	4/4	4/4	1/2	1/1	

Apart from the few past participle forms[11] and one past form of *sein* 'be' (Caroline 1;10a **war* instead of *waren* 'were'), all documented forms are in present tense and indicative mood. With respect to suppletive paradigms, both children use the 3s.pres.ind. *ist* 'is' of the auxiliary *sein* 'be'; Caroline also uses the 1s.pres.ind. *bin* 'am', the 1/3p.pres.ind. *sind* 'are' and the above mentioned past form *war*. Only one analytical construction is attested in Anna's data compared to 5 in Caroline's.[12] With the exception of one unclear occurrence with *darf* (1/3s of *dürfen* 'be allowed to' in 1;9.14) no modal verbs are found in Anna's premorphological stage. In contrast, Caroline uses *muß* 'have to', *soll/sollen* 'should', *dürfe* 'may', *kann* 'can', *mag* 'like', and w*ill/wollt* 'want' (*will* – her most frequent modal form – is recurrent since 1;8).

In the premorphological phase, most verbs are attested in only one morphological form (type), many of them occur only once (token). Of the 72 lemmas used by Anna 30 are documented as *-en* form, 18 as *-t* form, and 4 as pure stem form (*-Ø*) only. With Caroline, 51 of her 104 lemmas are used as *-en* form, 5 as *-t*, and 11 as stem (*-Ø*) form only. With both girls, we find a preference for verb forms ending in *-en*. However, whereas Anna concentrates on *-en* and *-t* forms (her verb usage is nearly reduced to these forms) Caroline doesn't show any preference for other than *-en* forms. Nevertheless, Caroline's verb lexicon contains a greater inventory of types than Anna's including a richer inventory of suppletive forms, modal verbs and analytic constructions. This difference in learning strategy (rather segmental vs. rather formulaic) also occurs with respect to the emergence of form contrasts which will be discussed in the next chapter.

5.2. Emergence of form contrasts

Two points are worth noting before discussing the documented form contrasts. First, at least in a language like German, emergence of different morphological types is not automatically correlated with acquisition of specific inflectional categories (s. discussion in section 7). Due to the syncretisms in German verb inflection, it is difficult for the child to find out which verb form is to use in which context: The *-en* form assigns the infinitive as well as all persons in plural. The *-t* form assigns 3s as well as 2p, additionally *-t* is the regular ending of the past participle. The stem form (*-Ø*) and the *-e* form assign 1s as well as 2s.imp. Thus, it is not surprising that non-target use of verb forms is frequent in the early phases of verb acquisition. Second, the syncretistic structure of German verb inflection causes a problem in analysing the acquisitional data. Due to minimal syntactic complexity of utterances (one- to two-word utterances), including widespread omission of the subject phrase, it is often hard to decide which person-number context has to be assumed for the verb used by the child.[13] In the given analyses, all verb forms for which person-number categories could not be identified, neither by the linguistic nor the non-linguistic context, have been classified as unclear. In the premorphological data of Anna, the person-number context of more than 50% of the *-en* tokens and more than 20% of the *-t* tokens appeared as unclear. In the data of Caroline, this holds for more than 60% of her *-en* tokens and nearly 50% of the *-Ø* tokens. For the remaining forms, one finds with both children *-en* forms used in nearly all person-number contexts whereas the -*t*, -*Ø* and -*e* forms mostly appear in an appropriate target context.

It is a well known fact that early verb acquisition in German is characterised by an extended use of the -*en* form.[14] So it is the case with Anna and Caroline too. The -*en* form is predominant among the lemmas occurring in only one morphological form. It is also predominant among the lemmas for which different inflectional types are attested. Tables 11 and 12 give the types and numbers of form contrasts found in premorphology with both children. The counting is cumulative, i.e. each type of a form contrast per lemma is counted once per recording and the resulting numbers are added up. Thus, the numbers do not reflect numbers of different lemmas.

Table 11. Two-member form contrasts in premorphology (p.part = past participle)

	-en/-t	-en/-Ø	-en/-e	-en/-st	-en/p.part	-t/-Ø	-t/p.part	-Ø/-st	suppl.
Anna	8	3				3	1		
Caroline	5	11	2	1	1	2		1	1

Table 12. Three-member form contrasts in premorphology[15]

	-en/-t/-Ø	-en/-t/-e	-en/-Ø/-e	suppl.
Anna	2			
Caroline	1	1	1	2

In most cases the non -*en* types are attested by only one token. It cannot be decided whether the respective forms are well established or occurred more accidentally. Due to the high degree of syncretism in German person-number inflection also -*t* and -*e*/-*Ø* types are frequent in adult language. The child can easily grasp them from the input but the functional differentiation between those types and the -*en* type is difficult to acquire. To avoid counting of occasional contrasts as (precursors of) miniparadigms, only those verb types which are attested in contrasting contexts and in more than one recording were counted as potential members of a paradigm.

The two-member contrasts which can be regarded as precursors of paradigmatic contrasts are given in table 13 and table 14. Of these contrasts, each type is attested more than once in premorphology and the non -*en* types tend to correlate with a specific person-number context.

Table 13. Anna – precursors of two-member contrasts in premorphology[16]

age	lemma	engl.	type	pers.-numb. context	recur-rence	pers.-number context
1;8.10	machen	'to do'	machen	(?)	1;9.14	(?)
			macht	3s	1;8.29	3s
					1;9.14	(?)
					1;10.0	3s + (?)
	malen	'to draw'	malen[17]	(?-request)	1;9.14	(?)
					1;10.0	*1s + (?-request)
			mal	(?)	1;10.0	1s
1;8.29	bauen	'to build'	bauen[17]	(?)	1;10.0	(?)
			baut	(?)	1;10.0	3s

One further form contrast with recurring tokens of each type is: *pullern* – *puller* 'to piddle' (1;9.14). But all of the tokens occur in 1s-contexts, thus, no functional contrast is intended.

Table 14. Caroline – precursors of two-member contrasts in premorphology

age	lemma	engl.	type	pers.-numb. context	recur-rence	pers.-number context
1;8	malen	'to draw'	malen	(?)	1;10a	*1s + (?)
					1;11b	(?)
			mal	1s + (?)	1;9b	1s
1;9b	auf-machen	'to open'	auf-machen	*2s + (?)	1;9a	2s-request
					1;10b	(?-request)
			aufmach	(?)	1;8	1s
1;10a	machen	'to do'	machen	(?)	1;9b	(?)
					1;11a	*1s + 2s-request + *3s + (?)
			mach	(?)	1;11a	1s

Among the three-member contrasts listed in table 12, recurrence of types and the tendency to use them in distinct contexts are attested for only one lemma used by Anna, cf. table 15. Additionally, there is one instance of a four-member contrast at the age of 1;9.14: *puttmach* 'break down' – *puttmacht* – *mache putt* – *puttemacht*. However, each of these types is attested by only one token.

Table 15. Anna – precursors of three-member contrasts in premorphology

age	lemma	engl.	type	pers.-number context	recurrence	pers.-number context
1;10.0	malen	'to draw'	malen	*1s + (?-request)	1;8.10	(?-request)
					1;9.14	(?-request)
			mal	1s	1;8.10	(?)
			malt	3s	1;9.14	(?)

With Caroline, only one of the suppletive three-member contrasts (table 12) appears to have recurrent tokens:

Table 16. Caroline – precursors of three-member contrasts in premorphology

age	lemma	engl.	type	pers.-number context	recurrence	pers.-number context
1;11b	sein SUPPL	'to be'	ist	(?)	1;11a	3s
			bin	1s	1;10a	1s
			sind	3p	1;10a	3p
					1;11a	3p

The identification of Anna being a more segmental learner and of Caroline being a more formulaic learner gets support by the earlier development with Caroline of the suppletive paradigm of *sein* 'to be' which can only be rote-learned. A further difference between the two girls in developing verbal inflection concerns the first form contrasts. Anna establishes the *-t* type (mainly used with 3s-contexts) in opposition to the *-en* type, whereas Caroline concentrates on the *-Ø* type (mainly used with 1s-contexts). This difference correlates with a higher rate of 3s-contexts in the data of Anna contrary to a higher rate of 1s-contexts in the data of Caroline. Among the identifiable person-number contexts 60% are 3s-contexts in Anna in opposite to 41% in Caroline. At the other hand, there are 22% 1s-contexts in Anna in opposite to 28% in Caroline. Obviously, Caroline is more self-oriented in her interactive/communicative behaviour whereas Anna is more object-oriented.

6. The transition to protomorphology
6.1. Development of the verb form repertoire

In case of Anna, a considerable spurt in verb usage can be inferred from the data at 1;11.6. Utterances containing a verb increases from about 30% before 1;11 to more than 50%. Additionally, a spurt in newly attested lemmas can be observed: at 1;11.6, 35 lemmas of 66 are newly attested lemmas (cf. table 7). With Caroline, we do not find comparable quantitative spurts. However, a clear increase in -*t*, -*Ø*, -*e* and past participle forms in contrary to a decrease of -*en* forms takes place after 1;11 (cf. table 10 and table 18). Before expanding the amount of verb lemmas and verb utterances, Caroline further develops the diversity of verb types. Only at 2;1b, the amount of verb utterances increases from 23% to 36% (cf. table 6), and a greater number of new verb lemmas occur (31 of 76, cf. table 8).

Table 17. Anna – formal analysis of non-suppletive verb forms (lemmas/tokens)[18]

age	-en	-t	-Ø	-e	past.part.	-st	-te (pret.)
1;11.6	48/85	18/27	5/10	1/1	4/7		
1;11.20	33/59	14/19	12/23	3/3	2/4		
1;11.30	26/43	18/21	6/6	1/1	1/1		
2;0.5	24/50	15/32	8/12		1/3	1/1	
2;0.29	64/119	27/44	17/43	2/2	5/8	3/6	1/1
2;1.13	34/63	22/28	17/48	5/6	2/2	4/4	

Table 18. Caroline – formal analysis of non-suppletive verb forms (lemmas/tokens)

age	-en	-t	-Ø	-e	past.part.	-st
2;0a	15/31	10/21	10/12	8/8	4/5	
2;0b	7/8	5/5	5/5	3/3	5/5	
2;1a	35/60	10/12	14/17	2/2	1/1	
2;1b	40/76	23/34	22/61	5/5	11/13	1/1
2;2a	43/65	22/44	17/39	7/7	7/9	1/1

At the end of the observed period both girls come to complete the range of present tense forms in acquiring the phonologically most complex form in -*st* (2s in adult language). They also start to use past tense forms in -*te* (1/3s.pret in adult language), cf. *klopfte* '(I/he) knocked', *wollte* 'wanted'. Anna seems to be a bit more advanced in this development than Caroline who only uses the modal verb with -*te* (*wollte*, see above). Interestingly, Caroline seems to be more advanced in the use of a -*ge*-like prefix in past participles that tends to become regular in her speech, cf. 2;2a: *umgefallt* (instead of *umgefallen*) 'fallen over', *drauf(g)emalt* 'drawn on', *puttdemacht* (target: *kaputtgemacht*) 'broken down'. Most of the formally perceptible past participles in Anna's speech still have only stem change, cf. *rein(ge)gossen* (inf. *reingießen*) 'poured in', *gang* (inf. *gehen*, target past.part. *gegangen*) 'gone'.

Clear developments can be stated in the emergence of a) modal verbs and the respective present tense forms, b) suppletive forms of the auxiliary *sein* 'be', and c) analytical verb constructions, cf.:

a) In premorphology, only one unclear token of the modal verb *darf* 'allowed to' was attested in the data of Anna. Then, at the age of 1;11, four modal verbs occur followed by two further lemmas in 2;0. At the age of 2;1, four of her six modal verbs are attested by more than one type per lemma, cf. table 19. Table 20 presents the respective data for Caroline, which will be commented below that table.

Table 19. Anna – modal verbs in the transition to protomorphology

	können 'can'	*dürfen* 'allowed to'	*müssen* 'have to/must'	*möchten* 'would like to'	*wollen* 'want'	*sollen* 'shall'
1;11	kann	darf	müssen muß	möchte		
2;0	kann		müssen muß mußt	möchte	wollen will wollte	soll
2;1	kann	darf	muß	möchte möchtest	wollen will willst	sollen

Table 20. Caroline – modal verbs in the transition to protomorphology

	wollen 'want'	*mögen* 'like'	*können* 'can'	*müssen* 'have to/must'	*dürfen* 'allowed to'	*sollen* 'shall'	*möchten* 'would like to'
2;0	will wollte	mag					
2;1	will	mag	kann	müssen muß	darf	sollten[19]	möchte
2;2	wollte	mag	kann	muß			

In accordance with her rather formulaic learning, Caroline already uses modal verbs in premorphology (s. 5.1.). Only one lemma was lacking in the class of modal verbs, i.e. *möchten* 'would like to', which emerges in 2;1a. However, her inventory of types of modal verbs only slightly enriches up to 2;2.

b) The acquisition of the suppletive forms of the auxiliary *sein* 'to be' parallels the development of modal verbs. In 1;11, Anna added the forms *sind* (1/3p.pres.ind.), *war* (1/3s.pret.), and *waren* (1/3p.pret.), followed by *sein* (inf.) in 2;0, to the previous single use of *ist* (3s.pres.ind.). Caroline, who has already employed *ist*, *bin* (1s.pres.ind.), *sind* and *war* in premorphology, arrived at a regular and frequent use of all the present tense forms. However, no recurrent use of the past tense forms is attested in her data.

c) The production of analytical constructions starts with Anna at 1;11. 6 present tense constructions (modal verb + inf.) are attested in the three recordings of that month. 24 occur in 2;0.29, and 11 in 2;1.13, cf. *ich will essen* 'I would like to eat'; *malen sollen wir* 'we shall drawing'. The first Perfect tense constructions (finite form of *sein* 'to be' or *haben* 'to have' + past part.) appears in the recording at 2;0.29, 5 appear at 2;1.13, cf. *gestern hab ich zu(ge)guckt* 'I was watching (it) yesterday', *(wir) lange spielt haben* '(we) were playing a long time'. Caroline again has used first analytical constructions in premorphology. Consistent use of present tense constructions starts in 2;1 when 9 instances are documented, cf. *muß aber uhu anmalen* 'have/has to draw the eagle owl', *reintun kann schon* '(I) can put (it) in'. The first considerable amount of perfect tense constructions is attested in 2;2a with 5 instances, cf. *Mami (ich) macht hab* 'Momy, (look what I) have done', *mann brunnen fallen ist* '(the/a) man was fallen into the fountain'.

6.2. Development of form contrasts in the transition to protomorphology

Also after premorphology, many verbs are attested by only one type and still a remarkable number of lemmas by only one token. With both girls, one-type verbs amount to 60% of the documented lemmas (Anna: 139 of 232 lemmas; 75x *–en*; 41x *–t*; 16x *-Ø* / Caroline: 115 of 194 lemmas; 75x *-en*; 18x *–t*; 13x *-Ø*). Nevertheless, a clear spurt of form contrasts can be stated. For each child, 47 instances of two-member contrasts are attested. Both girls focus on *–en/-t* and *–en/-Ø* contrasts. In addition, Caroline develops the *–t/-Ø* contrast, cf. table 21.

Table 21. Two-member contrasts in the transition to protomorphology

	-en/-t	-en/-Ø	-en/-e	-en/-st	-en/p.part.	-t/-Ø	-t/p.part.	-Ø/-e	suppl.
Anna	27	10	3	2	1	2			2
Caroline	9	12	5		2	11	4	2	2

The most remarkable development performs with contrasts consisting of more than two forms. 25 instances are attested with Anna, 21 with Caroline, cf. table 22. Moreover, also four- and five-member contrasts start to occur, 3 instances appear in the data of Anna, 4 in that of Caroline, cf. table 23.

Table 22. Three-member contrasts in the transition to protomorphology

	-en/-t/-Ø	-en/-t/-e	-en/-t/-st	-en/p.part.	-en/-Ø/-e	-en/-Ø/-st	-en/-e/p.part.	-t/-Ø/-e	-t/-Ø/-st	suppl
Anna	15	1	1	3		1			1	3
Carol.	8	4			5	1	1	1		1

Table 23. Four- and five-member contrasts in the transition to protomorphology

	-en/-t/-Ø/-e	-en/-t/-Ø/-st	-en/-t/-Ø/ p.part.	-en/-t/-Ø/ -e/-st	-en/-t/-Ø/ -e/p.part.
Anna	1	1		1	
Caroline	1		2		1

The most frequent three-member contrast is the *–en/-t/-Ø* contrast (table 22) and, consequently, this contrast comprises all of the four- and five-member contrasts (table 23).

The difference in the learning strategy of both girls is still existent. Anna continues in strong focussing on special contrasts. She merely extends her favourite *–en/-t* contrast in a clear sequential step by the *-Ø* type. Contrasts involving other types remain rare. Although the *–en/-t*, *-en/-Ø*, and *–en/-t/-Ø* are the most frequent form contrasts with Caroline too, she shows the strongest development with the *–t/-Ø* contrast. Beyond that, it appears a quite similar increase of all three-member contrasts she already performed in premorphology. Finally, past participle forms and *–e* forms are much more frequent in her form contrasts than in that of Anna.

6.3. Emergence of miniparadigms

The emergence of miniparadigms of non-suppletive verbs is considered to be one of the main criteria manifesting the onset of a protomorphological phase in language acquisition. In protomorphology, children detect and constitute morphological patterns and "a primitive system of morphology dissociates from phonology, syntax and the lexicon." (cf. Bittner et al. this volume; Dressler 1997). Kilani-Schoch and Dressler (2000) proposed five criteria for determining an inflectional contrast a miniparadigm. The respective verb forms must be 1) not imitative, 2) not formulaic, 3) articulatory accurate, 4) used in contrasting contexts, 5) recurring. In Bittner (2000: 33), I suggested a slight variation to these criteria. First, the last of the two criteria can be united to: recurrent in contrasting contexts. Second, in regarding languages with a high degree of polyfunctional and syncretistic forms, a further criterion should be added in order to keep miniparadigms an expression of form-function mapping and detection of morphology: except of the base or default form (cf. section 8), the tokens of each type must be used (mainly) in a certain functional context distinct from that of the other types of the same miniparadigm.

In the present study, the proposed variation of the miniparadigm criteria will be used. The analysis concentrates on the emergence of true miniparadigms, i.e. miniparadigms consisting of at least three contrasting inflectional forms. Tables 24 and 25 list the form contrasts which can be viewed as precursors of true miniparadigms, plus respective contrasts of suppletive verbs. With each lemma, at least two of the non-*en* types are used in target contexts mainly. However, recurrence is not documented for more than two types per lemma.

It is interesting to note that under the strong recurrence condition employed in this analysis (i.e. recurrence in contrasting contexts in different recordings within 6 weeks), the three-member paradigms documented first are of the same lemmas with both girls. Also with the Austrian German child investigated by Klampfer (this volume), these lemmas are the first to appear with miniparadigms. Clearly, this goes back to the high frequency of these forms in child (and adult) German. All of them are of small lexical content and belong to the so called light verbs. Thus, they are appropriate to be used in a great variety of contexts, and their high frequency results in an easier attesting in the data.

Taking a weaker recurrence condition (i.e. recurrence in contrasting contexts) all paradigms to be considered precursors of three-member mini-paradigms (tables 24 and 25) can be counted as true three-member miniparadigms. With respect to these lemmas, the development of paradigms shows differences between both children: Anna focuses on high frequency lemmas. The finite forms of *sein* 'to be', *haben* 'to have' and *wollen* 'to want' can be used in synthetic as well as in analytic constructions. The lemmas *essen* 'to eat', and *gehen/hingehen* 'to go/to go to' belong to the 'me first domain' (Mayerthaler 1981; A. Bittner 1996), which contains lexical items assigning basic human properties, and are therefore very frequent. Caroline shows a more individual sample of lemmas tending to paradigmatic use; e.g. *singen* 'to sing', *anmalen* 'to paint', *sagen* 'to say', and *tanzen* 'to dance'. These lemmas assign actions/ situations which are frequent in her play with her mother during the recordings. Thus, her sample is probably more situation bound than that of Anna's.

Table 24. Anna – precursors of three-member miniparadigms

age	lemma	engl.	type	person-number context
1;11.20	essen	'to eat'	essen	*3s + (?)
			*eßt (← ißt)	3s
			*eß (← ißt/iß-2s.IMP)	2s
			*esse (← ißt)	3s
1;11.30	sein SUPPL	'to be'	sind	3p + 1p-analyt.
			ist	3s
			war	3s-pret
2;0.5	machen	'to do'	machen	*1s
			macht	3s + (?)
			mach	1s
2;0.29	essen	'to eat'	essen	2s-request
			eß	1s
			ißt	2s
	hingehen	'to go'	hingehen	*3s + (?)
			hingeht	3s
			hingehst	2s
	haben	'to have'	hat	3s
			hab	1s
			hast	2s
	wollen MOD	'to want'	wollen	3p-analyt
			will	3s + 1/3s/(?)-analyt
			wollte	3s/(?)-analyt

Table 24. continued

2;1.13	gehen	'to go'	gehen	3p + (?)
			geht	3s
			*gangen (← gegangen)	3s-past part
	wollen	'to want'	wollen	1p
	MOD		will	1/3s
			willst	2s

Table 25. Caroline – precursors of three-member miniparadigms

age	lemma	engl.	type	person-number context
2;0a	singen	'to sing'	singen	(?)-request
			singt	3s
			singe	2s.imp
2;1b	halten	'to hold'	halten	*3s + (?)
			hält	3s
			halte	1s
	machen	'to do'	machen	*1s + 3p + (?)
			macht	3s + (?)
			mach	2s.imp + 1s +1p +3s-analyt.
			(g)emacht	1s/3s-past part
	anmalen	'to paint'	anmalen	*1s
			anmalt	(?)
			anmal	1s + (?)
			an(g)emalt	(?-past part)
	sagen	'to say'	sagen	(?)
			sagt	3s + (?)
			sag	2s.imp + 2/3s + 3p
	tanzen	'to dance'	tanzen	3s + 3p + 3s-inf-analyt
			tanzt	3s
			tanz	1s + (?)
			tanze	(?)

There are no precursors of true miniparadigms in the 2;2a recordings of Caroline. All the respective three-member contrasts resemble the suggested criteria for miniparadigms. Thus, all of them count as true three-member miniparadigms (cf. table 27). Table 26 and 27 list all of the true miniparadigms attested in the data of each child.

Table 26. Anna – emergence of miniparadigms

age	lemma	engl.	type	person-number context
2;0.5	haben	'to have'	haben	*1s
			hat	3s
			hab	1s
2;0.29	haben	'to have'	haben	1p-analyt + (?)-analyt
			hat	3s + 3s-analyt
			hab	1s + 1s-analyt
	machen	'to do'	machen	*1s + (?)
			macht	3s
			mach	1s + 2s-imp + (?)
2;1.13	haben	'to have'	haben	inf. + 1s-analyt
			hat	1s + 3s
			hab	1s + 1s-analyt
	sein SUPPL	'to be'	ist	3s + 3s-analyt
			sind	3p
			war	3s + (?)

Table 27. Caroline – emergence of miniparadigms

age	lemma	engl.	type	person-number context
2;1b	sein SUPPL	'to be'	ist	3s
			bin	1s
			sind	3p
2;2a	sein SUPPL	'to be'	sein	(?)
			ist	3s + 3s-analyt
			bin	1s
	haben	'to have'	haben	1s + (?)
			hab	1s-analyt.
			hast	2s
	machen	'to do'	machen	(?)
			macht	3s + 1s + 1s-analyt + (?)
			mach	1s + (?)
			mache	1s
			gemacht	3s-past part

The emergence of precursors of miniparadigms and true miniparadigms starts shortly after the assumed demarcation of pre- and protomorphology. The data suggest that with both children a developmental spurt resulting in the emergence of miniparadigms takes place. With Anna, it seems to happen after age 2;0.5; with Caroline after age 2;1a. Thus, it would be fair to assume a transition phase from pre- to protomorphology which begins with the developments mentioned in chapter 4. and 6. and lasts until the emergence of true miniparadigms.

7. On the emergence of inflectional categories

In order to detect the emergence of grammatical categories in child speech, it is most common to start from the target system and to count the instances of forms resembling the respective categories. This method will be used here as well. However, as has been discussed repeatedly (cf. Slobin 1985; Clahsen, Eisenbeiß, and Penke 1996; Tomasello 1992), we cannot be sure that the child assumes target form-meaning correlations from the very beginning. With respect to the category system, only broad cross-linguistic and very detailed research can answer the question as to whether child grammar is different from adult grammar and if so, to what extent. It is very likely that there are (pragmatic) domains in human life which crosslinguistically tend to be lexicalised and maybe also grammaticalised early, cf. 'grammaticizable notions' (Slobin 1985: 1172-1174). In order to assign basic pragmatic (i.e. semantic) oppositions, the child can only use the language material available from the input. Thus, a mismatch of child and adult categories is nearly preprogrammed in the linguist's analysis.

With this problem in mind, the figures 1 and 2 can be read as the order of emergence of appropriate forms in the adult categories. Black cells symbolize the regular occurrence of the target type-category correlation. Striped cells symbolize that around 50% of the respective tokens occur in a target category context (the calculation is based on tokens in clear person/ number contexts only).

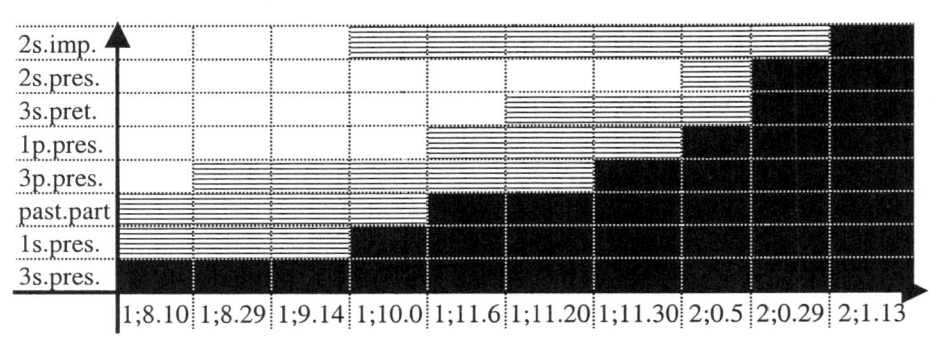

Figure 1. Anna – correlation of types and target categories

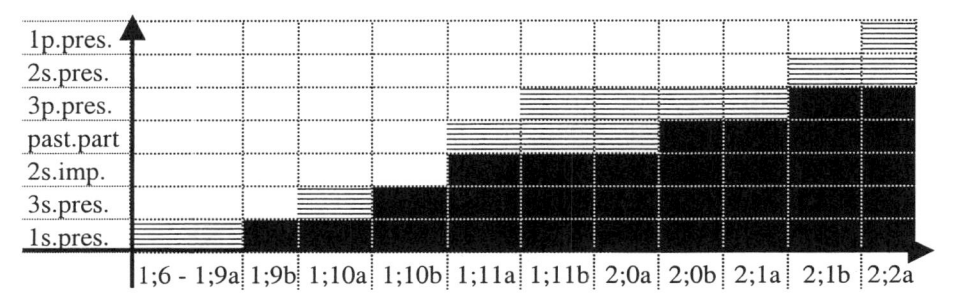

```
1p.pres.
2s.pres.
3p.pres.
past.part
2s.imp.
3s.pres.
1s.pres.
         1;6 - 1;9a 1;9b 1;10a 1;10b 1;11a 1;11b 2;0a 2;0b 2;1a 2;1b 2;2a
```

Figure 2. Caroline - correlation of types and target categories

It is doubtful, however, whether we may assume that the children have acquired the target inflectional categories when more than 50% of the respective forms are target-like. It is clearly ruled out for the premorphological phase when child speech is based on rote-learned forms. In the transition to protomorphology, a remarkable increase in the verb lexicon has been found with both children. Also, inflectional types and inflectional contrasts has been increased. Most likely, the children start to overcome rote-learning during the transition period. Certain patterns of non-target use of inflectional types emerge. Rather than emerging arbitrarily, these types are used according to first hypotheses on form-meaning relations (cf. chapter 8).

Still, it has been found that by the end of the investigated period, i.e. at the onset of protomorphology, 60% of the documented lemmas are attested with only one type. Also, use of the *-en* form in non-target contexts is still frequent. None of the inflectional types occurs without exception or at least up to 90% (cf. Brown's criterion for morphological productivity, Brown 1973) in the target category contexts,[20] and none of the latter is correlated with only one of the types. It is of no doubt that the children have acquired the distinction of speaker, hearer, and object spoken about, as well as for instance elementary mass distinctions (one vs. non-one vs. more than one). However, how is it that these pragmatic or perceptual categories correlate with the verb forms the children have extracted from the input? I would suggest that the children have not yet established the target categories of the present tense paradigm. What has probably been established is the relation of certain verb forms to very general or basic perceptual features, i.e. pregrammatic form-meaning relations. As mentioned above, evidence comes from non-target use of types and analogical formations which will be discussed in the next chapter.

8. Form analogies and form-meaning mapping

The strongest evidence that the child has started morphological analysis comes from overgeneralizations of inflectional forms. With both children, the main type of non-target use of verbs is the spread of *-en* forms over all types of grammatical contexts. Most likely, the children picked up this form from the input for reasons of frequency first. However, with both children, we found a disproportional increase in non-target use of *-en* forms in the transition period. This is especially noteworthy because there is also an increase in the number of inflectional types and the structural diversity of the utterances. It will be hypothesised that the non-target use of *-en* forms in the transition to protomorphology is an overgeneralisation which reveals the selection of a default form of the verb.[21]

This hypothesis is based in the following considerations: Among the increasing number of word forms which enter the lexicon of the child in this period, verb forms, possibly, reach the level of critical mass in both storing and processing (cf. the developments documented in the tables 5-8). This allows the separation of a verb domain. The most frequent form of that domain becomes the functional interpretation of assigning a verb character to a lexeme, i.e. to differentiate between forms that signal a verb concept/category and such which do not. This would be the first form-meaning correlation established with respect to verb grammar. However, what are verbs conceptually? Tomasello (1992: 11) has introduced the idea of the verb as a 'moving picture' contrary to the noun as a 'snapshot'. The verb prototypically signals that something exists (in a certain manner) in relation to time (Klein 1994, 1998). Thus, a perceptual property related to time is central to the concept of the verb. Furthermore, verbs express a (lexical) concept necessarily bound to entities which carry or mediate the properties of the concept. Even if a verb is uttered in isolation, it implies the presence of an entity acting out or affected by its conceptual properties. Thus, verbs assign concepts which exist in mutual relation to other types of concepts. Further, it is assumed that children acquire the category of nouns prior to that of verbs (e.g. Olguin and Tomasello 1993). The noun category is hypothesized to be earlier accessible to the child because it assigns prototypically concrete, clear shaped objects, i.e. because nouns have completely recognizable referents. In terms of semantics, they refer to bounded entities. However, if the child has acquired this classification it is inevitably aware of the counter property which is not bound. The feature, not bound, however, is a property which is related to time (note that time is not tempus!). Both features, 'not bound' and 'mutual relation' are rather directly to infer from perceptual features of experienced situations. Thus, it is possible to conclude that arriving at a critical quantity in verb use and storing, the child interprets the most significant formal pattern as a mean of information that the referent of the linguistic item is 'not bound' and in 'mutual relation' to entities.

Olguin and Tomasello (1993) deny the acquisition of a grammatical category of the verb up to the age of 25 month because the children in their experiments do not show any command of syntactic and morphological alternations the verbs possess in the target-language. However, under the hypothesis, that grammar emerges by assigning intention (Tomasello 2000a) or perspective (Leiss 2000: 246–250) via linguistic material, the extraction of word classes has to be viewed as a first grammatical or at least protogrammatical distinction. The linguistic sign gets related with a certain piece of information on the properties of the actual referent.

Another type of non-target use of verb forms is the occurrence of -*t* forms in contexts other than 3s.pres.ind (2pl contexts are not attested). It will be argued here that this is an overgeneralization based on the mapping of -*t* forms to a meaning related to perfectivity. Most of the non-target -*t* forms are used in perfective contexts, cf. *beide oben raufklettert* 'both climb up on top' instead of *raufgeklettert* 'has/have climbed up' uttered by Anna (1;11.30) after she and the interviewer had climbed up onto her bed. A common assumption is that in these cases the past participle prefix *ge-* is ommitted for phonological reasons (Weyerts and Clahsen 1994; Klampfer this volume). However, the children also overgeneralize the -*t* suffix to irregular verbs, i.e. to verbs which they never heard used as a past participle ending in -*t* ((4) and (5)) This is in strong contradiction to the observation that it is the -*en* form which typically replaces other verb forms.

(4) Anna:
(ich) auch ein geld gebt ← *gegeben* 'I also have given money' 1;9.14
opa (=NOM) geb ← *gegeben* 'grandfather has given' 1;11.6
wegschmeißt ← *weggeschmissen* 'thrown away'
auffreßt ← *aufgefressen* '(is) eaten up' 2;0.5
aufbeißt ← *aufgebissen* '(is) bit open'
runterfallt ← *runtergefallen* '(is) fallen down' 2;0.29
ausgeht ← *ausgegangen* '(is) gone out'

(5) Caroline:
reinefallt	← *reingefallen*	'(is) fallen into'	2;0a
wehdetut	← *wehgetan*	'(is) hurted'	
bißt	← *gebissen*	'(is) bit'	
stocht	← *gestochen*	'(is) pricked'	
reinakommt	← *reingekommen*	'(is) come into'	2;0b
analest (=vorgelest)	← *vorgelesen*	'(is) read out'	

In order to explain these forms, overgeneralization of the *-t* target past participle pattern has been assumed. However, for both girls, it is doubtful that they have acquired this pattern and can use it for overgeneralizations. In the early recordings of Anna, only 4 target-like past participle forms ending in *-t* (*kaputt(g)emacht* 'broken down', *ein(g)epullert* 'made wet oneself', 2x *weggemacht* 'got rid of') are attested. After age 1;11.6 no such form is attested at all. Due to the more formulaic learning strategy of Caroline, prefix *ge-* or phonological variants of it occur earlier in Caroline's data than in Anna's. However, the past participle pattern ending in *-t* is also rare. Up to the age of 2;1a, only 6 target like forms are attested (*undetellt* ← *hingestellt* 'putted', 2x *auf(g)ewacht* 'woken up', *hinnalegt* ← *hingelegt* 'laid down', *hinersatzt* ← *hingesetzt* 'sat down', *abaschaut* ← *angeschaut* 'looked at').

After all, does it make sense to assume homonymic use of *-t* forms for 3s.pres.ind and for perfectivity or is the child analysing a unified meaning with *-t*? It is worth noting that the person/number categories has to be considered as not yet acquired as long as the default form in *-en* is frequently used in non-target contexts. The overgeneralization of *-en* forms in 1/3sg contexts starts decreasing only at the very end of the observed period. Clahsen (1990) proposed that *-t* symbolizes intransitivity in early child German. This has been disproved by Weissenborn (1990) and others. However, the question as to whether *-t* forms in this early period are of a different nature than in the adult language, has not yet been resolved. My hypothesis is (cf. Bittner 2002) that the child initially associates the *-t* form with a meaning inherent in both 3s.pres.ind and in (past participle) perfectives. Both of the two domains exhibit an outside perspective on the referent, i.e. their referents are entities recognized as bounded wholes. In 3s.pres.ind, the referent is the entity spoken about, as opposed to the entities that are involved in speaking (speaker and hearer). In the (past participle) perfective, the described situation is completed in contrast to the situation of speaking. According to this assumptions, the overgeneralization of *-t* forms reveals the mapping of *-t* to the feature 'bounded (whole)'. By this step in form-function mapping, the domain of the verb receives a first subclassification. Whereas verbs prototypically assign referents which are to perceive as 'not bound', the *-t* form constitutes a marked subclass assigning referents which are to perceive as 'bounded (wholes)'.

A third type of non-target use of verbs is the lack of stem vowel change in 2/3sg of strong verbs, cf. forms in 3s.pres.ind contexts:

(6) Anna: *wascht* ← *wäscht* 'wash' 1;11.6
  gebt ← *gibt* 'give'
  eßt ← *ißt* 'eat' 1;11.20
  mitfahrt ← *mitfährt* 'drive with'
  auffreßt ← *auffrißt* 'eat up' 2;0.5
  runterfallt ← *runterfällt* 'fall dawn' 2;0.29

(7) Caroline: *runterfallt* ← *runterfällt* 'fall dawn' 1;11a
  wegfahrt ← *wegfährt* 'drive away' 2;0a
  fallt ← *fällt* 'fall'
  nehmt ← *nimmt* 'take' 2;1b
  stoßt ← *stößt* 'push'

The non-target use of these forms is based on the universal semiotic principle of the uniformity of signs (Dressler et al. 1987). According to this principle, it is more natural that the stem or root of a sign remains identical in its different usages. This is confirmed by the weak verbs which constitute the only productive class, and which represent the overwhelming amount of German verbs. The respective non-target treatment of strong verbs is, thus, motivated by universal and system-specific principles.

Of course, there are different possibilities to interpret the types of non-target verb use listed above. One of them is to regard them, especially the two first ones, as resulting from omissions of target language material, e.g. of modals in the case of *-en* forms or auxiliaries and the prefix *ge-* in the case of *-t* forms. In this perspective, they rather reveal constraints on complex syntactic processing than certain steps in the child's morphological analysis. Another possibility is to assume that the child is capable of establishing basic distinctions also in this early age. The common assumption of an early noun category is in line with that. It has been argued here that the child also detects the basic properties of the verb class early. Furthermore, the first steps towards subclasses within this verb class are possible. The early classifications are based on the feature opposition bounded vs. not bounded, which is abstracted from perception. If one excludes early categorizations in the verb domain one has to explain why the child can categorize the one and not the other. If one supports this way of explanation one has to show by which kind of learning processes the child is able to develop from rote-learning to analysis and classification of form-meaning correlations.

9. Conclusions
9.1. Steps towards mini-paradigms

The (morphological) steps towards mini-paradigms revealed by the data of Anna and Caroline can be summarised as follows:

premorphological steps:
- rote-learned inflectional forms in isolated use
- inflectional contrasts are attested merely occasionally with a few lemma
- no systematic correlation between inflectional forms can be assumed

steps in transition to protomorphology:
- increase of the attested verb lemmas beyond 100 lemmas
- increase of inflectional types
- overgeneralization of -en and -t forms : first form-meaning correlations
- increase of inflectional contrasts involving -en, -t, and -∅ forms
- first recurring three-member contrasts: unspecified -en vs. -t for 3sg or perfective contexts vs. -∅/-e for imp/1sg contexts or vs. past participle form
- emergence of modal verbs
- emergence of analytic constructions
- increase in the use of (potential) subjects[22]

steps at the onset of protomorphology:
- mastering of periphrastic perfect and periphrastic modal constructions
- emergence of past forms
- emergence of -st forms in 2s.pres.ind contexts
- increase of three-member contrasts (typically -en, -t, -∅)
- first recurring four-member contrasts (typically -en, -t, -∅, -st)
- emergence of true miniparadigms
- utterances containing (potential) subject, object, and the finite verb become regular

9.2. Form-meaning relations in early miniparadigms

In accordance with other investigations on early verb inflection, at the onset of verb use, no grammatical understanding of inflectional forms can be assumed for both of the investigated children. The acquisition of verbs starts with rote-learned infinite and finite forms. By the end of the investigated period, i.e. by age 2;2, still 60% of the verb lemmas in both corpora are attested by only one inflectional type. If we would assume that most forms are still rote-learned and stored as separate linguistic units, the emergence of miniparadigms would happen by chance. Miniparadigms would be a by-product of the storing of separate forms of one lemma – and exclusively a descriptional term.

However, it has been shown that at a certain point in development, i.e. in transition to protomorphology, an increase in morphological diversity as well as an increase in certain types of one and the same lemma is to observe. The most common contrasts of -en/-t and -en/-Ø forms, finally, include 21% of Anna's verbs (48 lemmas) and for 19% of Caroline's verbs (37 lemmas). it is worth noting that the 232 (Anna) and 194 (Caroline) verb lemmas attested in the data are only a small part of the children's active verb lexicon. The number of lemmas used with contrasting inflectional forms is, thus, actually much higher. Furthermore, already eight (Anna) and five (Caroline) inflectional types are consistently used (cf. figure 1 and 2). Everything considered, verb acquisition appears to be too developed to assume that all forms could still be rote-learned. But at the same time, 20% or even 30% of the verb lemmas showing the most frequent inflectional contrast are clearly not enough to assume a productive morphological relation between the respective forms, especially in regard to the still high amount of non-target -en forms.

The question arises as to what kind of verb usage lies between the phase of purely rote-learning and the phase of productive morphology? Most linguists dealing with the development from rote-learning to productive morphology,[23] assume a phase of analogical learning. However, it is still unclear what kind of analogies we have to assume, and, in particular, how these analogies differ from productive morphological processing.

The present analysis provides some evidence that in transition to and at the onset of protomorphology, the child finds out about basic oppositions between word classes and within inflectional systems. Very likely, the most frequent inflectional types are analysed and mapped according to perceptual features from which grammatical oppositions start to dissociate (cf. section 8). In respect of the German data, the observed overgeneralizations suggest that the *-en* form becomes mapped to the features 'not bound' and 'mutual relation', i.e. to properties which are the prototypical properties of the verb. Thus, it emerges as the default form of the verb. Both children, very likely, also mapped the *-t* and *-Ø* forms to special meaning. The *-t* form seemingly becomes related to the feature 'bounded whole'. With respect to *-Ø* forms which are used in 1.s.pres.ind and 2.s.imp contexts, both children may associate this form with a meaning like 'speaker', i.e. the speaker itself is acting out or initiating the expressed event.

These hypotheses on early form-meaning mapping are based on preliminary evidence only. Their confirmation would imply that miniparadigms in German-speaking children are the expression of first form-function mapping and as such reveal a developmental step in the detection of morphology and the target inflectional system. However, these miniparadigms are different from the paradigms assumed for adults. Neither form is specified for person/number as they are supposed to be in adult language.[24] They contain forms of a more general meaning. This can reveal that the child only step by step correlates features abstracted from the expressed situations with the forms extracted from the input.[25] (It can also reveal that our assumptions on the adult paradigm has to be examined.) One of the first steps could be to distinguish between ongoing and completed events (cf. Slobin 1985), as well as between referents actively involved in the actual communication vs. not involved. Hypothetically, the mapping process results first in the distinction of reference to bounded vs. unbounded entities.

Finally, I propose that the first form-meaning analysis in protomorphology follows on from analogical learning, in the sense that after purely rote-learning, the child accumulates forms of the type it was becoming familiar with by rote-learning. In other words, the mapping of forms to certain situations or contexts becomes easier the more instances of an inflectional type are already stored in connection with a comparable situation or context. For instance, the more lexemes the child has learned, which end in *-en* and have a verb meaning, the better access s/he has to new lexemes with the same combination of features. And the more the child becomes familiar with form contrasts like the *-en/-t* (/-Ø ...) contrast, the more s/he "expects" the same contrast with new lemmas. The appropriate forms are easier to extract from the input.[26] This way the child stores the necessary amount of instances of the same type ("critical mass") for changing to generalization and abstraction on grammatical features of the forms and structures acquired. These developmental steps are probably repeated with every new grammatical structure. Thus, after an initial phase of learning the very first structures purely by rote, one will find a coexistence of rote-learned structures, accumulated structures, and finally productive structures. After the first basic dissociations of modules, new developments leading to further dissociations within modules and submodules will also undergo the processes of the first dissociation and will do that in different domains at the same time. Accordingly, paradigm construction is a process of "representational redescription" (Karmiloff-Smith 1992) or repeated dissociation until the child has acquired the full set of paradigmatic relations.

Notes

* For helpful comments on a first version of this paper I would like to thank Heike Behrens, Wolfgang U. Dressler, Natalia Gagarina, Insa Gülzow, Marianne Kilani-Schoch and Sabine Klampfer as well as all participants of the workshop 'Early verbs. On the way to mini-paradigms' in late September 2000 in Berlin.
1. As A. Bittner (1996) showed, diachronic facts give evidence for systematic and strongly directed step by step change of strong to weak forms.
2. For further details see the description of inflectional classes of German verbs in Klampfer (this volume).
3. The data of Anna was audio- and partly videotaped by myself. The transcription and morphological coding of Anna's data was done with the CLAN program of CHILDES (MacWhinney 2000) by Franziska Bewer and Joerg von Thun. The data of Caroline is taken from the CHILDES data base. It has been collected by the language acquisition research group of Nijmegen, headed by Wolfgang Klein. Franziska Bewer helped me in processing and analysing the data.
4. Utterances which do not contain at least one meaningful lexical unit resembling a German word in form and meaning, as well as pure yes/no utterances, were excluded from the analyses.
5. For a discussion on verbal prefixes in German child language cf. Bennis et al. (1995), Vollmann et al (1997: 64-65).
6. For definitions see the Introduction to this volume.
7. In her remarks on Clahsen and Rothweiler (1992), Bybee (1995) criticised the counting of prefixed verbs derived from the same stem as different lemmas in a study on inflection because it is always the stem which determines inflection. There is no distinction in inflection between the base form and derived forms. Although I agree with that, base forms and prefixed forms are counted as dif-

ferent lemmas here too. First, in order to solve comparability of the analyses collected in this volume on the development of the verb lexicon. Second, because it is not sure when the child starts to realize the internal relation between the verb forms of the same stem. Third, it has been checked that an alternative analysis would not come out with a significant difference in the early developmental steps discussed in this paper.

8. To some extent, the comparatively late increase of utterances with verbs could be due to a different communicative strategy of Caroline. She uses demonstratives, deictics, proper names and other situation-bound forms more intensely than Anna. This difference could possibly be related to different recording situations: child and mother (Caroline) vs. child and non-parental interviewer (Anna).

9. In fact, the recording of Caroline began at the age of 10 month. However, there are no recordings at the ages of 1;5 and 1;7. In the recordings at 1;4 three verb tokens in frozen phrases are attested.

10. Only clear past participle forms, i.e. forms showing a stem change and/or the prefix -ge- or its reduced form -e-, have been counted.

11. Anna: *puttemacht* 'broken', *einepullert* 'made wet oneself', *raufemach* 'putted on the top', *iebn* 'written' (=*geschrieben*; inf. *schreiben*), *puttgangen* 'is broken down' (=*kaputtgegangen*; inf. *gehen*), *mitbracht* 'brought along' (=*mitgebracht*; inf. *bringen*); Caroline: *obefallen* (=*abgefallen*) 'fallen off', *umdefall* (=*umgefallen*) 'fallen', *undetellt* (=*hingestellt*) 'putted', *wehgetan* (inf. *tun*) 'hurted', *auff(g)ewacht* 'woken up', *aussesunken* (=*ausgetrunken*, inf. *trinken*) 'drunk out'.

12. Anna: 1;8.29 *hat kauft* 'has bought'; Caroline 1;6 *muß blau nehm* 'has/have to take blue'; 1;10a *will da bleiben* 'would like to stay here'; 1;10b *dürfe essen* 'can eat'; *doch gessen # haben gessen* 'of cours, have eaten'; 1;11b *ich will anhüpfen* 'I want hopping'.

13. Moreover, we have to keep in mind that the infinitive (or the *-en* form) can be used in various situations in adult language, for example, in answer to questions like 'what are you doing?' or as impersonal instructions, wishes and similar. (cf. Lasser 1997)

14. The cross-language preference for infinitives in early verb acquisition is discussed under the term 'optional infinitive stage', cf. Wexler (1994), for German Clahsen, Penke, and Parodi (1993), Weissenborn (1994).

15. The respective lemmas and types are: Anna: 1;10.0: *bauen* 'to build' – *bau* – *baut*; *malen* 'to draw' – *mal* – *malt*; Caroline: 1;9a: *waschen* 'to wash' – *wascht* – *wasche*; *anziehen* 'to put on' – *anzieh* – *anzieht*; 1;9b: *aufmachen* 'to open' – *aufmach* – *aufmache*; 1;10a: *sind* 'were' – *bin* 'am' – *war* 'was'; 1;11b *sind* 'were' – *bin* 'am' – *ist* 'is'.

16. An asterix in front of the category specification assigns that the given category specification is not the target one for the respective form.

17. The forms *malen/mal* 'to draw' and *bauen/bau* 'to build' at 1;10.0 are part of three-member contrasts, cf. footnote 15.
18. Modal verbs and the suppletive auxiliary *sein* 'to be' are excluded from tables 17 and 18.
19. The form *sollten* symbolizes 1/3p.pret. or 1/3p.pres.conj. in adult speech. In the speech of Caroline, this single occurrence of the lemma *sollen* in protomorphology appears in a 1s-context. The meaning of the whole phrase is unsure (*ich sollten um ma macht* perhaps 'I should tie round/put on').
20. Only the *-st* type occurs without any exception in the context of 2.s.pres.ind. However, only a few instances of this form are attested at the very end of the investigated period (cf. tables 17 and 18).
21. Note, that overgeneralization of one of the verb types has been attested for different languages in the transition to protomorphology, i.e. prior to paradigmatic contrasts (cf. Introduction to this volume and e.g. Berman and Armon-Lotem 1997).
22. Since 1;11.6 subject elements occur in more than 15% of Anna's utterances, cf. D. Bittner (2000).
23. Cf. MacWhinney (1978); Behrens (1993); Plunkett (1993); Dressler and Karpf (1995); Gentner and Markman (1997); Tomasello (2000b).
24. The first inflectional form which can be associated with person is the *-st* form, which only starts to emerge at the end of the investigated period.
25. Examples of a step by step differentiation of grammatical domains in language acquisition are discussed in D. Bittner (1998, 1999).
26. Some models of neural nets (e.g. ART nets, cf. Carpenter and Grossberg 1988) contain a separate level of nodes, which models the expectations of the learner in dealing with new input together with the value 'vigilance'. For an application on the acquisition of semantic relations in the lexicon, cf. Friedrich (2000).

References

Behrens, Heike
    1993   Temporal reference in the German child language: Form and Function of early verb use. Ph.D. thesis, Universiteit van Amsterdam.

Bennis, Hans, Marcel den Dikken, Peter Jordens, Susan Powers, and Jürgen Weissenborn
    1995   Picking up particles. *Proceedings of the Boston Conference on Language Development* 1994: 70–81.

Berman, Ruth, and Sharon Armon-Lotem
  1997   How grammatical are early verbs? *Annales littéraires de l'Université de Franche-Comté* 631: 17–56.

Bittner, Andreas
  1996   *Starke "schwache" und schwache "starke" Verben.* Tübingen: Narr.

Bittner, Dagmar
  1998   Entfaltung grammatischer Relationen im NP-Erwerb: Referenz. *Folia Linguistica* XXXI: 255–283.

Bittner, Dagmar
  1999   Erwerb des Konzepts der Quantifikation nominaler Referenten im Deutschen. In: Jörg Meibauer, and Monika Rothweiler (eds.), *Das Lexikon im Spracherwerb,* 51–74. Tübingen: Franke.

Bittner, Dagmar
  2000   Early verb development in one German-speaking child. In: Dagmar Bittner, Wolfgang U. Dressler, and Marianne Kilani-Schoch (eds.), *First Verbs: On the Way to Mini-paradigms,* 21–38. (ZAS Papers in Linguistics 18.) Berlin: Zentrum für Allgemeine Sprachwissenschaft, Typologie und Universalienforschung (ZAS).

Bittner, Dagmar
  2002   Emergence of grammatical complexity and markedness in the acquisition of verb and noun phrases in German. In: Katarzyna Dziubalska-Kołaczyk, and Jarek Weckwerth (eds.), *Future Challenges for Natural Linguistics,* 25–56. Wien: Lincom.

Brown, Roger
  1973   *A First Language: The Early Stages.* Cambridge, Mass.: Harvard University Press.

Bybee, Joan
  1995   Regular morphology and the lexicon. *Language and Cognitive Processes* 10: 425–455.

Carpenter, Gail A., and Steven Grossberg 1988 Neural dynamics of category learning and recognition: Attention, memory consolidation, and amnesia. In: Joel L. Davis, Ronald W. Newburgh, and Edward J. Wegman (eds.), *Brain Structure, Learning, and Memory,* 233–290. Boulder, CO: Westview Press.

Clahsen, Harald
1990   Constraints on parameter setting: A grammatical analysis of some acquisition stages in German child language. *Language Acquisition* 1: 361–91.

Clahsen, Harald, and Monika Rothweiler
1992   Inflectional rules in children's grammars: Evidence from the development of participles in German. In: Geert Booij, and Jaap van Marle (eds.), *Yearbook of Morphology 1992*, 1–34. Dordrecht: Kluwer.

Clahsen, Harald, Martina Penke, and Teresa Parodi
1993   Functional categories in child German. *Language Acquisition* 3: 395–429.

Clahsen, Harald, Sonja Eisenbeiß, and Martina Penke
1996   Lexical learning in early syntactic development. In: Harald Clahsen (ed.), *Generative Perspectives on Language Acquisition*, 129–159. Amsterdam/Philadelphia: John Benjamins.

Dressler, Wolfgang
1997   Introduction. In: Katarczyna Dziubalska-Kołaczyk (ed.), *Pre- and Protomorphology in Language Acquisition*, 7–14. (Papers and Studies in Contrastive Linguistics 33.) Poznań: Adam Mickiewicz University.

Dressler, Wolfgang U., Willi Mayerthaler, Oswald Panagl, and Wolfgang Ullrich Wurzel
1987   *Leitmotifs in Natural Morphology*. Amsterdam: John Benjamins.

Dressler, Wolfgang U., and Annemarie Karpf
1995   The theoretical relevance of pre- and protomorphology in language acquisition. *Yearbook of Morphology 1994*: 99–122.

Friedrich, Manuela
2000   Der sprachliche Einfluss auf das Auftreten von Exklusionen bei Kindern. *ZAS Papers in Linguistics* 15: 218-231.

Gentner, Dedre, and Arthur Markman
1997   Structure mapping in analogy and similarity. *American Psychologist* 52: 45–56.

Karmiloff-Smith, Annette
1992   *Beyond Modularity: A Developmental Perspective on Cognitive Science*. Cambridge, Mass./London: MIT Press.

Kilani-Schoch, Marianne, and Wolfgang U. Dressler
2000   Are precursors of morphemes relevant for morphological theory? In: Wolfgang U. Dressler, Oskar E. Pfeiffer, Markus Poechtraeger, and John R. Rennison (eds.), *Morphological Analysis in Comparison*, 89–111. Amsterdam: John Benjamins.

Klein, Wolfgang
1994   *Time in Language*. London: Routledge.

Klein, Wolfgang
1998   Assertion and finiteness. In: Norbert Dittmar, and Zvi Penner (eds.), *Issues in the Theory of Language Acquisition: Essays in Honour of Juergen Weissenborn*, 225–245. Bern: Lang.

Lasser, Ingeborg
1997   *Finiteness in Adult and Child German*. (MPI Series in Psycholinguistics 8.) Nijmegen: Max-Planck-Institute for Psycholinguistics.

Leiss, Elisabeth
2000   *Artikel und Aspekt: Die grammatischen Muster von Definitheit*. Berlin/New York: de Gruyter.

MacWhinney, Brian
1978   *The Acquisition of Morphophonology*. (Monographs of the Society for Research in Child Development 43, 1/2.) Chicago: University of Chicago Press.

MacWhinney, Brian
2000   *The CHILDES Project: Tools for Analyzing Talk.* Vol. I: Transcription, Format and Programs. Mahwah, New Jersey: Lawrence Erlbaum.

Mayerthaler, Willi
1981   *Morphologische Natürlichkeit*. Wiesbaden: Athenaion.

Olguin, Raquel, and Michael Tomasello
1993   Twenty-five-month-old children do not have a grammatical category of verb. *Cognitive Development* 8: 245–272.

Plunkett, Kim
1993   From rote-learning to system building. *Cognition* 48: 21–69.

Slobin, Dan I. (ed.)
1985   *The Cross Linguistic Study of Language Acquisition.* Vol. I: The Data; Vol. II: Theoretical Issues. Hillsdale, New Jersey: Lawrence Erlbaum.

Tomasello, Michael
1992   *First Verbs: A case Study of Early Grammatical Development.* Cambridge: Cambridge University Press.

Tomasello, Michael
2000a   First steps towards a usage based theory of language acquisition. *Cognitive Linguistics* 11: 61–82.

Tomasello, Michael
2000b   Acquiring syntax is not what you think. In: Dorothy Bishop, and Laurence B. Leonard (eds.), *Speech and Language Impairments in Children: Cause, Characteristics, Intervention and Outcome,* 1–15. Hove: Psychology Press.

Vollman, Ralph, Maria Sedlak, Brigitte Müller, and Maria Vassilakou
1997   Early verb inflection and noun plural formation in four Austrian children: The demarcation of phases an interindividual variation. In: Katarczyna Dziubalska-Kołaczyk (ed.), *Pre- and Protomorphology in Language Acquisition,* 59–78. (Papers and Studies in Contrastive Linguistics 33.) Poznań: Adam Mickiewicz University.

Wexler, Ken
1994   Optional infinitives, head movement, and the economy of derivations. In: David Lightfoot, and Norbert Hornstein (eds.), *Verb Movement,* 305–350. London: Cambridge University Press.

Weissenborn, Jürgen
1990   Functional categories and verb movement: The acquisition of German syntax reconsidered. In: Monika Rothweiler (ed.), *Spracherwerb und Grammatik,* 190–224. Linguistische Berichte, Sonderheft 3/1990.

Weissenborn, Jürgen
1994   Constraining the child's grammar: Local well-formedness in the development of verb movement in German and French. In: Barbara Lust, Margarita Suñer, and John Whitman (eds.), *Syntactic Theory and First Language Acquisition: Cross-Linguistic Perspectives,* 215–247. Hillsdale, New Jersey: Erlbaum.

Weyerts, Helga, and Harald Clahsen
　1994　　Netzwerke und symbolische Regeln im Spracherwerb: Experimentelle Ergebnisse zur Entwicklung der Flexionsmorphologie. *Linguistische Berichte* 154: 430–460.

Early phases in the development of Greek verb inflection

Anastasia Christofidou and Ursula Stephany

0. Abstract

In this paper we study the earliest phases of verb morphology in two children acquiring a highly inflectional-fusional language, Greek. We compare the inflectional development of a Greek boy from the age of 1;7.11 to the age of 2;1.27 to that of a rather precocious girl between 1;9.17 and 1;9.26. A verb-by-verb analysis of early inflectional forms shows that the grammatical categories of the Greek verb, i.e. aspect, mood, and tense as well as person and number, first develop in a lexicon-based way. Although acquisition seems to be piecemeal in the 'premorphological' phase, there is some systematicity inherent in the grammatical categories the children choose from the input already in the very beginning of development. Depending on the criteria applied, verbal inflectional categories appear to become productive quite early. A comparison of the children's speech to that of their mothers points to a strong connection of the cognitive, linguistic, and communicative characteristics of the input to the children's linguistic development.

1. Theoretical considerations

Basing themselves on the considerable linguistic achievements of the young bonobo Kanzi in comprehending spoken English, Savage-Rumbaugh, Shanker, and Taylor (1998: 73) conclude that "language is learned, not through speaking, but by coming to understand what others say to us." If this is true, the nature of the linguistic input children receive and "cultural (imitative) learning is more important in language development, especially in the early stages, than has traditionally been recognized" (Tomasello 2000: 71). In the light of usage-based theories of language acquisition, Jakobson's characterization of early language development in children as "creative imitation" regains special appeal:

> Was hier stattfindet, ist weder eine mechanische Übernahme noch eine wunderbare Schöpfung aus dem Nichts. Das Nachahmen öffnet den schöpferischen Kräften des Anfängers weite Möglichkeiten. Das vorhandene Muster gestattet eine Auslese der vollbrachten Entlehnungen und deren gesetzmäßige Reihenfolge, der zudanken das Kind anfangs das eine und dann erst das nächste sich anzueignen weiß (Jakobson 1977: 8).

On the basis of recent findings, "the assumption of a unidirectional and determinative relationship between cognitive and language development as it was conceived in the Piagetian tradition seems no longer tenable" (Behrens 2001: 458). As opposed to the Cognition Hypothesis,[1] the Language Specificity Hypothesis[2] "emphasizes the child's productive analysis of the form-function patterns of the target language" (Behrens 2001: 458) and "crosslinguistic diversity in patterns of grammaticization points to adult communicative practices as the most plausible source of form-function mappings in human languages, rather than prototypical events in infant cognition" (Slobin 2001: 412).

In this view, it seems reasonable to assume that the following general principles of learning posited by Bybee's (1991: 89) model of the acquisition of inflectional morphology may account for the acquisition of much of linguistic structure: (1) "The most often repeated experiences (in production and perception) have the strongest representation" and (2) "new experiences are analyzed and stored in terms of existing representations." What makes this model of language acquisition so attractive is "that it allows us to establish a relation between the way language is used – that is, how forms actually appear in natural discourse – and the way language is represented mentally" (Bybee 1991: 89).

One of the basic tenets of usage-based models of language acquisition is that young children want to use language to communicate. They therefore "begin by imitatively learning specific pieces of language in order to express their communicative intentions, for example, in holophrases and other fixed expressions," trying to use language the way they have heard it used by mature speakers in their environment (Tomasello 2000: 70–71). It is only sufficient experience with particular events of linguistic usage that will enable them to gradually induce ever more abstract linguistic regularities. Usage-based approaches to language acquisition thus "stress the *dynamic* properties of linguistic knowledge", not only the learner's ability "to induce categories and schemas", but also to restructure them continually in response to both changes in the input and pressure exerted by the growth of other categories in the learner's system" (Bowerman and Choi 2001: 498).[3] Although linguistic categories and schemas are at first only local, it seems necessary to posit that similar communicative functions play a major role in establishing linguistic categories from the very beginning (Mandler 1998; Tomasello 2000: 73). Once morphological patterns become larger, applying to an ever increasing number of lexical items, the corresponding schemas gain in strength and may attain the status of categorical rules (Bybee 1991: 86).[4]

In usage-based approaches to language acquisition, both type and token frequency of expressions occurring in the input serve important, but different goals: While the token frequency of an expression tends to "entrench" it, "enabling the user to access and fluently use the expression as a whole", "type frequency of an expression (i.e. the number of different forms in which the language learner experiences the expression or some element of the expression) determines the creative possibilities, or productivity, of the construction" (Tomasello 2000: 72).[5] Type variation of parts of an expression leads to the abstraction of linguistic patterns (Tomasello 2000: 76–77).

Since Greek is a language with a strict noun-verb distinction and the verb is especially rich in inflectional forms specific to this syntactic category, there is evidence for the grammatical category of verb, as opposed to the noun, early on in Greek child language (Stephany 1997a). Greek children develop inflected forms of verbs (and nouns) rather early due to the inflectional-fusional character of the language they are acquiring and to the perceptual salience of inflectional endings[6] (Stephany 1985, 1997a; see also section 2). In the early developmental stages, the inflectional categories of tense and aspect as well as person are tied to certain conglomerations of semantico-grammatical categories and only later generalize to all verbs. Thus, aspect and tense strongly depend on *aktionsart* and person is controlled by mood to a certain extent (Stephany 1981, 1985, 1997a).

Mastery of the rich inflectional system of the Greek language proceeds gradually and seems to be guided by semantic simplicity as well as frequency in the input, with the latter being a function of communicative needs and the way of "thinking for speaking" (Slobin 1990) peculiar to Greek culture. In the inflectional system of the Greek verb, the unmarked combinations of the categories of aspect, mood, tense, and *aktionsart* develop before the marked ones in child speech.[7] Guided by communicative needs and the endeavor to be understood by their immature interlocutors,

Greek mothers present a subset of the grammatical forms contained in the inflectional paradigms of verbs to their young children, which results in a manageable number of inflectional types of each verb lemma on the one hand and a considerable repetitiveness of verb form tokens on the other (Stephany 1985: 183–189; see also section 4).

The traditional word-and-paradigm model in which grammatical morphology "concerns relations among words" (Bybee 1991: 70) and "morphological patterns emerge through the comparison of words within and across paradigms" (Bybee 1991: 68), fits the morphological structure of an inflectional-fusional language like Greek especially well, since words do not have to be "pulled apart" in order to grasp their structure. In this view, "both the word and the paradigm to which it belongs are part of the grammar" rather than "derived by the grammar" (Bybee 1991: 68). Accordingly, the task of the child in acquiring inflectional morphology is to learn "many different words" and to develop "the ability to make more words" (Bybee 1991: 70).

Since the acquisition of inflectional morphology is lexicon-based, it seems more appropriate to postulate a phase model than a stage model of linguistic development. Adapting Karmiloff-Smith's model of "Representational Redescription" to the development of morphology it may be hypothesized that achievements in the mastery of verbal paradigms "occur recurrently within microdomains throughout development" rather than involving "fundamental changes across the entire cognitive system" as postulated by "stage models" (Karmiloff-Smith 1992: 18).

In this chapter, we will present a lemma-based, verb-by-verb analysis of early verb forms of the two children studied in order to show how the inflectional categories of the Greek verb, i.e. aspect, tense, and mood as well as person and number, emerge and become productive. As far as productivity is concerned we will show to what extent inflectional categories are learned piecemeal and to what degree more general patterns of usage can be documented.[8]

2. Greek verbal morphology

Greek verbal morphology is one of the richest among European languages and considerably more complex than the inflection of the Greek noun.

The grammatical categories expressed inflectionally by the Greek verb are mood, aspect, tense, and voice, as well as person and number. Modern Greek has no infinitive. There are three persons, both in the singular and plural. In finite verb forms, aspect is marked on the stem, while person and number are expressed by the verb ending, together with mood and/or tense (see below). Active and medio-passive voice are marked on the verb ending as well as the stem. Nearly all verbs formally distinguish between an imperfective and a perfective verb stem.[9] The main temporal opposition is past/non-past. Since the medio-passive is irrelevant for early verb development it will not be considered here. Table (1) exemplifies the main inflectional categories of the verb *líno* (1S) 'to solve, untie' in the active voice.

Table 1. The main inflectional categories of the Greek verb in the active voice

Mood	Tense	Aspect	
		Imperfective	Perfective
Indicative	Non-past	líno	–
	Past	élina	élisa
	Future	tha líno	tha líso
Subjunctive		na líno	na líso
Imperative		líne	líse

In Greek there are two main conjugational classes: class 1, bearing stress on the stem (e.g. *lín-o* 'solve:IPF-NONPAST:1S') and class 2, bearing stress on the ending (e.g. *aghap-ó* 'love:IPF-NONPAST:1S'). Most class 1 verbs form a sigmatic perfective active stem ending in *-s-* (e.g. *lín-o* 'solve:IPF-NONPAST:1S' → *é-lis-a* 'AUGM-solve:PFV-PAST:1S'). The rest of Class 1 verbs form an asigmatic perfective stem by various morphophonemic processes (e.g. *mén-o* 'stay:IPF-NONPAST:1S' → *é-min-a* 'AUGM-stay:PFV-PAST:1S'). All class 2 verbs form sigmatic perfectives, but most of them insert an *-i-* before the *-s-* (e.g. *aghap-ó* 'love:IPF-NONPAST:1S' → *aghápis-a* 'love:PFV-PAST:1S'). Since the past tense forms of most verbs are stressed on the antepenultimate syllable, syllabic augment (*é-lin-a* 'AUGM-solve:IPF-PAST:1S' vs. *lín-ame* 'solve:IPF-PAST:1P') is obligatory in the singular and third person plural forms of bisyllabic verbs.

The only difference between the two verb classes as far as their endings are concerned occurs in the imperfective non-past.[10] Class 2 comprises two subclasses which differ in the endings of the imperfective non-past (table 2).

Table 2. Verbal endings of the indicative and the imperative in the active voice[11]

PERS/NUM	PFV: NON-PAST Class 1/2	IPF:NONPAST Class 1	IPF:NONPAST Class 2	PAST Class 1/2	PFV:IMP Class 1/2	IPF:IMP Class 1	IPF:IMP Class 2
1S	-o	-o	-(a)o	-a			
2S	-is	-is	-as/-is	-es	-e	-e	-a
3S	-i	-i	-a(i)/-i	-e			
1P	-ume	-ume	-ame/-ume	-ame			
2P	-ete	-ete	-ate/-ite	-ate	-(e)te	-(e)te	-ate/-ite
3P	-un(e)	-un(e)	-an(e)/-un(e)	-an(e)			

3. Data

Two kinds of data have been analyzed for the present study: the longitudinal observation of the boy Christos from 1;7.11 to 2;1.27 and the more selective observation of the girl Mairi between 1;9.17 and 1;9.26.[12]

The longitudinal data of Christos consists in 25 (almost) weekly recordings of (approximately) 20 min. of (semi-)spontaneous speech (table 3).

Table 3. Christos' longitudinal data

Recording	Age	Utterances	Recording	Age	Utterances
1	1;7.11	162	13	1;11.27	109
2	1;8.21	114	14	2;0.4	150
3	1;9.3	23	15	2;0.7	214
4	1;9.12	85	16	2;0.15	145
5	1;9.24	111	17	2;0.16	97
6	1;10.1	86	18	2;1.2	115
7	1;10.9	237	19	2;1.9	96
8	1;10.24	81	20	2;1.14	213
9	1;11	162	21	2;1.22	54
10	1;11.10	104	22	2;1.23	200
11	1;11.13	80	23	2;1.26	168
12	1;11.19	108	24	2;1.27	83
			Total:		2,997

Recordings took place at the boy's or his grandparents' home while he was playing or looking at picture books familiar to him. Adult interlocutors were his mother and grandmother as well as other family members. Christos was then the only child of a Greek upper middle class family and is growing up monolingually in Athens. From a linguistic point of view, the boy may be characterized as an analytic ("referential") child, since formulaic and frozen forms are rare in his speech.

The verb forms occurring in the speech of the linguistically most advanced of the five children studied by Stephany (1985, 1997a) at an age comparable to that of Christos will be reanalyzed in the present study in order to show that Greek children may differ considerably in the rate at which their language develops. The child Mairi was first recorded between 1;9.17 and 1;9.26 with utterances analyzed amounting to 1,995 (MLU [words/utt.] 2.166). She was the only child of a lower middle class family at that time and grew up monolingually in Athens. She may be characterized as a "referential" child. Although at 1;9 her case system is barely beginning to emerge, she contrasts singular and plural forms of ten nouns (N = 107). Verbal inflection is much more advanced since two to seven different grammatical forms occur with more than half of her 64 verbal lemmas spontaneously and correctly used formally as well as functionally (see below).

4. Emergence of verb forms
4.1. Quantitative analysis

The verb is an extremely important category in Greek discourse and children encounter this syntactic category very frequently in the speech addressed to them even before the end of their second year. Thus, 85% to even 100% on average of the two mothers' utterances addressed to their children aged 1;8 and 2;0 (subject Christos) and 1;9 (subject Mairi), respectively, contain a verb form (table 4).[13]

Table 4. Number of verbal lemmas, types and tokens of grammatical verb forms, and percentages with respect to the number of analyzed utterances in child-directed speech

Subject	Input at age	Analyzed utter.	Verbal lemmas	Types	Tokens	Lemmas/ utter.	Types/ utter.	Tokens/ utter.
Chr.	1;8	812	53	131	727	6.55	18.00	89.55
Chr.	2;0	1,293	94	234	1,102	7.25	21.25	85.20
Mairi	1;9	1,792	110	337	1,817	6.14	18.81	100

Comparing the children's speech to their input it becomes clear that they receive a much higher input in both verbal types (lemmas and grammatical forms) and tokens than they themselves produce in the data studied (compare table 4 with tables 5a and 5b). These differences between the input and child speech are more pronounced with the less advanced child Christos than with Mairi. Also, Mairi uses verb forms in 39% of her utterances already at 1;9, while the child studied longitudinally arrives at nearly 33% of utterances containing a verb only by 2;1. One reason for this difference seems to be that in the first recordings Christos was particularly preoccupied with car brands so that these data are accordingly richer in nouns than verbs.

Table 5a. Number of verbal lemmas, types and tokens of grammatical verb forms in Christos' speech and percentages with respect to the number of analyzed utterances (with incorrect forms indicated in parentheses)

Age	Analyzed utter.	Verbal lemmas	Types	Tokens	Verbal lemmas/utter.	Types/ utter.	Tokens/ utter.
1;8	276	7	8 (3)	12 (4)	2.54	2.90	4.35
1;9	219	10	11 (2)	21 (3)	4.57	5.02	9.59
1;10	404	8	8 (2)	46 (2)	2.00	1.98	11.39
1;11	563	20	29 (9)	77 (16)	3.55	5.15	13.68
2;0	606	23	36 (13)	90 (17)	3.80	5.94	14.85
2;1	929	47	97 (34)	304 (48)	5.06	10.44	32.72
Total:	2,997	115	189 (63)	550 (90)	3.84	6.30	18.35

Table 5b. Number of verbal lemmas, types and tokens of grammatical verb forms in Mairi's speech and percentages with respect to the number of analyzed utterances

Age	Analyzed utter.	Verbal lemmas	Types	Tokens	Verbal lemmas/utter.	Types/ utter.	Tokens/ utter.
1;9	1,995	64	148	780	3.21	7.42	39.10

Since the subject Mairi of Stephany's data was observed at only one point before the end of her second year, early developmental aspects can solely be considered for the boy Christos. Fig. 1 shows that by age 1;8, when he was first recorded, he had already started to produce verbs.[14] His use of verbs increases steadily until the age of 2;0, when verb tokens rise from about 15% to 33% within one month.[15] The percentages of verbal lemmas and verb types momentarily drop at age 1;10 because in the recordings taken during this month, Christos uses the verb form *théli* 'want:IPF:NONPAST:3S*=1S' ('he wants' instead of 'I want') extremely often.

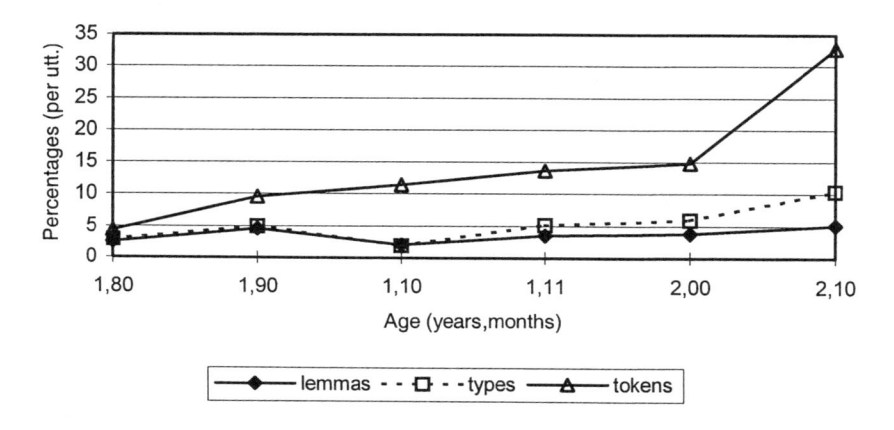

Figure 1. Christos' verb production: lemmas, types, and tokens (%)

4.2. Inflectional categories of the verb: Form and function
4.2.1. Introduction

In this section we will first study the system of the two children's grammatical categories of the verb and compare this to the input they receive. We will next examine the productivity of inflectional verb forms and address the question in how far the children's knowledge of Greek grammatical categories expressed inflectionally is systematic or piecemeal.

We are aware of the fact that, especially in early child speech, the categorization of child forms according to grammatical categories of the adult language is problematic. One main reason for using such categories in the description of child speech is to be able to identify the formal categories the child uses. In studying the children's language systems we will show in how far their categories differ from the target language both formally and functionally. Our approach is both synchronic (child-centered) and diachronic (goal-centered) and thus allows to account for the structure and function of children's linguistic systems at a given time as well as for the development of their language towards the target.

4.2.2. *Grammatical categories of the verb in early Greek child speech as compared to child-directed speech*

In order to better understand the early development of the syntactic category of the verb and the morpho-syntactic categories it expresses, we will sketch Christos' development of verb forms from 1;7.11 through 2;1 beginning with predecessors of verbs (pseudo-verbs) and holophrases (frozen forms). Onomatopoetic forms, such as *mam* 'to eat, food' (example 1) and *nani* 'to sleep, sleeping', which have both a nominal and a verbal function, as well as the pseudo-verb *bum* 'fell' already occur in the first recording.

(1)   SOU: *ti   kani   edho   to   scilaci?*
             what   does   here   the   doggie
             'What is the doggie doing here?'
    CHR: *mam.*
             'Eating'.

Interestingly, between the ages of 1;8 and 1;10, the form *bum* develops into a pseudo-past form *bume* 'it fell'. This form can be interpreted as a kind of blend of the pseudo-verb *bum* and the verb form *epese* (fall:PFV:PAST:3S) 'it fell/has fallen' and probably results from his mother's numerous corrections of Christos' form *bum* by *epese*. There will be 17 instances of this blend before the boy starts using the verb form *epese* in a more systematic way.

Since Christos is a non-formulaic child, there is little evidence for frozen forms[16] in his early speech from 1;8 to 1;10. The forms *cine* (for *eci ine* 'there is') and *tine* (for *ti ine* 'what is') are unanalyzed holophrases based on adult utterances comprising the verb form *ine* 'is/are'. At least until the emergence of two-member paradigms at 1;11, Christos' use of verb forms is lexically based since there is only a single form per lemma (examples 2 and 3).

(2)   a. *cita!*
        IMP:2S
        'Look!'
    b. *epese.*
        fall:PFV:PAST:3S
        'It has fallen.'
    c. *pai.*
        go:IPF:NONPAST:3S
        'Over/gone.'[17]

Greek 99

Three other lemmas used in the imperfective non-past 3rd singular from 1;8 to 1;9 seem to be context-bound, since they occur as (standard) reactions whenever Christos is asked to describe pictures in the books looked at during recording sessions (examples 3). Until 1;10, these forms are not always properly used as far as the category of number is concerned. In spite of the fact that Christos hears the contextually adequate 3rd singular or 3rd plural forms in the questions he is asked, he himself sticks to the form corresponding to the standard 3rd singular in his answers to both types of questions.

(3) a. *troi.*
       'He is eating.'[18]
    b. *vrechi.*
       'It is raining.'
    c. *clei.*
       'He is crying.'

At the age of 1;10.9, Christos mostly uses the 3rd singular *theli* (want:IPFV:NONPAST:3S) instead of the 1st singular *thelo* to refer to himself. This form also occurs in two-word constructions with different nominal and adverbial complements expressing the boy's needs and wishes (examples 4).

(4) a. *theli nero.*
       'He wants water.'
    b. *theli ghala.*
       'He wants milk.'
    c. *theli pano.*
       'He wants (to get) up.'

Christos first begins to use subjunctive forms at the age of 1;11. Although these forms occurring with three lemmas are not yet properly formed, they clearly contrast with the present indicative by vowel lengthening (example 5a) or reduplication (example 5b).[19]

(5) a. *koopi.*
       cut:PFV:NONPAST:3S
    for: *na   kops-is*
         MOD:PTL cut:PFV-NONPAST:2S
         'You shall cut (it).'

b. *kakani.*
   do:NONPAST:3S
for: *na   kan-is*
   MOD:PTL do-NONPAST:2S
   'You shall do (it).'

Moreover, at the age of 1;11, Christos' system of person-number categories develops and, except for the 2nd plural, all person-number combinations occur (almost across the three tense-aspect-mood categories past/non-past indicative and subjunctive). However, the 3rd singular remains dominant in these three tense-aspect-mood categories (henceforth TAM categories) and continues to be overgeneralized (see below). The secondly preferred person in Christos' speech is the 1st plural, but this is mainly used in the subjunctive mood serving a conative function.

Christos' development of the grammatical categories of the verb between 1;8 and 2;1 seems to divide into two periods the first of which lasts from 1;8 to 1;10 with the second setting in at 1;11. Up to 1;10, Christos uses three different tense-aspect-mood categories, namely the imperfective non-past ('present'), the perfective past, and the imperative (table 6a).

Table 6a. Types/tokens of Christos' adequately and inadequately used tense-aspect-mood and person-number categories[20]

Age	IPF:NONPAST				PFV:PAST			IMP	PFV:SUBJV		
	1S	3S	1P	3P	1S	3S	3P	2S	1S	3S	1P
1;8		6/8 (3/4)						2/4			
1;9		8/16 (1/2)				1/3 (1/1)		2/2			
1;10		7/41 (2/2)				1/5					
1;11	1/2	11/43		2/3		2/6	1/1	3/3	1/4	6/10 (1/1) (6/10)	2/5 (2/5)
2;0	1/2	12/50		3/3 (1/1)		7/15 (2/2)		2/5	2/2 (1/1)	5/5 (5/5)	4/8 (4/8)
2;1	6/11 (1/1)	20/115 (1/2)	3/9	1/1	2/2 (1/1)	14/81 (4/5)	8/20 (2/2)	3/3	30/43 (19/26)	10/19 (6/11)	

The perfective subjunctive only emerges at 1;11 and the imperfective subjunctive first occurs with two lemmas at 2;1, but a contrastive use with the perfective subjunctive cannot yet be attested.[21] While, up to 2;0, Christos uses the subjunctive exclusively in main clauses in order to express deontic modality, after 2;0 he starts using it in subordinate clauses as well (16 tokens from 2;0 to 2;1).[22]

In the period between 1;8 and 1;10, the categories of person and number are limited to the 3rd singular in the indicative (past/non-past) and the 2nd singular in the imperative, whereas the 1st singular and the 3rd plural begin to develop at 1;11 and the 1st plural emerges at 1;11 in the subjunctive. While, from the very beginning, there are almost no inadequacies in the use of TAM categories, the categories of person and number develop out of the 3rd singular more slowly and Christos continues to overgeneralize this person/number combination for quite some time (see below).[23] An explanation for these developmental differences may be found in the peripheral status of person/number as compared to TAM categories, which are semantically more central to the verb (Bybee 1991: 80–81). Since both person/number and tense (as well as mood) are marked by the verbal ending, only aspect is formally more central to the Greek verb.

The four main inflectional categories of the Greek verb, namely the imperfective non-past ('present'), the perfective subjunctive, the perfective past, and the imperative are all amply represented in Mairi's speech already by 1;9 (table 6b).

Table 6b. Numbers (second row) and percentages (third row) of types/tokens of Mairi's adequately used tense-aspect-mood and person-number categories at 1;9[24]

IPF:NONPAST					PFV:PAST				PFV:SUBJ				IMP
1S	2S	3S	1P	3P	1S	2S	3S	1P	1S	2S	3S	1P	2S
14/	9/	28/	3/	1/	4/	1/	5/	2/	19/	7/	10/	16/	20/
93	30	185	6	1	4	1	19	2	52	12	34	49	147
10.1/	6.5/	20.1/	2.6/	0.7/	2.9/	0.7/	3.6/	1.4/	13.7/	5.0/	7.2/	11.5/	14.4/
14.6	4.7	29.1	0.9	0.2	0.6	0.2	3.0	0.3	8.2	1.9	5.4	7.7	23.2

There are a few (recognizable) imperfective subjunctive verb forms (5 types/9 tokens) differing from the respective indicative non-past forms by the presence of a modal particle (see table 1 above). Except for the verb *vlepo* 'see', these are not contrasted to perfective forms, however. But even with this verb, it is not clear whether the child semantically distinguishes between the perfective form *na dhume* 'let's see' and the imperfective *na vlepume* 'let's see.' The imperfective past only occurs with the verb *kano* 'do', which usually makes no aspectual distinction. As with Christos, the TAM categories are nearly always adequately used. Since each of the three categories is only wrongly used in one or two tokens, these do not constitute systematic errors.

Unlike Christos, who, at 1;9, has only mastered verb forms corresponding to the standard 3rd singular, Mairi uses all person-number combinations except the 2nd plural.[25] As with Christos, when he begins to use the 1st plural mainly in the subjunctive, person-number combinations are not evenly distributed among the TAM categories of non-past, past, and subjunctive in Mairi's speech either. While the girl uses the 3rd singular most widely in the indicative mood ('present' and past) and the 3rd plural is restricted to the non-past, she prefers the 1st person singular and plural in the subjunctive. Still, the 1st person singular is already quite productive also in the present tense. The development of the categories of person and number will be studied in more detail below.

If the two children's verb forms are ranked according to the four TAM categories of the imperfective non-past, perfective past, perfective subjunctive, and the imperative, disregarding person-number distinctions, it becomes clear that the categories expressing deontic modality (subjunctive and imperative) play a much greater role in their utterances than the past (tables 7a and 7b).[26]

Although the precedence of the semantically unmarked imperfective non-past remains stable during the whole period for which Christos' speech has been analyzed and is also valid for Mairi at 1;9, the main contrasts among the early TAM categories are those of modal vs. non-modal forms (perfective subjunctive and imperative vs. imperfective non-past and perfective past) on the one hand and imperfective vs. perfective indicative forms (imperfective non-past vs. perfective past) on the other. As pointed out by Stephany (1997a: 245) "this verb-form inventory as well as the use to which it is put [...] is evidence that aspect is a more fundamental category than tense in child Greek as it is in the standard language (Seiler 1952, Stephany 1981, 1985)." While mood and aspect are the two fundamental verbal categories of early child Greek, "tense is initially only implicit" (Stephany 1997a: 249). The imperfective non-past occurs foremost with atelic-durative or stative verbs and typically refers to ongoing situations.[27] The perfective past is used more often with telic than with atelic verbs and characteristically has a resultative function implying pastness as far as the actions or events expressed are concerned (Stephany 1985: 141).[28] Since the future as it is used by young children has a more strongly modal rather than a temporal meaning most of the time, the categories of future and subjunctive are even more closely semantically related in early child Greek than in the standard language. While the opposition of past and non-past begins to develop in the indicative mood with the emergence of the imperfective past, the future gradually evolves from the subjunctive (Stephany 1997a: 249; see also Stephany 1985, 1992).

Table 7a. Ranking of aspect-tense-mood categories in Christos' speech from 1;11 to 2;1 (only formally and functionally correct forms)

TAM categories	Number of types	%	TAM categories	Number of tokens	%
IPF:NONPAST	57	40.42	IPF:NONPAST	235	51.31
PFV:SUBJ	53	37.58	PFV:SUBJ	99	21.61
PFV:PAST	20	14.18	PFV:PAST	98	21.39
IMPERATIVE	11	7.80	IMPERATIVE	26	5.67
Total:	141		Total:	458	

Table 7b. Ranking of aspect-tense-mood categories in Mairi's speech at 1;9 (only formally and functionally correct forms)

TAM categories	Number of types	%	TAM categories	Number of tokens	%
PFV:SUBJ	59	40.69	IPF:NONPAST	443	57.09
IPF:NONPAST	53	36.55	PFV:SUBJ	159	20.49
IMPERATIVE	20	13.79	IMPERATIVE	147	18.94
PFV:PAST	13	8.97	PFV:PAST	27	3.48
Total:	145		Total:	776	

Comparing the TAM categories of the verb used by Christos up to 2;1 and by Mairi at 1;9 to those of standard Greek the main difference is the following: The children's systems of verbal categories mostly consist of synthetic verb forms. They neither use the present perfect nor the past perfect (both constructed with the auxiliary *exo* 'have')[29] and their differentiation of the future/subjunctive from the 'present' indicative mainly relies on the synthetic part of the verb form (perfective stem + non-past ending) while the future and modal particles *tha* and *na* are often missing, sometimes not distinguished (*a* for both *na* and *tha*), or indicated by fillers (schwa), reduplication, or vowel lengthening (Christofidou and Kappa 1998). Mairi marks the difference between the future and the subjunctive in only 49% of the respective tokens (Stephany 1985: 96).

More illuminating than a comparison of the children's inventories of verb forms with that of standard Greek is a study of the relation between the input they receive and their own speech, both as far as verb form types and their use (tokens) are concerned. Not only do the inventories and ranking of TAM categories occurring in Christos' and Mairi's mothers' speech directed to their children in the second half of their second year closely correspond both type- and tokenwise (tables 8a and 8b), but there are also interesting relations between child-directed and child speech. Since Greek verbs comprise more than 130 different verb forms each, it can be seen that not only early child Greek but also Greek child-directed speech are severely limited in their inventories of TAM categories consisting of the communicatively most important of these.[30]

Table 8a. Ranking of aspect-tense-mood categories in the child-directed speech of Christos' mother at 1;8 and 2;0

TAM categories	Number of types	%	TAM categories	Number of tokens	%
IPF:NONPAST	179	49.58	IPF:NONPAST	1,213	66.83
PFV:SUBJ/FUT	76	21.05	IMPERATIVE	217	11.95
PFV:PAST	66	18.28	PFV:SUBJ/FUT	202	11.12
IMPERATIVE	40	11.08	PFV:PAST	183	10.08
Total:	361		Total:	1,815	

Table 8b. Ranking of aspect-tense-mood categories in the child-directed speech of Mairi's mother at 1;9

TAM categories	Number of types	%	TAM categories	Number of tokens	%
IPF:NONPAST	121	36.34	IPF:NONPAST	892	49.58
PFV:SUBJ/FUT	112	33.63	PFV:SUBJ/FUT	384	21.35
PFV:PAST	65	19.52	IMPERATIVE	384	21.35
IMPERATIVE	35	10.51	PFV:PAST	139	7.73
Total:	333		Total:	1,799	

Although until 1;10 Christos' ranking of TAM categories differs from that of his mother's child-directed speech due to the fact that he does not yet use the subjunctive, after the emergence of the subjunctive at 1;11 the boy's ranking coincides with that of his mother's speech typewise. Tokenwise there is a clear preference of both the subjunctive and the perfective past as compared to the imperative in the child's speech while in his mother's speech the three categories of the imperative, the perfective subjunctive/future, and the perfective past are more evenly distributed (see tables 7a and 8a). The high percentage of subjunctive tokens in Christos' speech as compared with imperative forms can be explained by his tendency to use subjunctive forms in imperative contexts (see below).

The TAM categories used by Mairi closely correspond to those occurring in her mother's child-directed speech, not only as far as the inventory of verb forms goes, but also concerning its use (tokenwise ranking in tables 7b and 8b). It is interesting to note that the two most important verb-form categories occurring in Mairi's mother's speech are almost evenly distributed typewise so that the child has a large opportunity to deal with different forms of the imperfective non-past and the perfective subjunctive as well as with the perfective past, which the girl herself does not yet use much at 1;9 but will in her third year (Stephany 1985: 115).

Let us now turn to the development of the category of person/number in more detail. As mentioned above, Christos exclusively uses verb forms corresponding to the standard 3rd singular imperfective non-past and perfective past, respectively, until the age of 1;10 (table 6a). It seems reasonable to interpret these verb forms as finite verb forms for the following reasons: The speech directed to the young Greek child nearly exclusively comprises finite verb forms.[31] The 3rd person singular <u>imperfective</u> non-past cannot possibly be interpreted as the (non-finite) *aparemfato* (Babiniotis and Kontos 1967) or "perfect formant" since the latter is "identical to the third person singular of the <u>perfective</u> non-past active or passive" (Mackridge 1985: 170; emphasis added, A.C. & U.S.) and therefore differs from the 3rd person singular imperfective non-past aspectually. Another reason to interpret the 3rd singular imperfective non-past as finite is the fact that this form emerges simultaneously with the 3rd singular perfective past in Christos' speech. Thus, Bybee's assumption "that a finite form is the basis of a verbal paradigm" (1991: 74), seems to be fully born out.[32] According to the criteria of markedness or semantic simplicity (Bybee 1991: 76) and frequency of use (Gathercole, Sebastián, and Soto 1999: 155) the 3rd person singular may be considered as a kind of basic verb form in Greek. It does not refer to the participants of the communicative event and therefore has more constant reference than the 1st and 2nd person. In child-directed speech, it is amply available,[33] since shifters tend to be avoided, and it therefore "has a stronger representation in the mental lexicon" (Bybee 1991: 73).

The 3rd person singular also has a special status as far as overgeneralizations are concerned since it continues to be the only category which is overgeneralized even after other person/number combinations have entered Christos' language (table 9a). Although in the beginning (1;8–1;9) the 3rd person singular is overextended to the 3rd person plural in the imperfective non-past, from 1;10 to 2;0 it is overused for the 1st person singular both in the indicative and the subjunctive mood in 39.53% of tokens. Since Greek is a pro-drop language we will not judge the child's overgeneralizations of the third person in terms of agreement but rather in terms of avoiding shifters.

Table 9a. Types/tokens of person/number categories inadequately used by Christos

Age	PERSON* 3S*=1S	%	3S*=2S[34]	%	3S*=3P	%
1;8					1/2	14.28/16.66
1;9					1/2	10.00/8.69
1;10	2/27	22.22/57.44				
1;11	3/5	15.78/8.47	5/10	26.31/16.94	1/1	5.26/1.69
2;0	5/8	20.83/11.42				
2;1	19/46	29.68/19.24	4/11	6.25/4.60	1/1	1.56/0.41

In the examples in which Christos uses the third person instead of the first he refers to himself by using his name along with a verb correctly agreeing with the subject in person and number (example 6).

(6) *to loo   to peticie   o   Picios.*
    for:
    to nero   to petakse   o   Christos
    the water   it throw:PFV:PAST:3S the Christos
    'Christos spilled the water.'

At 1;11, when the subjunctive emerges, Christos also overgeneralizes the third person singular to the second person singular in this mood. Contrary to standard Greek, where the subjunctive is more polite than the imperative for expressing directives, Christos extends the subjunctive to contexts of explicit directives where politeness is less important than the immediate accomplishment of an action. It must be noted however that the boy does not yet contrast both moods for expressing directives since lemmas used in the imperative do not occur in the subjunctive and vice versa (e.g. *ela* 'come!', *cita* 'look!', *fighe* 'go away!', *ase* 'leave/let (it)!').[35] Since, until

2;1, the 2nd person is limited to the few imperative forms quoted, it does not seem unlikely to assume that one reason why Christos prefers the subjunctive to the imperative is that the former mood allows for the use of the default form for person, namely the third singular.

Table 9b. Types/tokens of person/number categories used by Mairi at 1;9

PERS/NUM	1S	2S	3S	1P	3P
Correctly used	37/149	17/43	44/238 (+127 *ine* 'is/are')	21/57	1/1
	97.4%/99.3%	85.0%/91.5%	65.7%/83.2%	100%	100%
Incorrectly used	1S* = 2S 1/1	2S* = 1S 2/3	3S* = 1S 18/42	–	–
		2S* = 2P 1/1 (Imperative)	3S* = 2S 4/5		
			3S* = 3P 1/1		
Total incorrectly used	2.6%/0.7%	15.0%/8.5%	34.3%/16.8%	–	–

As is the case with the inventory of TAM categories used by Mairi at 1;9, her development of person and number is also more advanced than that of Christos. In contrast to the boy, she uses all person-number combinations except the 2nd plural. However, the 3rd person singular occurs most frequently and also shows traces of its former default use, since it is overextended to both the 1st and 2nd person, while the 1st and 2nd person singular are overextended (to the 2nd and 1st person, respectively) much less and never to the 3rd singular (table 9b). It should be noted that Mairi overextends the 3rd person singular to the 1st singular much more in the indicative (14 types/30 tokens) than in the subjunctive (4 types/12 tokens), in which the 1st person is better established.[36]

4.2.3. Productivity of inflectional categories and development of verbal paradigms

In order to understand the development of verbal inflection it is not sufficient to examine the grammatical forms of verbs spontaneously used by children but one must try to find out in how far systematic relations among verb forms and the grammatical categories they express have developed.

We will therefore apply two criteria of morphological productivity used by Pizzuto and Caselli (1994) and others[37] to the data of the two children studied and relate them to the notion of mini-paradigms elaborated by Bittner, Dressler, and Kilani-Schoch (2000).

According to Pizzuto and Caselli (1994:156, quoted in Gathercole, Sebastián, and Soto 1999: 144) a given inflectional form is considered to be productive when either or both of the following conditions hold: "(a) the same verb root appear[s] in at least two distinct inflected forms, and (b) the same inflection [is] used with at least two different verbs." As pointed out by Gathercole, Sebastián, and Soto (1999: 144), these criteria cannot underestimate a child's productivity of grammatical verb forms and therefore represent a minimal requirement for inflectional development.[38] In order to be able to compare the inflectional achievements of the more advanced child Mairi at 1;9 to Christos' development, we will first consider both of these criteria separately.

The first of the two criteria is linked to the notion of "mini-paradigms", which is defined by Bittner, Dressler, and Kilani-Schoch (2000: 5) as "an incomplete paradigm corresponding to a non-isolated set of minimally 3 accurate and distinct inflectional forms of the same verbal lexeme produced spontaneously in contrasting contexts." While criterion (b) of Pizzuto and Caselli (1994) stresses the productivity of a given grammatical form, criterion (a) and the notion of mini-paradigm take the establishment of paradigmatic relations characteristic of inflectional morphology into consideration. According to Bybee (1991: 78), "the learning strategy involved in constructing a paradigm [...] is the principle that new input is analyzed and stored in terms of existing structures. The first form of a paradigm to be acquired will be the most frequent and the semantically most coherent. Once this form is represented other less frequent and more complex forms may be analyzed and stored by reference to the existing form." This agrees well with the "default" status of the 3rd person singular noted in the preceding section.

We hope that by using both types of the criteria mentioned, we will be able to describe the children's grammatical achievements more properly. For the following analysis, only spontaneously and correctly used forms with stems and endings recognizably corresponding to those of standard Greek will be taken into consideration.

Although, up to 1;10, Christos uses his verbal lemmas in one grammatical form only and therefore does not yet meet Pizzuto and Caselli's (1994) productivity criterion (a) (table 10a), his two (out of three) inflectional forms of the imperfective non-past and the imperative occur with more than one lemma (see table 6a above) so that criterion (b) is fulfilled. At 1;11, Christos first meets both of Pizzuto and Caselli's (1994) criteria of productivity since now five of the 20 verbal lemmas (25%) occur in two forms (criterion (a)) and two of these 5 lemmas also occur in the same form (criterion (b)), i.e. the imperfective non-past third singular. At the age of 2;0, Christos uses 6 of his 23 verbal lemmas (26,08%) in two different forms and three grammatical categories occur with more than one of these lemmas. Finally, at the age of 2;1, the first three-member paradigms appear with 5 lemmas along with one four-member paradigm.

Table 10a. Inflectional forms and verbal mini-paradigms in Christos' speech

Age	Number of verbs	1 form per lemma	2-member paradigms	3-member paradigms	4-member paradigms
1;8	7	100%			
1;9	10	100%			
1;10	8	100%			
1;11	20	15 (75%)	5 (25%)		
2;0	23	17 (73.91%)	6 (26.08%)		
2;1	46	34 (73.91%)	6 (13.04%)	5 (10.87%)	1 (2.17%)

In the course of the boy's inflectional development, not only the number of verbs used with two or more inflectional forms increase, but also the number of different inflectional categories used with more than one lemma. While, at 2;0, the imperfective non-past 3rd person singular and 3rd person plural as well as the perfective subjunctive 3rd person singular occur with more than one lemma, at 2;1, the 1st singular of the imperfective non-past and the perfective subjunctive as well as the 3rd singular of the perfective past and the imperfective subjunctive are added to these.[39] A major achievement at the age of 2;1 seems to be that Christos uses the 1st person singular contrastively with more than one lemma in both the indicative and the subjunctive and thus begins to abandon the default use of the 3rd person singular.[40]

If Christos' morphological development is judged according to Bittner, Dressler, and Kilani-Schoch's (2000) criterion of paradigmatic development, productivity only sets in at 2;1, when the first three-member miniparadigms occur (table 10a), i.e. five months later than by Pizzuto and Caselli's (1994) criterion (b) (reached at 1;8) or at least two months later than by criterion (a) (fulfilled at 1;11). As is shown in table (11a), Christos uses 5 two-member paradigms at the age of 1;11. However, only two verbal lemmas of these paradigms share the same grammatical category (imperfective nonpast 3rd singular) and thus fulfill both of Pizutto and Caselli's criteria (a) and (b).

Table 11a. Inflectional categories occurring with at least 2 verbal lemmas every one of which also exhibits a mini-paradigm in Christos' speech (only correctly used forms)[41]

Age	TAM	1S	3S	1P	3P
1;11	5 verbs with ≥ 2 forms, Σ = 20 verbs				
	IPF:NONPAST		2 verbs		
	PFV:PAST				
	PFV:SUBJ				
2;0	6 verbs with ≥ 2 forms, Σ = 23 verbs				
	IPF:NONPAST		3 verbs		2 verbs
	PFV:PAST				
	PFV:SUBJ		2 verbs		
2;1	13 verbs with ≥ 2 forms, Σ = 47 verbs				
	IPF:NONPAST	2 verbs	4 verbs		
	PFV:PAST		7 verbs		
	PFV:SUBJ	4 verbs	7 verbs	3 verbs	
	IPFV:SUBJ		2 verbs		

When Pizzuto and Caselli's (1994) as well as Bittner, Dressler, and Kilani-Schoch's (2000) criteria of productivity are applied to Mairi's speech at 1;9, it becomes evident that the girl's morphological development is at least two months ahead of that of the boy Christos. Although 45.31% of her 64 verbal lemmas spontaneously and correctly used (both formally and functionally) occur in one grammatical form only, nearly 55% of her verbs are used with 2 to 7 forms demonstrating inflectional productivity in agreement with Pizzuto and Caselli's criterion (a) (table 10b).

Table 10b. Inflectional forms and verbal mini-paradigms in Mairi's speech at 1;9

Number of verbs	1 form	2 forms	3-member paradigms	4- to 5-member paradigms	6- to 7-member paradigms
64	29 (45.31%)	12 (18.75%)	11 (17.19%)	8 (12.5%)	4 (6%)

According to the stricter criterion of mini-paradigms which requires at least three contrastively used different inflectional forms of a verb, Mairi shows morphological development characteristic of the phase of protomorphology with 36% of her verbs.

Of the 43 verbs belonging to the 1st conjugation and spontaneously used by Mairi at 1;9, 23 (36% of all verbs) are used productively on both of the criteria (a) and (b) and 8 more 2nd conjugation verbs (12.5% of all verbs) (table 11b). In all, 48.5% of Mairi's 64 verbal lemmas are inflectionally productive on both of the criteria (a) and (b) and 36% according to the criterion of mini-paradigms requiring at least 3 contrastively used verb forms per lemma.

Of the bundles of grammatical categories expressed by Greek verb forms those represented in table (11b) occur with at least 2 lemmas in Mairi's speech, satisfying Pizzuto and Caselli's (1994) productivity criterion (b). The imperfective non-past ('present') and the perfective subjunctive are much more productive in both the 1st and 2nd conjugation than the perfective past. Also, the first conjugation is more developed than the second as far as the diversity of verb forms concerning both TAM categories and person/number are concerned. Medio-passive verbs are only beginning to be productively used according to criterion (b). In spite of a number of errors to be found in her use of verb forms (see section 4.2.2), Mairi has made a good headstart into the acquisition of verbal conjugation by 1;9.

Table 11b. Inflectional categories occurring with at least 2 verbal lemmas in Mairi's speech at 1;9 (only correctly used forms)

TAM	1S	2S	3S	1P
1st conjugation (23 verbs with ≥ 2 forms, Σ = 43 verbs)				
IPF:NONPAST	8 verbs	7 verbs	19 verbs	2 verbs
PFV:PAST	2 verbs	–	3 verbs	3 verbs
PFV:SUBJ	14 verbs	5 verbs	5 verbs	12 verbs
IPF:SUBJ	–	–	2 verbs	2 verbs
IMPERATIVE	–	13 verbs	–	–
2nd conjugation (8 verbs with ≥ 2 forms, Σ = 13 verbs)				
IPF:NONPAST	7 verbs	–	2 verbs	–
PFV:PAST	–	–	2 verbs	–
PFV:SUBJ	3 verbs	–	3 verbs	2 verbs
IMPERATIVE	–	3 verbs	–	–
Medio-passive (2 verbs, Σ = 6 verbs)				
IPF:NONPAST	–	–	2 verbs	

It is interesting to compare the results of the assessment of productivity of verbal inflections of the two children studied in this paper to the child-directed speech of their mothers in order to find out in how far a limited number of forms may be a result of studying a limited amount of data or of the mothers' adaptation to the communicative needs of adult-child interaction. As shown in tables (12a) and (12b), 61% of the verbs used by Mairi's mother and 67% (at 1;8) and 65% (at 2;0) of Christos' mother's speech occur in one or two forms only.

Table 12a. Inflectional forms and verbal mini-paradigms in child-directed speech (subject Christos)

Age	Number of verbs	1 form	2 forms	3-member paradigms	4- to 5-member paradigms	6- to 7-member paradigms	8- to 11-member paradigms
1;8	52	48.07%	19.23%	11.53%	17.30%	3.84%	–
2;0	95	47.36%	17.89%	13.68%	14.73%	3.15%	3.15%

Table 12b. Inflectional forms and verbal mini-paradigms in child-directed speech at 1;9 (subject Mairi)

Number of verbs	1 form	2 forms	3-member paradigms	4- to 5-member paradigms	6- to 7-member paradigms	8- to 13-member paradigms
110	36.36%	24.55%	10.91%	10.9%	7.28%	10.00%

Given that both mothers are native speakers of Greek, this finding cannot be explained by a limited knowledge of the language, but by their adjustment to the communicative needs of mother-child interaction. In view of the fact that Mairi uses up to 7-member mini-paradigms at 1;9, it seems to follow that the nearly 64% of her verbs occurring in only one or two forms (see table 10b) may at least in part be due to sample size. The picture is quite different with Christos, all of whose verbs occur in one form only until 1;10 and who continues to use his entire verbal inventory in at most two forms until 2;0 (see table 10a). Since it seems quite unlikely that his mini-paradigms comprising three or more verb forms were somehow missed in the recordings, the boy's data demonstrate a rather immature inflectional verbal system with different inflectional forms spread cross-lexically (see table 6a above) – except for sporadic instances which do not yet constitute true three-member paradigms with forms used in contrastive contexts.[42] It should be mentioned, however, that at the age of 1;9 the girl

Mairi is quite advanced in her inflectional development also in comparison to other Greek children (see Stephany 1985; Hyams 2002).

Although, by contrast with Christos, Mairi's use of inflectional forms of verbs seems quite comparable to that of her mother, the girl's still immature inflectional system becomes apparent when the size and number of her mini-paradigms are compared to those of her mother's child-directed speech. While there are 110 verbs in the mother's child-directed speech and mini-paradigms comprise up to 13 forms, Mairi only uses 64 verbs with at most 6 or 7 different inflectional forms of a given lemma. Also, the number of verbs used with 4 to 7 different inflectional forms by Mairi's mother is larger than the child's (20 vs. 12 verbs). In addition, the mother uses 11 verbs in 8- to 13-member paradigms. As for the boy Christos at 2;1, he also uses about half of the number of verbal lemmas as compared to his mother in child-directed speech at 2;0 (47 vs. 95 verbs). However, both the size of his mini-paradigms and the number of verbs used with 3 or more forms are much lower than those in his mother's speech. While his mother uses 31 lemmas (32.6% of verbs) with 3 to 11 different inflectional forms, only one verb occurs in 4 forms and five more occur in 3 forms in Christos' data (12.75% of verbs) (see tables 10a and 12a). It seems clear that the input of both children is far richer than their own speech both type- and tokenwise so that a mere artefact of sampling underrating the children's linguistic competence can be excluded.

5. Conclusion: Early phases in the acquisition of Greek verbal inflection

On the basis of our analysis of the early development of the inflectional categories of the verb in Christos' language from 1;8 to 2;1 and in Mairi's at 1;9, we will discuss the problem of establishing phases of the early development of Greek verbal inflection and address the question in how far this early acquisition is piecemeal or systematic.

5.1. Theoretical approaches to the development of inflection

There are different theoretical positions on the development of inflection to be found in the literature. One major point of discussion is the onset of inflection in child language, i.e. the demarcation of the "preinflectional" and the 'inflectional' stage (Stephany 1985), the "prefunctional" and "functional" stage (Radford 1990), and the "premorphological" and "protomorphological" stage (or phase) (Dressler and Karpf 1995; Bittner, Dressler, and Kilani-Schoch 2000).

Stephany (1985: 225) considers the process of language acquisition to be basically a process of morphologization and syntactization. The preinflectional stage is defined by the absence of contrasting inflectional forms of one and the same verb (Stephany 1985: 200). Although the forms used by the child may correspond to certain adult inflectional categories and do carry certain functional values in given pragmatic contexts (e.g. modal vs. nonmodal), the functions they carry are not yet formally distinguished. Thus, a German infinitive may either serve modal directive or commissive functions or nonmodal descriptive ones. The transition from the preinflectional to the inflectional stage is seen by Stephany (1985: 225) as an increase in grammaticization. The major achievement of the inflectional stage is not only that different functions are expressed by different forms, but that those forms offer the possibility of expressing further functional categories, such as aspect, tense, person, and number, so that the inflected forms serve their functional roles in a more differentiated way (Stephany 1985: 225).

It should have become evident in the course of our analysis that when the girl Mairi was first observed at 1;9, she had already entered the inflectional stage and proceeded quite far past the initial stages of the inflectional development of the verb.[43] It is therefore more interesting to turn to the early development of the boy Christos. Although, by the above definition, Christos could be taken to remain in the preinflectional stage until the age of 1;10, it seems more adequate to attribute some knowledge of the function of inflectional categories and thus some kind of local morphological awareness to the boy already by 1;8 when he was first observed. Unlike nouns[44], verbs do not occur in a single basic inflectional form fulfilling different TAM functions in the boy's early speech. By 1;8 Christos already uses two and by 1;9 three different verb forms carrying clear morphological markers (e.g. *pai* 'go:IPFV:NONPAST:3S' 'all gone', *ela* 'come:IMPER:2S' 'come!' or *epese* 'fall:PFV:PAST:3S' '(it) has fallen'). What is important is that these forms, although still lexically bound and not productively created, do not occur randomly, but are used in a largely functionally adequate way as far as their TAM categories are concerned.[45]

According to the "maturational position" held by certain proponents of theories of language acquisition situated within Universal Grammar (e.g.

Radford 1990) there is a "prefunctional" stage, in which functional categories (in the sense of generative grammar) are entirely lacking from child grammar. According to Hyams (2002: 229) this position "violates the continuity assumption, that is, the restrictive hypothesis that child grammars do not fall outside the limits of Universal Grammar." What is more important in the framework of the present paper is the fact that Hyams (2002: 226) also provides convincing empirical evidence from Greek child language for the finding of Early Morphosyntactic Convergence (Hoekstra and Hyams 1998), i.e. the fact that "children acquire the specifics of the target language at a strikingly early age", a position similar to that advocated by proponents of usage-based theories of language acquisition (see the references quoted in section 1).

This leads us to Dressler's and co-workers' theory of morphological acquisition, in which the "premorphological" stage (or phase[46]) precedes the stages of protomorphology and (modularized) morphology proper. In spite of its name, the premorphological stage is not devoid of morphological phenomena. Rather, it is characterized by "extragrammatical" morphological operations, "whose only unifying property is that some principle of morphological grammar is violated" (Dressler and Karpf 1995: 101). Examples of such operations which, according to Dressler and Karpf, are characteristic of early child language, are blends, back-formations, surface analogies, truncations, and reduplications (Dressler and Karpf 1995). In addition, the stage of premorphology is characterized by "morphological operations" which are "precursors of later grammatical rules" consisting of rote-learned forms (Bittner, Dressler, and Kilani-Schoch 2000: 5). In the protomorphological stage, the system of morphological grammar and its subsystems start to develop, without however reaching "the status of modules and submodules" (Dressler and Karpf 1995: 104). Bittner, Dressler, and Kilani-Schoch (2000: 5) characterize protomorphology as "the phase where children start to construct creatively morphological patterns of analogies and first rules." In what follows we will only be concerned with the premorphological and protomorphological stages and have nothing to say about an eventual modular dissociation of morphology.

5.2. The development of Greek verbal inflection

Based on the data of the Greek children studied in this paper we will try to find empirical evidence for the theoretical concepts of a premorphological and a protomorphological stage in the development of verbal inflection and for a possible demarcation of these stages. As far as the extragrammatical operations characteristic of the premorphological stage are concerned, there are the isolated blend *bume* (*bum* + *epese*) and a few other pseudo-verbs in Christos' speech between 1;8 and 1;10 (see section 4.2.2) and, between 1;11 and 2;2, reduplications such as *kakani* for *na kani* 'MDL.PTL make:NONPAST:3S' '(he/she) should do' and *pepetsume* for *na peksume* 'MDL.PTL play:PFV:NONPAST:1P' 'let's play' are used rather extensively (Christofidou and Kappa 1998). Since, after 1;11, such reduplications systematically mark the function of modality rendering the preverbal modal particle *na* (Christofidou and Kappa 1998) they are not to be classified as premorphological operations, but belong to the protomorphological phase. At least with the referential children studied by Stephany (1985), truncations of verbal endings are relatively rare in the best established TAM categories of the imperfective non-past and the perfective subjunctive (2% to 7.4% of verb form tokens from 1;8 to 1;11) and somewhat higher in the perfective past for three of four children (5% to 29%). Therefore, in Greek child language studied so far, extramorphological operations seem to play a minor role in early inflectional development. Furthermore, this type of operations represents "blind alleys" as far as the acquisition of morphological operations of the standard language is concerned, since reduplication, back-formation, or blending do not occur in the inflectional system of Modern Greek. It therefore seems more adequate to describe the above phenomena as morphophonemic so that they will not block further language-specific morphological development. Although it is certainly true that the verb forms occurring in this early period are lexically bound and that paradigmatic contrasts have not yet begun to develop within lemmas, it can be maintained that the occurring forms will easily pattern once the child will recognize that different verbs may form the same bundles of inflectional categories. It is in this sense that rote-learned forms used during the premorphological stage may be termed "precursors of later grammatical rules" (Bittner, Dressler, and Kilani-Schoch 2000: 5) or rather precursors of later inflectional patterns or regularities. The period of Christos' development between 1;7.10 and 1;10 could therefore be described as premorphological regarding the development of both verbal and nominal inflection (see also Kilani-Schoch et al. 1997; Christofidou 1998; Christofidou and Stephany 1997).

As far as the development of Greek verbal inflection is concerned, we consider patterning of inflectional forms to be the most important achievement showing that the children have entered the protomorphological "stage".[47] Since this patterning and the evidence for mini-paradigms develops in a lemma-based way, i.e. locally and not across the board, we think of this development as proceeding in phases rather than stages (see section 1). It is at 1;11 that Christos' speech gives evidence of the beginnings of a new phase of development: He starts to use the 1st person singular of the modal verb *thelo* 'to want' (*thelo* 'want:IPFV:NONPAST:1S' vs. *theli* '3S') in the imperfective non-past and also of two full verbs in the perfective subjunctive besides the old 3rd person singular. In spite of the fact that there is functional overlap – the 3rd singular continues to be also used for the 1st singular – the new 1st singular is not overextended to the 3rd person. This shows that a grammatical contrast is beginning to emerge. Besides, the 3rd person plural is contrasted to the 3rd singular with the verb *troo* 'to eat' (*troi/trone* 'eat:IPFV:NONPAST:3S/3P'). Another two-member mini-paradigm developing at this age consists of the forms *kani* 'do:NONPAST:3S' and *kakani* (for *na kani* 'MDL.PTL do:NONPAST: 3S') formally marking a modal contrast. At this age, Christos also meets both of Pizutto and Caselli's (1994) criteria of productivity for verbal inflection and case marking of nouns sets in (Kilani-Schoch et al. 1997: 21). It therefore seems well-founded to assume that the age of 1;11 represents the onset of the protomorphological phase in Christos' development, since the first signs of systematic and contrastive use of some inflectional forms emerge at this time. It is only at 2;1 that Christos meets the more rigid criterion of true mini-paradigms, when five 3-member-paradigms are first observed (see section 4.2.3). If one is interested in tracing the very development of inflectional competence it seems more adequate to say that until the age of 2;1 Christos has made important progress in his inflectional development so that his competence may certainly be termed protomorphological. We would rather not place Christos at the beginning of the protomorphological stage of development since in order to demarcate stages of morphological development one would have to find evidence of "turning points" in language acquisition. The picture presented by Christos' inflectional development is rather one of smoothly gliding developmental phases, however.

5.3. Piecemeal and systematic inflectional development

Is the inflectional development of the Greek verb piecemeal or systematic? A sibylline answer to this question would be "both", since morphological development is piecemeal on the one hand and systematic on the other. In view of Christos' and Mairi's early inflectional development of the verb, there is no doubt that it is piecemeal in the sense that not all morphological contrasts occurring in the input are at once acquired. Rather, only certain inflectional forms of certain verbal lemmas are at first taken in by the children, such as the 3rd person singular of the imperfective non-past, the perfective subjunctive, or the perfective past. The initial phase of inflectional development studied in this paper, the premorphological phase, is strongly lexically based. In this phase, acquisition may be called piecemeal because paradigmatic patterns have not yet started to develop within verbal lemmas and the inflectional forms used by the children are only correct as far as the central combinations of TAM categories are concerned but may be overgeneralized with respect to the peripheral categories of person and number. As soon as the kinds of TAM and person/number categories used by the children and the aspectual categories (*aktionsart*) of the verbs occurring with different TAM are taken into consideration, it becomes evident that some systematicity is inherent already in this early period of inflectional acquisition: Neither are the inflectional categories children use randomly selected nor is there much interindividual variation in this respect. The first combinations of TAM and person/number categories occurring in child Greek are the most unmarked and therefore also the most frequent ones in child-directed speech (Stephany 1985; see also Dressler and Karpf 1995: 114; Gathercole, Sebastián, and Soto 1999: 161). Once evidence for paradigmatic patterns appears in the protomorphological phase there is no doubt that development has become systematic in the stricter sense of the establishment of paradigmatic contrasts within lemmas and classes of these.

We consider the results of our study of the early inflectional development of the Greek verb as consistent with usage-based models of language acquisition such as those mentioned in the introduction and therefore see no reason for explaining language acquisition on the basis of early innate knowledge of grammatical categories. Also, rather than slicing the process of language acquisition into neat and clearly delimited developmental stages, we think that the following image taken from Gathercole, Sebastián, and Soto (1999: 160–161) captures the characteristics of the process of language acquisition in a more adequate way:

> A better image would be one of drops of water falling down, to eventually form a river. Each drop adds to the whole, until there is a substantial, critical mass to establish a whole, which both functions as a stable unit and at the same time continually changes as new drops fall and old ones dry up or roll away. At no point is it possible to say that before that point there was no river, while after it there is.

As the authors mention, this idea is consistent with dynamic, self-organizing systems "capable of generating stable patterns of enormous complexity, without pre-existing programs or prescribed processes" (Gathercole, Sebastián, and Soto 1999: 161).[48]

Appendix

Christos' two-member paradigms from 1;11 to 2;1

Age	Lemma	Gloss	Form	Category
1;11	kano	do	kani	NONPAST:3S
			kakani (=na kani)	SUBJ:3S
	pefto	fall	epetse (=epese)	PFV:PAST:3S
			petane (=pesane)	PFV:PAST:3P
	pezo	play	petun (=pezun)	IPF:NONPAST:3P
			a peciome (na peksume)	PFV:SUBJ:3P
	thelo	want	thelo	IPF:NONPAST:1S
			(th)eli	IPF:NONPAST:3S
	troo	eat	troi	IPF:NONPAST:3S
			trone	IPF:NONPAST:3P
2;0	kano	do	kani	NONPAST3S
			kakani (=na kani)	SUBJ:3S
	kathome	sit	katse	PFV:IMP:2S
			kacici (=na kathisi)	PFV:SUBJ:3S
	odhigho	drive	(o)dhighai	IPF:NONPAST:3S
			(o)dhighu(n)	IPF:NONPAST:3P
	pao	go	pi(gh)e	PFV:PAST:3S
			ela	PFV:IMP:2S
	pezo	play	petun (=pezun)	IPF:NONPAST:3P
			a patume (=na peksume)	PFV:SUBJ:3P
	thelo	want	thelo	IPF:NONPAST:1S
			theli	IPF:NONPAST:3S

Appendix continued: Christos' two-member paradigms from 1;11 to 2;1

2;1	ferno	bring	efere	PFV:PAST:1S
			ta feghi (=tha feri)	PFV:FUT:3S
	fevgho	leave	efighe	PFV:PAST:3S
			fighe	PFV:IMP:2S
	odhigho	drive	odhighai	IPF:NONPAST:3S
			dhogho (=odhigho)	IPF:NONPAST:1S
	pefto	fall	epese	PFV:PAST:3S
			t(h)a pesi	PFV:FUT:3S
	vazo	put	na valo	PFV:SUBJ:1S
			na vali	PFV:SUBJ:3S
	xalao	destroy/ spoil	xalai	IPF:NONPAST:3S
			xalace (=xalase)	PFV:PAST:3S

Christos' first three-member paradigms at 2;1

Age	Lemma	Gloss	Form	Category
2;1	pao	go	pai	IPF:NONPAST:3S
			(na) pame	PFV:SUBJ:1P
			tha pao	PFV:FUT:1S
	pezo	play	na peciume (=na peksume)	PFV:SUBJ:1P
			a pecio (=na pekso)	PFV:SUBJ:1S
			a peci (=na peksi)	PFV:SUBJ:3S
	perno	take	palo (=na paro)	PFV:SUBJ:1S
			na pali (=na pari)	PFV:SUBJ:3S
			pile (=pire)	PFV:PAST:3S
	pino	drink	na pii	PFV:SUBJ:3S
			na pini	IPF:SUBJ:3S
			ipse (=ipje)	PFV:PAST:3S
	troo	eat	na/t(ha) fai	PFV:SUBJ:3S
			(n)a/t(h)a fame	PFV:SUBJ:1P
			tatoi (=na troi)	IPF:SUBJ:3S

Christos' first four-member paradigm at 2;1

Age	Lemma	Gloss	Form	Category
2;1	kano	do	kano	NONPAST:1S
			kani	NONPAST:3S
			ekana	PAST:1S
			ekane	PAST:3S

Notes

1. See, for example, Slobin (1973; 1979).
2. See Bowerman (1985); Choi and Bowerman (1991); Gopnik and Choi (1995).
3. See also Bybee (1985, 1991); MacWhinney (1987); and Dressler and Karpf (1995).
4. Work on distributional learning by Lieven, Pine, and Baldwin (1997); and Pine, Lieven, and Rowland (1998) mainly supports the views expressed in usage-based approaches to language acquisition.
5. See also Bybee (1991) and the references quoted by Tomasello (2000).
6. Especially as far as verbs are concerned.
7. On markedness in Greek verbal inflection see Stephany (1985: 43–44).
8. On this approach, see also Lieven, Pine, and Baldwin (1997); and Gathercole, Sebastián, and Soto (1999).
9. Exceptions are the auxiliaries *exo* 'to have' and *ime* 'to be' and a few other verbs like *ksero* 'to know', *kano* 'to do' and *pao* 'to go'.
10. For different views concerning the segmentation of verb endings cf. Mackridge (1985: 174); Kleris and Babiniotis (1999: 132); and Holton, Mackridge, and Philippaki-Warburton (1997: 119).
11. The endings of the future and the subjunctive coincide with the endings of the non-past indicative.
12. Computer-assisted coding and analysis were effected within the CHILDES Project (MacWhinney 2000).
13. The high average percentage of utterances containing a verb in the child-directed speech of Mairi's mother is due to the fact that besides utterances without a verb she uses many utterances containing two or even three verb forms (e.g. *ja na pai o thios na su pari to tilefono na milisis me ton papuli sto tilefono* PTL PTL go:SUBJ:3S the uncle PTL you:GEN take:SUBJ:3S the telephone PTL speak:SUBJ:2S with the grandfather on.the telephone 'Uncle shall go and bring you the phone so that you can speak to grandfather on the phone').
14. Age 1;8 comprises Christos' first two recordings at 1;7.11 and 1;8.21 (see table 3).
15. The absolute numbers corresponding to fig. 1 are indicated in table (5a).
16. For definitions of frozen forms see Tomasello (2000: 65) and Kilani-Schoch (this volume).
17. These uses of the verb form *pai* are also characteristic of Greek baby talk.
18. The progressive aspect is not expressed by the Greek forms.
19. The modal particle *na* is incorporated into the verb by reduplication until the age of 2;2.
20. The subsets of forms inadequately used are indicated in parentheses; frozen forms have been excluded.

21. In standard Greek, the categories of future tense and subjunctive mood are formally distinguished by a particle accompanying the verb (*tha* for the future, *na* for the subjunctive). Since the two categories are not consistently differentiated in early child Greek and the future has an even stronger modal meaning than in the standard language the child category of the subjunctive has a rather global (deontic) modal/temporal meaning and only develops into the two distinct grammatical categories of future and subjunctive later on (for details see Stephany 1985: 93–102, 1997a: 247–249).
22. In standard Greek, the subjunctive is used both in main and subordinate clauses and can serve the expression of epistemic or deontic modality (see Philippaki-Warburton 1992; and Kleris and Babiniotis 1999).
23. Although, at 1;11, Christos uses the verbal ending of the 1st plural subjunctive adequately he fails to use the proclitic modal particle *na* correctly; this explains the high percentage of errors in the subjunctive (100%) indicated in table 6a.
24. N = 139 types, 635 tokens (excluding 127 tokens of *íne* 'is, are')
25. The second person plural will have developed one year later at 2;9 (Stephany 1985).
26. The perfective past is also much less used than the other three TAM categories by the other three children studied at 1;8, 1;9, and 1;11 by Stephany (1985: 115).
27. For details on the functions of the imperfective non-past in early child Greek see Stephany (1985: 130–139).
28. For details on the functions of the perfective past in early child Greek see Stephany (1985: 139–148).
29. In Katis' (1984) extensive longitudinal data of one Greek girl as well as in her cross-sectional data, both the present and past perfect remain exceptionally rare until about 3;2.
30. A comparison of the child-directed speech of four Greek mothers to their adult-directed speech shows that not only the inventory of verb-form categories is much larger in adult-directed speech as compared to child-directed speech, but also that the rankings differ, especially as far as the imperative and the perfective past are concerned (Stephany 1985: 185, table 8.2).
31. The present perfect comprising the non-finite *aparemfato* is nearly absent from child-directed speech in the early phases. Of the four mothers studied by Stephany only one uses it at all, but extremely rarely (1985: 187).
32. We consider Varlocosta, Vainikka, and Rohrbacher's (1998) interpretation of the early Greek child forms which we describe as perfective and imperfective non-past 3rd person singular finite verb forms as non-finite "root infinitives" at least as empirically unfounded (see also Hyams 2002).
33. In the child-directed speech of Christos' mother 63% of the imperfective non-past categories are in the 3rd person singular at the age of 1;8 and even 73% at

the age of 2;0. – Mairi's mother uses the 3rd person singular with nearly 60% of (non-imperative) verb form tokens in child-directed speech, while the 1st person singular occurs in 9.7% and the 2nd person singular in 18.7% of tokens. The 1st and 3rd person plural occur in 7.5% and 4.3% of tokens, respectively, and the 2nd person plural is not used at all (N = 1,431 non-imperative verb form tokens).

34. This error only occurs in the perfective subjunctive.
35. These imperatives also belong to the most common ones in Stephany's data (see Stephany 1985: 231–244, 1986: 382).
36. There is no evidence in Greek for Bybee's finding that the 1st person singular is formed by using the 3rd person singular as a base (Bybee 1991: 74–75), since both forms end in different vowels (1st Sg -*o*, 3rd Sg -*i* [or -*a*]).
37. See Gathercole, Sebastián, and Soto (1999: 144) for references.
38. Dressler (p.c.) distinguishes between "linguistic productivity" (the ability to apply morphological rules to new lemmas) characteristic of mature speakers and "acquisitional productivity" (Kilani-Schoch and Dressler 2002). In this paper, we use the notion of productivity as it applies to the development of the inflectional system.
39. For details see the appendix.
40. Although the forms of the imperfective and the perfective subjunctive mentioned in table (11a) seem to be adequately used, it cannot be attested from the context if they are really in contrast in Christos' system.
41. Since Christos uses only one lemma of the second conjugation and only in forms which do not differ from the first conjugation, we will not concern ourselves with the formal distinction between first and second conjugation.
42. According to the criteria set up by the editors of this volume, only forms constituting paradigms are indicated in the 3rd, 4th, and 6th columns of table (10a): These forms are neither imitative, nor formulaic, suppletive, or analytical and occur in contrastive contexts within the same month.
43. Number and case distinctions had also emerged in Mairi's language by 1;9 (Stephany 1997a).
44. Until the age of 1;10, Christos uses nouns exclusively in their basic form ending in a vowel and corresponding to the accusative singular for masculines (*baba* ACC vs. *babas* NOM 'Daddy') and to the nominative/accusative singular for feminines (*mama* NOM/ACC vs. *mamas* GEN 'Mummy') (Kilani-Schoch et al. 1997).
45. The fact that the 3rd person singular is used as a kind of basic verb form in all of Christos' early TAM categories (except, of course, the imperative), does not represent counter-evidence to our claim of inflectional awareness, since the formal differences of both stems and endings do have functional values in the child's language and person and number are more peripheral categories of the verb than tense, aspect, and mood.

46. The terms "stage" and "phase" seem to be used interchangeably in their works. At least the pre- and protomorphological sections of morphological development seem to have characteristics of entire stages as well as mere phases of development (see Dressler and Karpf 1995).
47. We have nothing to say here about the development of the subdivision into inflectional and derivational morphology in the acquisition of Greek. On word formation in child Greek see Stephany (1997a, 1997b).
48. See Smith and Thelen (1993) and Thelen and Smith (1995).

References

Babiniotis, Georgios, and Panajotis Kontos
    1967   *Sinchroniki grammatiki tis koinis neas ellinikis: Theoria, askisis* [Contemporary grammar of Modern Greek Koine: Theory, Exercises]. Athens.

Behrens, Heike
    2001   Cognitive-conceptual development and the acquisition of grammatical morphemes: The development of time concepts and verb tense. In: Bowerman and Levinson 2001, 450–474.

Bittner, Dagmar, Wolfgang U. Dressler, and Marianne Kilani-Schoch
    2000   Introduction. In: Dagmar Bittner, Wolfgang U. Dressler, and Marianne Kilani-Schoch (eds.), *First Verbs: On the Way to Miniparadigms*, 1–6. (ZAS Papers in Linguistics 18.) Berlin: ZAS.

Bowerman, Melissa
    1985   What shapes children's grammars? In: Dan I. Slobin (ed.), *The Crosslinguistic Study of Language Acquisition*. Vol. 2, 1257–1319. Hillsdale, New Jersey/London: Lawrence Erlbaum.

Bowerman, Melissa, and Soonja Choi
    2001   Shaping meanings for language: Universal and language-specific in the acquisition of spatial semantic categories. In: Bowerman and Levinson 2001, 475–511.

Bowerman, Melissa, and Stephen C. Levinson (eds.)
    2001   *Language Acquisition and Conceptual Development*. Cambridge: Cambridge University Press.

Bybee, Joan L.
    1985   *Morphology: A Study of the Relation between Meaning and Form*. Amsterdam: John Benjamins.

Bybee, Joan L.
1991   Natural morphology: The organization of paradigms in language acquisition. In: Thom Huebner, and Charles A. Ferguson (eds.), *Crosscurrents in Second Language and Linguistic Theories*, 67–91. Amsterdam/Philadelphia: John Benjamins.

Choi, Soonja, and Melissa Bowerman
1991   Learning to express motion events in English and Korean: The influence of language-specific lexicalization patterns. *Cognition* 41: 83–121.

Christofidou, Anastasia
1998   Number or case first? Evidence from Modern Greek. In: Ayhan Aksu-Koç, Eser Erguvanli-Taylan, A. Sumru Oezsoy, and Aylin Kuentay (eds.), *Perspectives on Language Acquisition. Selected Papers from the VIIth International Congress for the Study of Child Language*, 46–59. Istanbul: Bogazici University.

Christofidou, Anastasia, and Ioanna Kappa
1998   Pre- and protomorphological fillers in Greek language acquisition. In: Steven Gillis (ed.), *Studies in the Acquisition of Number and Diminutive Marking*, 193–214. (Antwerp Papers in Linguistics 95.) Universiteit Antwerpen: Universitaire Instelling Antwerpen, Departement Germaanse, Afdeling Linguistiek.

Christofidou, Anastasia, and Ursula Stephany
1997   The early development of case forms in the speech of a Greek boy: A preliminary investigation. In: Katarzyna Dziubalska-Kołaczyk (ed.), *Pre- and Protomorphology in Language Acquisition*, 127–139. (Papers and Studies in Contrastive Linguistics 33.) Poznań: Adam Mickiewicz University.

Dressler, Wolfgang U., and Annemarie Karpf
1995   The theoretical relevance of pre- and protomorphology in language acquisition. *Yearbook of Morphology* 1994: 99–122.

Gathercole, Virginia C. Mueller, Eugenia Sebastián, and Pilar Soto
1999   The early acquisition of Spanish verbal morphology: Across-the-board or piecemeal knowledge? *The International Journal of Bilingualism* 3: 133–182.

Gopnik, Alison, and Soonja Choi
1995   Names, relational words, and cognitive development in English and Korean speakers: Nouns are not always learned before verbs. In: Michael Tomasello, and William E. Merriman (eds.), *Beyond*

Names for Things: Young Children's Acquisition of Verbs, 63–80. Hillsdale, New Jersey: Lawrence Erlbaum.

Hoekstra, Teun, and Nina Hyams
1998   Agreement and finiteness of V2: Evidence from child language. In: Annabel Greenhill, Mary Hughes, Heather Littlefield, and Hugh Walsh (eds.), *Proceedings of the 22nd Annual Boston University Conference on Language Development*. Vol. 22/1, 360–373. Sommerville, Mass.: Cascadilla Press.

Holton, David, Peter Mackridge, and Irene Philippaki-Warburton
1997   *Grammatiki tis Ellinikis Glossas* [Grammar of the Greek Language]. Athens: Ekdosis Patakis.

Hyams, Nina
2002   Clausal structure in child Greek: A reply to Varlokosta et al. and a reanalysis. *The Linguistic Review* 19: 225–269.

Jakobson, Roman
1977   *Der grammatische Aufbau der Kindersprache*. (Rheinisch-Westfälische Akademie der Wissenschaften. Vorträge, G 218.) Opladen: Westdeutscher Verlag.

Karmiloff-Smith, Annette
1992   *Beyond Modularity*. Cambridge: Cambridge University Press.

Katis, Demetra
1984   The acquisition of the Modern Greek verb: With special reference to the imperfective past and perfect classes. Unpublished Doctoral dissertation, University of Reading, England.

Kilani-Schoch, Marianne, Anna de Marco, Anastasia Christofidou, Maria Vassilakou, Ralf Vollmann, and Wolfgang U. Dressler
1997   On the demarcation of phases in early morphology acquisition in four languages. In: Katarzyna Dziubalska-Kołaczyk (ed.), *Pre- and Protomorphology in Language Acquisition*, 15–32. (Papers and Studies in Contrastive Linguistics 33.) Poznań: Adam Mickiewicz University.

Kilani-Schoch, Marianne, and Wolfgang U. Dressler
2002   The emergence of verb paradigms in two French corpora as an illustration of general problems of pre- and protomorphology. In: Maria D. Voeikova, and Wolfgang U. Dressler (eds.), *Pre- and Protomorphology: Early Phases of Morphological Development in Nouns and Verbs*, 45–59. München: Lincom.

Kleris, Christos, and Georgios Babiniotis
1999   *Grammatiki tis Neas Ellinikis* [Grammar of Modern Greek]. Vol. II. Athens: Ellinika Grammata.

Lieven, Elena V. M., Julian M. Pine, and Gillian Baldwin
1997   Lexically-based learning and early grammatical development. *Journal of Child Language* 24: 187–219.

Mackridge, Peter
1985   *The Modern Greek language: A Descriptive Analysis of Standard Modern Greek.* Oxford: Clarendon Press.

MacWhinney, Brian
1987   The competition model. In: Brian MacWhinney (ed.), *Mechanisms of Language Acquisition*, 249–308. Hillsdale, New Jersey: Lawrence Erlbaum.

MacWhinney, Brian
2000   *The CHILDES Project: Tools for Analyzing Talk.* 3rd ed. Mahwah, New Jersey: Lawrence Erlbaum.

Mandler, Jean
1998   Representation. In: Deanna Kuhn, and Robert S. Siegler (eds.), *Handbook of Child Psychology.* Vol. 2: Cognition, Perception, and Language, 255-308. Fifth edition. New York: Wiley.

Philippaki-Warburton, Irene
1992   I sintaktiki taftotita tu *na* [The syntactic status of *na*]. In: *Meletes ja tin elliniki glossa* [Studies in Greek linguistics]. *Proceedings of the 13th Annual Meeting of the Department of Linguistics, Faculty of Philosophy, Aristotle University of Thessaloniki*, 255–274. Thessaloniki: Kiriakidis.

Pine, Julian M., Elena V. M. Lieven, and Caroline F. Rowland
1998   Comparing different models of the development of the English verb category. *Linguistics* 36: 807–830.

Pizzuto, Elena, and M. Christina Caselli
1994   The acquisition of Italian verb morphology in a cross-linguistic perspective. In: Yonata Levy (ed.), *Other Children, Other Languages: Issues in the Theory of Language Acquisition*, 137–187. Hillsdale, New Jersey: Lawrence Erlbaum.

Radford, Andrew
    1990   *Syntactic Theory and the Acquisition of English Syntax*. Oxford: Basil Blackwell.

Savage-Rumbaugh, Sue, Stuart G. Shanker, and Talbot J. Taylor
    1998   *Apes, Language, and the Human Mind*. Oxford: Oxford University Press.

Seiler, Hansjakob
    1952   *L'aspect et le temps dans le verbe néo-grec*. Paris: Les Belles Lettres.

Slobin, Dan I.
    1973   Cognitive prerequisites for the development of grammar. In: Charles A. Ferguson, and Dan I. Slobin (eds.), *Studies of Child Language Development*, 175–208. New York: Holt, Rinehart and Winston.

Slobin, Dan I.
    1979   Prototypical event and canonical sentence forms in language acquisition. Paper read at the meeting *Beyond Description in Child Language*, Max Planck Institute for Psycholinguistics, Nijmegen, June 10–16, 1979.

Slobin, Dan I.
    1990   Learning to think for speaking: Native language, cognition, and rhetoric style. Plenary Address: International Pragmatics Conference, Barcelona, July 9–13, 1990; Fifth International Congress for the Study of Child Language, July 15–20, 1990.

Slobin, Dan I.
    2001   Form-function relations: How do children find out what they are? In Bowerman and Levinson 2001, 406–449.

Smith, Linda B., and Esther Thelen
    1993   *A Dynamic Systems Approach to Development: Applications*. Cambridge, Mass.: MIT Press.

Stephany, Ursula
    1981   Verbal grammar in early Modern Greek child language. In: Philip S. Dale, and David Ingram (eds.), *Child Language: An International Perspective*, 45–57. Baltimore: University Park Press.

Stephany, Ursula
1985 *Aspekt, Tempus und Modalität: Zur Entwicklung der Verbalgrammatik in der neugriechischen Kindersprache.* (Language Universals Series 4). Tübingen: Gunter Narr.

Stephany, Ursula
1986 Modality. In: Paul Fletcher, and Michael Garman (eds.), *Language Acquisition: Studies in First Language Development*, 2nd ed., 375–400. Cambridge: Cambridge University Press.

Stephany, Ursula
1992 Grammaticalization in first language acquisition. *Zeitschrift für Phonetik, Sprachwissenschaft und Kommunikationsforschung* 45: 289–303.

Stephany, Ursula
1997a The acquisition of Greek. In: Dan I. Slobin (ed.), *The Crosslinguistic Study of Language Acquisition.* Vol. 4, 183–333. Mahwah, New Jersey/London: Lawrence Erlbaum.

Stephany, Ursula
1997b Diminutives in early child Greek: A preliminary investigation. In: Wolfgang U. Dressler (ed.), *Studies in Pre- and Protomorphology*, 153–163. Wien: Verlag der Österreichischen Akademie der Wissenschaften.

Thelen, Esther, and Linda B. Smith
1995 *A Dynamic Systems Approach to the Development of Cognition and Action.* Cambridge, Mass.: MIT Press.

Tomasello, Michael
2000 First steps toward a usage-based theory of language acquisition. *Cognitive Linguistics* 11: 61–82.

Varlokosta, Spyridoula, Anne Vainikka, and Bernhard Rohrbacher
1998 Functional projections, markedness, and 'root infinitives' in early child Greek. *The Linguistic Review* 15: 187–207.

The early verb development and demarcation of stages in three Russian-speaking children*

Natalia Gagarina

0. Introduction

The goal of this paper is to investigate verb inflection development in the early stages of the acquisition of Russian and to trace the sequential steps on the way to productive use of verb inflection. I will address the problem of the demarcation between pre- and protomorphology and argue that the acquisition of paradigm construction rules in Russian is correlated with (and influenced by) such aspects of verb acquisition as changes in children's verb lexicon, perfective and imperfective verb production, development of diverse Aktionsarten, the use of the infinitive forms and other facts discussed below. The absence of homonyms in the verbal inflectional endings, their perceptual phonological distinctness and the low rate (and importance) of the analytical constructions in the morphological verb system facilitate the process of the acquisition of the paradigm construction rules and the development of productivity. When tracing the steps in the transformation of early contrastive forms into a true paradigm, we shall see that one must take into consideration the state of the whole grammatical system of a child at a given moment and analyse the respective morphological features in connection with changes in the production of verb forms and in the structure of utterances containing verbs.

1. Verb morphology in the target language

Russian is known to have "rich" verb morphology. Three tenses – past, present and future – are distributed between two aspects – perfective (henceforth, PERF) and imperfective (henceforth, IPFV) – in the following way:

	PAST	PRESENT	FUTURE
PERF	+	−	+
IPFV	+	+	+

(byt' 'to be' + main verb in the infinitive)

Forms of IPFV in the present and of PERF in the future (also the auxiliary *byt'* 'to be' in the compound future with IPFV) have three persons in SG and PL (there is no person distinction in the past). Past forms are marked for gender (only in SG) and number. The main categories are displayed in the table below:

Table 1.[1] System of verb categories

	1 Infinitive	2 Finite forms			3 Participle	Verbal adverb
aspect (PERF and IPFV)	+	+			+	+
voice (active, passive)	+	+			+	+
mood		indicative	imperative	conditional		
tense (past, present, future)	−	+	−	−	pres. and past	pres. and past
person (1st, 2nd, 3d)	−	+ (except past)	+ (only 2nd pers.)	−	−	−
number (SG, PL)	−	+	+	+	+	−
gender (MASC, FEM, NEUT)	−	+ (SG – in the past)	−	+ (in SG)	+ (in SG)	−
case	−	−	−	−	+	−

One important peculiarity of the inflectional system is the presence of two bases for the verbs. The open base (henceforth, OB) (often stem-based) usually ends in a vowel, e.g., *smotr'e-t'* – 'to look', *igra-t'* – 'to play' and serves as a platform to build past tense forms. The closed base (CB) (often root-based) ends in a consonant: *smotr'-u* – 'look-1S.PRES.', *igraj-u* – 'play-1S.PRES'. Present/future forms in the indicative and imperative are constructed from this base. Alternations between OB and CB are an important device for constructing verb forms which belong to different inflectional classes. Although both bases belong to one (full) paradigm (as defined in most traditional Russian grammars) it is not very easy for children to discover the correlation between the two bases because there are different implicative paradigm structure conditions for different verb classes.[2]

The traditional alternation between the OB of the infinitive and the CB of the present/future (1S) has been taken by us as a platform to define 45 inflectional microclasses (henceforth, MC) (see Dressler and Gagarina 1999). Only four of them are fully productive:

1st MC (alternation between OB and CB is a/aj), *obeda-t'* – *obedaj-u* 'to have dinner',
7th MC (with the alternation: ova/uj), *risova-t'* – *risuj-u* 'to draw',
17th MC (with the alternation: consonant + i/consonant), *kuri-t'* – *kur'-u* 'to smoke',
38th MC (with the alternation: consonant + vowel is part of the pluriphonemic thematic suffix *nu*/consonant *n*), *prygnu-t'*– *prygn-u* 'to jump once'.

The main basic rule is "j correlation": "add to the OB consonant *j* (and do not change anything in the OB)". Children often overgeneralise this rule, especially if the OB of the infinitive ends in *-a*. Thus, they use mainly the 1st productive class for overgeneralisation.

The table below presents the paradigm[3] of an aspectual counterpart of the verb *obeda-t'*–IPF/*poobeda-t'*–PF 'to have lunch':

As we see from the table, person is assigned only in the present (IPFV) and future (PERF) synthetic forms. In the process of acquiring verb inflection, children have more difficulty in mastering inflected forms of the present than of the past. This is because various changes occur in the stem of present forms (see the alternation between an OB and the CB in the inflectional MC), while past forms are predominantly marked only with the inflectional suffix *-l* (which is added to the OB of the infinitive) and gender/number inflection. There are not many irregularities in the formation of past tense forms, and children acquire them rather quickly (as soon as the category of gender/number is acquired).

Table 2. The paradigm

mood	tense	number	pers./gender	IPF/PF lexeme
imperative		SG	2	(po)obedaj
		PL	2	(po)obedaj-te
indicative	past tense	SG	masc.	(po)obeda-l
		SG	fem.	(po)obeda-l-a
		SG	neutr.	(po)obeda-l-o
		PL	–	(po)obeda-l-i
	present tense (for PERF forms – future)	SG	1	(po)obedaj-u
		SG	2	(po)obedaj-eš'
		SG	3	(po)obedaj-et
		PL	1	(po)obedaj-em
		PL	2	(po)obedaj-ete
		PL	3	(po)obedaj-ut
	future analytical[4] tense (only IPFV forms)			*byt'* (1.2.3. sg or pl) + infinitive *obeda-t'*

The imperative, like the present tense, presents more challenges. Jakobson (1987: 8) compared it with vocative case and wrote that "the imperative stands out clearly within the Russian verbal system, not only syntactically, but also morphologically, and even phonologically ... the unmarked imperative represents the present tense stem without any grammatical ending". However, the CB of the present tense may differ from OB of the infinitive and children have to detect this difference and apply it while constructing imperative and (other) inflected forms.

2. Data description

The paper is based on the data from one girl and two boys.[5] The two boys, Vanja (V.) and Roma (R.), are the only children in middle-class families in St. Petersburg, where the standard "Petersburg" version of colloquial Russian is spoken. Liza (L.) is the second child (her brother is ten years older) in a family of linguists. All three children were more or less systematically recorded and/or video-taped two-five hours a month, from the onset of speech till the age of three (except for R.). The mean length of recordings per month is about 150 minutes (2.5 hours). During the period of crucial lexical and inflectional development recording sessions reached six hours a month. These sessions were united into two or three sections so that each section of data per month has (a) relatively equal quantity, (b) the minimal interval between the sessions. The distribution of recordings into groups of files and the number of analysed utterances (with verbs) is given in Appendix 1 and 2.

L. is the earliest to develop inflectional morphology. Her first inflected verbs appear already at 1;7–1;8 and their number increases more steadily than by the boys. Her first utterances consist mainly of one (almost always inflected) component. The first multi-component utterances with verbs occur only at 2;0. L. is rather careful in pronouncing different inflectional endings although her pronunciation cannot be said to be "accurate". She often preserves the syllabic structure of the word and changes its phonemic representation. For example, *igigiki* (1;8) – for *ogurchiki* 'cucumbers-DIM', *gajaiki* (1;9b) – for *goroshinki* 'pears-DIM', *abatii* (1;9b) – for *rabotajut* 'work-3S.PRES'.[6] L.'s speech is also characterised by a number of so-called 'family specific' words registered during the whole period of recordings which are declined and serve as basic forms for derivation, for example, the name of her brother *Aljosha* (liter.) – *Apka* (family specific). She also possesses more (pro)nominal and verb inflection and in comparison with the two boys she is relatively late in the construction of multi-component utterances. Probably the quantity and the diversity of inflected forms which a child possesses correlates with the number of components in the sentences that s/he produces: the more diverse inflectional forms of verbs, nouns and pronouns a child has, the fewer sentence components s/he needs in order to express the meaning. Thus, the morphological richness the child possesses compensates for the syntactical poverty (and vs.).

V.'s corpus consists of more than 100 hours of recordings.[7] For the purpose of the present study I analysed the data collected during the time from 1;5–2;1 till 2;3 – the period of the emergence and onset of the productive use of verb inflection. V., unlike L., is a late talker and is generally slow (in comparison with the two other children) in his language development. The number of child-specific words in his data corpus is not as frequent as in L.'s, but these words are more 'stable'. They are used for a longer period and are not easily superseded by their counterparts from the adult language, for example *mashina* – *bizinja* is used (from 2;1b to 2;3b) for 'car'. In comparison with L., there are also more verbs whose last vowel(s) or consonant(s) (or the whole inflectional endings) are not clearly distinct, like *poexa* for *poexali*-'start-go-by-car.PAST.PL'. These forms (but not lemmas) whose inflectional endings were affected by inaccurate pronunciation were excluded from the analysis. The lexical and inflectional diversity shown by V. is lower than L.'s, but he leads her in constructing multi-component sentences and combining words in utterances. Thus, poverty in verb and (pro)nominal inflection is compensated by the number of utterance components in V.'s speech. This difference seems to be an important peculiarity in the development of productive verb morphology.

R.'s data are not as representative as those of the other children: the whole corpus consists of about 18,3 hours of recordings during the period from 1;1 till 2;11. For the present contribution we used only the speech of R. that was registered between 1;10 and 2;1b (see Appendixes 1 and 2).[8] R.'s pronunciation is more accurate than with L.'s and V.'s pronunciation and the number of unclear forms is very low. He starts combining words in utterances later than V. (if the onset of verb production is taken for the counting out point) and has almost no child- or family-specific words. The analysis below shows that in the short period investigated he passes through the stage of premorphology (1;10 to 2;0a) and after the overlapping phase (2;0b to 2;1b) reaches the protomorphological stage.

3. Stages of early verb development

The "standing point" of the article is the theoretical assumption that in "the pre-morphological phase no system of grammatical morphology has yet become dissociated from a general cognitive system that handles, inter alia, words of whatever form (including morphological forms), i.e. pre- and at least early protomorphology are part of the lexicon" (Dressler 1997: 11). Thus, all contrastive forms at these periods are considered to be rote-learnt. This means that only by the "peak" of protomorphology contrastive forms may be treated as not rote-learnt. These assumptions are the basis of the preliminary schemata (with brief explanations) of the stages of the development of the grammatical system in Russian sketched below.

The schemata shows two stages, corresponding to pre- (system 1) and protomorphology (system 2); the half-dark part of the schemata is the overlapping part of the two stages, where features of both pre- and protomorphology may be found.

For example, contrastive forms in Russian occur both during two stages and the overlapping phase. These contrastive forms satisfy the five criteria elaborated by Kilani-Schoch and Dressler (2000) already during the overlapping period, but we consider them true paradigms only during stage 2 (protomorphology). We need, thus (in order to estimate when any three contrastive forms become true MP), to find out what features of the children's grammatical system manifest themselves only in one given stage. These features/characteristics will provide the additional "independent" criteria in defining stages and the overlap of (demarcation) borders.[9]

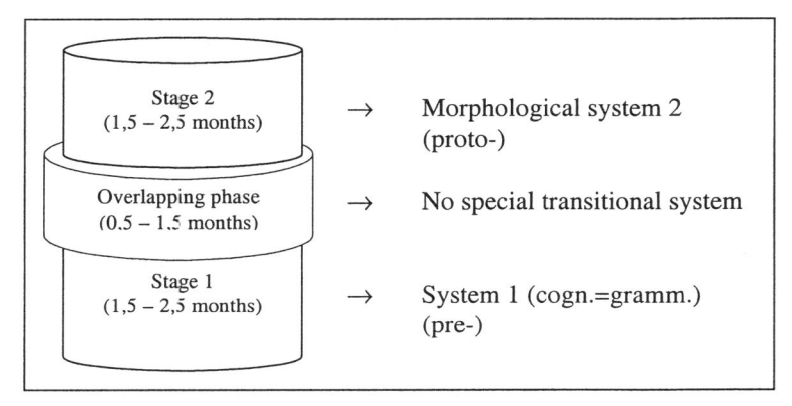

```
┌─────────────────────────────────────────────────────────────┐
│   Stage 2                                                    │
│  (1,5 – 2,5 months)   →   Morphological system 2             │
│                           (proto-)                           │
│                                                              │
│   Overlapping phase                                          │
│  (0.5 – 1.5 months)   →   No special transitional system     │
│                                                              │
│   Stage 1                                                    │
│  (1,5 – 2,5 months)   →   System 1 (cogn.=gramm.)            │
│                           (pre-)                             │
└─────────────────────────────────────────────────────────────┘
```

Figure 1. Early stages of grammatical development

Actually one may also think of the overlapping phase as a "transition" stage. However, it is important to note that there is no "special transitional grammatical system" between the stages. In this overlapping (or transitional) phase, features of both systems may be found. But with further development, the features of the earlier system will lose their validity and disappear, while features of the next system (for example, use of different lemmas and their inflected forms) will become closer to the target morphological system.[10]

So, the period under investigation envelopes two main stages: pre- and proto-morphology (and the overlap between them). The table below synthesises the results of data analysis:

Table 3. Early stages of the morphological development in three children: age

	Liza	Vanja	Roma
Premorphology (before emergence of verbs)	$1;0^{11} – 1;7$	1;5 – 2;1a	1;3 – 1;10
Premorphology (onset of verb production)	1;7 – 1;9b	2;1a – 2;2b	1;10 – 2;0b
Overlapping phase (emergence of the protomorphology "features")	1;9c – 1;11	2;2c – 2;3a	$2;1a – (2;1b)^{12}$
Protomorphology (disappearance of the premorphology "features")	after 1;11	after 2;3a	after 2;1b

As will be shown below, the premorphological period lasts (for each of three children) for about eight-ten months and includes two phases: (a) before the emergence of verbs (six-eight months) and (b) after the emergence of verbs (one-two months).[13] It is interesting to note that the duration of the first two phases, and the beginning of protomorphology, is similar in all children despite the differences in the rate/tempo of their general (and language) development. After the emergence of verbs the development of the grammatical system accelerates. The premorphological stage then lasts one - one and a half month: a bit longer for L. than V. (and probably longer than for Roma[14]). And the protomorphological stage develops three to four months after the onset of verb production.

The main criterion of the demarcation between periods employed by the contributors of this volume has been considered while establishing and describing these early periods. Additionally (when the main criterion did not absolutely work out) some (lexical and syntactical) "items" relevant for the acquisition of Russian were considered:[15]

(I) verb lemmas: (a) emergence and increase of the utterances with verbs (henceforth, VU), (b) emergence of new verb lemmas, (c) quantitative correlation of PERF and IPFV verbs, (d) emergence of aspectual pairs and verbs of complex (morphemically characterised) Aktionsarten;
(II) verb forms: (a) infinitives and their use, (b) inflected forms of PERF and IPFV, cluster of tense and aspect, (c) contrastive forms, development of mini-paradigms (henceforth, MP), (d) morphological overgeneralisations, (e) syntactic use of inflected forms;
(III) interrelation between (I) and (II);
(IV) development of the syntactical complexity of VU.

4. Verb predecessors in the predicative function

From the onset of the recordings, all three children use onomatopoeia. At the beginning the children use them to denote whole – not partitioned – situations. For example, L. (1;6) is looking at the water running from the tap and says: 'Kap-kap', where *kap-kap* can denote the water, the tap, the process of falling: everything that is connected with the water.

Later (shortly before the verb occurs) onomatopoeia are used more specifically for denoting either a perceived entity or a perceived event (action). At this stage of language development (before a verb occurs) the mother's questions determine in a way a predicative function of onomatopoeia and may play a role in the formation of the class of verbs. See example (1),[16] where the mother first repeats the child's word *fuu* – imitation of blowing up – and then adds the equivalent from the adult language *naduvaet* 'blow up-IPFV.3S':

(1) *MAM: Liza, chto brat delaet?
          Liza what brother-NOM do-IPFV.3S
          'Liza, what is the brother doing?'
     *LIZ: Fuu.   (1;7)
            fuu-imitation of blowing up
     *MAM: A, on fuu, naduvaet mjachik.
          a he-NOM fuu blow-up-IPFV.3S ball-DIM.ACC.SG
          'Ah, he is doing fuu, he is blowing the ball.'

The adult's question "what is s/he doing" and uttering the *correct* verb after the child's answer helps L. to identify "the place" of onomatopoeia and verbs in the group of word classes, and facilitates the acquisition of the lexeme itself. The child follows the "teaching" strategy of the mother and often repeats the appropriate form.

The use of onomatopoeia is an important phase in the acquisition of verb morphology, because it helps a child a) to learn to differentiate between events (actions) and entities, b) to recognise various types of situations (with the help of the interlocutor's commentaries) and to denote them first with sound-imitations, and later with the appropriate verbs (see Gagarina 2000). The strategy of adults selectively repeating onomatopoeia or the correspondent verbs and nouns may additionally catalyse the process of the formation of word classes.

The long period of use of onomatopoeia in the predicative function serves as the starting-off "platform" for the emergence of verbs. With the emergence of verb production we observe a decrease in the use of onomatopoeia in the data of all three children. Thus, L. with the emergence of verbs (and their contrastive forms) sharply reduces the use of onomatopoetics from 6,9%[17] at 1;9c to only 0,5% at 1;10 (later on the number of onomatopoetics does not exceed 2,7%). In V.'s data we find a decrease in the use of onomatopoeia after 2;0b (when the first contrastive verb forms occur) from 54,6% to 36,8% and a further decrease to 5,1% at 2;2b. R. actively uses onomatopoeia only till 1;11 when the number of onomatopoeia drops from 4,5% to 0,7%. Changes in the number and in the use of onomatopoeia (and the their final disappearance in the predicative function) may be an additional criteria for establishing the demarcation between stages. (The sharp decrease in the use of onomatopoeia takes place *during/at the very end of* overlapping phase when protomorphological features emerge).

5. Verb lemmas
5.1. Lexicon by the onset of verb production

Seven to eight months after the onset of meaningful speech production children use their first verbs. How does their lexicon look by this time? According to the diary of L., her lexicon at 1;8[18] consisted of 94 words in active use and 451 in passive use (understanding). Among the words in active use there are many 'proto'-words invented by L., like *Apka* for the brother and 'baby-talk' words with very general meaning, like *aja* – something unfamiliar or suspicious, *vava* – a wound, a creme, a pimple. Eleven words which are accurate phonetically and have one referent are categorised as *nouns*. Table 4 below integrates the data from all three children and shows the absolute number of noun lemmas and tokens by the onset of verb production. Russian children show not only the same tendency of noun predominance in the early lexicon as found, for example, in French (Bassano 2000), Italian (D'Odorico et al. 2001), and in English (Bates, Bretherton, and Snyder 1988 among others), etc., but also the earlier emergence of words denoting entities (nouns) in relation to verbs. The lead is held by V. who even used contrastive SG and PL forms of the noun: *gaga* (normative *jagoda*-NOM) for 'a/the berry' and *gagi* (normative *jagody*-NOM) for '(the) berries' when no verbs were documented.

Table 4. The number of noun lemmas and tokens by the onset of verb production

	Liza 1;7	Vanja 2;0b	Roma 1;8
lemmas/tokens	11/34	28/82	7/21

The onset of verb production is followed by dramatic changes in the whole grammatical system: contrastive forms occur – oblique cases (in nouns), inflected forms of both aspects (in verbs); changes in sentence structure are observed (sentences with subjects and verbs emerge); and the children start an intensive movement towards the generalisation of grammatical rules.

5.2. Emergence of verb lemmas

The number of VU doesn't increase steadily, and the verb lexicon is not enriched with an equal number of new lemmas at regular intervals. In all three children we register shifts from a more intensive increase in VU and new verb lemmas to a less intensive increase or even decrease and fall[19] (see figure 2 – the curves "VU" and "new lemmas"[20]). The slowing down in the increase of VU and the decrease in the emergence of new lemmas take place – as shown in figure 2 – simultaneously (L. 1;9b–1;9c) or consequently (V. 2;2a–2;2c).

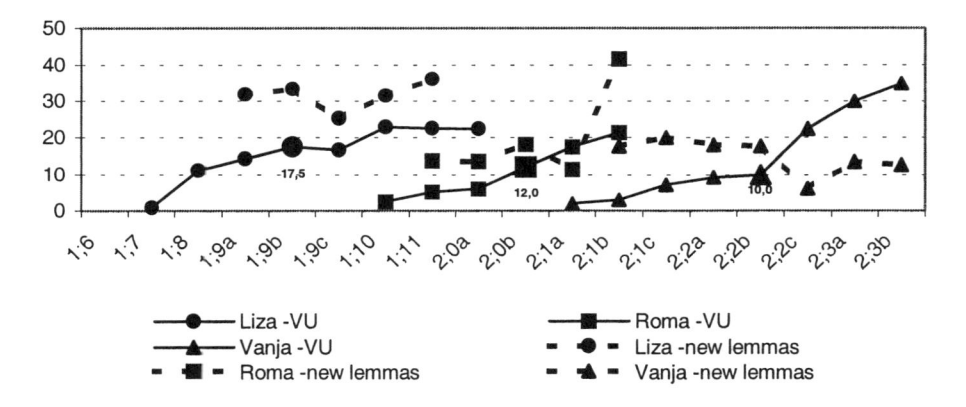

Figure 2. Emergence and development of VU and new lemmas (axis x = percentage, axis y = age) (the onset of the use of contrastive IPFV and PERF forms is indicated with respective numbers under VU curves)

Documented changes in the development of the verb lexicon probably are connected with the emergence of contrastive verb forms (as the diagrams of all three children show). Simultaneously with (or shortly after) the emergence of the first contrastive forms of both aspects, a clear fall in the number of new lemmas is observed. Probably it is difficult for a child to actively develop both – grammar and lexicon – simultaneously during the intensive development of the early grammatical system. During the early stages investigated in the present article, children enrich crucially either the number of words or the number of forms. In other words, when a period of intensive morphological acquisition begins, the development of lexicon is weakened, thus, the "shift of the children's attention" between the two language constituents, morphology and lexicon, takes place.[21] These changes coincide (and correlate) with the movement from pre- to protomorphology. What we observe is that the children's lexical and grammatical system develop rather steadily within each period and is exposed to "non-stable" changes shortly before, during and after the transition from one period to another in the overlapping phase.

During the premorphological stage children increase production of VU from only a few instances to 18% (L.), 12% (R.), and 10% (V.) of all analysed utterances. The number of new verb lemmas produced during this period rises to 7 (R.), 17 (L.) and 24 (V.). Verbs of both aspects occur simultaneously, however for two children IPFV lemmas outnumber PERF (L. 13/11 and V. 24/17). Although the morphemic structure of both PERFs and IPFVs remains not very complex, IPFVs are still morphemically more simplex and, thus, easier to operate with. In PERFs children use almost only pure-aspectual affixes. There are no aspectual pairs[22] or verbs of morphemically characterised Aktionsarten, i.e. verbs denoting special types of actions, characterised by spatial, temporal, etc. boundedness. The IPFV verbs denote as a rule a perceived ongoing process and PERFs – the perceived (or experienced) result of a concrete action taken place in the nearest past.

The movement to protomophology is characterised by a further increase of VU. The quantitative correlation between PERF and IPFV lemmas changes, as PERF verbs begin to be more actively produced. The first aspectual pairs occur: this shows the children's ability to treat the same situational context from different perspectives (regarding boundedness and temporal interpretation). The emergence of aspectual pairs and of various inflected verb forms of one aspectual pair (as well as verb synonyms) indicate the further development of the child's grammatical system.

6. Emergence of forms
6.1. Infinitive

Infinitives occur in the children's speech together with inflected forms and are very "stable". They are used along with inflected forms during the whole period under observation.[23] For the purpose of the present study it is important to note that changes in the meaning of infinitives may indicate the demarcation of the pre- and protomorphology stages (and thus, indirectly the onset of the productive use of inflected forms). Only during premorphological stage do children use infinitives to express the general "idea" of an action connected with the perceived entity, example (2):

(2) Situation: Mama and L. (1;10) are playing with a car with a small ladder:
*LIZ: Lestnica.
       ladder-NOM.SG
*MAM: Eto   lesenka   u   mashinki?
       this   ladder-NOM.SG   by car-DIM.GEN.SG
       'Is it the car's ladder?'
*LIZ: Podnimat's'a.
       go-upstairs-INF
*MAM: Da,   podnimat's'a   po takoj   lesenke
       yes, go-upstairs-INF   on such-LOC.SG   ladder-LOC.SG
       mozhno.
       possible
       'Yes, one can go upstairs on such ladder '

During the longer period (premorphological stage and overlapping phase) infinitives are used to denote a situation which refers to the past (example (3)), present (example (4)), or future/intention/request – 'irrealis' (examples (5), (6)):[24]

(3) Situation: Mama asks if L. (1;8) remembers how they picked mushrooms:
*MAM: I   ela   Liza   sup
       and   eat-IPFV.PAST.SG.FEM   Liza   soup-ACC
       potom,   da?
       afterwards yes?
       'And did Liza eat the soup afterwards, ah?'
*LIZ: Chistit'.
       peel-INF
*MAM: Mama chistila   griby,   da.
       mama peel-IPFV.PAST.SG.FEM   mushrooms-ACC.PL   yes
       'The mother was peeling mushrooms, yes'.

(4) Situation: grandmother says to V. (2;2c) that it is not possible to open the doors of the small car and that V. has broken already some doors.[25]
*VAN: Slomal=jamaj   net=e~a.
       break-PERF.PAST.SG.MASC   no
       'I did not break'

Situation: V. starts to break another door of the car, commenting his action:
*VAN: Slomat'=sjamat'.
       break-INF

(5) Situation: R. (2;0a) (together with his mother) approaches the table with the sugar-bowl on it and requests with the firm intonation:
*ROM: Otkryt'=kit'.
       open-INF
       'Open!'

(6) Situation: R. (2;1a) is sitting on the sofa holding the pen and intends to write on the magazine:
*ROM: Pisat'=pasjat'.
       write-INF
       'Write'
*MAM: Pisat'?   Chto ty   budesh' pisat'?
       write-INF what you   be-2S   write-INF
       'Write? What will you write?'

During the premorphological stage (and overlapping phase) infinitives are often used instead of inflected forms in contexts which are set up by the adult's questions (infinitives occur more rare in self-initiated utterances). Even when the child possesses an appropriate inflected form which is necessary to answer a question an infinite verb form may occur. Such frequent use of infinitives lasts only for a certain period, namely, till the beginning of protomorphology. The "peak" of protomorphology may be said to be reached when the analytical forms of the future occur and infinitives of IPFVs are used in constructions like *budu slushat'* 'be-1S.+listen-INF' (L.'s first use of the analytical future at 2;1). The first use of the same construction in V.'s data is documented at 2;3a with a sound-imitation instead of the proper infinitive *budu pryg* 'be-1S+jump-ONOM' and in R's data (diary notes) at 2;1b *budu streljat'* 'be-1S+shoot-INF'. By the "peak" of protomorphology the non-normative use of the perfective and imperfective infinitives drops under 10% of all verb tokens (for more details on non-target use of infinitives, see Gagarina 2002).

What is important to stress regarding true MP is that as long as infinitives are used instead of other inflected forms one should be cautious to claim that the child has constructed a verb paradigm. It is more probable that s/he is only on the way to learning the appropriate morphological rules. The child may posses one or another inflected form connected with a set of familiar/repeated contexts and use infinitive instead of an appropriate finite form in any new unfamiliar (situation or) context (see example (4)). Thus, such instances of contrastive inflected forms, areas in (3), (4), should not necessarily be counted as rote-learnt, but the pair s*lomal – slomat'* 'break-PERF.PAST.SG.MASC – -INF' would be a precursor of true MP and not yet a set of forms which may be considered a MP.

6.2. Single inflected forms (before the occurrence of true MP)

From the onset of verb production we record forms in two moods – the imperative and the indicative employing two verb stems. In all three children, inflected forms of both aspects occur simultaneously. The (traditional) cluster of tense and aspect is also observed in all children: first PERF verbs are marked for the PAST and IPFV verbs have the PRES inflectional endings.

All children are rather careful in the use of inflected forms. Errors occur when they answer adult questions containing verbs inflected for the past or present. Example (7) is rather typical for the pre- and the beginning of protomorphology stage when the child's grammatical system is not "stable" yet. Dialogues, namely forms used in adults' questions, may influence the form used by the child in the answer. In self-initiated utterances such errors do not occur. When the mother uses a non-inflected form in the question, L. uses the correct 3S form (example (8)):[26]

(7) *MAM: Chto ty delaesh'?
         what you do-IPFV.2S
         'What are you doing?'
    *LIZ: Pishesh'=pisis', karandash=kajajas'   (1;9a)
          write-IPFV.2S   pencil-NOM
    correct pishu-IPFV.1S
          '(I'm writing, pencil'

some utterances later:

(8) *MAM: Pisat',   da?
          write-IPFV.INF yes?
          'Are you going to write?'
    *LIZ: Pishet
          write-IPFV.3S
          '(Liza) is writing'

At the beginning 3S forms predominate in the data. Other person and/or number forms come later. Table 5 shows the emergence of different inflected forms in L.'s and V.'s speech. Figures in bold indicate the overlapping phase when "pre-" still manifests itself and "proto-" does not yet rule all morphological processes, to the left and to the right from the overlapping phase pre- and proto- periods are given, respectively. Some forms that come to be regularly used in protomorphology occur only sporadically in the overlapping phase. For example, 1S *em* 'eat' occurs for L. at 1;9c then disappears for two months and "returns" again as the regular inflected form after 2;0. Many new forms emerge by L. and V. after the overlapping phase (at 2;0 and 2;3b, respectively) when morphological rules start to be generated and first stem-shift errors occur.

Table 5. Emergence of inflected forms in two children: Liza and Vanja (lemmas/tokens)

LIZA

	Asp	1;7	1;8	1;9a	1;9b	**1;9c**	**1;10**	**1;11**	2;0
IMP.2S	IPFV	1/1				**2/3**	**1/2**		2/2
	PERF		1/2	2/3	1/1	**2/9**	**2/7**	**2/2**	2/2
PRES.3S	IPFV		2/3	4/7	3/12	**11/14**	**11/18**	**15/21**	12/21
PAST.SG	PERF		2/2	2/2	6/11	**5/15**	**13/32**	**13/17**	7/8
PAST.SG	IPFV		1/1		3/3	**1/1**	**1/1**		2/2
PAST.PL	PERF		1/1		1/1	**3/3**	**1/3**	**1/1**	1/1
PRES.3P	IPFV							**~3**	2/2
PAST.PL	IPFV							**1/1**	
FUT.1S	PERF					**1/1**			3/3
FUT.3S	PERF						**2/2**		2/3
PRES.1P	IPFV								
PRES.1S	IPFV								1/1
FUT.1P	PERF								1/2
IMP. PL.	IPFV								2/2
PART. PAST.PL.									1/1
PRES.2S	IPFV								1/1
ANAL. FUT overgen.	IPFV						1		

VANJA

	Asp	2;1a	2;1b	2;1c	2;2a	2;2b	2:2c	2;3a	2;3b
IMP.2S	IPFV		1/3	4/17	3/10	2/14	**4/6**	2/4	4/5
	PERF	1/1	1/1		1/1			1/7	4/16
PRES.3S	IPFV		1/2		2/2	2/4	**5/29**	13/39	20/60
PAST.SG	PERF	1/1	1/1	2/3	4/8~1²⁷	1/1~9	**9/20~13**	12/37~20	34/68~32
PAST.SG	IPFV					1/1	**1/1**	4/5	2/2
PAST.PL	PERF				1/5	1/1	**3/4**	5/26~1	3/3~1
PRES.3P	IPFV						**2/13**	1/3	4/13
PAST.PL	IPFV							**1/1**	1/1
FUT.1S	PERF								1/1
FUT.3S	PERF								3/5
PRES.1P	IPFV								2/2
PRES.1S	IPFV								3/4
FUT.1P	PERF								1/2
IMP. PL.	IPFV							1/9	
PART. PAST.PL.									
PRES.2S	IPFV								
ANAL. FUT	IPFV							**1/1²⁸**	
overgen.									1

As for R., from the beginning of the observed period (the age 1;10) he uses inflected forms (which are either frosen or rote-learnt) as well as infinitives. Forms of seven different inflectional types are found in the data in the first three sections: SG.PERF (masc., fem.) and PL.PERF in the PAST, 3S in the present and SG and PL in the imperative. At 2;0b one can see a qualitative spurt in the occurrence of inflected forms: four new types of forms (all of them apparently rote-learnt) are registered. The repertoire of paradigmatic forms has become richer. After the age of 2;0 occurrences of the analytical future are recorded in the diary.

Forms of 2S.IMP and of the infinitive of PERF and IPFV in R.'s speech occur simultaneously. Regarding other inflectional forms, I noticed slight differences in the time of occurrence: PERF forms with the PAST inflectional endings emerge earlier than IPFV and are used more often. IPFV verbs (*exat'* 'to go by car', *prygat'* 'to jump') occur only in the last group of recordings: 2;1b. It is interesting to note that from 2;0b R. starts to use PERF (which have the meaning of the nearest future), but the amount of lemmas is not high, only one for each data session: at 2;0b – *poexat'* 'to go by car', 2;1a – *postavit'* 'to put, to place', 2;1b – *dat'* 'to give'.

6.3. Emergence and development of contrastive forms

Contrastive forms occur at different intervals after the emergence of the first verb. With V. they occur a bit less than one month later, with R. after exactly one month, and with L., after two months. These first contrastive forms are displayed in table 6. One can see that the repertoire of these forms is not very diverse. It consists of: (a) infinitive and IPFV verbs inflected for 3S.PRES or PERF verbs inflected for the PAST, (b) infinitive and imperative verbs of both aspects. As the past forms have adjectival (type of) conjugation and imperatives consist of a bare CB without an inflectional affix we record only small number of contrastive forms where both contrastive forms are inflected for person/number. Among the first contrastive forms, no PERF verbs marked for person/number or IPFV verbs marked for the past are recorded and no true MP are observed.

Table 6. First occurrence of contrastive forms in three children

LIZA

lemma	a		engl.trans.	1;9[29]	1;10	1;11	2;0
kopat'	i	2	dig	inf/3S (1;9b)			
rvat'	i	2	tear	inf/past.f (1;9b)			
ubezhat'	p	2	run away	past.f/m (1;9b)			
katat'	i	2	roll	inf/3S (1;9c)			
myt'	i	2	wash	inf/3S (1;9c)			
myt's'a	i	2	wash-refl.	inf/3S (1;9c)			
vstavat'	i	2	stand up	inf/imp (1;9c)			
s''est'	p	2	eat	past.f/m (1;9c)		inf/past.m/pl	
guljat'	i	2	walk	inf/3S			
odevat'	i	2	dress	inf/3S			
est'	i	3	eat	inf/1S/3S (1;9b)			
chistit'	i	3	clean	inf/3S (1;9a) /past.f			
sobirat'	i	3	collect	inf/3S/past.m			
sosat'	i	2	suck		inf/3S		
polozhit'	p	2	put		past.f/pl	inf/imp	
poexat'	p	2	start going by car		inf/past.f		
snjat'	p	2	put off		inf/past.f		
upast'	p	2	fall down		past.f/m		
zalezt'	p	3	climb up		inf/past.f/m		
sest'	p	4	sit down		inf/imp/past.f/m		

Table 6. continued. LIZA

chitat'	i	2	read			inf/1S	
povesit'	p	2	hang up			inf/past.f	
uskakat'	p	2	jump away			past.f/m	
postavit'	p	2	put			inf/1S	
sprjatat's'a	p	2	hide-refl.			past.f/m	
2 contrastive forms				10	5	4	2
3 contrastive forms				3	1	1	–
4 contrastive forms				–	1	–	–

VANJA

lemma	a		engl.trans.	2;1	2;2	2;3a	2;3b
spat'	i	2	sleep	inf/3S	inf/3S (2;2c)	inf/3S	inf/3S
upast'	p	2	fall down	past.f/m	past.f/m/pl	past.f/m/pl	3S/past.f/m/pl
risovat'	i	2	paint		inf/imp		
goret'	i	2	burn		3S/3P[30] (2;2c)	3S/	**/3P**
rulit'	i	2	drive		inf/3S (2;2c)		
stojat'	i	2	stand		3S/3P (2;2c)		inf/**3S/3P**
otkryt'	p	2	open		inf/partic. (2;2c)		
poexat'	p	2	start going by car		past.f/pl (2;2c)		3S/past.f/m/~pl
propast'	p	2	escape		past.f/pl (2;2c)		
slomat'	p	2	break		inf/past.m (2;2c)	past.m/pl	past.f/m/part
zakryt'	p	2	close		inf/part. (2;2c)	part./	inf/past.m/pl
chinit'	i	3	repair		inf/imp/3S		inf/imp
bezhat'	i	2	run			past.f/m	
bolet'	i	2	be ill			3S/3P	/past.pl
sadit'sja	i	2	sit down-refl.			imp.sg/pl	
sidet'	i	2	sit down			inf/3S	3S
vezti	i	2	carry			inf/3S	
postroit'	p	2	build up			past.m/pl	imp/past.m
vstat'	p	2	stand up			inf/past.m	past.f/m
dat'	p	3	give			inf/imp/1S	inf/imp/1S
byt'	i	2	be-aux.				1S/3S
igrat'	i	2	play				inf/imp
krichat'	i	2	shout				imp/**3S**
lechit'	i	2	treat				inf/3S
pit'	i	2	drink				inf/3S
stroit'	i	2	build				imp/1S
zhdat'	i	2	wait				3S/3P

Table 6. continued. VANJA

dostat'	p 2	get			inf/past.m
kupit'	p 2	buy			inf/past.f
priexat'	p 2	arrive			past.f/m
snjat'	p 2	put off			inf/past.f
ubrat'	p 2	put away			inf/past.f
est'	i 3	eat			inf/3S/past.m
najti	p 3	find			inf/past.f/m
pochinit'	p 3	repair		past.pl/	inf/imp/past.f
pojti	p 3	start on going			1S/1P/past.m
prijti	p 3	come			3S/past.f/m
2 contrastive forms			2	10	19
3 contrastive forms			–	2	9
4 contrastive forms			–	–	5

ROMA

lemma	a		engl. trans.	1;11	2;0	2;1
upast'	p	3	fall down	past.f/m/pl	past.f/m	past.f/m
pit'	i	2	drink		inf/3S	inf/3S
spat'	i	2	sleep		inf/**3S**	inf/3S
dat'	p	2	give		inf/imp	
otkryt'	p	2	open		inf/imp	
pojti	p	2	start going by foot		past.f/m	1P/past.f/m
vkljuchit'	p	2	switch on		inf/imp	
kopat'	i	3	dig		inf/imp/3S	
poexat'	p	4	start going by car		2P/3S/past.f/pl	1P/past.m
myt's'a	i	2	wash – reflex.			inf/3S
pisat'	i	2	write			inf/3S
sidet'	i	2	sit			3S/3P
popit'	p	2	drink a bit			inf/past.m
prijti	p	2	come			3S/past.f
2 contrastive forms				–	7	9
3 contrastive forms				1	1	1
4 contrastive forms				–	1	–

The most displayed in the table contrastive forms occur during the overlapping phase and beginning of proto-morphology. Although they are not imitative, not formulaic, are accurately pronounced and recur in different contexts (see the criteria elaborated by Kilani-Schoch and Dressler 2000), in my opinion they should not be treated as true MP till the age when the overlapping phase is over; i.e. after the age of 1;11 for L., the age of 2;1 by R. and the age of 2;3a for V. The only person inflectional ending which is used is 3d singular and only with IPFV verbs (one instance of 1S for L., one use of 2P for R., and one form of 3P for V. is recorded) and very few contrastive forms are used in sentences with a subject. There are no aspectual pairs and, finally, no active morphological productivity[31] can be generally seen.

In Roma's data the first three differently inflected forms of one PERF verb *upast'* 'to fall down' occurred already at the age of 1;11:

(9) Upal   upala   upali
     MASC   FEM   PL
     12 times   6 times   1 time

However, I cannot consider these forms to be the first true MP. One reason would be that all these inflected forms were created from the OB, by adding the inflectional suffix for the past *-l* and different markers for either feminine or masculine in SG or PL: *-a, -Ø* or *-i* (adjectival tape of inflection). No evidence has been found that at this age R. differentiates between gender (and number). Moreover, sometimes he uses the masculine and feminine endings of the verb in the wrong contexts, examples (10)–(12):

(10) Situation: A wheel (neuter gender: *upalo*) fell from R.'s hands
     *ROM: xxx upal.
                fall-MASC.SG

(11) Situation: R. threw down a plastic tube (feminine gender: *upala*) and watched it rolling:
     *ROM: Upal.
                fall-MASC.SG

(12) Situation: R. approaches the armchair, takes the cover (feminine gender: *upala*) and throws it on the floor:
     *ROM: Upali.
                fall-PL

Two contrastive forms of other verbs *pit'*-IPFV 'to drink' (5th MC) and *spat'*-IPFV 'to sleep' (26th MC), infinitive and 3S, are documented. In order to produce these forms the child has to switch between OB and CB. However, due to the small number of lemmas with two forms (which appear mainly in 3S.PRES (rarely PL.), past (SG. and PL.) and in the imperative), and the general "level" of R.'s grammatical system I would consider such forms as rote-learnt, not constructed by the child.

At 2;0b R. uses 17 lemmas (seven IPFV plus ten PERF), and four new types of inflected forms (IPFV – PAST.SG. and PRES.3S and PERF – FUT.2S and 3S) occur. The number of lemmas that have two to four forms increases to seven. However, some of the forms appear to be strongly connected with the situations (context-dependent) to which these verbs refer. For example, R. often uses two forms of the verb 'to give' *dat'*-PERF.INF (two times in recordings, one time in diary) and *daj*-PERF.IMP.2S (five times in recordings, nine times in the diary). However, this verb is always used in similar situations, when R. wants to get something or to open a box.[32]

A bit later, the first three- and four contrastive forms emerge.[33] R. starts to use more actively both OB and CB for constructing different inflected forms. At 2;1b another six new lemmas (five IPFV plus one PERF) occur, and the number of inflectional types increases to nine (forms of 1S and 1P occur). The mother notes in the diary the emergence of the imperfective future – *budet ščitat'* 'will-3S count' and *budet streljat'* 'will-3S shoot', showing R. has started to construct analytical morphological forms. Thirteen verbs (in the diary and the recordings) are used in two or more inflected forms. R. also starts to produce sentences with subject and verb inflected for agreement. Three aspectual pairs are documented. R.'s whole grammatical system seems to change. As a result, contrastive forms produced by R. by this point may be considered as true MP.

6.4. True MP

As mentioned above, contrastive forms occur in our data already during premorphology, and their number increases steadily during the next stages. It is rather difficult (in the case of Russian) to establish the demarcation of stages (only) on the basis of the emergence of true MP. In cases when the criterion of true MP does not work I would rather suggest to pay attention to a) the types of the bases employed by children (both OB and CB or only one of the two bases), b) "quality" of the members in a true MP (for example, additional criterion "no optional infinitive form" within a true MP), and c) the "indirect evidence", see part 3, e.g. to treat contrastive forms as true MP when they are produced at a certain level of development of the grammatical system of a child (when the transition from pre- to proto- is finished), and there is an "independent" evidence that the child has moved from one grammatical system (premorphology in our case) to another one (protomorphology).

However we may find some forms that may be treated as candidates to true MP already during the overlapping phase. These forms are: for L. (1;10) forms of three lemmas (*zalezt'* 'climb up', *sest'* 'sit down' and *snjat'* 'put off'), for R. (2;0) forms of three lemmas (*spat'* 'sleep', *kopat'* 'dig' and *poexat'* 'start going by car') and for V. (2;2) forms of two lemmas (*goret'* 'burn' and *stojat'* 'stand'). One of the candidates for MP either agrees with subjects in person/number (V. 2;2c: *spit garazh* 'sleep-3S garage'), or employs different stems with considerable stem alternations (L. 1;10: *sest'-sjad'-sel* 'sit down-INF-IMP-PAST.FEM'), or is an overgeneralisation (L. 1;10 *snimila* instead of *snjala* 'put off-PAST.FEM'). I also considered as a candidate to MP lemmas with four forms (R. 2;1 *poedem-poedet-poexala-poexali* 'start going by car 2P.-3S.-PAST.SG.FEM-PAST.PL'). Due to the R.'s small sample size (and limited number of lemmas), only a small number of contrastive forms in his data are considered to be true MP (or even candidates to be true MP): twelve lemmas with two and more different forms – recordings and five lemmas – diary. During the age of 2;1 R. used four verbs in three or more forms; this is one IPFV verb(-particle) *davat'* 'to give', 'let's (+INF)' and three PERFs: *dat'* 'to give', *pojti* 'to start going' and *vkljuchit'* 'to switch on'. (See the above discussion for other problems in considering R.'s early verb forms candidates for true MP).

True MP after the peak of the protomorphology stage may still not fulfil the five requirements specified by Kilani-Schoch and Dressler (2000); but then they have to be correctly used in sentences with subjects, form an aspectual pair and/or be the result of the overgeneralisation. The first true MP also consists of "atypical", for the early grammatical development, sets of forms, for example PERF verbs inflected for person/number, IPFV verbs inflected for 1S. In L.'s data the true paradigmatic forms occur after 1;11 and in V.'s data – at 2;3a. Although the variety of inflectional forms is still not very high, the children possess more verb lemmas and operate with them more freely, combining them with different subjects and objects and trying various word combinations. In both children, shortly after true MPs occurs the variety of contrastive forms sharply increases (see table 5 L. at 2;0 and V. at 2;3b). It seems that the ability to construct the minimal set of contrastive forms of a MP provides the stimulus for the acquisition of the other forms of a paradigm.

7. Emergence of categories

When tracing the emergence of categories it is very important to consider their complex nature, both their grammatical meaning and their formal expression (see, for example, in the Russian tradition Maslov (1978), Švedova (1980), Ceytlin (1989), Bondarko (1995)). For example, in Russian aspect is considered to be a "more" lexical category than tense and more grammatical than Aktionsarten. In the description below I treat separately the emergence of the formal marking and the grammatical meaning of some verb categories. The emergence of an inflected form signals in a way the forthcoming emergence of a given category, but one cannot say (especially, in the early stages of language acquisition) that a given inflectional category is acquired when a respective inflected form, which may be rote-learnt, occurs. For example, the emergence of the 1S form of the verb *em* 'to eat' at 1;9c does not mean that L. possesses the category of first person. We may conclude that the (inflectional) category is acquired or is in the process of acquisition when the form where the given category is displayed (a) constitutes true MP, (b) is produced at the age when the child's grammatical system enters (at least) the peak of the proto-morphological stage.

In the period under observation forms of only two moods (imperative and indicative) are documented. One peculiarity has been found in R.'s data. From 1;10 he uses verbs of two moods, indicative and imperative, but during 1;10 and 1;11 no "correct" imperatives with the inflectional suffix *-i(te)* or the zero suffix are used. Moreover, R. produces infinitives with the imperative meaning. The first correct imperatives occur at 2;0a: *kopaj*-IPFV 'dig!' and *daj*-PERF 'give!'. The late occurrence of the correct imperative forms can be due to the fact that in order to construct an imperative a child has to learn how to switch from the OB to the CB. This is a rather complicated operation, and the switch between an OB and a CB may be obfuscated by the root/stem alternations, like in the infinitive *pis-a-t'* 'to write' and imperative *pish-i*, or the infinitive *otkry-t'* 'to open' and imperative *otkroj*.[34] Such forms cannot be constructed by the child in the premorphological stage. Thus, the (grammatical) meaning of the imperative mood occurs before the correct morphological marking.[35]

Aspect is probably one of the most complicated verb categories, and its investigation is characterised by a variety of (sometimes controversial) definitions and approaches (like in Isačenko 1960; Švedova 1980; Verkuyl 1993; Li and Shirai 2000). Due to the lack of space it is possible to remark only on the emergence of PERF and IPFV verbs (for the discussion on grammatical aspect or viewpoint aspect, see Smith 1983, 1997; Sasse 2001) and some Aktionsarten.[36] Verbs of both aspects occur simultaneously in our corpus. The first PERF verbs are marked for past: *upal* 'fell down-SG.MASC', *slomal* 'broke-SG.MASC', and IPFV verbs – for present: *kapaet* 'dig-3S', *kataet* 'roll-3S'. PERF verbs denote resultative actions, the perceived result of which was reached at the time of speech and belong mainly to the group of achievements. IPFV verbs denote ongoing actions (that may have potential telic meaning and belong to activities or states).[37] This connection between the inherent semantics of verbs (i.e., lexical aspect or Aktionsart) and tense marking has been reported for other languages as well (see, for example, Antinucci and Miller (1976) for Italian and English, Shirai & Anderson (1995) for English, Aksu-Koç (1978) for Turkish, Champaud et. al 1997 for French).

Gradually connections between verbs of either PERF or IPFV aspect and tense marking become weaker, and clusters between tense and aspect disappear. Already at the overlapping phase IPFV verbs become inflected for the past, for example, *exal* 'was going-SG.MASC', and children are able to use these verbs in a generalised-factual sense, denoting any (not necessarily concrete) event that had happened in the past. PERF verbs occur with various person markers, for example, 3rd or 1st person: *postavit-postavlju* 'will put-3S-1S'.

Basic notions of "result-process" (see Slobin 1985) underlie children's very early denotation of (perceived) various actions (events, processes, states, etc.). However, this does not mean that the child constructs aspectually contrastive forms and is completely "aware" of aspectual distinctions. I would claim that mastering of aspect begins when the child starts to produce/use a) PERF and IPFV verbs in all (three) tenses, b) modifications of the basic meanings of PERF and IPFV aspects, c) counterparts of one lexeme, d) one and the same stem with different prefixes (diverse Aktionsarten) in various contexts with different partial meanings of PERF and IPFV aspect. It seems that, generally, as long as finite verb forms are rote-learnt, their development (and choice) would be determined much more by extralinguistical (and external situational) and contextual factors then when rule-based learning starts.

The morphotactically transparent verbs of a few (non-morphemically characterised) Aktionsarten comprise the early verb lexicon. These are telic verbs with the meaning of dynamic actions, aiming to achieve a result, such as *kopat'* 'to dig', *est'* 'to eat', *stirat'* 'to wash', etc. (accomplishments). Atelic state verbs are less common (in the adult and children speech production): *sidet'* 'to sit', *spat'* 'to sleep'. A few verbs (of motion) with prefix *po-* denoting ingressive meaning were found in the data: *poexat'* 'to start going by car', *pojti* 'to start going by foot'. No verbs with semantically "complicated" affixes, like *perečityvat'* 'to reread – iterative', *peresolit'* 'to put too much salt' or *nadlomit'* 'to break partially, not to the end' were found.[38]

Present and past tense forms occur simultaneously, but the past marker *-l* is attached in the beginning only to perfective verbs. The here-and-now result of an action is expressed by early past forms. Thus, the formal opposition of the contrastive forms of present and past does not really reflect the presence of two tenses – past and present. The acquisition of the past tense can be said to develop actively when children split the aspect-tense cluster and start to denote processes (and different activities) by the past IPFV forms. The contrastive future forms of PERF and especially the analytical IPFV strengthen the "idea" of tense, even though the future forms of both aspects denote an unreal state-of-affairs or intention to perform an action. Lexical devices, such as temporal adverbials *yesterday, tomorrow, before* enrich the further acquisition of tense.

Inflectional forms of the 3rd person are the first to occur in the data of all three children. The emergence of these forms does not mean, as mentioned already, the immediate emergence of the category of person. The category of person is used productively when a child not only produces contrastive forms of, let's say, third and first person, but when at least one of the following conditions is fulfilled: a) the inflected verb form agrees with the subject in a VP, b) the (personal) pronouns are correctly produced, c) the inflectional endings of at least any two persons are used with different lexical types of verbs (and with two aspects). Of course, recurrence in diverse contexts is necessary. The criteria (a) and (c) are also valid for determining which verb inflected forms are productive.

To sum up, each form represents a conglomerate of categories which are – at the early stages of language acquisition – not separable. As long as inflected forms are rote-learnt and the categories are "clustered" in an inflected form, one cannot claim that the child possesses a given category. Only when the child starts to construct by him/herself inflectional forms and one can ascertain the productive use of contrastive forms, it is possible to claim that the categories assigned to these forms have been acquired.

8. Morphological substitutions
8.1. Agreement

In the observed period, only a few agreement errors were found.[39] It is interesting to note that these errors occur mainly in children's answers to adult questions. Thus, they were influenced by the inflected forms used by adults or were predetermined by the adult's questions.

For example, at 2;1b R. uses an infinitive after the mother's question containing the past tense form because he is not able to build correctly a sentence with subject and object (and inflected verb):

(13) *MAM: Kogo   ty   tam   videl?
             whom   you   there see-IPFV.PAST.MASC
             'Whom did you see there?'
     *ROM: Djadja Sergej sobachka kormit'
             uncle   sergej dog-NOM   feed-INF
     correct uncle   sergej dog-ACC   feed-IPFV.PAST.MASC
             'Uncle Sergej fed the dog'

In the sentences initiated by the children these types of agreement errors were almost never recorded.

8.2. Stem shift and class shift

Children employ both bases (as rote-learnt) from the onset of verb production. Errors in switching from one base to another occur simultaneously with the emergence and development of true verb paradigms (two months later after the onset of verb production), "naturally" precede class shift errors, and signalise the beginning of the productive use of the inflected forms. Two wrong past constructions are documented. One is by L. 1;10: *snimila* instead of *snjala* 'put off clothes-PERF.PAST.FEM'. L. constructed the past form not from the OB *snja-*, but from the SG imperative form *snimi*.[40] Another example of the stem mixture is by V. 2;3a: *ubaj* instead of *uberi* 'put away-IMP'. V. constructs the CB of the imperative by j-addition (the most frequent type of correlation between OB and CB) and the stem vowel alternation is absent. R. at 2;1b uses the OB of the verb *otkryt'* 'open' to construct the imperative, thus ignoring the normative CB variant *otkroj*: *okij* instead of *otkroj* 'open-IMP'.

At 1;10 one example of a class shift (from the 13th unproductive MC to the 1st productive MC) is registered by L.: *sosaet* instead of *sosjot* 'suck-

IPFV.3S'; *sosat'* 'suck-INF'.[41] No class shifts for R. and V. were registered in the observed period. Apparently, class shifts in Russian occur mainly during the later stage (of transitional morphology). Interestingly, Kiebzak-Mandera, Smoczyńska, and Protassova (1997), in their investigation of the acquisition of the early stages of Russian verb morphology, write that "processes of class shifts and regularizations could be observed ... well after the emergence of the basic verb system. [...] In the very earliest phases of building tense, aspect and mood distinctions they were extremely infrequent and did not reveal any systematic pattern".

It seems that in Russian class shifts and overgeneralisations in constructing OB and CB forms as well as aspectual pairs of verbs occur later than in other languages observed in this volume. The complex nature of alternations within one paradigm (there are more than 40 verb microclasses) along with the rich system of prefixation (with numerous Aktionsarten), probably slow down the emergence of "creative" class shift errors in children. Only once they are able to deal with the basic (minimal) system of verb inflectional endings the children start to produce overregularisations in the alternations between MCs. Later overgeneralizations in derivation of various Aktionsarten occur.[42] The consequence in the emergence of errors may probably serve as an indirect evidence for the subsequent way of the acquisition of the parts of grammatical system.

9. Conclusion

The main problems discussed in the article are: (a) when and how children move from pre- to protomorphology, (b) what contrastive forms are considered to be true MPs or candidates to true MP and when do they occur, (c) what linguistic evidence, regarding verbs, does one have in the data to be able to claim that the grammatical system of a child moves from one "level" to another "level". That is, what evidence do we have in order to say that (each) form of a verb paradigm is the result of the (productive) application of already mastered grammatical rules/features. The problem of establishing steps towards the emergence of a true paradigm and mastering the grammatical rules was discussed in connection with general development of the verb lexicon and morphology.

If we consider that the child cannot acquire with equal (and simultaneous) intensity two components of a (morphologically rich) language: inflectional morphology and the lexicon, then we may assume that the onset of the dramatic development of either the lexicon or grammar should alternate. The Russian data seem to confirm this supposition. What we observe in the data of all three children is that the number of new verb lemmas dramatically drops after the first contrastive forms. These crucial changes take place in the transition phase when protomorphology start to conquer the leading place in the grammatical system of the children, and the rudiments of the previous period disappear with the end of the overlapping phase.

We observe that in Russian contrastive forms occur already during the pre-morphological period, however, they are extracted from *inflecticon*[43] as rote-learnt forms. When the whole grammatical system of a child moves to another level, the level of abstract grammatical rules and operations with morphological patterns – children start to build true MP. I think that at this level the criteria elaborated by Kilani-Schoch and Dressler (2000) become less decisive because the whole child's system is operating already with abstract grammatical rules. These criteria are more important for the overlapping phase, when premorphology is still manifesting itself and protomorphology does not totally predominate in the grammatical system of the children. However, as soon as we can establish, using such linguistic evidence (regarding verbs) as use of infinitives, development of agreement, syntactic structure of VU, word classes, emergence of aspectual pairs, etc., that the child has no rudiments of premorphology, we can conclude that contrastive forms produced by the children are already pattern-derived and constitute true MPs.

Appendix 1. The recordings of each data file

Liza	File name	Age of recording	Roma	File name	Age of recording
	1;9a	1;9.0		2;0a	2;0.3
		1;9.4			2;0.12
		1;9.6		2;0a	2;0.24
	1;9b	1;9.10		2;1a	2;1.3
		1;9.15		2;1b	2;1.18
	1;9c	1;9.20			
		1;9.23			
		1;9.24			
		1;9.25			
		1;9.27			

160 *Natalia Gagarina*

Vanja	File name	Age of recording	Recording interval (in minutes)
	2;0a	2;0.2	20
		2;0.4	35
		2;0.15	30
	2;0b	2;0.20	30
		2;0.23	45
	2;1a	2;1.2	30
		2;1.6	45
	2;1b	2;1.12	65
		2;1.20	65
	2;1c	2;1.25	30
		2;1.27	30
		2;1.28	90
	2;2a	2;2.5	90
		2;2.8	35
	2;2b	2;2.17	60
		2;2.21	30
	2;2c	2;2.23	45
		2;2.25	45
	2;3a	2;3.4	90
		2;3.9	90
	2;3b	2;3.19	60
		2;3.24	80
			1140 min. (19 hours)

Appendix 2. The data (recordings) in the period under investigation

age	Liza anal. utter.	V utter.	V utter. (%)	Vanja anal. utter.	V utt. (s *dat'* 2;2a)	V utter. (%)	Roma anal. utter.	V utter.	V utter. (%)
1;5				69					
1;6	86			88			9		
1;7	123	1	0,8	110			11		
1;8	117	13	11,1	428			36		
1;9a	140	20	14,3	153			–	–	
1;9b	280	49	17,5						
1;9c	466	78	16,7						
1;10	377	86	22,8	426			154	4	2,6
1;11	306	69	22,5	368			305	16	5,2

Appendix 2. continued

2;0a	285	64	22,5	198			359	22	6,1
2;0b				142			415	50	12,0
2;1a				206	4	1,9	388	68	17,5
2;1b				471	14	3,0	112	24	21,4
2;1c				481	35	7,3			
2;2a				366	34	9,3			
2;2b				432	43	10,0			
2;2c				446	100	22,4			
2;3a				640	192	30,0			
2;3b				747	262	35,1			
Total	2180	380		5771	684		1789	184	

Notes

* I would like to thank W.U. Dressler, D. Bittner and M. Kilani-Schoch for their helpful comments on the earlier version of this paper. I express my gratitude to L. Downing for checking my English. All mistakes are mine.
1. Participle, verbal adverb and forms in the conditional mood and in the passive voice occur only sporadically in the period under observation.
2. For more about different implicative paradigm structure conditions see Wurzel (1987).
3. The participle and verbal adverb forms are not given in the table.
4. Analytical forms occur only at the end of the investigated period and are not analysed in the present study.
5. Transcription and coding of data was done in CLAN format.
6. This last form is calculated as unclear, because phonetic inaccuracy has spread to the inflection, and it is not possible to judge what inflected form is produced by the child.
7. This is the biggest corpus of the longitudinal tagged data for Russian collected so far.
8. Beginning with the age of 2;2 when the crucial development continues we have, unfortunately, the gap of three months in the recordings.
9. About some problems of demarcation between pre- and protomorphology see, for example, Kilani-Schoch et al. (1997).
10. For example, the meaning of the infinitives, which occur with the onset of verb production.
11. Age specification is given as in CHILDES: first figure shows number of years, second indicates months, the letter at the end – group of sessions.
12. There is the gap in the recordings after 2;1b.

13. In the present article we draw our attention mainly to the period after the emergence of verbs and will shortly comment on the period when children use predecessors of verbs in a predicative function.
14. When the information about R.'s speech production is omitted, this means that we have no documented evidence for the facts under discussion.
15. The more detailed schemata is given in Gagarina (2001).
16. All examples are given in CHILDES transcription, see MacWhinney (2000). At the end of the first line of the child's utterance in each example the age of the child is given (if it was not specified before).
17. I calculated the percentage of sound-imitations in relation to all analysable utterances.
18. I do not consider here Liza 1;7 when the only one use of *otdaj* 'give back-IMP' is documented.
19. The verb vocabulary differs between children qualitatively and quantitatively. The high rate of the variability in the verb vocabulary development has been documented for other languages as well (for the definition of a *'vocabulary spurt'* and for the discussion on the variability of the verb vocabulary, see D'Odorico et al. (2001).
20. The percentage of VU is calculated in relation to all analysed utterances. The percentage of new lemmas is calculated in relation to all VU. "New lemmas" are defined as verb lemmas that occur in speech production for the first time.
21. There are differences in the co-development of the noun/verb lexicon and the acquisition of the inflected (contrastive) forms of these word classes. The correlation (co-dependence) between the acquisition of the verb lexicon and verb morphology is stronger than the correlation between the acquisition of the noun lexicon and noun morphology, because verbs serve as the compositional centre of VP and, generally, play more decisive role (than nouns) in the acquisition of the grammatical system.
22. By aspectual pair in language acquisition we mean two verbs – PF and IPF – with the same root and different (not only pure aspectual, but also slightly semantically aggravated) affixes. This definition is broader than for the adult language (see Švedova 1980; Smirnov 2001; Wiemer 2001, etc.). In the period investigated children build mainly pairs with pure-aspectual affixes, and affixes slightly modifying the meaning of the derived verb.
23. For discussion of the optional infinitives stage in Russian see Snyder and Bar-Shalom (1998); Brun, Avrutin, and Babyonyshev (1999); Bar-Shalom and Snyder (1999).
24. It is often difficult to differentiate between child's intention to perform an action by him/herself and a request addressed to an adult.
25. It is interesting to note that V. uses the past form of the same verb correctly.
26. At this age L. always speaks about herself in the 3rd person.

27. The sign ~ means that the inflectional suffix (or the whole form) was not clear enough pronounced by the child. Such forms were calculated separately.
28. The example is b*udu pryg* 'byt'-1S+jump-ONOM' 'I will jump'.
29. As noted above, forms constituting true MP may be taken from different recording sessions within a single month.
30. Forms marked in bold are used in sentences with a subject (correct person/number agreement in the present).
31. For the discussion of productive forms and relevant problems see Weist (2002).
32. Other children use this verb if they want something to start working or to switch the light on or off or to achieve any result. V. used *dat'* 'to give' in three inflected forms during the seven months from the age of 1;5 till the age of 2;1 when the other verb lemmas occur.
33. The IPFV verb *kopat'* 'to dig' occurs not only in the infinitive and imperative, but also with the 3.SG inflection; the PERF verb *poexat'* 'to start going by car' appears in four inflected forms: 2.SG and 3.SG of the present and feminine and masculine of the past.
34. In the second example the verb *otkryt'* 'to open' was produced by R. in two different ways: correctly as *'okoj'* (the adult norm *otkroj*) and with the phonological error *'okij'* (consonant clusterer *'tkr'* was not produced in this period). The infinite form *otkryt'* was used with imperative meaning.
35. In the data of the other children we also find the infinitive used with imperative meaning. However, such use gradually and slowly disappears.
36. More to this issue see, for example, Vendler (1967); Šeljakin (1987).
37. The same tendency has been reported also for other children learning Russian: Gvozdev (1949); Gagarina (1997); Pupynin (1998).
38. The acquisition of these verbs and their paradigms is the next step which the child climbs having mastered basic inflectional operations with the more simplex verbs and Aktionsarten.
39. Agreement errors are also rare in the data of Kiebzak-Mandera (2000).
40. The CB of the verb is *snim-* (the overgeneralization with the same verb was found in V. 2;4a, the period not under observation in the present article; V. mixed two stems and constructed imperative from the OB *snja-*, having not used stem alternation and inflectional suffix *i*, the normative form is *snimi-*).
41. Overgeneralization of the pattern of the 1st productive MC "a-aj correlation" is frequent, in fact, not only in children's data, but also in adult spoken Russian (*iskat'* – **iskaju* instead of *ishchu* 'seek for-IPFV.1S') and in diachronic change (compare *mjaukat'*- *mjaukajet* 'to miau-INF – IPFV.3S', arch. *mjauchit* 3S).
42. The overgeneralizations in the Aktionsarten derivation last till the age of seven to nine years, see Ceytlin (1989).

43. Under *inflecticon,* a parallel term to lexicon, I understand the number of stored inflectional forms. The child extracts single inflected forms for his speech production from *inflecticon* like s/he extracts lemmas from the lexicon.

References

Aksu-Koç, Ayhan
    1978   Aspect and modality in the children's acquisition of the Turkish past tense. Dissertation, University of California, Berkley.

Antinucci, Francesco, and Ruth Miller
    1976   How children talk about what happened. *Journal of Child Language* 3: 167–189.

Bar-Shalom, Eva, and Willian Snyder
    1999   On the relationship between Root Infinitives and Imperatives in Early Child Russian. In: Annabel Greenhill, Heather Littlefield, and Cheryl Tano (eds.), *BUCLD 23: Proceedings of the 23rd Annual Boston University Conference on Language Development,* 56–67. Boston: Boston University.

Bassano, Dominique
    2000   Early development of nouns and verbs in French: Exploring the interface between lexicon and grammar. *Journal of Child Language* 27: 521–559.

Bates, Elisabeth, I. Bretherton, and L. Snyder
    1988   *From First Words to Grammar: Individual Differences and Dissociable Mechanisms.* New York: Cambridge University Press.

Bondarko, Aleksandr V.
    1995   Semantika glagol'nogo vida v russkom jazyke [Semantics of aspect in Russian]. (*Beiträge zur Slavistik XXIV.*) Frankfurt am Main/Berlin/Bern/New York/Wien: Lang.

Brun, Dina, Sergej Avrutin, and Marina Babyonyshev
    1999   Aspect and its Temporal Interpretation during the optional Infinitive Stage in Russian. In: Annabel Greenhill, Heather Littlefield, and Cheryl Tano (eds.), *BUCLD 23: Proceedings of the 23rd Annual Boston University Conference on Language Development,* 120–131. Boston: Boston University.

Ceytlin, Stella N.
1989   Detskaja rech': innovacii formoobrazovanija i slovoobrazovanija (na materiale sovremennogo russkogo jazyka) [Language acquisition: inflectional and derivational innovations (the case of modern Russian)]. Habilitation, State Pedagogical University of Russia, St. Petersburg.

Champaud, Christian, Wolfgang U. Dressler, Maria Sedlak, and Natalia Gagarina
1997   Acquisition of verbal categories in French, German, Russian. Paper presented at the Symposium on comparative studies in language acquisition: 7. European Conference on Developmental Psychology. France, Rennes: 5.9.1997

D'Odorico, Laura, Stefania Carubi, Nicoletta Saleri, and Vincenzo Calvo
2001   Vocabulary development in Italian children: A longitudinal evaluation of quantitative and qualitative aspect. *Journal of Child Language* 28: 351–372.

Dressler, Wolfgang
1997   Introduction. In: Katarczyna Dziubalska-Kołaczyk (ed.), *Pre- and Protomorphology in Language Acquisition*, 7–14. (Papers and Studies in Contrastive Linguistics 33.) Poznań: Adam Mickiewicz University.

Dressler, Wolfgang U., and Natalia Gagarina
1999   Basic questions in establishing the verb classes of contemporary Russian. In: Lila Fleishman, Michail Gasparov, Tatjana Nikolaeva, Alexander Ospovat, Vladimir Toporov, Ronald Vroon, Alexei Vigasin, and Andrej Zaliznjak (eds.), *Essays in Poetics, Literary History and Linguistics: Presented to Viacheslav Vsevolodovich Ivanov on the Occasion of His Seventieth Birthday*, 754–760. Moscow: Ob''edinjonnoje Gumanitarnoje Izdatel'stvo.

Gagarina, Natalia
1997   Aspektual'naja semantika i funkcionirovanije vidov russkogo glagola v detskoj rechi [Aspectual semantics and functioning of the aspects of Russian verbs in language acquisition], Unpublished Ph.D. dissertation, State Pedagogical University of Russia, St. Petersburg.

Gagarina, Natalia
2000   The acquisition of aspectuality by Russian children: The early stages. *ZAS Papers in Linguistics* 15: 232–246.

Gagarina, Natalia
2001   Etapy razvitija grammaticheskoj sistemy jazyka v zerkale osvoenija grammatiki glagola (opyt predvaritel'nogo analiza). [The stages of the development of the grammatical system as a reflection of the acquisition of verb grammar]. *Proceedings of the conference on theory of Functional Grammar*, 260–271. St. Petersburg.

Gagarina, Natalia
2002   Thoughts on optional infinitives [in Russian]. In: Daniel Hole, Paul Law, and Niina Zhang (eds.), *Linguistics by heart, Web-fest for Horst-Dieter Gasde*, 1-23. Berlin: Zentrum für Allgemeine Sprachwissenschaft, Typologie und Universalienforschung (ZAS).

Gvozdev, Aleksandr
1949   *Formirovanije u rebenka grammaticheskogo stroja russkogo jazyka*. [The construction of the grammatical system of Russian by the child]. Moscow: Akademija Pedagogicheskih Nauk RSFSR.

Isačenko, Aleksandr N.
1960   *Grammatičeskij stroj russkogo jazaka v sopostavlenii so slovackim*. [The Russian grammar in comparison with the Slovac] Morfologija, Čast' 2. Bratislava: Izd-vo Slovackoj Akademii Nauk.

Jakobson, Roman
1987   Structure of the Russian verb. In: Linda R. Waugh, and Morris Halle (eds.), *Russian and Slavic grammar*, 1–14. Berlin: Mouton de Gruyter.

Kiebzak-Mandera, Dorota, Magdalena Smoczyńska, and Ekaterina Protassova
1997   Acquisition of Russian verb morphology: The early stages. In: Wolfgang U. Dressler (ed.), *Studies in Pre- and Protomorphology*, 101–114. Wien: Verlag der Österreichischen Akademie der Wissenschaften.

Kiebzak-Mandera, Dorota
2000   Formation of the verb system in Russian children. *Psychology of Language and Communication* 4: 27–46.

Kilani-Schoch, Marianne, Anna De Marco, Anastasia Christofidou, Maria Vassilakou, Ralph Vollmann, and Wolfgang U. Dressler

1997   On the demarcation of phases in early morphology acquisition in four languages. In: Katarzyna Dziubalska-Kołaczyk (ed.), *Pre- and Protomorphology in Language Acquisition*, 15–32. (Papers and Studies in Contrastive Linguistics 33.) Poznań: Adam Mickiewicz University.

Kilani-Schoch, Marianne, and Wolfgang U. Dressler
2000   The emergence of verb paradigms in two French corpora as an illustration of general problems of pre- and protomorphology. Poster presented at the 9th International Morphology Meeting, Vienna, February 2000.

Li, Ping, and Yasuhiro Shirai
2000   *The Acquisition of Lexical and Grammatical Aspect.* Berlin/New York: de Gruyter.

MacWhinney, Brian
2000   *The CHILDES Project: Tools for Analyzing Talk.* Vol. I: Transcription, Format and Programs. Mahwah, New Jersey: Lawrence Erlbaum.

Maslov, Jurij S.
1978   *Ocherki po aspektologii* [Drafts on aspectuality]. Leningrad: Leningradskij Gosudarstvennyj Universitet.

Pupynin, Jurij A.
1998   Elementy vido-vremennoj sistemy v detskoj rechi. [The elements of the system of tense and aspect in language acquisition]. *Voprosy jazykoznanija* 2: 102–116.

Sasse, Hans-Jürgen
2001   *Recent Activity in the Theory of Aspect: Accomplishments, Achievements, or just Non-progressive State?* (Arbeitspapier Nr. 40. Institut für Sprachwissenschaft, Universität zu Koeln.) Köln: Universität.

Šeljakin, Mihail A.
1987   Sposoby dejstvija v pole limitativnosti [Actionsarten in the field of limitedness]. In: Aleksandr V. Bondarko (ed.), *Teorija funkcional'noj grammatiki*, 63–85. Leningrad: Nauka.

Shirai, Yasuhiro, and Roger Andersen
1995   The acquisition of tense-aspect morphology: A prototype account. *Language* 71: 743–763.

Slobin, Dan (ed.)
1985   *The Crosslinguistic Study of Language Acquisition.* Vol. I. Hillsdale: Lawrence Erlbaum.

Smirnov, Jurij B.
2001   O vidovoj pare (v svjazi s razgranichenijem ponjatij "slovoizmenenije" i "slovoobrazovanije") [About an aspectual pair (in context of the demarcation of derivation and inflection)]. In: Alexander V. Bondarko, Marija K. Sabaneeva, Stella N. Ceytlin, Sad'je A. Shubik, Michail J. Dymarskij, Natalia V. Gagarina, Elena V. Andreeva, Jana E. Ahapkina (eds.), *Proceeding on the Conference "Theoretical Questions of Functional Grammar"*, 84–90. St. Petersburg: Nauka.

Smith, Carlota
1983   A theory of aspectual choice. *Language* 59: 479–501.

Smith, Carlota
1997   *The Parameter of Aspect.* 2nd ed. Dordrecht: Kluwer.

Snyder, Willian, and Eva Bar-Shalom
1998   Word order, finiteness, and negation in early child Russian. In: Annabel Greenhill, Mary Hughes, Heather Littlefield, and Hugh Walsh (eds.), *Proceedings of the 22d annual Boston University Conference on Language Development*, 717–725.

Švedova, Natalja J. (ed.)
1980   *Russkaja grammatika.* Moskva: Nauka.

Vendler, Zeno
1967   Verbs and times. In: Vendler, Zeno (ed.), *Linguistics in Philosophy*, 97–121. Ithaca, NY: Cornell University Press.

Verkuyl, Henk J.
1993   *A Theory of Aspectuality: The Interaction between Temporal and Atemporal Structure.* Cambridge: Cambridge University Press.

Weist, Richard
2002   The first language acquisition of tense and aspect: A review. In: Rafael Salaberry, and Yasuhiro Shirai (eds.), *The L2 Acquisition of Tense-aspect Morphology*, 21–78. Amsterdam: John Benjamins.

Wiemer, Bjoern
2001 Aspektual'nyje paradigmy i leksicheskoje znachenije russkix i litovskix glagolov [The aspectual paradigms and lexical meaning of verbs in Lithuanian and Russian]. *Voprosy jazykoznanija* 2: 26–58.

Wurzel, Wolfgang U.
1987 System-dependent morphological naturalness in inflection. In: Wolfgang U. Dressler (ed.), *Leitmotifs in Natural Morphology*, 59–98. Amsterdam/Philadelphia: John Benjamins.

A case study of the early acquisition of verbs in Dutch

Steven Gillis

0. Introduction

In this paper we report on one child's morphological development. The child acquires Dutch as a first language, and her language acquisition is followed from 1;5 till 2;5. Naturalistic observational data from bimonthly observation sessions are analyzed. We start with a global quantitative characterization of the child's use of verbs: cumulative overviews if the child's verb lexicon in terms of lemmas, verb types and her verb usage in terms of tokens will be presented. The child's developing verb lexicon is described in terms of the verb categories *main verb*, *auxiliary* and *copula*, and in addition verb use is analyzed from a syntagmatic perspective. A developmental analysis of the morphology of main verbs, auxiliaries and copulas is presented. It turns out that a relatively clear delineation of a premorphological and a protomorphological stage can be made on a purely quantitative basis. Against this background the child's cumulative lexicon is analyzed in terms of the emergence and elaboration of verbal mini-paradigms.

1. The Dutch verbal system

This introduction covers a number of basic facts about the verb phrase in Dutch as far as they are relevant for the early stages of acquisition.[1] Like other Germanic languages, Dutch has a two-term tense distinction on the basis of inflectional contrasts: present and past. Furthermore, the verb encodes the grammatical categories of person and number.

The imperative does not distinguish between singular and plural and is generally expressed by the verb stem without an explicit subject (as in (1)). If the addressee is to be foregrounded, the second person (singular (2) or plural (3)) pronoun may be combined with the indicative verbal form. The clause then has inverted word order, as in interrogative clauses (as in (4)):

(1) kijk!
    'look!'
(2) kijk jij daar maar eens!
    'look you-SG there!'
(3) kijken jullie daar maar eens!
    'look you-PL there!'
(4) kijken jullie daar eens?
    'look you-PL there?'

A distinction between on the one hand lexical verbs, and, on the other hand modals, copulas, and auxiliariesis in order. On the whole, the inflection of lexical verbs is regular, while the inflection of auxiliaries, copulas, and modals is (largely) irregular (through the use of suppletive forms).

Regular Dutch lexical verbs have a stem, to which bound morphemes can be added as an affix. The present indicative has three forms: (1) the verb stem, used for the first person singular (and for the second person singular in clauses with inversion); (2) the verb stem plus -*t* for the second and the third person singular (except for the second person in inversion, see (1)); and (3) the verb stem plus -*en* (/∂(n)/[2] for plural forms irrespective of person. This paradigm is illustrated in (5).

(5)

Person	Lexical verb	Example (werken 'to work')
1S	stem	werk
2S (inversion)	stem	werk
2S	stem+t	werkt
3S	stem+t	werkt
1-3P	stem + en	werken

But, for the copula / auxiliary *zijn* 'to be', the auxiliary *hebben* 'to have' and the modal *kunnen* 'can', the corresponding present indicative forms look as follows:

(6)

Person	zijn 'be'	hebben 'have'	kunnen 'can'
1S	ben	heb	kan
2S (inversion)	ben	heb	kan
2S	bent	hebt	kan
3S	is	heeft	kan
1-3P	zijn	hebben	kunnen

Dutch has two infinitives, viz. a bare infinitive and a *te*-infinitive. The former consists of the stem followed by the suffix /ə(n)/ or /n/, which yields the same form as the plural present form. The *te*-infinitive consists of *te* plus the bare infinitive. The distribution between the two infinitives depends on their syntactic environment. In present day Dutch, the *te*-infinitive appears to be constantly gaining ground on its bare counterpart (De Schutter 1994): the *te*-infinitive is required with prepositions and with a growing number of auxiliaries.

The simple past (preterit) of weak verbs, the regular case, is derived from the stem by adding /tə/ or /də/ in the singular (as in (7) and /tə(n)/ or /də(n)/ in the plural as in (8). The suffixes /tə/ and /tə(n)/ are restricted to stems ending in a voiceless obstruent.

(7) Ik/jij/hij werkte
 'I/you/he worked'
 Ik/jij/hij voelde
 'I/you/he felt'

(8) Wij/jullie/zij werkten
 'We/you-PL/they worked'
 Wij/jullie/zij voelden
 'We/you-PL/they felt'

The simple past form of strong verbs shows vowel alternation: a fairly large number of formal classes can be distinguished, though only a few of them contain more than ten verbs (Geerts et al. 1984). Most of these verb classes with vowel alternation in the simple past are not productive, and consist of high frequency verbs (see below).

The past participle in Dutch is formed by adding the prefix /ɣə/ and the suffix /t/ or /d/ to the stem.[3] The prefix is not added when the stem is already preceded by prefixes such as *ver-*, *be-*, *ont-*, etc. Weak verbs undergo regular past participle formation. Strong verbs show a more complicated pattern, with vowel and/or consonant alternation.

The standard Dutch grammar ANS (Geerts et al. 1984) distinguishes several classes of strong verbs, depending on the (ir)regularity of the simple past and/or the past participle. In addition to the fully regular paradigm, a semi-irregular paradigm and a fully irregular paradigm are distinguished. Semi-irregular verbs are those of which either the simple past (9) or the past participle (10) are irregular.

(9) vragen   vroeg   gevraagd
    'to ask' 'asked' 'asked'
(10) bakken   bakte   gebakken
     'to bake' 'baked' 'baked'

Fully irregular strong verbs are those verbs of which both forms are irregular, as in (11):

(11) smijten   smeet   gesmeten
     'to throw' 'threw' 'thrown'

     kopen   kocht   gekocht
     'to buy' 'bought' 'bought'

Verb phrases in Dutch can be 'simple' or 'complex'. A simple verb phrase consists of one verb element only. A complex verb phrase consists of up to four verb elements. In principle, every verb phrase, whether simple or complex, contains one and only one finite element, which shows congruence with an overt or elided subject. In principle the finite form always occupies the second sentence position, while the non-finite part of the verbs phrase occupies the final position. More precisely: Dutch is a verb-second language with an (underlying) SOV structure. Clauses have the main verb at the end. But, leaving out unnecessary complicating facts, there is a rule that moves the finite verb to the first position of the main (interrogative or imperative) clause or to the second position of the (declarative) main clause. This means that if there is no auxiliary in the clause, the finite form of main verb has to occupy the first or second position of the clause. Consequently, the canonical sentence final position of the verb remains 'empty' (see (12)). However, complex verbs leave behind their phrasal particles in sentence final position (see (13)).

(12) ik neem een appel
     'I take an apple'
(13) ik neem een appel **mee**
     'I take an apple with-me'

2. Data

The data analyzed in this paper stem from longitudinal observations of the Flemish Dutch-speaking girl Jolien. She was recorded at her home twice a month in an unstructured setting, interacting with her mother and the observer, and occasionally with her father, older sister and grandparents. The child was followed twice a month between the ages of 1;5 and 2;5. In what follows, all observations will be grouped per month.

The data were transcribed in CHAT format. The audio tapes were transcribed orthographically. In addition to the orthographic transcription of all participants' utterances, a phonemic transcription of the child's utterances was produced. The data were further annotated morpho-syntactically: all wordforms were lemmatized, part-of-speech tagged and morphologically decomposed using the full-form version of the CLAN program MOR. The tag set and the formal definitions of the tags were adapted from the standard Dutch reference grammar ANS (Geerts et al. 1984) and from the CGN ('Spoken Dutch Corpus') tagset (Van Eynde 2000). For this coding the actual form of the child's utterance was decisive. For instance, if the child uttered /vɑl/ (stem: /vɑl/, infinitive: /vɑlə/, past participle: /ɣəvɑlə/), the form was coded as a bare stem, even if in the next turn the child's mother replied with an infinitive or a past participle.

Data reduction: the following types of utterances were excluded from the data analysis: all utterance consisting exclusively of a babbles (indicated with the suffix @b in the transcript), utterances marked as incomprehensible (yy, yyy, xx, xxx) in the transcript, and utterances marked as 'www'. This step of data reduction yields the set of analyzable utterances, see table 1.

Table 1. Overview of the child's analyzable utterances, number of words and MLU (as calculated by CLAN on the orthographic transcription tier), the number and percentage of utterances with verbs and the number of tokens of verbs

	Number of analyzable utterances	Number of words	MLU	# Utterances with verb(s)	% Utterances with verb(s)	# Verb tokens
1;5	113	114	1.009	14	12.4	14
1;6	365	379	1.038	43	11.8	43
1;7	107	113	1.056	17	15.9	17
1;8	182	201	1.104	33	18.1	33
1;9	227	275	1.211	34	15.0	35
1;10	158	244	1.544	44	27.8	52
1;11	85	154	1.812	30	35.3	32
2;0	180	364	2.022	64	35.6	71
2;1	411	837	2.036	94	22.9	101
2;2	291	567	1.948	106	36.4	115

Table 1. continued

2;3	130	357	2.746	63	48.5	82
2;4	342	864	2.526	171	50.0	202
2;5	288	714	2.479	117	40.6	141

3. Precursors of verb forms

The first words that children acquire are closely linked with their direct experience: children's first words function in interaction with other people, they are part of games children play, they are used in connection with specific people and things, and they are expressions of affect such as comfort and discomfort (see Gillis 1984; Gillis and De Schutter 1986; De Houwer and Gillis 1998; Elbers and Van Loon-Vervoorn 1998, 2000 for Dutch examples, and Barrett 1995 for a selective overview of children's early words in languages other than Dutch).

These first 'words' (the term 'protowords' or 'phonetically consistent forms' may be more appropriate, cf. Gillis (1984); De Houwer and Gillis (1998)) have two defining characteristics: they recur in the child's vocal repertoire in a relatively consistent phonetic form and they occur in particular situations or are tied to particular events. In other words, these early 'words' are clusters of consistent sounds exhibiting a functional content.

There are two types of words that may be considered as precursors of verbs in Jolien's data. The first one is exemplified by the adult verb *kijk!* 'look!' which is actually used as an attention getting or an attention directing device (Dore et al. 1976, Dore 1985). Although formally it is a bare stem, the word probably only has a pragmatic function for Jolien, comparable to a demonstrative (like 'that!') used by other children (see De Houwer and Gillis 1998). Hence it is not quite clear if these words function as genuine verbs for the child. From 1;5 (the beginning of the observations) until 1;6 Jolien only uses the bare stem of the verb *kijken* 'to look' most frequently in one word utterances (*kijk!*) and she does not use another form of the verb. From 1;6 onwards, the stem alternates with the infinitive, thus yielding clearer evidence for the status of the word as a verb, see (14)–(15).

(14) *JOL: kijk.   (1;6)
      %mor: v:main|kijken&IMP&SG
      %eng: look

(15) *JOL: (h)ier kijken.   (1;9)
      %mor: adv|hier v:main|kijken-INF.
      %eng: here look

The second type of early words that can be seen as precursors of verbs, is closely tied to the specific objects and/or events. The term 'event' must be understood here in a very broad way as it may include social-interactional routines such as the give-and-take game or someone entering or leaving the room, or specific child activities such as throwing things or pushing toy cars around. Or it may be a perceptually salient event such as the noise of cars in the street or a dog barking. Jolien uses onomatopoeia such as *kwaak* for ducks, *beu* for cows, *boem* for hammering, etc. Some of these are lexical verbs in adult Dutch (e.g., *kwaken* 'to quack'), others are onomatopoeia (cf. in the adult language they can only be used in conjunction with alight verb such as *doen* 'to do').

Gillis (1984) and Gillis and De Houwer (1998) discuss these precursors in detail. They conclude that especially in the early stages it is rather difficult to pinpoint their exact reference. For instance, does *kwaak* 'quack' refer to the noise a duck makes, or to aduck quacking, or to a duck (see Barrett 1986 for highly similar examples and an analysis along the same line).

A similar observation holds for genuine (adult) verbs like *drinken* 'to drink', *eten* 'to eat' which are homophonous nouns / verbs. Hence when the child uses these words in single word utterances (ex. 16 and 17), it is very difficult to decide if she intends them as a verb ('I want *to drink*') or as a noun ('I want to have *something to drink*'), or as an ambiguous noun/verb of which the reference (and the category) is not clear. It is not until 2;4 that we find unambiguous evidence for a clear differentiation between noun-like and verb-like usage (ex. 18 and 19): in (18) *drinken* en *eten* are preceded by the determiner *de* 'the', and can thus be considered as nouns, and in (19) the verb *drinken* occurs with a surface subject (*die* 'that-one')and object (*wortel* 'carrot'.

(16) *JOL: drinken.   (1;8)
      %mor: v:main|drinken-INF^n|drinken.
      %eng: drink
(17) *JOL: drinken water hebben.   (1;11)
      %mor: v:main|drinken-INF^n|drinken n|water v:main|hebben-INF.
      %eng: drink water have

(18) *JOL: met de drinken met de eten. (2;4)
%mor: prep|met det:def|de n|drinken prep|met det:def|de n|eten.
%eng: with the drink with the eat [= food].

(19) *JOL: die drinken wortel uit zo. (2;4)
%mor: pro:deic|die v:main|uit#drinken-INF n|wortel adv|zo.
%eng: this-one drink carrot like-this out.

A last precursor of early verbs is the child's use of verbal particles. In Dutch, like in English and German, verbs can be prefixed with an adverb (e.g., *buitenwippen* 'to throw out') or a preposition (e.g., *uitdoen* 'to take off'). The so-called verbal particle of these separable verbs is often used in isolation by children, leaving the verb unexpressed (20)–(21). Examples (22) and (23) illustrate the use of the verb *aandoen* 'to put on'. In (22) the child uses only the verbal particle, while in (23) she uses the particle as well as the verb.

(20) *JOL: open. (1;5)
%mor: part|open.
%eng: open

(21) *JOL: ik heb die uit +... (2;1)
%mor: pro:pers|ik v:aux|hebben&PRES&1/2SG pro:deic|die part|uit.
%eng: I have that-one off

(22) *JOL: ik wil ook een trui aan. (2;2)
%mor: pro:pers|ik v:mod|willen&PRES&1/2/3SG adv|ook det:indef|een n|trui part|aan
%eng: I want also a sweater on

(23) *JOL: kap aandoen. (1;8)
%mor: n|kap v:main|aan#doen-INF.
%eng: hood put on

In the analyses presented in the following sections, these precursors of verbs will not be considered unless there are sufficient evidence for their use as verbs. The attention getting/directing word *kijk!* 'look!' will only be considered when the child's cumulative vocabulary also contains another form of the verb in addition to the bare stem. A similar approach will be taken for ambiguous words like *drinken* 'a drink – to drink' (see examples

(16)–(19)): when the syntactic context makes clear that the word is used either a noun or a verb, the word will be considered as such, otherwise, it will not be considered in the cumulative counts of the child's vocabulary. The onomatopoeia will not be considered as verbs unless they are also verbs in the adult language and unless a clear referential meaning can be established.

4. Global characterization of the child's use of verbs

In this section we will analyze the child's acquisition of verb lemmas, types, and tokens. The acquisition of verbs will be compared with the acquisition of nouns (lemmas, types and tokens) so as to be able to appreciate the relative amount of verbs and the relative pace of their acquisition. In section 5.1. we will look at the types of verbs that enter the child's vocabulary (main verbs, auxiliaries, copulas) and in section 5.2. the sentential context of the child's verbs will be touched upon.

4.1. Verb lemmas and types

In table 2 a cumulative overview of the child's verbs is presented. In the first observation session (at 1;5), Jolien uses 5 verbs (lemmas). Gradually her stock of verbs increases and reaches 105 verb lemmas at 2;5. Proportionally speaking, this means that the share of verbs in the complete cumulative lexicon increases steadily from less than 10 %[4] to 18% in the last month. For the sake of comparison, table 2 also contains the data for nouns. At 1;5 the child has 25 noun lemmas, and that amount has increased to 367 noun lemmas at 2;5. Thus, the growth rate of nouns and verbs is very different: for noun lemmas there is an average increase with 28.5 lemmas per month while for verb lemmas the average increase is 8.3 lemmas.

Table 2 also shows the data for the child's verb types: the number of different types increases from 5 at 1;5 to 179 at 2;5, in the same period the number of noun types increases from 25 to 459. This means that the average growth rate for verbs is 14.5 and for nouns 36.2. Thus for lemmas as well as word types, the contingent of nouns growths much faster than the contingent of verbs.

Table 2. Cumulative number of verbs (lemmas and types) and noun (lemmas and types) with their increase in consecutive months

Age	Lemmas			Types		
	Verbs	Nouns	Total	Verbs	Nouns	Total
1;5	5	25	39	5	25	39
1;6	8	73	98	11	73	102
1;7	11	95	123	14	97	129
1;8	20	122	162	24	126	171
1;9	27	161	216	35	169	234
1;10	43	182	263	53	197	292
1;11	49	198	292	61	219	330
2;0	57	231	341	73	254	389
2;1	67	264	403	95	304	489
2;2	77	290	451	112	343	560
2;3	81	308	479	125	365	603
2;4	92	341	538	154	419	704
2;5	105	367	584	179	459	777
Mean increase	8.3	28.5		14.5	36.2	61.5

In terms of the relative amount of nouns and verbs on the total number of word lemmas, the increase of verbs is gradual (see figure 1, in which only nouns and verbs are shown).

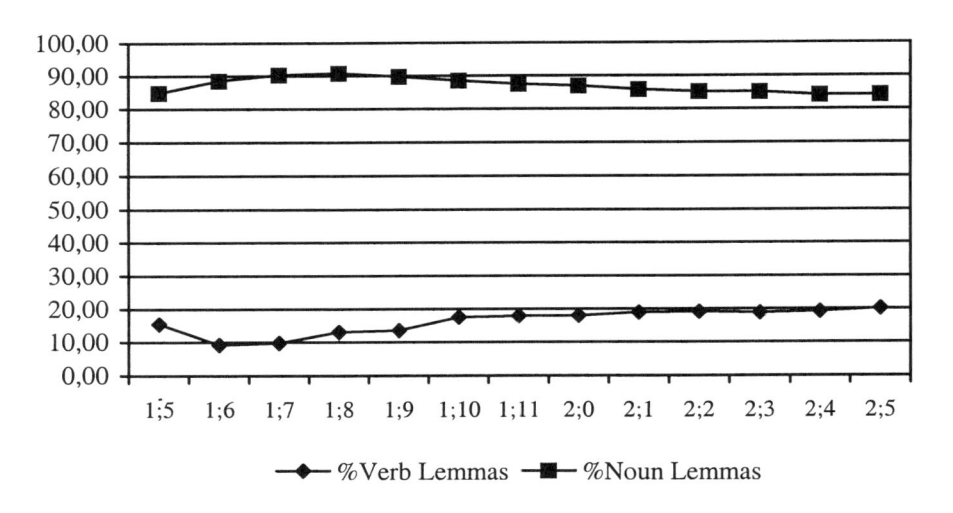

Figure 1. Percentage of noun and verb lemmas in the child's cumulative lexicon

Verbs represent a relatively stable proportion of the lemmas. The relative amount of nouns increases up to 80% of all words at 1;7, and from then on it decreases to around 65%. The proportion of verbs is much lower: at the very beginning it is below 10% and then steadily increases to ca. 20%. Thus judging from the child's cumulative lexicon, there is no verb spurt, i.e., an abrupt increase of the number of verb lemmas relative to other word classes. However there is an increase in the number of new verb lemmas per month. The mean number of new verb lemmas per month is 8.33. The figures in table 2 show that while this mean value is hardly or not attained in the first months, it is readily exceeded in the second half of the observation period. For verb forms a similar observation holds: the mean number of new verb forms per month is 14.5. This number is exceeded in the second half of the study, but not in the first months. Thus, there are clear indications of an acceleration of the pace with which Jolien acquires new verbs (both lemmas and forms).

The most interesting comparison is that between the new lemmas and the new verb types in the child's cumulative lexicon. In figure 2 the absolute number of new verb lemmas and verb types is plotted. We compared the cumulative number of verb lemmas in two consecutive sessions, and the difference between them is in the plot. The same was done for verb types. At the beginning of the observation period, the two lines are virtually identical: when the child acquires a new lemma, there is only one type representing that lemma. However, the two lines start deviating dramatically between 2;0 and 2;1. Thus, we may safely conclude that until the age of 2;0 the child has hardly any morphological oppositions within a verb lemma. Oppositions turn up from 2;0 onwards.

By way of comparison, the same exercise was done for noun lemmas and noun types (simplex, plural, diminutive and diminutive plural forms of a noun were taken as separate types). It appears that for nouns, the discrepancy between the line representing lemmas and the one representing forms is minimal at the very beginning, which suggests that the child has only one noun type for each lemma. Morphological variation turns up from 2;0 onwards: as for verbs, lemmas start occurring in different 'disguises', i.e. for several noun lemmas there are different types.

These comparisons indicate that at the beginning of the third year of life, the child starts using different forms of the same verb lemma, so that the discrepancy between the number of new word types relative to the number of new lemmas increases. At the same moment, a similar development can be seen for nouns. This means that around 2;0 morphology makes its first appearance, in the sense that there is a first upsurge of variations of word forms (for nouns as well as verbs). This may indicate the transition between premorphology and protomorphology.

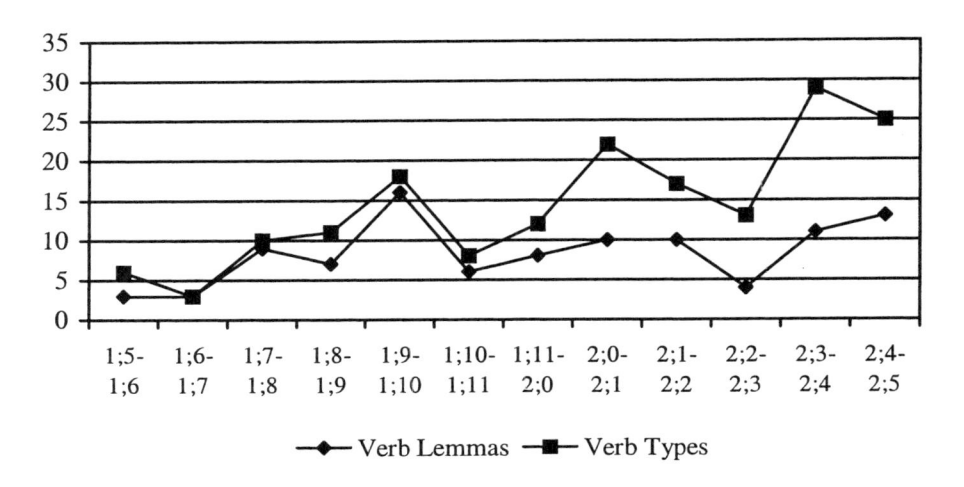

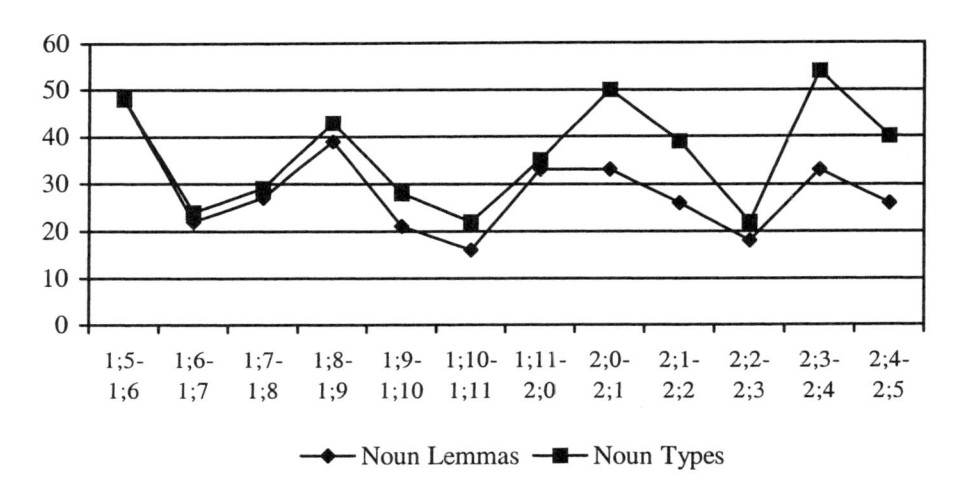

Figure 2. Number of new verb lemmas and forms and number of new noun lemmas and forms in the child's cumulative vocabulary

4.2. Category analysis: Paradigmatic

Which verbs does the child use? In table 3 a cumulative overview is provided of the main verbs, auxiliaries (including modals) and copulas that the child uses spontaneously. It is quite clear that the major proportion of the child's cumulative vocabulary consists of main verbs. From the very beginning of the observation period main verbs comprise an average of 90% of all verb lemmas. There is a break between 2;0 and 2;1: until 2;0 the child's lexicon consists almost exclusively of main lexical verbs. After that the auxiliaries and the copula *zijn* ('be') come in.

Table 3. Cumulative number of lemmas of main verbs, auxiliaries and copulas, cumulative number of verb lemmas and cumulative number of all lemmas.

Age	Main verbs	Auxiliaries	Copula	Total verb lemmas	Total lemmas
1;5	4	1		5	39
1;6	7	1		8	98
1;7	10	1		11	123
1;8	19	1		20	162
1;9	25	2		27	216
1;10	40	3		43	263
1;11	46	3		49	292
2;0	53	3	1	57	341
2;1	58	8	1	67	403
2;2	68	8	1	77	451
2;3	72	8	1	81	479
2;4	81	10	1	92	538
2;5	93	11	1	105	584

This break between 2;0 and 2;1 is also evident when we consider the actual verb tokens. In figure 3 the percentage of verb tokens relative to the total number of verb forms is displayed: till 2;0 the majority of tokens of verbs are tokens of main verbs. This number starts decreasing rapidly after 2;0, and since the number of auxiliaries and copulas is very restricted, this means that these latter categories are repeated relatively often.

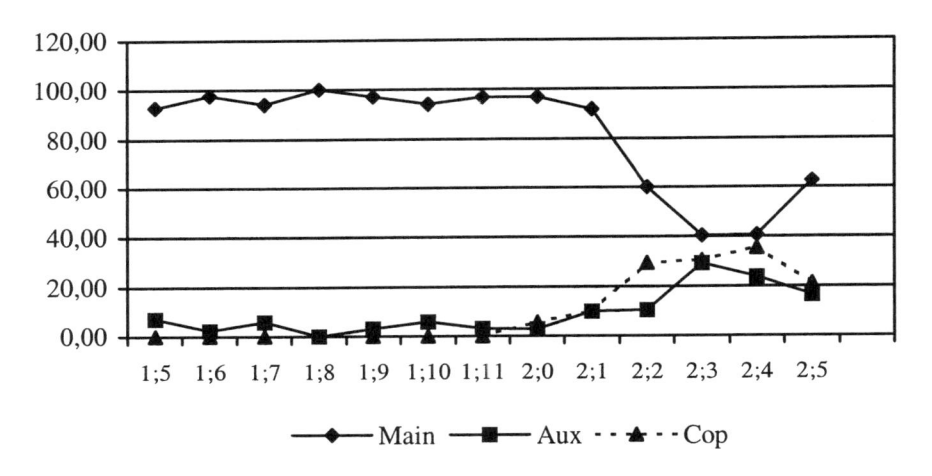

Figure 3. Percentage of tokens of main verbs, auxiliaries and copulas relative to the total number of verb tokens

4.3. Category analysis: Syntagmatic

The use of auxiliaries is especially interesting. It is not only the case the child acquires auxiliaries, and starts using them more frequently at a particular moment, there is also a prominent syntactic development. In table 4, utterances that contain a verb are split into four categories: utterances with one verb form versus utterances with more than one verb form. The former category is further divided according to the type of verb: main lexical verbs, auxiliaries and copulas. The latter category represents periphrastic verb phrases which consist of an auxiliary and a main verb. There is a clear developmental pattern: at the onset of the observation period, the child uses only one verb per utterance, and most of these verbs are main lexical verbs. From 2;0 onwards, the child starts using the copula 'be' in a productive way, especially in combination with a demonstrative or a locative adverb. Periphrastic verb phrases are only used with reasonable frequency from 2;3 onwards in the typical pattern with the finite verb form (auxiliary, modal) in the second sentential position and the non finite verb form in sentence final position. Note that auxiliaries are not only used in periphrastic verb phrases, they also occur as single (finite) verbs forms in sentences.

Table 4. Percentage of utterances with a main verb, auxiliary, copula and a periphrastic verb phrase

Age	% Main verb	% Auxiliary	% Copula	% Auxiliary + Main verb
1;5	92.86	7.14		
1;6	97.67	2.33		
1;7	94.12	5.88		
1;8	100.00			
1;9	97.06			2.94
1;10	93.33	2.22		4.44
1;11	96.77			3.23
2;0	80.60		16.42	2.99
2;1	80.20	3.96	9.90	5.94
2;2	60.00	4.35	29.57	6.09
2;3	40.00	7.50	31.25	21.25
2;4	39.90	10.10	36.36	13.64
2;5	62.77	3.65	20.44	13.14

From a syntagmatic perspective, there is still another important factor that needs examination, viz. congruence: in Dutch the finite verb should agree in person and number with the subject. Thus we may expect that from the child's perspective different forms of the same lemma are far less functional if no subject is expressed than when an overt subject occurs. Consequently, the more overt subjects, the more different verb forms we expect. Or conversely, the more different verb forms the child has mastered, the more need there is for discovering a function for these forms, and, hence, the more overtly expressed subjects we may expect. Whatever the direction of causality (morphology driving syntax or syntax driving morphology), we expect a close relationship in time between the development of both aspects.

First of all, there is a clear progression in the realization of overt subjects: Figure 4 shows the percentage of utterances with and without an overt subject. From 1;10 onwards more and more subjects are realized overtly. At age 2;4 there is an overt subject in 75% of the utterances. Thus in a majority of cases the syntactic prerequisite for realizing agreement between the subject and the finite verb is present. In figure 5 we connect the presence / absence of an overt subject with the nature of the verb, i.e. finite versus non finite verb form. Figure 5 shows that from 2;2 onwards, there is an overt subject with a finite verb form in a majority of the sentences the child produces. Subjectless sentences have a finite or a non finite verb (with no clear preference for either of them) but sentences with a subject overwhelmingly prefer a finite verb. Moreover, the number of sentences with correct agreement is considerable: from 1;11 onwards the percentage of sentences with an overt subject in which the verb agrees with the subject in number and person, increases from 71% to more than 95%.

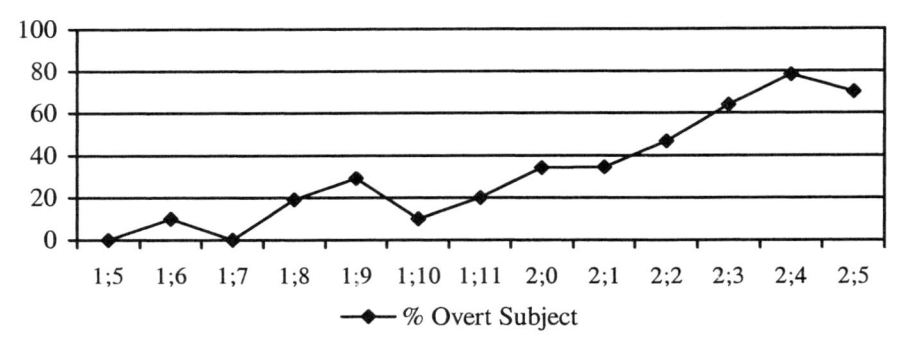

Figure 4. Percentage of utterances with an overt subject

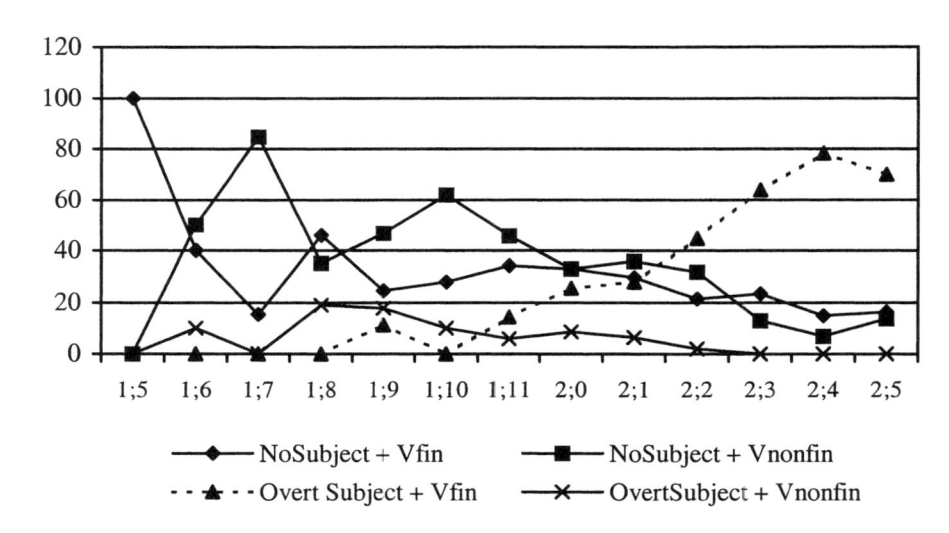

Figure 5. Percentage of sentences with/without an overt subject and the accompanying finite / non finite verb form

From this short analysis of the syntagmatics and paradigmatics of verbs, it can be concluded that for the child's verb use, 2;0 – 2;1 is an important turning point: around that moment, the child's verb usage seems to undergo a major transition both qualitatively and quantitatively. In what follows, we will discuss the morphology of verbs and also from this respect the beginning of the child's third year of life will appear to be critical.

5. Main verb forms

In table 5 an overview is provided in terms of lemmas and tokens of the verbs that the child uses during the period studied. For this analysis the actual forms produced by the child were considered and their formal properties were analyzed. The following verb forms were distinguished:

- *0* morpheme: this category comprises both the indicative and the imperative such *loop* 'run' which are formally not distinguishable; also verbs ending in *-t* (or underlying /d/) that have a homophonous form for the first, second and third person indicative present, were categorized as zero morpheme or (bare) stem forms.
- *-en* infinitive morpheme: this category comprises all verb forms with an *-en* ending. They can be formally distinguished as such, though they are formally ambiguous between the infinitival form and the present indicative plural form. For the present analysis all *-en* forms were collected in the same category, except for the verb forms ending in *-en* that had a clear plural subject. These are indicated in the table as *-en (PL)*.
- *-t* morpheme: all verb forms with a stem that does not end in an alveolar stop, were categorized under the heading *-t* morpheme.
- Past participles are categorized as such if they are formally unambiguous. This means that for regular past participle the presence of a prefix *ge-* was required (e.g., *geval* instead of the adult form *gevallen* was nevertheless categorized as a past participle, while *vallen* was categorized as an *-en* infinitive).

Table 5. Overview of affixes (Le = lemmas, To = tokens)

Age	-0		-e		-t		Past PP		-en (PL)	
	Le	To	Le	To	Le	To	Le	To	Le	To
1;5	4	13								
1;6	2	3	4	5						
1;7	2	7	4	9						
1;8	4	18	8	14						
1;9	2	8	13	23	2	2				
1;10	3	8	16	35	1	1	2	4		
1;11	3	10	9	16			2	4		
2;0	5	21								

Table 5. continued

Age	-0		-e		-t		Past		PP		-en (PL)	
	Le	To	Le	To	Le	To	Le	To	Le	To	Le	To
2;1	3	23	17	44	4	6	2	2	1	1		
2;2	3	19	18	37	3	8			5	5		
2;3	3	5	5	14	1	1	1	1	2	4		
2;4	5	25	23	34	2	4			6	8	1	1
2;5	5	30	19	35	5	5			3	8	1	2

The child starts out with two forms: first the bare stem (at 1;5) and the infinitive (at 1;6). Except for the first month, the -en infinitive occurs much more frequently and with many more verbs (lemmas) than the bare stem. Other types of verb forms come in later: the -t form at 1;9, the past form at 1;10, the past participle at 2;1, and the present plural at 2;4. All of the latter are rather infrequent when they first appear, both in terms of the lemmas and tokens.

In order to further appreciate these findings, the cumulative number of lemmas appearing as an infinitive (-en morpheme), a bare stem (-0 morpheme), a second/third person singular (-t morpheme), a plural form (present indicative -en morpheme), as a simple past form (past) and as a past participle (pp) are plotted out in figure 6.

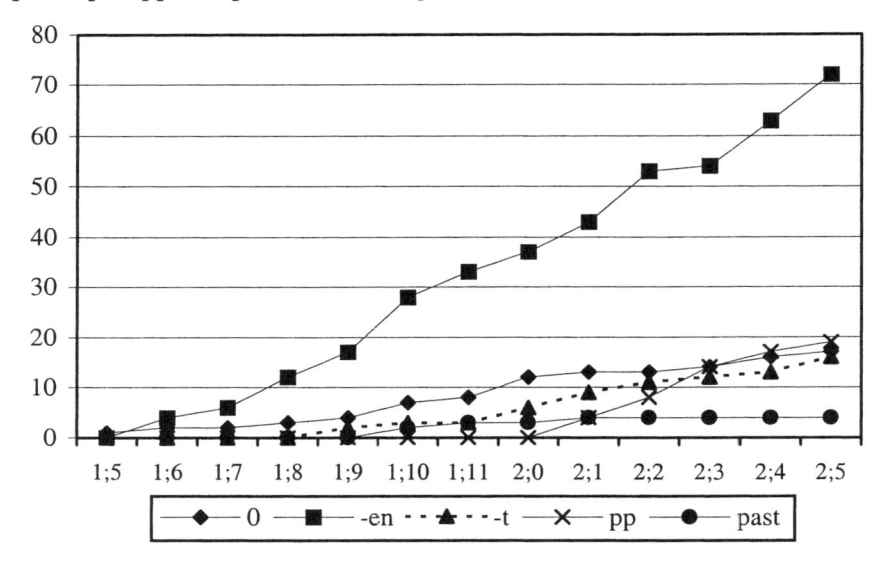

Figure 6. Number of lemmas for each morphological form

It is quite clear – once again – that the infinitive is pervasive. Around the child's second birthday, -*t* morphology as well as the past participle start occurring with an increasing number of verbs. This can be taken to indicate that only from then onwards the child discovers variations of verb forms and reflects them in her own productive verb usage.

Bare stems occupy a rather peculiar place in the child's production. First of all they appear early. And although far less lemmas occur as bare stems than as infinitives over time, the fact that they occur alongside infinitives (see below for the mini-paradigms in which bare stems enter) is rather troublesome at first sight. These bare stems are especially noteworthy since in the literature it has been reported that the earliest stage of verb development can be characterized as a 'root infinitive stage' during which infinitives and other verb forms hardly overlap (Jordens 1990; Wijnen and Verrips 1998). In other words, -*en* infinitives are expected, but stems (or other forms of the verb) are not expected to occur. In this respect three remarks are crucial. First of all, bare stems are used to express the first person, of the present indicative as well as the imperative singular. Formally they are not distinguishable. So it may be the case that all these stems are actually imperatives. In a number of cases this may well be the case, but it is highly speculative assumption. Secondly, especially in the earliest observation sessions, bare stems may be the result of phonological processes: truncations of multisyllabic word forms are reported frequently in the earliest stages of acquisition. These truncations typically take the form of the deletion of non-final weak (or unstressed) syllables. More specifically, multisyllabic words are often reduced to a trochaic pattern (Fikkert 1994, 1998; Gillis 2000). But these typical truncation patterns do not explain the reduction of a trochaic infinitive to a monosyllabic stem. However, Taelman and Gillis (2001) point at a high incidence of intra word (as well as inter word) variation in children's early multisyllabic productions. Children's productions are highly variable in the sense that a particular word can occur in various forms even in consecutive utterances. This phenomenon of intra word variation may explain the occurrence of a verb as an infinitive and a bare stem. A third remark concerns the phonological structure of these verbs. A closer examination of the bare stems that occur in the later sessions, reveals that most of them end in a dental stop (e.g., *lust* 'likes', *zit* 'sit', *eet* 'eat', *fluit* 'whistles', *weet* 'know'). In these verb forms, the stem and the second/third person singular present indicative are not distinguishable: the stem ends in a -*t* and the second/third person normally takes a -*t* as suffix, but due to degemination there is no difference between the two forms. Thus, the occurrence of these forms may actually be instances of the -*t* suffixation instead of -*0*suffixation.

6. Auxiliaries and copulas

In table 3 a cumulative overview was provided of the number of verb lemmas, including the auxiliaries and the copula(s). In figure 3 it was shown that the proportion of tokens of the auxiliaries and the copula starts rising rapidly around the child's second birthday. In table 6 an overview is provided of the child's use of auxiliaries and copulas. In terms of lemmas (per session as well as cumulatively) 2;0 – 2;1 again proves to be a turning point: the child uses twice as many auxiliaries (lemmas) than before and the cumulative count doubles. In the same vein, there is a considerable increase of the number of types and tokens of auxiliaries. Given this background, we will have a look at the child's acquisition and use of these verb forms in more detail.

Table 6. Number of lemmas, types and tokens of auxiliaries and copulas and cumulative number of lemmas of auxiliaries and copulas

Age	# Auxiliary			# Copula			Cumulative Number of Lemmas
	lemmas	types	tokens	lemmas	types	tokens	
1;5	1	1	1				1
1;6	1	1	1				1
1;7	1	1	1				1
1;8							1
1;9	1	1	1				2
1;10	3	3	3				3
1;11	1	1	1				3
2;0	2	2	2	1	1	11	4
2;1	5	8	10	1	1	10	8
2;2	6	6	12	1	2	34	8
2;3	5	7	24	1	2	25	8
2;4	7	12	48	1	5	72	10
2;5	6	10	23	1	2	30	11

The first auxiliary shows up at 1;5: the child uses *kunnen* 'can' in the phrase (amalgam) *kan niet* 'can not' (*kan* is the present indicative form for singular). This usage recurs in the following sessions, and it is the only auxiliary that shows up until 1;9. At 1;9 the auxiliary *laten* 'let' is used. Also *laten* has only one form for the first, second and third person singular present indicative, viz. *laat* 'let' and it occurs in the phrase (amalgam) *laat eens zien* 'let once see' which means 'show me!' At 1;10 *willen* 'want' and at 2;0 the copula *zijn* 'be' are introduced. The big step comes at 2;1 when four new auxiliaries enter the child's vocabulary: *gaan* 'go', *moeten* 'have to', *hebben* 'have', and the auxiliary *zijn* 'be' (in addition to the copula *zijn* 'be'). The example of *zijn* 'be' is important: it clearly shows that the child's use of these auxiliaries is not like the formulaic usage mentioned with respect to *kunnen* 'can' en *laten* 'let' above. In fact the child uses the same verb in two grammatically different ways: as a copula and as a temporal auxiliary (to form the perfective). Similarly, when we follow an auxiliary such as *kunnen* 'can' we see that it becomes less formulaic (i.e., tied to a specific phrase): *kan* appears as *kan niet* 'can not' (1;6 – 1;10) and after that in *kan hard bijten* 'can bite hard' (2;0), *kan het niet vertellen* 'can not tell it' (2;2), *die kan staan* 'that-one can stand' (2;4), and the like.

The introduction of the auxiliaries also permits the child to form complex verbs (a finite form of a modal auxiliary plus a main verb in its non finite form). Moreover temporal auxiliaries are used in the indicative perfective (which occurs in addition to the indicative present and imperfectum, see section 6). From 2;1 onwards the child uses the verb *hebben* 'have' as a main verb and as a temporal auxiliary: *mama heeft verteld hier* 'mama has told (a story) here' versus *lepel hebben* 'spoon have' (2;1).

7. Emergence of mini-paradigms

Bittner, Dressler, and Kilani-Schoch (this volume) and Bittner (2000) propose criteria for determining if an inflectional type is a potential member of a paradigm. These criteria include that the verb form is (1) not imitative, (2) not formulaic, (3) articulatory accurate, (4) used in contrasting contexts, (5) recurring. In the present study some of these criteria were strictly adhered to: only those verbs used non imitatively were considered, i.e. the verb should not occur in the turn preceding the child's turn in which the verb occurs. It should not be formulaic in the sense that it should not be surrounded by exactly the same lexical material in a majority of cases. The criterion of articulatory accuracy is dealt with in the sense that as a target the adult form was taken that most closely resembled the child's rendition in a / some critical feature / features (see the discussion of past participles in section 3). The criterion of recurrence was adhered to in the sense that a contrast was validated if it occurred in more than one session. The criterion of 'contrasting contexts' was also adhered to in the sense that 'contrasting contexts' were strictly taken to mean 'contrasting lexical contexts': if as Tomasello (1992) and Theakston et al. (2001) claim, acquisition is a lexically driven process, productivity should be defined in terms of lexically non identical contexts. The major departure from the criteria is that we are using a cumulative approach to the occurrence of verb paradigms instead of considering the occurrence of verb forms session per session or month per month. The main rationale behind this is that the data collection is so sparse that limiting the child's production abilities to one single observation session or to one single month will greatly underestimate her abilities.

Given these considerations we arrive at the cumulative overview of mini-paradigms in table 7. Per month the cumulative number of verb lemmas is indicated, the cumulative number of mini-paradigms, as well as the cumulative number of 2-, 3-, 4- member paradigms. The first 2 member mini-paradigm appears at 1;6, at 1;10 the first 3 member mini-paradigm appears, and at 2;3 the first 4 member mini-paradigm. Thus, in the child's production, verb form oppositions start appearing very slowly with a first acceleration at 1;9 and a second one at 2;1.

Table 7. Cumulative overview of the child's mini-paradigms

Age	# Mini Paradigms	#Main verb lemmas	2 members	3 members	4 members
1;5		4			
1;6	2	7	2		
1;7	2	10	2		
1;8	2	19	2		
1;9	5	24	5		
1;10	6	38	5	1	
1;11	7	44	6	1	
2;0	9	51	6	3	
2;1	13	59	8	5	
2;2	18	69	13	5	
2;3	20	74	14	4	2
2;4	25	83	18	4	3
2;5	28	95	18	7	3

The kinds of oppositions that the child produces are displayed in table 8. The overview is cumulative: every month the oppositions that meet the criteria mentioned above were examined for all the verbs produced during that month as well as all the months before. In this way the sparse data problem (i.e., only a very limited sample of the child's productions is available for each month) is reduced somewhat. Table 8 clearly shows that most mini-paradigms contain the infinitive. This is really not surprising since most lemmas show up as an infinitive in the child's vocabulary, and the infinitive is the verb form that the child produces most frequently.

Table 8. Cumulative overview of the morphological oppositions (empty cells denote zero number of instances)

Age	2 Oppositions						3 Oppositions					4 Oppositions	
	Inf + stem	Inf + 2/3S Pres	Inf + S Past	Inf + Perf	Inf Stem + 2/3S Pres	Inf + 1-3P Pres	Inf + stem + S Past	Inf Stem + Inf + 2/3S Pres	Inf + 2/3S Pres + Perf	Inf Stem + 2/3S Pres + Perf	Inf Stem + 2/3S Pres + SPast	Stem + Inf + 2/3S Pres + Perf	Stem + Inf + 2/3S Pres + SPast
1;5													
1;6	2												
1;7	2												
1;8	2												
1;9	4	1											
1;10	4	1					1						
1;11	5	1					1						
2;0	4	2					2	1					
2;1	3	2	1	1			2	3	1				
2;2	5	2	1	4	1		2	2			1		
2;3	6	2		4	1		2	1		2	2		
2;4	6	3		7	1	1	2	1	1	1	2		
2;5	4	3	1	9		1	2	3	1	1	2		1

The first 2 member mini-paradigms are composed of the infinitive and the bare stem. Two verbs are involved, viz. *kijken* ('look') and *wenen* ('cry'). Both verbs occur as a bare stem and as an infinitive (*kijk – kijken* and *ween – wenen*). These pairs are the only ones in the corpus until 1;9, when two additional bare stem – infinitive pairs appear (*zie – zien* 'see/watch' and *speel – spelen* 'play') as well as the first pair with a second/third person singular present form and the infinitive: *valt – vallen* 'fall (down)'. While the first mini-paradigms may be disputable on phonological grounds (see the explanation in section 7), the verb forms entering mini-paradigms are solid evidence that the child makes a formal opposition between several verb forms. The early forms of *kijken* and *wenen* can be explained on the basis of intra word variation: the bisyllabic infinitive results into the monosyllabic bare stem as a consequence of the phonological process of truncation. However the alternation of *zie* and *zien*, and the alternation of *vallen* and *valt* cannot be explained in that way, and hence these pairs form the first genuine examples of mini-paradigms.

When the child is 1;10, the first 3-member mini-paradigm occurs: the verb *zien* ('see / watch') is used in the simple past singular form, viz. *zag* 'saw', in addition to its usage as an infinitive (*zien*) and a bare stem (*zie*). The contexts in which the three forms of the verb are used are clearly different (imperative for the stem, future action for the infinitive and reporting an event for the simple past).

The beginning of the child's third year of life mark a number of new types of oppositions: the opposition between the infinitive and simple past singular form (*zitten* 'to sit' – *zat* 'sat') and the perfective or past participle form (*kleuren* 'to color' – *gekleurd* 'colored'). There are also two new types of 3-member mini-paradigms: stem – infinitive – 2/3SgPres (*ween* 'cry' – *wenen* 'to cry' – *weent* 'cries') and infinitive – 2/3SgPres – perfective (*doen* 'to do' – *doet* 'does' – *gedaan* 'done').

The verb *doen* 'to do' is also the first one to enter a 4-member paradigm (*doen* 'to do', *doe* 'do', *doet* 'does', *gedaan* 'done') at 2;2, followed at 2;3 by another high frequency verb, viz. *slapen* (*slapen* 'to sleep', *slaap* 'sleep', *slaapt* 'sleeps', *geslapen* 'slept').

8. Discussion and conclusion

In this paper we attempted to trace one child's morphological acquisition from 1;5 to 2;5. We mapped out aspects of her development over a year during which one or two observation sessions per month were held. In this concluding section we want to broaden the perspective in two directions: first of all, we will focus on what this study can contribute to the study of morphological development and more specifically on the study of the premorphological and the protomorphological stages. Secondly, we will compare the findings in the present paper with the quite extensive literature on the acquisition of Dutch morphology and more specifically the literature of the acquisition of verbs.

In terms of the delineation of a premorphological and a protomorphological stage, we have applied a data-driven approach. The analysis of the child's cumulative vocabulary showed a gradual increase, without a real 'verb spurt', though the pace of acquisition increases during the period studied. A comparison of the absolute number of lemmas with the absolute number of verb types reveals a jump around 2;0 and 2;1: for verbs as well as nouns the ratio of lemmas over types decreases, which means that there are much more verb types relative to lemmas, or in other words, morphological variation increases. At the same time, there is a diversification in the types of verbs that the child acquires: until ca. 2;0 the child's verb lexicon consists almost exclusively of lexical verbs (used mainly as infinitives). Around her second birthday the copula *zijn* 'be' and a growing number of (modal) auxiliaries are acquired and used with a relatively high token frequency. This is also the period when marked finite forms (second and third person singulars, as opposed to bare stems) are used with growing frequency. These findings seem to point at a development at the morphological level around 2;0, which runs parallel with syntactic developments, i.e. the overt marking of subject-verb agreement. As to the formation of mini-paradigms, the data do not show a sudden upsurge in the acquisition of various forms of the same lemma, on the contrary, the child shows a more gradual profile in this respect.

The data presented here show a lot of commonalities with previous reports on verb acquisition in the literature. The preponderance of infinitives in the early productions is an often remarked aspect of child Dutch (see for instance De Houwer and Gillis 1998; Wijnen and Verrips 1998 for overviews of the literature). Moreover, most children initially use a small number of infinitives (small number of verb lemmas) with a relatively high frequency. Later on, the frequency of infinitives will decline: in their third year of life children use a restricted number of auxiliaries and modals with high frequency and the lexical verbs appear with a much higher type / token ratio, which is exactly the same in adult Dutch. The copula *zijn* 'be' is the first copula to be acquired (other copulas occur much later) and it is used very frequently. Moreover, the copula as well as the modals and the auxiliaries are first acquired in finite form in Dutch (as in German, Behrens 1993). In the literature there is also a consensus that present tense indicative singular is acquired earlier than the present tense plural and the past tense indicative, which occur more or less simultaneously with the past participle (used in the present perfect).

One of the main issues that has been dealt with in the literature is the acquisition of the verb second position of the verb: in Dutch main clauses a finite verb form has to occupy the second position in a sentence and all other (non-finite) verb forms have to be in sentence final position. Thus there is a clear correspondence between verb morphology and verb placement. However, children acquiring Dutch show a strong preference for using infinitival verb forms during the early stages of grammatical development. Moreover, in terms of the order of acquisition, it has often been remarked that children start with a so-called 'optional infinitive stage': Wijnen (1998) claims that at the outset of multiple word speech, children exclusively use non-finite verb forms in utterance final position, without a finite verb which is compulsory in adult Dutch.

Children do not only use infinitives with high frequency, at the outset of acquisition, they seem to use only one verb type for each lemma: only a finite or a non finite type appears in the early stages of acquisition. Mini-paradigms, as they are called here, appear only later. This non-overlap has been remarked in the earliest studies of verb acquisition in Dutch: a.o. De Haan (1987) and Jordens (1990) note that children either use a finite verb form, which they place in first / second position in an utterance, or a non finite form of a verb, which they place almost without exception in utterance final position.

Now there are two important questions cropping up from these observations: first of all, why do children show positional preferences in their early multi word utterances, and why do they show the position – form correlations? In the present context, a still more important question is: why do children acquire the forms that they acquire? In the literature various attempts have been made to answer this second question. The most straightforward answer is: it is easier for children to learn the forms that they hear more frequently. However this answer is far too simple: Gillis and Verlinden (1988) already showed that the most frequent verbs that a Dutch speaking child hears are modals, auxiliaries and copulas (they are among the ten most frequent verbs in the input), and these are not the verbs that a Dutch learning child acquires first. All of these items are acquired later than a lot of infinitives which are used far less frequently. A standard argument to counter this frequency argument is that such 'functional verbs' are less salient in the input than lexical verbs: they are perceptually less salient because unstressed, they are positionally less salient than lexical verbs, their meaning is less concrete, etc.

This does not mean, however, that frequency does not play a role in acquisition: in a recent study, Wijnen, Kempen and Gillis (2001) showed that there is a negative correlation between the frequency of lexical verbs in the input and the age of acquisition, that is, the more frequent the verb occurs in the input, the earlier the verb is acquired. Schlichting (1996) found that not all forms of a verb are equally frequent and children tend to acquire the verb form that occurs most frequently in the input: "A verb which is more frequent in finite form(s) than in nonfinite form(s) in Child Directed Speech is (first) acquired in finite form(s); a verb which is more frequent in nonfinite form(s) than in finite form(s) in Child Directed Speech is first acquired in nonfinite form(s)." Schlichting (1996: 118) Thus, there seems to be a relationship between the frequency of lexical verbs and the order of acquisition. However, that relationship is not as straightforward as the quote from Schlichting (1996) may suggest. Wijnen, Kempen, and Gillis (2001: 657) explicitly address this issue: "Is there a role to play for frequency of exposure, at the level of lexical items? Our analyses have yielded moderate correlations (at best) between frequency of verb forms in the input and age of first appearance." They analyzed the order of acquisition of finite and non finite forms of lexical verbs in relation to their input frequency: the lexical verbs that occurred both as infinitives and as finite forms in children's speech were identified, their frequency in child directed speech was determined, and these data were related to the order of acquisition. They found that for the verbs that occur in the children's productions as an infinitive and as a finite form, the infinitive was almost always acquired before the finite form although for a considerable number of verbs the infinitive was not the most frequent form in the input.

These findings lead us to the conclusion that there is more to it than mere token frequency of the verb. Wijnen, Kempen and Gillis (2001) investigated two factors that they considered to contribute to the salience of verbs in final position in the input. First of all, they considered type/token ratio as an index of informativity. It appears that infinitives have a much higher TTR than finite verbs in the input. On a low TTR, the likelihood of encountering the same verb in two arbitrarily selected utterances is higher than on a high TTR. Consequently, infinitives contribute more often to a difference in meaning between two randomly selected sentences than verbs in utterance initial position, and hence infinitives are more informative than verbs in utterance initial position. In other words, it pays more for the child to attend to infinitives (verbs in utterance final position) than to finite verbs (verbs in utterance initial position).

In addition to this information theoretic measure, Wijnen, Kempen, and Gillis (2001) also followed a lead by Jordens (1990) who claimed that verbs with finite morphology in first / second sentence position differ semantically from verbs in sentence final position that take non finite morphology. Schlichting (1996) found a relationship between the degree of transitivity of the verb (as defined by Givon 1984) in relation to position and finiteness: She found a strong correlation between the degree of semantic transitivity of the lexical verb and its position and morphology: verbs with strong prototypical transitivity such as *bouwen* 'build' are rarely found in first/second position in finite form. Verbs with weak semantic transitivity such as *zien* 'see' are found both in first/second position and in sentence final position. Wijnen, Kempen, and Gillis (2001) also classified lexical verbs on semantic grounds into statives and eventives.[5] It appears that eventive and stative verbs do turn up in utterance initial as well as in utterance final position. However, while eventive verbs outnumber stative ones in utterance initial position three to four times, eventives outnumber statives in utterance final position ten to twenty times. Thus, verbs in sentence final position are significantly more often semantically transparent than those in utterance initial position.

In sum, this means that the set of verbs in utterance final position is not only more informative than the set of verbs in utterance initial position, the former is also much more semantically coherent. This may explain why children learning Dutch acquire infinitives earlier than finite verbs.

Turning back to frequency, Wijnen, Kempen, and Gillis (2001) eliminated the variables position and semantic transparency, and calculated the correlation between frequency in the input and age of appearance for finite lexical verbs only. They report a markedly higher correlation between input frequency and age of acquisition than the one they achieved for the complete class of lexical verbs. In other words, everything else being equal, the more frequent a verb occurs in the input, the easier it is for the child to pick it up.

There are still a number of aspects of early morphological development that are in need of an explanation. To name just a few: we have seen that the role of frequency in the input is modulated by a other factors. This may explain why infinitives are acquired before finite forms, though in a majority of cases the finite forms are more frequent. But when we look at development, we see that actually finite forms only start being acquired and used regularly once the child has detected two verb positions in the sentence, and this seems to coincide with the discovery of agreement between subject and verb. So, the question is, which development is the driving force, or in other words, how are these developments interconnected?

Another unresolved problem concerns the relative contributions of characteristics of the input and the child's own processing. If indeed the input (both frequency and relative transparency or salience) plays a crucial role, it still needs to be determined what the role is of the "critical mass hypothesis" (Marchman and Bates 1994) in the acquisition of verbs and verb (mini-)paradigms. Does a child need a particular number of verbs in order for morphological development to take off, or in other words: is that 'critical amount' a prerequisite? Or is morphological development a simple consequence of the mere addition of more word forms to the lexicon?

Notes

1. More elaborate introductions may be found in Geerts et al. (1984); De Schutter (1994); De Houwer and Gillis (1998); Booij and Van Santen (1995), De Haas and Trommelen (1993).
2. Stems ending in a vowel or a diphthong always take /n/, stems ending in a consonant take /ən/. The final /n/ following /ə/ is optional.
3. Note that this suffix will undergo final devoicing.
4. Except for the first datapoint (age 1;5) when the child has 5 lemmas on a total of 39 lemmas.
5. Eventives are verbs that refer to dynamic changes that occur within a relatively bounded interval, involving one or more actors. Transitive action verbs, which denote exchanges between an agent and a patient (e.g., 'hit', 'kiss') are the prototypical examples. Statives such as 'love', 'know', denote relatively stable, unbounded conditions or situations. Besides meaning, various diagnostics for the classification of verbs into these two categories are discussed by Wijnen (1998).

References

Barrett, Martyn
    1986   Early semantic representations and early word use. In: Stan A. Kuczaj, and Martyn Barrett (eds.), *The Development of Word Meaning*, 362–392. New York: Springer.

Barrett, Martyn
 1995 Early lexical development. In: Paul Fletcher, and Brian MacWhinney (eds.), *The Handbook of Child Language*, 362–392. Oxford: Blackwell.

Behrens, Heike
 1993 Temporal reference in the German child language: Form and Function of early verb use. Ph.D. thesis, Unniversiteit van Amsterdam.

Bittner, Dagmar
 2000 Early verb development in one German-speaking child. In: Bittner, Dagmar, Wolfgang U. Dressler, and Marianne Kilani-Schoch (eds.), *First Verbs: On the Way to Miniparadigms,* 21–38. (ZAS Papers in Linguistics 18.) Berlin: ZAS.

Bittner, Dagmar, Wolfgang U. Dressler, and Marianne Kilani-Schoch (eds.)
 2000 *First Verbs: On the Way to Miniparadigms.* (ZAS Papers in Linguistics 18.) Berlin: Zentrum für Allgemeine Sprachwissenschaft, Typologie und Universalienforschung (ZAS).

Booij, Geert, and Arianne Van Santen
 1995 *Morfologie: De woordstructuur van het Nederlands.* Amsterdam: Amsterdam University Press.

De Haan, Ger
 1987 A theory-bound approach to the acquisition of verb placement. In: Ger De Haan, and Wim Zonneveld (eds.), *Formal Parameters of Generative Grammar.* Utrecht: OTS.

De Haas, Wim, and Mieke Trommelen
 1993 *Morfologisch handboek van het Nederlands: Een overzicht van de woordvorming.* 's-Gravenhage: SDU Uitgeverij.

De Houwer, Annick, and Steven Gillis
 1988 Dutch child language: An overview. In: Steven Gillis, and Annick De Houwer (eds.), *The Acquisition of Dutch*, 1–100. Amsterdam: John Benjamins.

De Schutter, Georges
 1994 Dutch. In: Ekkehard König, and Johan van der Auwera (eds.), *The Germanic Languages*, 439–477. London: Routledge.

Dore, John
1985 Holophrases revisited: Their 'logical' development from dialogue. In: Martyn Barrett (ed.), *Children's Single-word Speech*, 23–58. Chichester: Wiley.

Dore, John, Margery Franklin, Andrea Ramer, and Robert Miller
1976 Transitional phenomena in early language acquisition. *Journal of Child Language* 3: 13–28.

Elbers, Loekie, and Anita Van Loon-Vervoorn
1998 Acquiring the lexicon: Evidence from Dutch. In: Steven Gillis, and Annick de Houwer (eds.), *The Acquisition of Dutch*, 301–377. Amsterdam: John Benjamins.

Elbers, Loekie, and Anita Van Loon-Vervoorn
2000 Lexicon en semantiek. In: Steven Gillis, and Annemarie Schaerlaekens (eds.), *Kindertaalverwerving: Een handboek voor het Nederlands*, 185–224. Groningen: Martinus Nijhoff.

Fikkert, Paula
1994 *On the Acquisiion of Prosodic Structure*. The Hague: Holland Academic Graphics.

Fikkert, Paula
1998 The acquisition of Dutch phonology. In: Steven Gillis, and Annick De Houwer (eds.), *The Acquisition of Dutch*, 163–222. Amsterdam: John Benjamins.

Geerts, Guido, Walter Haeseryn, Jan de Rooij, and Maarten van den Toorn
1984 *Algemeen Nederlandse Spraakkunst*. Groningen: Wolters-Noordhoff.

Gillis, Steven
1984 De verwerving van talige referentie. Unpublished Ph.D., University of Antwerp.

Gillis, Steven
2000 Fonologische ontwikkeling. In: Steven Gillis, and Annemarie Schaerlaekens (eds.), *Kindertaalverwerving: Een handboek voor het Nederlands*, 131–184. Groningen: Martinus Nijhoff.

Gillis, Steven, and Annick de Houwer (eds.)
1998 *The Acquisition of Dutch*. Amsterdam: John Benjamins.

Gillis, Steven, and An Verlinden
   1988   Nouns and verbs in early lexical acquisition: Effects of input frequency? *Antwerp Papers in Linguistics* 54: 1988.

Gillis, Steven, and Georges de Schutter
   1986   Transitional phenomena revisited: Insights into the nominal insight. In: Bjorn Lindblom, and Ralf Zetterström (eds.), *Precursors of Early Speech*, 127–142. New York: Stockton Press.

Givón, Talmy
   1984   *Syntax, a Functional Typological Approach*. Amsterdam: John Benjamins.

Jordens, Peter
   1990   The acquisition of verb placement in Dutch and German. *Linguistics* 28: 1407–1448.

Kilani-Schoch, Marianne, and Wolfgang U. Dressler
   2000   Are precursors of morphemes relevant for morphological theory? In: Wolfgang U. Dressler, Oskar E. Pfeiffer, Markus Poechtraeger, and John R. Rennison (eds.), *Morphological Analysis in Comparison*, 89–111. Amsterdam: John Benjamins.

Marchman, Virginia, and Elizabeth Bates
   1994   Continuity in lexical and morphological development: A test of the critical mass hypothesis. *Journal of Child Language* 21: 339–366.

Schlichting, Liesbeth
   1996   *Discovering Syntax: An Empirical Study in Dutch Language Acquisition*. Nijmegen: Uitgeverij Katholieke Universiteit Nijmegen.

Taelman, Helena, and Steven Gillis
   2001   Variation in children's early production of multisyllabic words: The case of truncations. In: Sophie Kern (ed.), *Early Lexicon Acquisition: Normal and Pathological Development. CD ROM*. Lyon: Université Lumière Lyon 2.

Theakston, Anna, Elena Lieven, Julian Pine, and Caroline Rowland
   2001   The role of performance limitations in the acquisition of verb-argument structure: An alternative account. *Journal of Child Language* 28: 127–152.

Tomasello, Michael
  1992   *First Verbs: A Case Study of Early Grammatical Development.* Cambridge: Cambridge University Press.

Van Eynde, Frank
  2000   *Part of Speech Tagging en Lemmatisering.* Leuven: CCL.

Wijnen, Frank
  1998   The temporal interpretation of Dutch children's root infinitivals: the effect of eventivity. *First Language* 18: 379–402.

Wijnen, Frank, Masja Kempen, and Steven Gillis
  2001   Root infinitives in Dutch early child language: An effect of input? *Journal of Child Language* 28: 629–660.

Wijnen, Frank, and Maaike Verrips
  1998   The acquisition of Dutch syntax. In: Steven Gillis, and Annick de Houwer (eds.), *The Acquisition of Dutch*, 223–299. Amsterdam: John Benjamins.

Early development of verbal morphology in an English-speaking child

Insa Gülzow

0. Introduction

In this paper the first results concerning the development of early verb morphology in an L1-English speaking child are presented. Adopting the framework of morphological development of Dressler (1997), the data of a girl from the CHILDES database, Nina of the Suppes corpus, is analysed with regard to the emergence of early verbal categories. Due to the fact that English is a language with little verbal morphology, the status of the emergence of first mini-paradigms will be discussed. It will be shown that the few English verbal suffixes appear at different times in development due to their status in terms of belonging to an adjectival or verbal conjugational system. In a phase in which mini-paradigms are not yet present, the child Nina shows clear signs of an awareness of the inflectional non-finite ending *-ing*. This is documented in the specification of the suffix in terms of person and number and the production of overgeneralisations with *-ing*. The inflectional finite suffixes *-s* and *-ed* on the other hand gain a morphosemantic status not until a few months later and hardly contribute to the new types of morphological contrasts that begin to appear from an age of 2;5 onwards. It will be argued that results from both an analysis of the interverbal morphological development such as the general appearance of verbal affixes including overgeneralisations and the analysis of verbspecific morphological development such as the formation of paradigmatic pairs and sets contribute to the identification of the onset of protomorphology in the sense of Dressler. It will be shown that a quantitative change in lemma and token numbers both of verbs bearing the *-s* and *-ed* suffix and of strong past tense formations can be correlated with qualitative change such as the appearance of overgeneralisations with *-ed* and the appearance of first three-member mini-paradigms.

1. Description of verb morphology in the target language

English is a language which has lost most elements of its once rich inflectional system. All in all about ten inflectional suffixes have survived the Middle English period when most inflections were lost. Verb morphology is reduced to a few suffixes marking person, number, tense and aspect. In the absence of inflectional suffixes, the categories person and number are mainly marked by personal pronouns; English auxiliaries also mark person and number along with tense, mood and voice. The morphology of English auxiliaries is opaque and a number of syncretic forms exist. Present indicative presents the only case in which the categories person and number are marked simultaneously by a suffix: third person singular invariably occurs with the inflection -s (table 1). Past tense forms are in the case of weak verbs identical with the past participle (table 1) and are marked for tense only. Some strong past tense forms/past participles display an opaque or suppletive morphology. Progressive aspect is constructed analytically and consists of the present participle marked by the ending -*ing* and a finite form of the verb *to be*. In the case of present progressive this is the present participle and a present finite form of the verb *to be* (table 1). In the present study only a few constructions are relevant. The child in this study used the base form of verbs and the present participle which later on occurred in targetlike present progressive constructions. Some weak and some overgeneralized past tense forms occurred together with a number of strong past formations. Third person singular -s was used sporadically but not in a systematic way until the end of the recordings analysed in this study. Some modal and some future constructions were used.

Table 1. To walk

	1/2S	3S	1/2/3P
present indicative	walk	walk-s	walk
simple past	walk-ed	walk-ed	walk-ed
present progressive	am walk-ing	is walk-ing	are walk-ing

Apart from pronominal elements English noun phrases are not inflected for case. The personal pronouns of first and third person singular and plural differ in nominative and objective case. Consequently, word order is crucial for identifying the subject in a sentence. English sentences must have subjects which occur in preverbal first position. Unless a sentence is passive, the most agentive member will appear in subject position. While it is impossible to give an indepth analysis of all verbal constructions in English, two aspects that seem to be relevant in the present analysis should be mentioned. First, despite the fact that only a few suffixes can be attached to English verbs, an adjectival and a verbal conjugation type can be distinguished. Parallel to many other languages English participles can be used as adjectives. When participles are used as adjectives, the imperfective or perfective aspect of the action performed is preserved. Unlike in languages like French, English does not mark gender neither in participles nor when the form is used as an adjective. It is however important to notice that the possibility that participles can be marked for the nominal category gender and the fact that they are non-finite distinguishes participles from other verbal elements in English that display a purely verbal inflection type.

2. Data description

The data were taken from the CHILDES database. For the present study the 52 recordings of the girl Nina of the Suppes corpus were analysed. In the first session of the recordings Nina has reached an age of 1;11.16. In the last session she is 3;3.21.

Table 2. Age at recording and number of child utterances

age	number of recordings	total number of child utterances
1;11	3	2.177
2;0	4	2.202
2;1	4	2.752
2;2	3	2.213
2;3	4	2.721
2;4	4	1.800
2;5	5	3.452
2;6	0	0
2;7	0	0
2;8	0	0
2;9	3	2.215
2;10	4	2.976
2;11	3	1.736
3;0	4	2.665
3;1	4	2.088
3;2	4	2.355
3;3	3	1.847
Total	52	27.799

It should be mentioned at this point that there is a two-and-a-half month gap in the recordings between the ages of 2;5.28 and 2;9.13. This must not necessarily be regarded as a disadvantage of the data as there are numerous signs in the five recorded sessions when Nina is two years and five months old that she is moving on to a new phase of morphological development. The trends that can be observed in the last five sessions before the gap occurs are well-established in all recordings following the gap from an age of 2;9 onwards. In the first session of the recordings, Nina still produces a lot of one-word-utterances, but has begun to put words together in longer sequences and also uses a number of verbs. The first recording takes place at Nina's home with only her mother being present. Other sessions were taped when Nina's grandparents or some of her friends were visiting.

3. Predecessors of verbs in predicative function

At the onset of the recordings (1;11.16), Nina is already using a number of lexical verbs. In early stages of language development it has been claimed that relational words such as *more*, *gone* or prepositions such as *in* and *out* can also be considered verblike predicates as long as their conceptualization is a process and their use is as a predicate (Tomasello 1992). Often documented as predecessors of verbs these expressions still exist in the data of Nina. Only some can be discussed briefly. Initially, *more* was used to indicate general recurrence of objects (1), food (2) and activities (3). In session 9 Nina begins to use *more* as a quantificational modifier as demonstrated by her use of the expression in utterances containing a "true" verb (4). From session 10 onwards the majority of utterances containing *more* also has a verb (5)–(6).

(1) *CHI: more rabbit. (1;11.16)
(2) *CHI: more cookie. (1;11.16)
(3) *CHI: more reading. (2;0.3)
(4) *CHI: my want more coffee. (2;1.6)
(5) *CHI: my have more things in my box. (2;1.15)
(6) *CHI: he got more food. (2;1.15)

If context is lacking, it is not always easy to decide if a preposition is used as a verb or not. Most utterances in which a preposition seems to be used as a verb, see (7a) and (8a), are constructed parallel to other utterances which are produced by Nina with a lexical verb in place of the preposition, see (7b)–(7c) and (8b)–(8c). Utterance (9) was produced by Nina when she was getting up, because she wanted to go out. That prepositions are indeed conceived as verblike predicates by children is illustrated in (10) where Nina productively uses the suffix of the present participle. The utterance was a comment of Nina at age 2;0.3 as she watches her mother taking the pieces of a puzzle out. The production of the non-target form *outing* will be discussed in section 4.2.2. since it serves as an example that Nina is capable of some morphological generalisation in a phase of language acquisition when she is not yet making use of a more complex system of English verbal affixes. It is hard to say at which point Nina stops to use prepositions in place of verbs, but in the course of the recordings, examples such as (7a), (8a) and (9) become less frequent and even if an utterance is produced without a verb, the preposition tends to occur as an appropriate member of a prepositional phrase, see (11).

(7) a. *CHI: off Mommy (2;0.17)
 b. *CHI: draw # Mommy (2;0.24)
 c. *CHI: talk Mommy (2;1.6)
(8) a. *CHI: off a eye (poking teddy's eyes) (2;1.6)
 b. *CHI: pulling a bus (2;0.10)
 c. *CHI: see the nail (2;1.15)
(9) *CHI: out up. (1;11.16)
(10) *CHI: Mommy's outing. (2;0.3)
(11) *CHI: on the chimney (2;1.15)

4. Emergence of verb-forms

It is a well-known fact that children learning English as their first language are relatively late in the acquisition of verbal affixes. In his study, Brown (1973) investigated the order of acquisition of a number of bound and free morphemes; (12) is adapted from Brown (1973: 274) and lists the order of acquisition of the verbal morphemes relevant in the present study. The further to the left an element is listed, the earlier is it acquired by the children in Brown's study.

(12) present progressive, past irregular, past regular, third person

According to Brown's 90 % criterion (cf. Brown 1973: 271) *-ing* is the first verbal affix to be acquired by the three children in his study, Adam, Eve and Sarah. All three children begin to use the suffix *-ing* in 90% of obligatory contexts in stage II when their MLU is not higher than 2.25. For comparison, the last verbal affix to appear, inflectional -*s*, is acquired in stage V by the two children Adam and Eve (MLU = 4.00) and in stage IV by Sarah (MLU = 3.50). Both Adam and Sarah acquire the regular past inflection -*ed* approximately at the same time as inflectional -*s*, after they have established irregular past references.[1] The relatively early emergence of English verb forms ending with -*ing* is a well-known fact and has been reported repeatedly (for an overview see Li and Shirai 2000). With respect to the use of inflectional -*ed* it has been argued by various researchers that initial tense morphology does not encode a temporal contrast, but that children use it to mark the aspectual relationship of completion (e.g. Bronckart and Sinclair 1973; Bloom, Lifter, and Hafitz 1980; Antinucci and Miller 1976). This "aspect before tense" hypothesis rests on the analysis of early tense marking in relation to the aktionsart of the verb used by the child. In their study of the first language acquisition of Italian and English children, Antinucci and Miller (1976) found that before they have reached an age of 2;1. children can only use tense morphology to encode past events that result in a present state. Relating to this position, Weist (1986), who coined the term "defective tense hypothesis" (Weist and Wysocka 1984) has shown in his investigation of three children acquiring Polish as their first language that the children did not use only telic verbs with past tense inflections. Weist (1986) offers convincing evidence from studies of a number of languages including Greek (Stephany 1981), Polish (Smoczyńska 1978) and Finnish (Toivanen 1980) that a categorical inability of children to make past reference must be rejected. In more recent studies (cf. Shirai and Andersen 1995) the tendency to use past morphology predominantly with telic verbs and progressive inflections with activity verbs is explained as mirroring the distributional bias that can also be found in child-directed speech of caretakers.

Despite his rejection of the "defective tense hypothesis", Weist proposes a stage model that corresponds in parts to the predictions made by the "aspect before tense" hypothesis. According to this model, children pass through four stages the first of which is characterized by the fact that the children use -*ing* to make aspectual but not temporal distinctions. In this first stage of Weist's model, the speech time system, children make no distinction between speech time, event time and reference time (Weist 1986). It is only later when children have passed on to the event time system that they use morphological contrasts productively for encoding temporal relationships. Along with an early appearance of verbs with a progressive inflection, children acquiring English as their first language also use the base form of the verb frequently. For other languages such as German (e.g. Behrens 1993) and Dutch (e.g.Wijnen, Kempen, and Gillis 2001) it has also been attested that children in early stages of language acquisition use non-target nonfinite verbal forms. A well-known position among the explanations offered for this phenomenon is that of Wexler (1994) who argues for a so-called "optional infinitive stage". Wexler claims that the grammars of young children are constructed in a way that they allow both finite and non-finite variants in identical positions. Without morphological or semantic motivation finite and non-finite constructions can co-occur until the emergence of the tense feature [+TNS] which is represented in the past tense and marks the end of the optional infinitive stage. This position has been recently challenged by Wijnen, Kempen, and Gillis (2001) in that they claim that the use of infintives by children in non-target positions can be shown to be semantically motivated. Wijnen, Kempen, and Gillis (2001) argue that infinitves are more salient in comparison to finite forms in child-directed speech which the language learning child filters regarding such factors as frequency, distribution in terms of the syntactic postion of an element and conceptual transparency. The change of the children's grammar towards a more targetlike version is explained not by a structural alteration of the language faculty, but as a reflection or function of the way in which the child filters the input.

For the present analysis two aspects of the previous results concerning the verbal morphological development of children will be regarded as being especially relevant. First, the fact that there is a semantic bias to encode telic events with past inflectionsand altelic events with progressive inflections, but not a categorical inability of children that confines them to a restricted use of a certain verbal inflection is a necessary basis for the emergence of mini-paradigms in the sense of Dressler (1997). Were the acquisition of verbal affixes restricted as radically as proposed by Antinucci and Miller (1976), the formation of mini-paradigms with regard to a certain verb including both past and progressive inflection would be generally impossible at early stages of language acquisition. Second, there seems to be a systematic difference between children who acquire a language with a clear distinction between infinitival and finite verb forms. If the infinitival verb forms appear in structures that are used in child-directed speech, the general tendency of children acquiring such languages is that they pass through a stage in which infinitves are used in a variety of non-target positions.[2] Together with the early appearance of the -*ing* affix in the language of children acquiring English it seems a valid question to ask if the children's use of the base form of the verb is a phenomenon that can be interpreted independently or if the base form of verbs and verbs with the progressive inflection emerge as part of a verbal system that is still lacking a more systematic integration of finite verb forms. Recent studies (cf. Behrens 1993; Wijnen, Kempen, and Gillis 2001) have stressed the importance of the structure of the target system and that one has to be careful to distinguish general developemental processes from those that mirror the characteristics of the adult system that the child is acquiring. In the present study the question how Dressler's model that takes the emergence of mini-paradigms as an important milestone can contribute to the description of morphological development in a language with only a few verbal inflections will be of central importance (Dressler 1997).

4.1. Demarcation of pre- and protomorphology

Of the languages which are analysed in this volume, English represents one end of the continuum and can be characterized as an analytic rather than a synthetic type of language regarding its verbal morphology. There is no overlap concerning the categories encoded by the inflectional endings *-ing*, *-ed* and *-s*. The three suffixes do not contrast within one category. While the majority of the other languages discussed in this volume have person and number contrasts within paradigms like the simple present paradigm, English marks only one member of the present paradigm, third person singular. All remaining five forms of the present paradigm are the base form. As will be demonstrated in section 4.2., person and number distinctions emerge in the data of Nina as nominal categories. That is, before Nina discovers grammatical means of agreement, she begins to make person and number distinctions in subject noun phrases. At the beginning these are mainly used together with base verb forms and verbs ending in *-ing*. Although it is difficult to speculate at which point an English default like *walk* reaches the status of a finite form, an attempt to describe this transition will be made in section 4.3.1. From the onset of the study, Nina uses two main verb forms: the base form (13)–(14) and the present participle (15)–(16), a quantitative analysis can be found in table 3. The first fully inflected forms that appear with some regularity are analytical constructions with third person singular present progressive verb forms (17)–(19).

(13) *CHI: bunny dance too. (1;11.16)
(14) *CHI: drink dolly. (1;11.16)

(15) *CHI: bunny dancing.   (1;11.16)
(16) *CHI: drinking dolly   (1;11.16)
(17) *CHI: he's sleeping.   (2;0.24)
(18) *CHI: he's eating his cereal. (2;1.6)
(19) *CHI: he is sleeping.   (2;2.12)

Table 3 shows the total amount of verb lemmas and tokens used by the child Nina including base forms and verbs with the inflectional endings *-ing*, *-s* and *-ed*.[3] In the case of inflectional *-ing*, the adjectival use of the participle was excluded from the analysis. For the suffix *-ed* two columns are shown, one listing non-finite uses, these were mainly copula constructions like *I'm tired* or *she's called Becca*. The second column lists cases in which the verb ending in *-ed* represents the finite form of target past tense constructions.

Table 3. Lemma/token occurences

	infinitival	-ing	-ed (participle)	-ed	-s	ratio[4]
1;11	59/272	23/86	2/2		7/14	17%
2;0	77/250	38/106	1/4		2/2	16%
2;1	80/472	30/60	1/2	1/1	2/2	20%
2;2	75/462	46/129	2/5	4/11	6/7	28%
2;3	105/840	47/131	6/11	8/13	4/7	37%
2;4	89/472	27/61	5/8	6/4	2/3	30%
2;5	[5]	51/174	10/15	11/20	8/11	
2;9		42/101	7/10	15/27	19/38	
2;10		51/137	10/17	24/41	16/44	
2;11		38/64	5/9	13/19	12/30	
3;0		52/145	7/15	24/30	13/28	
3;1		41/93	7/15	10/18	15/32	
3;2		33/72	16/38	17/31	13/20	
3;3		58/103	11/14	12/19	18/38	

The most obvious trends that can be seen in this simple chart are illustrated in figure 1 and figure 2 which give lemma numbers only. Note that the gap in the recordings between 2;6 and 2;8 is included with zero values in the figures. As must be expected in a child still learning new verbs and other lexical items, lemma and token numbers rise during the recordings. However, the quantitative analysis shows that the rise in lemma and token numbers is not identical in style for each of the different verb forms. A closer look at figures 1 and 2 reveals that while the rise of verb forms ending in

214 *Insa Gülzow*

-ing as well as the rise of participle verb forms ending in *-ed* displays a number of ups and downs the general trend is steadily upwards. Verb forms ending in *-s* and finite *-ed* on the other hand display a sudden rise of lemma numbers towards a higher niveau when Nina reaches an age of 2;5.

Note that in figure 1 overgeneralized and weak verb forms ending in *-ed* are differentiated. It can be seen that overgeneralized forms such as **falled* or **taked* are not documented in a regular manner until Nina reaches an age of 2;9. However, Nina produces an overgeneralized form with inflectional *-ed* in month 2;1 before she begins to produce weak past forms (see section 4.2. for further discussion). It seems worth noting that all non-finite forms are present in the data of Nina right from the beginning. Verb forms ending in *-ing* are numerous in lemma and token numbers right from the beginning with no obvious quantitative change.

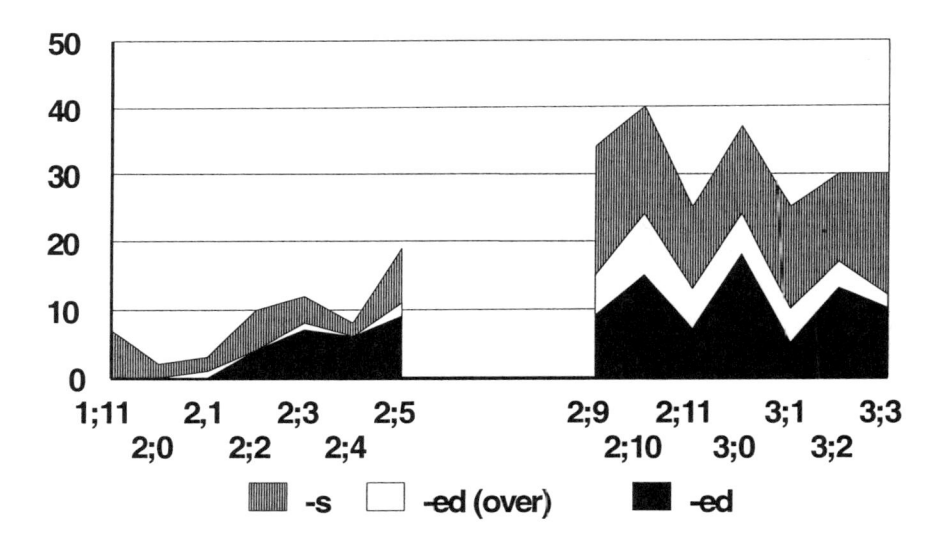

Figure 1. Finite affixes

The same is true for non-finite verb forms with *-ed* although the numbers are generally lower (figure 2). Finite *-s* and *-ed* on the other hand show quite an obvious change when Nina reaches an age of 2;5. For both verb forms lemma numbers are around five for all months between the ages of 1;11 and 2;4. These numbers begin to rise to 15 and more from month 2;5 onwards. The ratio between lemmas and tokens changes in a way that token numbers usually double lemma numbers. In the majority of cases this is not true for the months before Nina reaches an age of 2;5 showing that the use of the forms is rather isolated and not generalized to more than one context. In accordance with results from previous studies (cf. previous section), the data show that in the first months of the recordings, Nina uses the verbal suffix -*ing* and produces a large quantity of the base form of the verb. Together with the finding that in this phase Nina also uses non-finite verb forms with -*ed* it can be argued that until age 2;5 the verbal system of Nina is predominantly non-finite.[6]

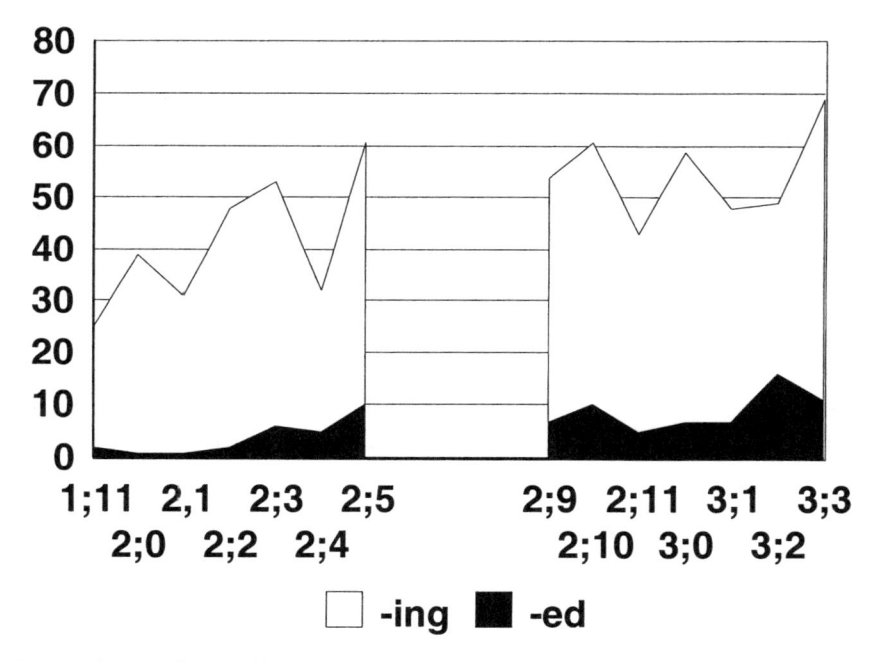

Figure 2. Non-finite affixes

The change in the verbal morphological system as documented from age 2;5 onwards is towards the use of more finite verb forms. While the two phases in the morphological development of Nina are obvious, the question that needs to be answered with regard to Dressler's theory (1997) is whether the non-finite and the finite phase correspond to pre- and protomorphology. Protomorphology is characterized by the children's detection of morphological patterns. Apart from the emergence of mini-paradigms, overgeneralisations begin to occur. Keeping this in mind, the emergence of first paradigmatic contrasts and overgeneralisations until and after month

2;5 will be discussed in the next sections. It will be argued that both in a phase in which predominantly non-finite verb forms are used and in a phase in which finite verb forms are documented more regularily, the child in the study shows some awareness of the morphological operations in her target language.

4.2. The non-finite verbal system

In the following section the development of verb constructions in the data of Nina until she reaches an age of 2;5 will be discussed. For several reasons named below the recordings discussed in this section are believed to represent a phase in the (verbal) morphological development of Nina display a number of characteristics which are typical for premorphology in the sense of Dressler (1997). However, there are also some processes that according to Dressler are more typical for the protomorphological phase. This seeming contradiction directly reflects that the non-finite and the finite verbal affixes develop somewhat independently in the language systems of a child acquiring English as her first language. As both non-finite and finite verb forms in English can bear suffixes, even if the system of the child is still lacking a more systematic integration of finite forms, morphological contrasts between different non-finite verb forms can be established.

Before an age of 2;5 Nina has some basic knowledge that affixes can occur on verbs. That the inflection *-ing* in this phase has a morphosemantic status is documented in her use of a few overgeneralisations of the suffix. Although the *-ing* suffix is not marked for person and number categories, Nina seems to develop some awareness that inflectional affixes can be used to make such distinctions. In the following sections (4.2.1.–4.2.4.) the different verb forms that occurred in the data of Nina until she reached an age of 2;5 will be discussed individually. For the majority of verb forms a form-function analysis will show which verbal categories emerge and if any of the verbal suffixes show early signs of specification. As it is mostly impossible to determine the intended referent unless a subject is given, only those utterances which contained a verb plus an identifiable subject were considered in the form-function analysis. The results of the English-speaking child Nina are summed up in tables 4, 5 and 7–9 and will be discussed in turn.

4.2.1. Base forms

The data in table 4 represents predominantly non-target utterances concerning Nina's use of the base form. While a non-target use is straightforward in the case of third person singular where inflectional -*s* is missing, this might not be as obvious in the case of first person singular references. The examples given in (20)–(22) show that the use of the simple present might look targetlike on a formal basis but seldom is in the discourse of the child. All utterances are comments on the child's activities. In many instances more than one interpretation is possible concerning the fact whether the child has just completed an action, is commenting on an ongoing action or anticipating an action. Despite these various possibilities, use of the base form of the verb is not targetlike in any one of them.

(20) *CHI: my make a house.   (2;0.10)
(21) *CHI: me eat (th)em.   (2;1.6)
(22) *CHI: I slide down too.   (2;1.15)

Table 4 gives a listing of the kind of referents of the subject noun phrases in Nina's language when producing utterances with base forms. The results will be discussed together with occurences of verbs ending in -*ing* in the next section (4.2.2.).

Table 4. Base forms with subject (lemmas/tokens)

age	1S	2S	3S	1P	3P	IMP
1;11	9/10	4/4	25/49	2/2	3/4	3/8
2;0	16/23		27/46		1/1	6/6
2;1						
2;2	30/118	17/42	33/88	3/3	6/7	14/37
2;3						
2;4	46/168	20/37	26/53	6/10	7/9	20/30

4.2.2. The -ing affix

A closer look at form-function relationships within the two main verb forms used by Nina reveals two interesting tendencies. The general trend of form-function pairings in table 4 and 5 can be summed up as follows: the child Nina uses two verb-forms for present tense references, the base from and the -*ing* form. While both are not specified in terms of person and number, one of the two verb-forms is more general than the other, this is the base form of the verb. The use of the base form is spread more generally across person and number categories while the -*ing* form is mainly used for third person singular references. The main contrast that Nina establishes at this stage of development is a proximal vs. non-proximal one. While the base form appears as a default form in all cases that have not yet been specified, the -*ing* form is almost entirely reserved for third person singular reference. In other words, reference to a non-proximal participant that is a member of the child's discourse and thus is neither speaker nor hearer is marked by the use of a first verbal affix: the -*ing* form of the verb.

Regarding Nina's use of the present participle there are clear signs that some generalisation process is taking place and that the suffix -*ing* is gaining a morphosemantic status. Apart from the example which was stated in (10), Nina produces some more creative usages of the suffix -*ing*. The example in (23) is produced while Nina is looking at a bug that is walking on an apple, (24) while she is looking at a picture in which a dog is sleeping in a house the door of which is closed, Nina is pointing at the keyhole, in (25) Nina is commenting on the activity of ducks:

(23) *CHI: bugging. (2;0.3)
(24) *CHI: locking. (2;0.3)
(25) *CHI: duck's wetting. (2;2.6)
(26) *CHI: she came oystering with us. (2;9.13)

Table 5. -*ing* verb forms with subject (lemmas/tokens)

age	1S	2S	3S	1P	3P
1;11	1/1		10/33		3/3
2;0	5/5		20/35		4/4
2;1	6/8	1/1	13/23		1/1
2;2	4/4	1/2	26/75		3/4
2,3	7/13	3/4	22/61	1/3	4/9
2;4	6/10	1/2	12/22	1/1	1/1

All examples involve the use of the suffix -*ing* together with what is categorized as a noun or adjective in the target system. Although it is impossible to tell what Nina's exact intended meaning is, in all cases it is quite possible to identify an event in the context that Nina could be relating to.

Concerning her early specification of *-ing*, the instances are consistent with her system, all referents are third person singular. Table 6 shows in which months overgeneralisations with the verbal affix *-ing* occurred. While the instances are not numerous, the majority of examples can be found in month 2;0. In later recordings only one other utterance was found (25) and an additional example in which Nina used *-ing* to form a non-target nominalization (26). Overgeneralisations with the past suffix *-ed* are hardly represented until month 2;9 when they begin to appear in greater numbers (cf. 4.3.4.). This finding is taken as further evidence that the infinite suffix *-ing* and the finite suffix *-ed* develop somewhat independently. Alternatively it could of course be argued that the past inflection *-ed* occurs later than the affix *-ing*, because reference to past events becomes relevant at a later stage in development. While this kind of position is of course justified the important point to note in the present analysis is that Nina establishes morphological contrasts between non-finite verb forms before she begins to use finite verb forms contrastively. Overgeneralisations mark a phase in which the child is coming to terms with analogous processes in her language. When overgeneralized forms begin to disappear again, the child is believed to have mastered another step in language development. In section 4.3.2. it will be shown that in a phase in which Nina is not yet producing overgeneralisations with *-ed* or using inflectional *-s*, she is making considerable progress concerning agreement factors in present progressive constructions.

Table 6. Overgeneralisations

	1;11	2;0	2;1	2;2	2;3	2;4	Total
-ing		3/3		1/2			4/5
-ed			1/1		1/1		2/2

4.2.3. *Inflectional* -s

Concerning Nina's usage of inflectional *-s* nothing much can be said at this stage. Only a few examples are documented in the data. Of the examples that could be found in which Nina used a verb with inflectional *-s* together with a subject noun phrase, the majority displayed targetlike agreement. Non-target utterances had a first person singular or third person plural referent. Although the examples are not numerous, a possible interpretation of the data is that third person singular *-s* is not yet specified in terms of the categories person and number. A closer look at the data however reveals that in the case of first person singular referents, Nina uses not a pronoun but her own name in two of the examples (27a) and (27b).

(27) a. *CHI: Nina says Honey.   (1;11.16)
     b. *CHI: Nina loves Snoopy.   (2;1.22)
(28)   *CHI: those my tickles.   (2;2.28)

The third example is not easy to interpret although there is a possibility that *tickles* is used as plural noun instead of as a verb (28). The important fact to note is that from the point of view of the form used in all but one example Nina is making non-proximal reference when using a verb with the *-s* suffix. This includes examples in which she is referring to herself by using noun phrase that typically marks non-proximal reference.

Table 7. Inflectional *-s* with subject

age	1S	3S	3P
1;11	1/1	2/7	1/1
2;0		1/1	
2;1	1/1		1/1[7]
2;2	1/1	4/5	
2;3		4/7	
2;4		2/3	

4.2.4. *Past reference and non-finite -ed*

The most interesting fact that emerges from Nina's first past reference is that while strong past tense forms are present from the beginning (table 8), it is not until three months later that the first weak past tense forms occur (table 9). Although not as numeroues as her use of the base form and *-ing*, Nina also produces a number of non-finite verb forms with the *-ed* suffix. As will be discussed in more detail below (cf. 4.2.5.), none of the non-finite verb forms ending with *-ed* belong to the same lemma as the type pairs consisting of the base from and the present participle. Only one of the weak past tense forms was used in opposition with another paradigm member. Of the strong past verb forms, four entered into paradimatic relations with other types of the lemma. Two strong past forms were used together with the base form and the other two formed a three member mini-paradigm together with the base form and the progressive form. In both three-member mini-paradigms the past form only occurred isolated in a specific context. The two paradigmatic sets *eat-eating-ate* and *go-going-went* were therefor not counted as occurences of first three-member mini-paradigms. However, it seems worth mentioning that both lemmas are among the first to occur in paradigmatic contrasts with three verb types, cf. 4.3.5.

Table 8. Strong past verb forms with subject

age	1S	2S	3S	1P
1;11	1/1		1/2	
2;0			2/14	
2;1	3/6	1/1	2/4	
2;2	4/5		4/6	
2;3			2/3	1/1
2;4	2/3		2/2	

All in all past tense reference with appropriate froms is relatively rare in this phase. One interesting fact to mention is that of the strong past tense forms that occurred in the data until month 2;5. many were verbs like *ate, made, gave* all including [ei]. While phonological influences in the acquisition process cannot be discussed here it is possible that Nina has detected a pattern which she is sensitive to for a limited period of time. Regular past tense forms are very rare, but appear with no obvious preference regarding person and number categories, see table 8 and table 9.

Table 9. Weak past verb forms with subject

age	1S	2S	3S	3P
1;11				
2;0				
2;1				
2;2	3/3	1/1	3/7	
2;3	2/2		4/5	1/1
2;4	3/3		1/1	

Table 10 lists the lemma and token numbers of non-finite *-ed*. None of the forms were in contrast with either another non-finite form or a finite verb form.

222 *Insa Gülzow*

Table 10. Non-finite -ed

age	-ed forms
1;11	2/2
2;0	1/1
2;1	1/2
2;2	2/5
2;3	6/11
2;4	4/7

4.2.5. Paradigmatic contrasts

In table 11 verb types are listed that fulfill the criterion for appearance in a mini-paradigm (cf. Bittner et al. this volume).

Table 11. Paradigmatic contrasts

	1;11	2;0	2;1	2;2	2;3	2;4
bite	9	1	5	6	2	1
biting	1		7	6		2
catch		5	5			2
caught			3			
crying	4	5	3	1	4	2
cried					4	1
drink	11	4	3	1	15	2
drinking	6	6	3	4	4	1
eat	9	9	13	19	16	14
eating	9	7	2	8	4	4
ate	3		3	1		
fall	16	16	27	7	14	14
falling			5	2		
give	1	1	5	3	11	1
gave		13	3			
go	1	2	21	48	62	40
going	1	2	5	5	35	7
went				3	1	1
hang			2			5
hanging						3
hop	5	1	2	4		
hopping	2			3		
hops	6					

Table 11. continued

	1;11	2;0	2;1	2;2	2;3	2;4
hurt	8	2	3	2	1	1
hurts	3	1				
make	7	8	26	15	21	13
making		2			3	2
play	4	5	8	4	13	18
playing	2	5	1	4		3
put	1	12	27	15	67	34
putting				1	1	4
sleep	1	3	2	41	24	4
sleeping	1	8	3	19	18	5
talk	1	1	4	2	2	
talking	5	2	3			
touch	2		12		1	
touching			3			
want		1	7	11	107	72
wants					4	
types	9	8	15	13	16	12
lemmas	4	4	7	6	8	6

Apart from *eat-eating-ate* in month 1;11 and 2;1 and *go-going-went* in month 2;2 all pairs have only two members and consist mostly of the base form and the present participle. The five pairs *sleep-sleeping, play-playing, go-going, eat-eating* and *drink-drinking* are the only verb forms that appear with some regularity. All other pairs occur in isolation, in many cases they are produced in a special context. The fairly numerous examples of the past form *gave* in month 2;0 and 2;1 for instance are all embedded in the same context, the recordings in which the verb form occurs are all close to Christmas that year. This is also true for *ate* in the three-member set. Nina produces three tokens of *ate* in each the third and the tenth recorded session, in a context in which the mother is pretending that a chicken just ate Nina's food and in a context in which mother and child talk about eating out in a restaurant some days ago. It has already been mentioned that despite the context-bound use of *ate* and *went* these two verb forms are among those that qualify as members of first mini-paradigms a couple of months later (cf. 4.3.5.). The data in the present study confirm the claim that the suffix *-ing* is at first mainly used with activity verbs (cf. Shirai and

Andersen 1995). Activity verbs that are inherently atelic like *fall*, *catch*, or *give* appear only in low numbers until month 2;5.

To sum up what has been said so far, until Nina reaches an age of 2;5 she mainly produces nonfinite verb forms. Of these, the base form and the present participle appear in greater numbers than the past participle. Regarding first signs of an emerging awareness of morphological operations, a number of overgeneralisations with the *-ing* suffix show that Nina is using the affix somewhat productively. According to Dressler (1997) overgeneralisation such as discussed in section 4.2.2. (cf. table 6) are rather expected to occur in protomorphology than in premorphology. Overgeneralisations mark that the child is beginning to make generalisations which is characteristic for the protomorphological phase. It thus needs some explaining what the status of the affix *-ing* and examples like (23)–(26) is in a phase of morphological development that clearly does not display further signs of the onset of protomorphology. From a typological perspective not all languages make a similar distinction between finite and infinite forms compared to languages such as English and German. It can therefore not be argued universally that children pass through an non-finite phase before they acquire finite inflections. On the other hand it has been shown by Behrens that children acquiring German tend to pass through a stage in which they predominantly use infinitival forms (Behrens 1993). For English, Weist has proposed a stage model in which a phase of uncoded temporal reference is followed by a phase in which the deictic tense marker is encoded (Weist 1986). A similar picture emerges from the data of Nina. As was illustrated in the previous section, not only the base form of the verb and verbs ending in *-ing* are present until Nina reaches an age of 2;5, but regarding the affix *-ed*, it is also produced from the beginning when used as a participle or adjective. The finite use of the inflection *-ed* appears not before Nina reaches an age of 2;2 and only becomes more regular when she is older than 2;5. It seems to be the case that for the child Nina a non-finite phase can be recognized before she moves on to a finite phase. In Dressler's terms the non-finite phase matches premorphology to the extent that with one exception, morphological generalisations are largely absent from the data. The interesting point to note is that during the non-finite or premorphological phase Nina is beginning to make some generalisations regarding the affix *-ing* which shows that Nina has acquired some knowledge of the morphosemantic status of this affix. Regarding this seeming contradiction to Dressler's theory it is important to acknowledge that the premorphological generalisation processes occurs within the adjectival or non-finite verbal system. Nina has established categories such as person and number and to a certain degree past reference. She has learned that verbal elements can have affixes and that affixes can be used to mark person and number distincions. While her system in large parts does not yet fit the target system the observed processes lay the ground for the kind of development that occurs from age 2;5 onwards.

4.3. The finite verbal system

In the following sections the transition from a phase in which Nina predominantly uses non-finite verb forms to a phase in which her production of finite forms becomes more regular will be discussed. Regarding the forms documented in the data of Nina it will be shown that at an age of 2;5 not only a quantitative but also a qualitative change is taking place. The trends occurring in month 2;5 are well established when Nina reaches an age of 2;9 and continue in a similar fashion until the end of the recordings at age 3;3.

4.3.1. Base forms

It was shown in section 4.2.1. (table 4) that person and number distinctions are established relatively early in utterances with base verb forms. Therefore, a similar analysis of form-function pairings is not presented here. Instead, a part of all base verb forms used by Nina will be analysed concerning their status as a finite or non-finite verb form. figure 3 lists token numbers of a subset of the verb lemmas that occurred in the data of Nina. The finite/base category includes targetlike utterances such as (29a)–(29b) and non-targetlike utterances in which the infinitival verb form is used without a further verbal element (29c)–(29d). The non-finite category includes a variety of constructions with both target and non-target uses in which Nina uses the infinitival verb form together with another expression, usally a verb to form a compound construction (29e)–(29f).

(29) a. *CHI: Nina loves Snoopy. (2;1.29)
    b. *CHI: those bite. (2;1.29)
    c. *CHI: I close the doll door. (2;1.15)
    d. *CHI: my read a book. (2;0.24)
    e. *CHI: I will hold panda # Mommy. (2;3.14)
    f. *CHI: oh you can make a snowman. (2;1.22)

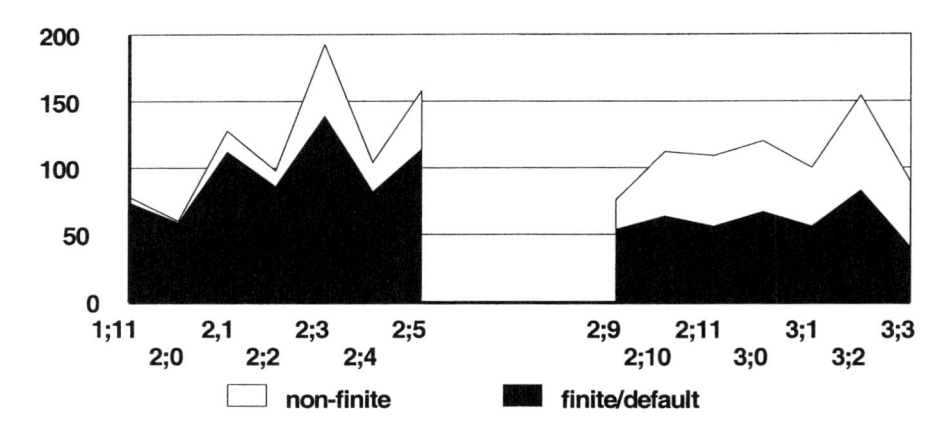

Figure 3. Infinitival forms

The quantitative development of base forms runs contrary to that of all other forms. While there is no obvious trend in 2;5 that is still prevalent in 2;9, it can be said that lemma and token numbers of base forms increase at first and then decrease to reach a fairly stable niveau from age 2;9 onwards. A possible interpretation of this trend is that in early stages of language acquisition base forms are used in place of a variety of analytical verbal constructions. Therefore, the number of utterances with the base form rises due to lexical learning within the first months of the study. Once the base forms begin to occur with modal and non-modal auxiliaries, utterances become more targetlike and the ratio between finite base forms that are targetlike and base forms as members of compound constructions becomes stable. It should be mentioned that even in the very last sessions, Nina uses numerous non-target base forms, but considerably less than in the first sessions of the recordings.

4.3.2. The -ing affix

Concerning the quantitative occurrence of the *-ing* affix, nothing much changes between the non-finite and the finite phase (table 12). It was already discussed in the previous section that the child uses the infinite member of analytical constructions involving the present participle at early stages. Regarding the overall development of verbal morphology it seems to be interesting to note that agreement in analytical constructions with the present participle seems to be acquired in a process that is largely not affected by the qualitative changes occurring from month 2;5 onwards. Below a brief discussion of subject noun phrases in utterances with verbs ending in -*ing* will be given. Three individual months, two in the non-finite phase (1;11 and 2;1) and one in the finite phase (2;9)were chosen.

Table 12. -*ing* verb forms with subject (lemma/token)

age	1S	2S	3S	1P	3P
2;5	10/21	1/2	34/77		13/20
2;9	7/8	6/7	24/43		8/10
2;10					
2;11	4/4	2/2	20/35		9/10
3;0	15/26	4/5	30/72	7/7	6/7
3;1	13/16	7/8	12/20		13/24
3;2	6/6	2/2	13/31	6/8	11/18
3;3	9/15	1/1	27/37	2/2	9/11

Figure 4 shows which kind of subject noun phrases were produced by Nina when referring to third person singular. The three types of construction that appeared in the data are listed below, see (30)–(32). Figure 4 below shows that in month 1;11 a total of 32 tokens in which Nina combined a third person singular subject with a verb form ending in -*ing* appeared.

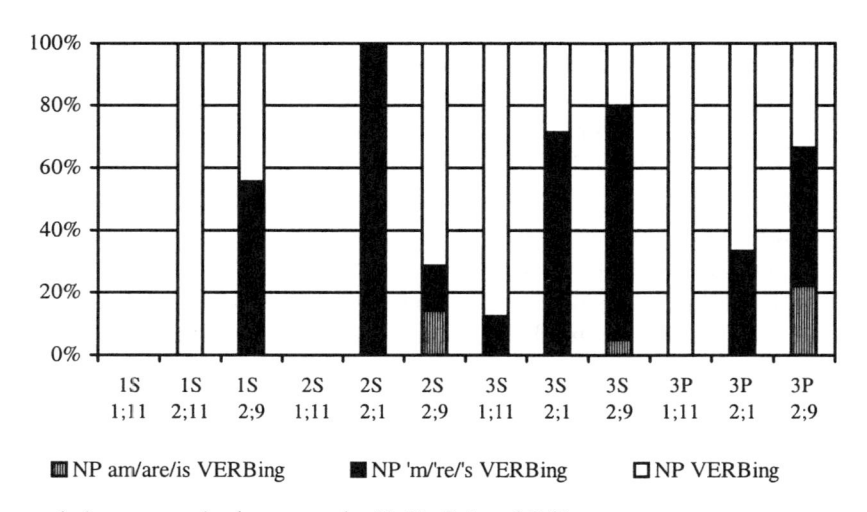

Figure 4. Agreement in three months (1;11, 2;1 and 2;9)

Only a total of three third person plural references was found. First person singular references were documented in the data not before month 2;1. in month 2;9 also second person singular references with subject-verb combinations involving a progressive form appeared. Ultimately, the usage of the present progressive has to show subject-verb agreement. Regarding third person singular referents, only a small percentage, ~12%, appears with target-like agreement in month 1;11. Two months later the situation has changed dramatically and ~70% of the utterances are targetlike. In the third month that was analysed the 80% targetlike utterances are divided between 30 utterances in which agreement is reached by the attachment of a suffix: in these cases 's is attached to the subject noun phrase. Another two utterances were found in which the present progressive is used in its full analytical form. The other kinds of subject noun phrases, 1S, 2S and 3P show a similar kind of development. All in all agreement becomes more accurate in months 2;1 and 2;9. In the majority of cases the progressive is not used fully analytical, but the finite member occurs suffixed to the subject.

(30) *CHI: she swimming.   (2;9) NP VERBing
(31) *CHI: she's smiling.   (2;9) NP'm/'re/'s VERBing
(32) *CHI: my little hand is moving # Mommy. (2;9) NP am/are/is V-ing

Regarding the child's first steps towards the acquisition of the inflectional suffixe *-ing* plus agreement elements like the respective auxiliary the following trend can be observed. The child sets off by using an *-ing* form when referring to third person singular, at first these constructions involve no auxiliary. References to first person singular involving the suffix *-ing* are less numerous, reference to second person is almost non-existent. The next step is the acquisition of agreement factors. At this early stage these are reduced to the affixed version of auxiliaries. First and second person references with *-ing* forms are not used together with auxiliaries at all. In the process of the acquisition of verbal morphology the child first concentrates on third person singular references, which are specified by the use of a verb with the suffix *-ing*. Parallel to the slowly emerging use of *-ing* with first person and finally with second person references agreement factors begin to play a role in third person singular references. The use of the auxiliary *is* or its affixed version is established before agreement with first and second person singular references is reached.

4.3.3. Inflectional -s

One of the most obvious changes that occur in month 2;5 is that lemma and token numbers of verbs bearing the *-s* affix rise (table 13). Table 14 lists all verbs with inflectional *-s* that had a total token number of more than 10 instances in the whole period of the recordings. The five verbs *to go, to like, to need, to say* and *to want* match this criterion. The first point to be mentioned is that the three perceptual verbs *to like, to need* and *to want* cannot be used in the progressive under normal circumstances. Thus a mini-paradigm like *want-wants-wanting* is impossible in these cases. The verb forms *saying* and *says* are the only possible candidates for a mini-paradigm. An interesting point to note is that perceptual verbs *to like, to need, to want* are established relatively late. While it is not surprising that the child's system shows sensitivity to the use of inflectional *-s* in the adult system, it seems worth noting that in the non-finite phase the few examples with inflectional *-s* that do occur are verbs that also take the *-ing* affix while the highest lemma and token numbers of verbs with inflectional *-s* that are introduced to the system from month 2;5 onwards show a semantic pattern and cannot be used in the *-ing* form. Regarding the transition to a phase in which finite verb forms are beginning to occur with some regularity in the language of Nina the quantitative change in verb form with the *-s* affix can thus be correlated with a qualitative change in the system which must be interpreted in a way that the child is showing greater sensitivity to inflectional processes in her target language including restrictions on semantic verb types.

Table 13. Inflectional -s with subject

age	2;5	2;9	2;10	2;11	3;0	3;1	3;2	3;3
3S	8/10	15/33	16/44	11/29	13/26	16/31	12/19	16/34

Table 14. Verbs used with -s with high token numbers

age	1;11	2;0	2;1	2;2	2;3	2;4	2;5	2;9	2;10	2;11	3;0	3;1	3;2	3;3	T
goes	1		1	1	2		7	6	9	5	3	2		3	40
likes								5	1	1	3			1	10
needs											4	3		5	12
says	1		1			1	3	3	4	2				1	16
wants				4			5	15	6	8	6	2		6	52

4.3.4. Past reference

Three facts need to mentioned concerning the changes in Nina's system of past references. First, lemma and token numbers of weak past formations rise but not as dramatically as in the case of inflectional -s. Second, strong past formations also rise regarding lemma and token numbers but also not as dramatically as inflectional -s (table 15). Third, overgeneralisations with -ed begin to occur in greater numbers (table 16).

Table 15. Weak and strong past tense formations (token/lemma)

		1;11	2;0	2;1	2;2	2;3	2;4	2;5	2;9	2;10	2;11	3;0	3;1	3;2	3;3
weak	token			1	11	13	6	20	27	41	19	30	18	31	19
	lemma			1	4	8	6	11	15	24	13	24	10	17	12
strong	token	3	14	11	13	5	7	33	29	35	17	22	21	29	25
	lemma	1	2	4	7	4	4	8	8	9	10	8	6	9	10

It has already been mentioned that the occurrence of overgeneralisations must be interpreted as a symptom that the child is specifically interacting with a structure of her target language. The high lemma and token numbers in table 16 from month 2;5 onwards document that the child is detecting analogous inflectional processes regarding the formation of weak past forms. An interesting point to note is that along with a higher number of strong past forms in this phase, overgeneralized forms with -ed involve examples in which the suffix -ed is attached to the target irregular past form, like *broked and *felled. With *branged Nina produces a form that is overgeneralized in two ways. First the attachment of the suffix -ed and second, a vowel change analogous to verbs like *ring-rang-rung*, or *sing-sang-sung*. Nina produces one example in which she treats a preposition like a verb, similar to *outing, she uses *uped.

Table 16. Overgeneralisations with -ed

	1;11	2;0	2;1	2;2	2;3	2;4	2;5	2;9	2;10	2;11	3;0	3;1	3;2	3;3	T
blowed					1						1				2
branged							1								1
breaked						1						1			2
broked									1						1
buyed											1	1			2
doed						1									1
drinked								1							1

Table 16. continued

	1;11	2;0	2;1	2;2	2;3	2;4	2;5	2;9	2;10	2;11	3;0	3;1	3;2	3;3	T
falled				1			1	1	1			1	3	1	9
feeled													1		1
felled					1										1
goed											1	1	1	2	5
hanged									1						1
runned								2							2
sayed							1	1							2
seed			1							1					2
swimmed							2	1							3
taked								7	2	2		1	6		18
telled								1		1					2
uped						1									1
waked												1			1
weared									1						1
total	0	0	1	0	1	0	2	7	15	7	7	5	11	3	59

4.3.5. Paradigmatic contrasts

As must be expected, paradigmatic pairs of the sort base form-present participle become more numerous in the second phase of morphological development discussed here. These pairs are mainly activity verbs and increasingly inherently telic verbs and will not be discussed further. Apart from these pairs other types of paradigmatic sets beginn to emerge. Table 17 lists all verb types that contributed to such sets involving at least two different verb types of one lemma. Only those sets that occurred with some regularity were included. In table 17 three major patterns can be detected. First, two member pairs like *eat-eating* and *make-making* now appear together with a third form, a strong past formation like *ate* or *made*. Second, a new type of two-member pairs is established consisting of the base form and the third person singular present indicative, like *need-needs* or *want-wants*. Third, of a number of verbs four types are documented consisting of the base form, the present participle, a strong past form and the third person singular present indicative form.

232 Insa Gülzow

Table 17. Paradigmatic contrasts

	2;5	2;9	2;10	2;11	3;0	3;1	3;2	3;3
come	18	3	14	6	12	19	27	15
coming	4	2	6	3	5	1		1
came			2		2	3	1	4
eat	53	15	70	6	25	20	34	20
eating	19	3	18	3	8	9	2	4
eats	1					1	1	5
ate	1	1	10		2	4	8	3
give	3	6	9	20	11	8	25	5
gave	2	14	4	1	7	8	3	3
goes		7	6	9	5	3	2	3
went	8		4		1		1	2
make	42	28	50	10	15	11	23	16
making	3	5	5		1			6
made	1	4	5		3	2	2	2
need	1			1	4	6	27	22
needs						4	3	5
play	9	28	48	7	24	9	25	7
playing	9	6	2	3	4	4	3	9
played	1	4	3	1	2	3	1	1
say	6	6	9	3	10	2		6
saying	1		2	3	3			1
says	1	3	3	4	2			1
said		3	4	4	4		6	3
take	46	12	29	16	20	26	25	15
taking	4	2	4	2	1	3		
*taked			7	2	2	1	6	
want	1	1	3	11	105	>100	>100	>100
wants		5	15	6	8	6	2	6

Regarding such paradigmatic sets as *eat-eating-ate* and *make-making-made* it seems worth noting that despite the general emergence of the suffix *-ed* as a past marker (cf. table 3) which was regarded as a major developmental step in this phase, the third member of the set is not a weak past formation but the targetlike strong past form. It was already mentioned in section 4.2. that Nina seems to be sensitive to [ei] as a pattern of past formation. In month 2;10 Nina produces the three sets *eat-eating-ate*, *make-making-made* and *take-taking-*taked*. Along with the form *played* which is produced as a member of the set *play-playing-played* in month 2;9 for the first time, **taked* and *played* are the only weak past forms that appear as members of paradigmatic sets. This is an intersting point to note as Nina produces numerous past forms with *-ed* in this phase including a number of overgeneralisations. In comparison to past forms like *made* and *ate*, **taked* and *played* share the [ei] sound with the strong forms. Also both *made* and *ate* end in [d] or [t], both allomorphs of the past marker *-ed*. Although not produced in greater numbers, table 16 gives two token instances of an overgeneralized past form that shares the same pattern, *sayed*. With regard to pairs like *need-needs*, *like-likes* and *want-wants* it has already been mentioned that Nina's productions mirror a semantic bias of the target language that does not regularily include verb types like *needing*, *liking* or *wanting*. The two-member sets lack a past from until the end of the recordings when Nina has reached an age of 3;3. Within the paradigmatic sets discussed here, another three third person singular present indicative forms are documented, *goes*, *eats* and *says*. The three cannot be related in terms of belonging to a similar semantic verb type as *need*, *want* and *like* since they do not depict mental states. To the contrary, all three are somewhat different in their use. The inclusion of *goes* in the same paradigm as *go-going-went* seems somewhat problematic as *goes* was used by Nina in sentences such as (33). It could therefor be argued that *goes* belongs to a different lemma than *go-going-went* as it is not used with the meaning of moving someplace but rather meaning that something belongs someplace. The verb type *says* mainly occurred in a fixed phrase like (34) and it is therefor difficult to argue that it represents a form that is morphologically analysed. The form *eats* is different form the other forms with the suffix *-s* as it is used with a habitual meaning, see (35).

(33) *CHI: that goes on the house. (1;11.24)
(34) *CHI: chicken says cook+a+doodle+doo (2;9.26)
(35) *CHI: he eats mud (3;3.21)

5. Conclusion

The scarcity of inflectional affixes in English considerably reduces the probability of different inflectional verb forms occurring that belong to one lemma. Additionally, semantic factors contribute to the absence of paradigmatic pairs like *needs-needing* in the data. Therefore, in the case of

English, mini-paradigms cannot serve as a safe indicator that the child is making a transit from pre- to protomorphology. This is not to say that a child acquiring English as her first language does not pass through stages that can be called pre- and protomorphology with justification. It was shown that a number of other factors that are recognized by Dressler (1997) as symptomatic for phases in children's morphological development can be identified in the data of Nina. These included the rise of token and lemma numbers from month 2;5 onwards and the occurrence of overgeneralisations. The parallel analysis of the data both from a perspective of interverbal and verbspecific paradigmatic development showed that Nina's transition from one phase of morphological development to the next could be correlated with a number of developmental steps. In a phase of morphological development in which Nina predominantly uses non-finite forms, the base form and the present participle combine into two-member mini-paradigms only in a very limited number of cases. In the next phase of morphological development token and lemma numbers rise dramatically. Nina uses finite verb forms more regularily, these are mostly weak past forms and the third person singular present indicative form. Nina's use of strong past forms rises only slightly in token and lemma numbers. Despite this finding, with regard to paradigmatic contrasts, the two-member mini-paradigms of phase one develop into a few three-member mini-paradigms and two instances of a four-member paradigm. Apart from two examples, *came* and *went*, all mini-paradigms that have more than two members have integrated a past form that includes an [ei] sound and final [d] or [t], like *ate*, *made*, *played* and *taked*. One other past form that Nina uses during this phase combines an overgeneralisation of both patterns, vowel change and final dental plosive, *sayed* ([seid]). While a verb independent analysis of verbal affixes could be interpreted in a way that Nina is concentrating on the *-ed* affix in her acquisition of past reference forms, the past reference forms that occur most frequently and therefor end up as members of mini-paradigms, display both the pattern of weak and strong past inflection. Overgeneralisations on the other hand are mainly with *-ed*, only one example with an overgeneralised vowel change could be found in *sayed*. Together with Nina's increasing use of *-s* from month 2;5 onwards, this phase of morphological development can be interpreted to represent protomorphology in the sense of Dressler (1997). The preceeding phase until month 2;5 displays the characteristics of premorphology in so far as apart from the *-ing* affix, verbal suffixes hardly occur. The fact that in this phase *-ing* could be regarded as having an independent status as an affix which was documented in a couple of overgeneralised uses was interpreted as directly reflecting the fact that in English the non-finite and the finite verbal system develop somewhat independently.

Compared to the other children analysed in this volume, Nina reaches protomorphology relatively late, beginning her transition at an age of 2;5. In the present volume and another study reported by Kilani-Schoch (Kilani-Schoch et al. 1997) only a minority of children enters the phase of protomorphology comparatively late, these are the German child Bernd (cf. Kilani-Schoch et al. 1997) and the Austrian child Katharina (Klampfer 2000). Bernd leaves premorphology at an age of 2;6, Katharina at an age of 2;3. In the majority of languages discussed in this volume, in premorphology the children start with only some affixes used in isolation and move on "picking up" inflections on their way to a first mini-paradigm which is believed to be one factor that signals the onset of protomorphology. Among the first categories to be established, third person singular and the imperative are recurrent. The forms used to mark these categories are in many cases the infinitival, imperative and third person singular form of the verb. In the case of English the form-function pairings at the very beginning in month 1;11 display these characteristics. In subsequent months other person/number categories are also established by Nina but no affixes are "picked up" on the way as there are no inflectional person/number distinctions. During the following months, Nina's morphological system keeps changing but not in a way that can be counted as symptomatic for the onset of protomorphology. It is only half a year later at an age of 2;5 that Nina's data shows clear indications of a quantitative and a qualitative change that was interpreted as the onset of protomorpholgy. In an alternative interpretation of the data in the present study it could be argued that premorphology ends at the end of month 1;11 which displayed all the characteristics typical for early premorphology. As little happens from the point of view of morphological development regarding synthetic verbal forms until 2,5, the period between 2;0 and 2;4 could be regarded as a prolonged transitional phase between pre- and protomorphology. This interpretation is in accordance with an observation made in many of the studies in this volume. That the transition from pre- to protomorphology is not abrupt but a gradual process is recognized in all contributions. As Klampfer (this volume) and Wójcik (this volume) observe regarding the morphological development of an Austrian and a Lithuanian child, the children go through a phase in which numerous two-member paradigms are documented before the first true mini-paradigms occur.

Notes

1. As verb forms like *ring-rang-rung* and *sing-sang-sung* are constructed somewhat parallel, in the present analysis these verbs will be refered to as "strong" rather than "irregular". What Brown calls "regular" verbs will be refered to as "weak" verbs here.
2. In the following, the term "base form" will be used rather than "infinitive form".
3. Note that in table 3 and subsequent tables and figures there is some effect of the total number of recorded utterances per month as they vary from month to month. Some peaks and lows in lemma and token numbers are to be interpreted as an effect of the high or low total number of child utterances. It goes without saying that the trends that will be discussed in this paper are visible despite high or low values for the total number of utterances per month. Recurrent peaks that must be interpreted as an effect of the total number of utterances occur in the months 2;3, 2;5, and 2;10. Somewhat lower values can be expected for the months 2;4 and 2;11.
4. In this column, percentages are given with respect to the proportion that the total token numbers with verbs as listed in this table represent in relation to the total number of utterances recorded in each month as listed in table 2. For age 2;5 onwards see section 4.3.1.
5. A discussion of Nina's use of infinitival verb forms from an age of 2;5 onwards can be found in section 4.3.1.
6. In the present study, an indepth discussion of the concept of finiteness is impossible. The present analysis rests on the assumption that English has three nonfinite forms: the infinitive *(to) walk*, the present participle *walking* and the past participle *walked*. Nonfinite forms are not inflected for number and person and predominantly occur in compound constructions in which they combine with a finite auxiliary or modal verb to constitute the sentence predicate.
7. The two examples in which Nina uses third person singular -*s* together with a plural subject noun phrase are listed below. From an age of 2;2 onwards these examples disappear from the data.
   *CHI: deers walks. (1;11.29)
   *CHI: those bites. (2;1.29)

References

Antinucci, Francesco, and Ruth Miller
    1976   How children talk about what happened. *Journal of Child Language* 3: 167–189.

Behrens, Heike
1993   Temporal reference in German child language. Ph.D. thesis, Universiteit van Amsterdam.

Bloom, Lois, Karin Lifter, and Jeremy Hafitz
1980   Semantics of verbs and the development of verb inflection in child language. *Language* 56: 386–412.

Bronckart, Jean Paul, and Hermina Sinclair
1973   Time, tense and aspect. *Cognition* 2: 107–130.

Brown, Roger
1973   *A First Language*. Cambridge: Cambridge University Press.

Dressler, Wolfgang
1997   Introduction. In: Katarczyna Dziubalska-Kołaczyk (ed.), *Pre- and Protomorphology in Language Acquisition*, 7–14. (Papers and Studies in Contrastive Linguistics 33.) Poznań: Adam Mickiewicz University.

Kilani-Schoch, Marianne, Anna De Marco, Anastasia Christofido, Maria Vassilakou, Ralf Vollmann, and Wolfgang U. Dressler
1997   On the demarcation of phases in early morphology acquisition in four langugaes. In: Katarczyna Dziubalska-Kołaczyk (ed.), *Pre- and Protomorphology in Language Acquisition*, 15–32. (Papers and Studies in Contrastive Linguistics 33.) Poznań: Adam Mickiewicz University.

Klampfer, Sabine
2000   Early verb development in one Austrian child. In: Dagmar Bittner, Wolfgang U. Dressler, and Marianne Kilani-Schoch (eds.), *First Verbs: On the Way to Miniparadigms*, 7–20. (ZAS Papers in Linguistics 18.) Berlin: Zentrum für Allgemeine Sprachwissenschaft, Typologie und Universalienforschung (ZAS).

Li, Ping, and Yasuhiro Shirai
2000   *The Acquisition of Lexical and Grammatical Aspect.* Berlin/New York: Mouton de Gruyter.

Shirai, Yasuhiro, and Roger W. Andersen
1995   The acquisition of tense/aspect morphology: A prototype account. *Language* 71: 743–762.

Tomasello, Michael
  1992   *First Verbs: A Case Study of Early Grammatical Development.*
           Cambridge: Cambridge University Press.

Weist, Richard
  1986   Tense and aspect: Temporal systems in child language. In: Paul Fletcher, and Michael Garman (eds.), *Language Acquisition*, 356–374. Cambridge: Cambridge University Press.

Weist, Richard, and Hanna Wysocka
  1984   The defective tense hypothesis: On the emergence of tense and aspect in child Polish. *Journal of Child Language* 11: 347–374.

Wexler, Kenneth
  1994   Optional infinitives, verb movement and the economy of derivation in child grammar. In: David Lightfoot, and Norbert Hornstein (eds.), *Verb Movement,* 305–350. Cambridge: Cambridge University Press.

Wijnen, Frank, Masja Kempen, and Steven Gillis
  2001   Root infinitives in Dutch early child language: An effect of input. *Journal of Child Language* 28: 629–660.

Early verb development in one Croatian-speaking child*

Antigone Katičić

0. Introduction

This paper shows the early development of verb morphology of one Croatian girl. Focus will be laid on the emergence of verb paradigms. Furthermore the aim is to analyse and interpret the child's verb development in terms of the transition from pre- to protomorphology (Dressler and Karpf 1995).

1. Description of Croatian verb morphology
1.1. Grammatical categories

The verbal system of the Croatian variety which is acquired by the child under investigation, can be described with the following verbal categories: person (1., 2., and 3.), number (singular and plural), mood (synthetic: indicative, imperative, analytic: conditional I and II), aspect (perfective, imperfective), tense (synthetic: present, analytic: perfect, pluperfect, future I, and future II), infinitive and the adjectival past participle agent.[1]

Although we have no systematic evidence from the child's input regarding the frequency of the use of verbal categories, one can assume that conditional II, the optative, the patient participle and pluperfect are either not used at all or very rarely. Except for elliptic contexts, e.g. in answers to questions, infinitives and participles hardly appear without finite auxiliary verbs. Although, in a special stylistic use and also in colloquial speech, past participles, especially when used in third singular contexts, can be used without an auxiliary verb.

Croatian is a pro-drop language. The finite verb agrees with the subject in regard to person and number. Participles (in analytic tense forms) are marked for gender and number. The child is acquiring an urban variant, usually referred to as Zagreb Kajkavian dialect (ZKD). This dialect differs in many respects from the Štokavian standard variant (c.f. Magner 1966; Šojat 1979). For the purposes of this work it is important to mention that the only form expressing the past is the analytic perfect. Forms of exact future (future II) have the same temporal reference as future I. They are usually used in ZKD to express future tense and not future perfect as in the standard language. In addition, it is typical for ZKD that overt pronouns in contexts which require pro-drop in the standard language do not imply emphatic interpretation.

Examples for categories which show up in the child's speech productions in the analysed period are given below exemplified by forms of the verb *gledati* 'to look' (infinitive).

Table 1. Morphological marking in Croatian synthetic moods[2]

	Present indicative		Imperative	
	Singular	Plural	Singular	Plural
1P	*gled-a-m*	*gled-a-mo*		
2P	*gled-a-š*	*gled-a-te*	*gled-a-j*	*gled-a-j-te*
3P	*gled-a*	*gled-a-ju*		

	Active past participle		
	Masculine	Feminine	Neuter
Singular	*gled-a-o*	*gled-a-la*	*gled-a-lo*
Plural	*gled-a-li*	*gled-a-le*	*gled-a-la*

Aspect: imperfective: *pre-gled-av-a-ti* 'search through'
        perfective: *pre-gled-a-ti*

Aspect is mostly expressed derivationally: typically by suffixes and prefixes. The latter are occasionally combined with ablaut. Prefixation plays an important role in perfective formation, but it hardly has exclusively grammatical function, because it almost always also modifies the lexical meaning of the verb.

Tense: synthetic: present *gledam, -aš* ... (see table 1)
        analytic: future I is formed by the clitic forms of the verb *htjeti* 'want' and the infinitive (see table 2).
                    future II consists of the perfective forms of *biti* 'be' and the active past participle (see table 3). Perfect tense is also formed with the latter participle and clitic forms of *biti* 'be' (see table 4).

Table 2. Future I formation

	Infinitive	Singular	Plural
1.	gledat(i)	ću	ćemo
2.		ćeš	ćete
3.		će	će

Table 3. Future II formation

	AUX³	Participle
1S	budem	gledao, -la, -lo
2S	budeš	
3S	bude	
1P	budemo	gledali, -le, -la
2P	budete	
3P	budu	

Table 4. Perfect formation

	Participle	AUX
1S	gledao, -la, -lo	sam
2S		si
3S		je
1P	gledali, -le, -la	smo
2P		ste
3P		su

1.2. Inflectional classes

As a typical Slavic language Croatian is a fusional-inflecting language and is considered to be morphologically rich. The verbal inflectional system consists of many distinct morphological classes.[4] Dressler, Dziubalska-Kołaczyk, and Katičić (1996) establish in their classification of verbal paradigms on the basis of inflectional productivity, 4 major macroclasses with productive microclasses and one recessive class with root inflection and many irregularities. In table 5 only those classes are listed, which show up in the child's production. Classes are referred to by numbers: the first number indicates the respective macroclass, the second number the class, capital letters indicate subclasses and small letters microclasses. The forms given are: infinitive, 1s.pres.ind, 3p.pres.ind, imperative, fem.s.active/past participle. In the following row the plus or minus sign shows whether the respective class is productive or not.

Off all classes 4/a is the most frequent, homogeneous, transparent and productive microclass, which integrates almost all loan words. Thematic vowels or consonants can be the same in present and infinitive stems as in microclass 4/a and 3/1/a or they can differ as in all other classes. In the 3/1/a microclass, 3s.pres and 2s.imp are homophonous, e.g. *nosi* 'carry-3/2s'. In ZKD many verbs belonging to class 3/2/a and 2/2/b are inflected like verbs from class 3/1/a and 4/a respectively, e.g. *kašljem > kašljam* 'cough' and *voljeti > voliti* 'love'.

Table 5. Verb-classes

Class	Infinitive	1S	3P	IMP	PART	Prod.	English
4/a	gled-a-ti	gled-a-m	gled-a-ju	gled-a-j!	gled-a-la	+	look
3/1/a	nos-i-ti	nos-i-m	nos-e	nos-i!	nos-i-la	+	carry
3/2/a	vid-je-ti	vid-i-m	vid-e	vid-i!	vid-je-la	–	see
3/3/a	drž-a-ti	drž-i-m	drž-e	drž-i!	drž-a-la	–	hold
1/2/a	pi-ti	pi-j-e-m	pi-j-u	pi-j!	pi-la	–	drink
2/1/A/a	ski-nu-ti	ski-n-e-m	ski-n-u	ski-n-i!	ski-nu-la	+	take down
2/2/a	pis-a-ti	piš-e-m	piš-u	piš-i!	pis-a-la	–	write
2/2/b	kašlj-a-ti	kašlj-e-m	kašlj-u	kašlj-i!	kašlj-a-la	–	cough
2/2/c	pr-a-ti	per-e-m	per-u	per-i!	pr-a-la	–	wash
Suppl.	biti	(je)sam	(je)su	budi!	bila	–	be
Isolated	htje-ti	hoć-u	hoć-e	–	htje-la	–	want
Root-class	pas-ti	pad-n-e-m	pad-n-u	pad-n-i!	pa-la	–	fall down

2. Data description

Verb productions treated in this study are taken from a longitudinal corpus of a first-born girl. Antonija is growing up in Zagreb and her input is a Croatian urban koine, also called the Zagreb (Kajkavian) dialect (see section 1.).

The analysis includes recordings from the age of 1;6.15, when the child produced the first clearly identifiable verb productions, until the age of 2;0, when mini-paradigm formation can be clearly identified. The recordings have been transcribed and coded following the norms of CHILDES (MacWhinney 2000).[5] Table 6 shows details of the Antonija corpus.

Note that there is a period of almost two months where no recordings were made (between 1;7.27 and 1;9.15). The column "overall productions" covers all transcribed units except for babbling, paralinguistic material (e.g. laughing) and unintelligible vocalisations.

The column "analysed utterances"[6] includes all productions except citations (e.g. nursery rhymes and songs), direct imitations and repetitions[7]. Utterances with formulaic or phatic forms, e.g. znaš! ('you know!', meaning warning and displeasure), molim ('I ask', meaning 'please') were also excluded from the analysis. Furthermore numbers of utterances which include verbs are given. In order to achieve a better overall view, from now on figures will be given per month of life. There has been no striking linguistic development between the single recordings in the particular months which would be an obstacle to such a grouping of sessions.

Table 6. Data

Session	Age (y;m)	Age (y;m.d)	Overall productions	Analysed utterances	Utterances with verbs
AB06	1;6	1;6.15	65	58	18
AB07		1;7.2	80	77	24
AB08	1;7	1;7.15	142	116	27
AB09		1;7.27	123	89	20
AB10	1;9	1;9.15	249	197	112
AB11		1;10	153	146	66
AB12	1;10	1;10.10	77	56	19
AB13		1;10.21	81	74	34
AB14		1;10.30	56	54	16
AB15		1;11.10	48	34	8
AB16	1;11	1;11.17	60	60	16
AB17		1;11.25	77	75	38
AB18	2;0	2;0.2	104	85	47
AB19		2;0.12	93	90	38
Total			1408	1211	483

3. Verbs in the input

As regards the input of the child, no quantitative systematic analysis can be provided for the purpose of this study. The mother's productions can be characterised as follows[8]:

Synthetic verb forms appear predominantly in the singular as indicative present and imperative. In the indicative present all three person categories are represented, whereas 3s. and 2s. forms exceed by far 1s. forms. Synthetic plural forms are comparatively rare and appear as 1. and 3. person in indicative present and 1. plural in imperative. Among analytic forms, future I and especially perfect constructions are very frequently used. A few instances of conditional I are also produced by Antonija's mother in the analysed period. Future II forms expressing future tense, a characteristic of ZKD, are used very rarely by the mother. Nevertheless, we have evidence that other participants of the family confront the child regularly with future II forms.

During any single session the mother produces relatively often form contrasts. These contrasts appear with suppletive and irregular verbs, which usually are grammatic verbs, and also with verbs of classes with a varying degree of transparency. Examples are given below.[9]

(1) a. AB 6   *pisati: pišem* 'write': 2/2/a: *piše* (3s.pres) – *pišeš* (2s.pres) – *nije pisala* (3s.neg.perf.fem.sg)

     b. AB 8   *baciti: bacim* 'throw, pfv.': 3/1/a: *baci* (2s.imp) – *baciš* (2s.pres) – *bi bacila* (3s.cond.I.fem.sg) – *ste bacili* (2p.perf.masc.pl) – *bacimo* (1p.pres) – *je bacio* (3s.perf.masc.sg)

     c. AB 10   *biti: sam* 'be': suppletive: *sam* (1s.pres) – *si* (2s.pres) – *je* (3s.pres) – *smo* (1p.pres)

     d. AB 16   *imati: imam* 'have': 4/a: *imaš* (2s.pres) – *ima* (3s.pres) – *budeš imala* (2s.fut.II.fem.sg)

     e. AB 19   *čuti: čujem* 'hear': 1/2/a: *čuješ* (2s.pres) – *čuj* (2s.imp) – *si čula* (2s.perf.fem)

4. Emergence of verb forms

4.1. Verb production

Table 7 shows figures about Antonija's verb usage. It shows numbers of all analysed utterances, utterances with verbs and their relation to all analysed utterances. Furthermore, numbers of verbs as lemmas[10] (in brackets the proportion of new lemmas)[11], types[12] and tokens in absolute numbers are presented.[13]

Table 7. Verb production

Age	Analysed Utterances	Utterances with verbs	%Utt. with verbs/ ana-lysed utt.	Lemmas (new lemmas)	Types	Tokens
1;6	58	18	31	6 (6)	6	18
1;7	282	71	25	27 (23)	33	74
1;9	197	112	57	28 (17)	39	131
1;10	330	135	41	40 (19)	58	156
1;11	169	62	37	31 (12)	48	80
2;0	175	85	49	33 (11)	56	116
Total	1211	483	40	165 (88)	240	575

Sample size varies strongly between different sections and therefore the rate of verbs (tokens, lemmas and types) cannot easily be interpreted on the basis of absolute numbers. In order to make figures for each month suitable for comparison they are set into relation to the number of all analysed utterances. The relation of lemmas types and tokens is presented in figure 1.

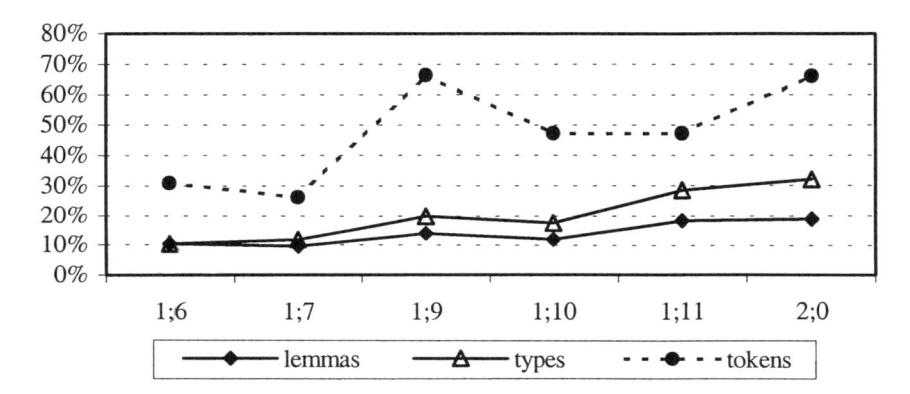

Figure 1. Tokens, types, and lemmas in relation to all analysed utterances

From the moment on when verbs emerge in Antonija's productions their rate is considerably high. Utterances with verbs and verb tokens represent 31% of all analysed utterances. This rate shows a small decrease at 1;7 before verb usage in general increases.[14] In the analysed period the quantity of different verb lemmas and types grows gradually. No huge spurt can be observed. In regard to the general use of verbs, which is represented by the numbers of tokens and utterances with verbs, two peaks appear in the curve. At 1;9 we assume that the quantitative distribution is connected with a development in Antonija's verbal system, especially with regard to syntax and morpho-syntax. The fact that no striking increase shows up with different verb lemmas can be explained by her extensive use of grammatical verbs (copula and auxiliaries) and by the occasional omission of lexical verbs in analytic constructions (see section 4. and 5.). Table 8 shows numbers of grammatical verb lemmas, types and tokens for each session and their rate percentage in relation to the number of all verb lemmas, types and tokens. At 2;0 there is another increase in the use of verbs, although this time the rate of grammatical verbs is not conspicuously growing. At this point the child's verbal lexicon and inventory of verb forms has expanded. Furthermore, subordination shows up, which occasionally results in utterances with four verb tokens. It is necessary to consider recording sessions which show the child's further development in order to detect, whether the increased verb production at 2;0 represents the beginning of a qualitative change in the verbal system.

Table 8. Grammatical verbs

Age	Lemmas	% Lemmas	Types	% Types	Tokens	% Tokens
1;6	1	17	1	17	6	33
1;7	2	7	3	9	26	35
1;9	4	14	7	18	69	53
1;10	5	13	9	16	56	36
1;11	4	13	8	17	21	26
2;0	5	15	15	27	37	32
Total	21	13	43	18	215	37

4.2. Verb forms and categories (1;6–1;7): Premorphology

The first verb forms appearing in the corpus and their correspondence with verbal categories of the target language are shown in numbers of lemmas/tokens in table 9. The rate of the copula is given in brackets.

Table 9. Verb categories 1;6–1;7

	1;6	1;7
1S IND	1/1	3/4 (1/2)
3S IND	3/10 (1/6)	16/39 (2/23)
2S IMP	1/6	7/22
INF + 1P IMP		1/1 + 1/1
PAST PART.+AUX-3S		1/1 + 1/1
Ambig. 3S PRES/2S IMP	1/1	1/1
Ambig. 1P IMP/IND		1/2
Infinitive		1/1
Root		1/1

First verb forms are in most cases present 3s and imperative 2s, the former being more frequent in lemmas and tokens than the latter. Forms of the 3s correspond in lexical verbs to the base form, which is the least marked form[15]: *p(r)iča* 'tells', *kupa* 'bathes', *g(l)eda* 'looks', *čita* 'reads'. Verb forms in 3s frequently also show up with the affirmative enclitic and the negated copula: (ni)je.¹⁶ The forms *baci* 'throw' and *p(r)imi* 'grasp' are ambiguous (pres.3s/imp.2s). They are also base forms (root+thematic -*i*) and belong to the productive microclass 3/1/a (see section 4.4.). Clear instances of imperatives occur with the verbs *čekati* 'wait' and *dati* 'give'. The respective forms are *čekaj!* and *daj!* Antonija also uses the shortened imperative form *g(l)e!* 'look' (instead of *gledaj!*) which is very frequently used in colloquial speech.¹⁷

In the present indicative 1. person marking was observed with three verbs: *bacim* 'I throw', *nisam* 'I'm not' and *neću* 'I don't want'. Other categories appear very rarely and mostly in a single lemma.

Plural can be found only with presumably formulaic and rote-learnt expressions in imperative or ambiguously imperative or indicative mood: *idemo p(j)evati* 'let's sing' and *bacimo* 'throw' (1p.pres.pfv. or 1p.imp). Moreover one single analytic verb form appears, context bound 3s.perf.masc: *pao je* 'he fell down'.

When looking at context and meaning of these early verb forms it becomes apparent that 3s forms are used also instead of other categories, e.g. 1s¹⁸ and imperative. Examples are:

(2) Situation: Antonija insists in taking her father's keys from the table.
 *MOT: ne   maco ne.
          'no   kitty no.'
 *MOT: to   je tatino.
          this is paternal
          'this belongs to daddy.'
 *ANT: (h)oće.
          want-3S

(3) Situation: Antonija brings a picture-book to her mother and asks her to read.
 *ANT: čita!¹⁹
          read-3S

Generally, Antonija's verb productions in sessions 1;6–1;7 indicate that she is in the premorphological phase, devoid of any specific morphological activity. In this period verb forms appear to be non-analysed and rote-learnt (see MacWhinney 1978; Dressler and Karpf 1995). Lemmas show up in just one single form. Exceptions in this respect are the verb *baciti* and the negated copula (auxiliary) *ne biti* (see section 6.). Suffixes marking person and number in the target language are often skipped in lexical verbs, hence

248 *Antigone Katičić*

replaced descriptively speaking by 3s. present which may be interpreted as the default verb form. Infinitives and participles are very rare and when used they seem to be strictly context-bound.

4.3. Verb forms and categories (1;9–2;0): Protomorphology

After a long recording interval of almost two months, Antonija produces more and new verb (sub)categories. She already produces repeatedly multi-word utterances (cf. section 5.). Table 10 shows categories, which are realised by synthetic verb forms (present and imperative) and furthermore constructions with infinitives (i.e. various lexical or modal verbs plus infinitive). Numbers in the cells are to be interpreted as lemmas/tokens. Infinitives which have been produced in constructions with finite verbs are referred to underneath the respective categories. Since the rate of the copula is relatively high, figures in brackets refer to copula productions.

Table 10. Synthetic categories (present and imperative), constructions with the infinitive

	1;9 PRES	IMP	1;10 PRES	IMP	1;11 PRES	IMP	2;0 PRES	IMP
1S + INF	8/17 (1/1) 1/1	–	10/34 (1/4) 1/1	–	6/12 (1/1) 2/3	–	7/14 (2/4) 1/1	–
2S + INF	3/4 (1/2)	4/12	7/15	7/12 1/1	8/12 (2/5) 1/1	4/5	5/7 3/3	9/34
3S + INF	7/44 (2/38)		8/45 (2/26) 1/1		8/10 1/1		5/14 (2/8)	
1P + INF		1/2 1/2	1/2			1/1	1/1	1/4 1/1
3P		1/1	1/1				1/1	

From the age of 1;9 in addition to 3. person, also other persons, especially 1. singular, are used in singular indicative mood. Lexical verbs are marked with the respective suffixes (*-m, -š*), e.g. *zezam* 'tease-1s', *znam* 'know-1s', *nemam* 'not have-1s', *imaš* 'have-2s', *p(r)ičaš* 'tell-2s'. Verbs, which appeared in premorphology as base forms in imperative context, show up with the imperative suffix. E.g. forms of the verb *čitati, -am* 'read': *čita* at 1;7.2 and *čitaj*! at 1;10.10.

Plural forms remain rare until the end of the analysed period. They are predominantly represented in 1p. imperative forms and appear with the same lemma *ići* 'go' as in the earlier sessions: *idemo p(j)evati!* 'let's sing!'.

First analogical errors appear. The verb *htjeti* 'want', which has an irregular suffix (*hoć-u*) in the target language, is repeatedly realised as *hoćem* in 1s. The form used by the child shows that she has identified the "theme plus *–m*" suffix as 1s marking.[20] Furthermore, at the age of 1;10.30 the first 3p.pres form emerges with the most transparent suffix *-ju*, which results in the "erroneous" verb form *(l)jubiju* 'kiss/love-3p.pres' (see section 7.2.) instead of the target form *ljube*. The above mentioned errors show that Antonija has begun to detect already properties of the inflectional system she is acquiring.

Table 11a presents figures of the production of analytic categories, i.e. future I, II, and perfect (cf. tables 2, 3, and 4).[21] Finally, table 11b shows the amount of non-finite verb forms, which have been produced without corresponding finite ones.

Table 11a. Categories: analytic (perfect, future I and II)

	1;9		1;10		1;11		2;0	
Future I	AUX	+ INF	AUX	+ INF	AUX	+ INF	AUX	+ INF
1S	2/25	5/9	3/6	3/3	2/3	3/3	1/1	1/1
2S	1/1	1/1						
3S			1/2	2/2	1/2	2/2		
1P								
Future II	AUX	+ PART	AUX	+ PART	AUX	+ PART	AUX	+ PART
1S			1/5	2/2			1/1	
2S					1/5	2/3	1/2	1/1
3S	1/4	2/2	1/3	3/3	1/4	1/3	1/1	
1P							2/2	1/1
Perfect	AUX	+ PART	AUX	+ PART	AUX	+ PART	AUX	+ PART
1S	1/1	1/1	4/11	5/5	1/1	1/1	3/9	4/6
2S	1/1	1/1					2/5	3/4
3S	1/1				1/1	1/1		
1P							1/1	1/1

Table 11b. Infinite verb forms

	1;9	1;10	1;11	2;0
PART FEM SG			3/3	
PART PL MASC	1/1		1/1	
Infinitive		2/2	2/2	

All analytic forms with infinitives (fut.I) and participles (fut.II and perf.) are used spontaneously:

(4) a. *ja ću   bombicu   popapati.*
        I   AUX-FUT I   candy-DIM.AKK   eat up-INF
        'I will eat up.'
     b. *bude   jodija [: rodila]   mama.*
        AUX-FUT II   give birth-PART.FEM.SG   mummy
        'mummy will give birth.'
     c. *ja   san [: sam]   dobija [: dobila]   c(v)ijeće.*
        I   AUX-PERF   get-PART.FEM.SG   flowers
        'I got flowers.'

As can be seen in table 11b infinitives and participles without corresponding finite verbs are very rare in Antonija's data. In most cases these forms are elliptic answers to questions as they are often used also by adults. Otherwise participles and infinitives appear in analytic verb forms. Gender marking on participles is in most cases feminine, presumably because the girl refers usually to herself or to female subjects. Nevertheless, no gender or number errors have been detected. In the few cases, when referents and subjects are masculine and/or plural the child used the corresponding "correct" forms of the participle.

Antonija's morpho-syntactic development shows up not only in the use of analytic forms. Generally, she seems still to have a preference for grammatical verbs (see section 5.). 72 (64%) of the 113 analysed tokens in 3s.pres. are copulas. Moreover, in the first two months (1;9–1;10) when analytic forms are elliptic, the lexical part tends to be omitted. This holds especially for future I forms, such as in the following example at 1;9.15:

(5) Situation: In displeasing her mother Antonija announces that she intends to press the button of the tape recorder.
     *ANT: *ja ću ovak.*
            'I will like this.'
     *MOT: *pritisnuti.*
            push-INF

In sum, Antonija shows new verb categories and erroneously regularised verb forms. Furthermore her category substitutions and agreement errors almost totally disappear. Due to these observations one can assume that at the age of 1;9 the child has entered the protomorphological phase.

4.4. Verb classes

The following table 12 provides an overview of the distribution of inflectional classes in Antonija's production (cf. table 5). The numbers in the cells correspond to lemmas/types/tokens. Numbers in brackets correspond to the part of tokens which were forms not existing in the target language.

Table 12. Inflectional classes in Antonija's verbs

Class	Example	1;6	1;7	1;9	1;10	1;11	2;0
4/a	gledati, -am	1/1/6	11/13/28	13/17/31	15/20/30	13/18/27	10/18/47
3/1/a	nositi, -im	1/1/1	5/7/9	4/4/4	10/11/13 (1*)	5/5/5	4/5/7 (1*)
3/2/a	vidjeti, -im		2/2/2		2/2/3	1/1/1	1/1/1
3/3/a	držati, -im			1/1/5			1/1/1
1/2/a	piti, pijem		1/1/1	1/1/1			
2/1/A/a	skinuti, -nem				2/2/2 (1*)		2/2/3 (1*)
2/2/a	pisati, -šem	1/1/1(1*)	1/1/1	1/1/1	1/2/2		2/2/2
2/2/b	kašljati, -em					2/3/4 (3*)[22]	
2/2/c	prati, perem					2/3/6 (1*)	2/2/2
Sup-plet.	biti, (je)sam	1/1/6	4/6/29	4/8/53	5/12/71	5/12/29	5/17/43
Isolated	htjeti, hoću	2/2/4	2/2/3	4/7/36 (3*)	4/8/34 (11*)	3/6/8	4/5/7
Root-cl.	pasti, padnem		1/1/1		1/1/1		2/3/3
Total		6/6/18	27/33/74	28/39/131	40/58/156	31/48/80	33/56/116

Within lemmas, types and tokens throughout the analysed sessions there is a dominance of two types of classes: on the one hand suppletive and isolated paradigms, and on the other hand the two most homogeneous and transparent classes, microclasses 4/a and 3/1/a. The preference for non-homogeneous and morphotactically opaque suppletive and irregular verbs (56% of all tokens) are connected with the extensive use of grammatical verbs, which have high token frequency also in the target language, e.g. copula and modal or auxiliary (*ne*) *htjeti* '(not) want'. On the other hand Antonija's lexical verbs throughout the sessions show a preference for transparent patterns. The most productive, homogeneous, transparent and frequent class in the target language is also by far the best represented class (29% of all tokens) in the child's lexical-verb productions. The less productive, but also very transparent and frequent class 3/1/a is continuously used by the child, though to a smaller extent (7% of all tokens). Furthermore, the emergence of form contrasts shows up with verbs of these two classes and also with suppletive and irregular verbs. The increase of these contrasts is shown by the growing difference between the numbers of lemmas and types in table 11 (cf. section 6.).

At the beginning of protomorphology, when the child begins to use also infinitive and participles, these categories show up with verbs of the 4/a and 3/1/a class, which have no (present – infinitive) stem alternation, e.g. *pjevala* 'sing-part.fem.sg' and *pjeva* 'sing-3s.pres' (cf. table 5).

After the age of 1;10, when the verbal lexicon has expanded, the amount of verbs belonging to various other microclasses grows. Although, these verbs mostly show up in those forms which do not differ from forms of class 4/a and 3/1/a:

(6)   a. 1;9.15   *dužati* [: držati]   'hold, inf.'
      b. 1;10   *p(l)akaja* [: plakala]   'cry, part.fem.sg.'
      c. 1;10.21   *p(l)akati*   'cry, inf.'
      d. 2;0.12   *p(l)esala*   'dance, part.fem.sg.'

On the basis of these forms alone, without any opposition to other forms which involve different bases (e.g. *drži* 'hold-3s.pres' and the infinitive *držati*), there is no evidence that the child differentiates those classes from the homogeneous ones.

Finally, class shifts, dialectal preferences, and analogies indicated with an asterisk in table 12 also show a preference for these transparent patterns (see section 7.).

5. Syntactic usage

First verb forms appear as one-element utterances. This holds for the sessions at 1;6 and 1;7.2. At 1;7.15 and 1;7.27, Antonija has both one- and two-element utterances. Verbs with predominantly grammatical meaning, i.e. copula and auxiliary verbs, are among the earliest forms. Out of 92 verb tokens (at 1;6 and 1;7), 32 (35%) are grammatical verbs.

It has already been shown in section 4.2. that the context, in which early verb forms appear (1;6.15–1;7.27), indicates that Antonija does not use grammatical categories according to the target language. This holds especially for the 3s.pres (see section 7.) (cf. also Anđel et al. 2000).

In cases with an overt pronoun and a non-agreeing verb also the syntactic context shows that 3s.pres -being the default verb form- replaces other categories (in this case 1s):

(7) a. 1;7.15 *ja prima.*
I grasp-3S
b. 1;7.27 *vidi ja.*
see-3S I

At 1;9.15, Antonija's productions show that a striking syntactic development has taken place: Utterances with more than three elements recur. Although Antonija is acquiring a pro-drop language she produces considerably often pronominal subjects (cf. Katičić 1997). Except for 3 obvious agreement errors in one session (1;10.21), from the age of 1;9.15 onwards, all finite verbs show person and number agreement, participles also show gender agreement with their subjects. Furthermore, the use of grammatical verbs increases at 1;9.15. There are 69 (53%) grammatical verb tokens out of total 131 verb tokens in the recorded session. Moreover adverbs, direct and indirect object pronouns and analytic tense forms emerge in these sessions:

(8) a. *neću tebi dati.*
NEGAUX-1S you-DAT give-INF
'I will not give to you.'
b. *i ja ću ovo dužati* [: *držati*].
and I AUX-1S this-ACC hold-INF
'And I will hold this.'

The child also starts using constructions consisting of modal verbs and infinitives:

(9) *(h)oću (o)vako dužati* [: *držati*].
    want-1S like this hold-INF
    'I want to hold like this.'

At 1;10 Antonija shows the first co-ordinate clause:

(10) *nisam pevaja* [: *pjevala*] *nego ja sam pakaja* [: *plakala*].
     'I did not sing but I cried.'

Finally, at the age of two the child produces her first relative and subordinated clauses:

(11) a. *oni koji jadiju [: radiju] kuću.*
        'those, who make a/the house.'
     b. *jesi vid(j)e(l)a kad sam ja bi(l)a mava* [: *mala*]?
        'have you seen, when I was (a) little (child)?'

6. Emergence of mini-paradigms

This section focusses on the child's paradigmatic form-meaning distinction on the basis of lemmas. Criteria for defining the onset of a paradigm are in accordance with Kilani-Schoch and Dressler (2000), Bittner, Dressler, and Kilani-Schoch (2000) and the introduction of the present volume. The emergence of mini-paradigms is taken to be an indicator for the fact that the child has identified morphology. In this sense the question arises, whether the emergence of mini-paradigms coincides with other factors which indicate or which accompany the child's developmental changes.

6.1. Qualitative analysis

In the premorphological period (at 1;7), Antonija shows already variations of the same lemma. In particular, she produces *baci, bacim, bacimo* and the root *bac*, which are forms of the lemma *baciti* 'throw'. These variations do not match all the criteria in order to constitute a mini-paradigm, e.g. they do not show up in contrastive contexts and they have no clear category specification. Thus, they can be regarded as precursors of mini-paradigms. Following the proposed criteria we find the first true mini-paradigms (three-types of the same lemma) and furthermore also two-member mini-paradigms as candidates for true mini-paradigms at the age of 1;9.

The following tables provide information about the child's paradigm formation activity. Table 13 shows the emergence of true mini-paradigms.

Table 13. True mini-paradigms

Age	Lemma	Forms	Category	Class	English
1;9	biti, clitic COP/AUX-PERF	sam si je	1S PRES 2S PRES 3S PRES	suppletive	be
	ići	idem ide idemo	1S PRES 3S PRES 1P PRES/IMP (ZKD)	suppletive	go
1;10	znati	znam znaš zna	1S PRES 2S PRES 3S PRES	4/a	know
	ići	ići idem ideš ide idemo	INF 1S PRES 2S PRES 3S PRES 1P PRES/IMP (ZKD)	suppletive	go
	htjeti	(h)oćem* (h)oćeš (h)oće	1S PRES 2S PRES 3S PRES	irregular	want
1;11	ići	ići idemo idem išla	INF 1P PRES/IMP (ZKD) 1S PRES PART FEM SG	suppletive	go
2;0	biti, pfv. AUX-FUT II	budem budeš bude budemo	1S PRES 2S PRES 3S PRES 1P PRES	suppletive	be
	biti, clitic COP/AUX-PERF	sam je smo	1S PRES 3S PRES 1P PRES	suppletive	be
	biti COP/AUX-PERF	jesam jesi bila	1S PRES 2S PRES PART FEM SG	suppletive	be
	ne biti COP/AUX-PERF	nisam nisi nije	1S PRES 2S PRES 3S PRES	suppletive	not be

Table 13. continued

2;0	gledati	gledala	PART FEM SG	4/a	look
		gledao	PART MASC SG		
		gle	2S IMP (colloquial)	irregular	
	pjevati	pjevaj	2S IMP	4/a	sing
		pjevati	INF		
		pjevala	PART FEM SG		
	snimati	snimaj	2S IMP	4/a	record
		snimati	INF		
		snima	3S PRES		

Two-member mini-paradigms are listed in table A1 in the Appendix. In order to allow comparability of different languages and different corpora, mini-paradigms were counted per month of life. Therefore three-member mini-paradigms, which appear in a short interval but not in the same month of life were not counted as true mini-paradigms.

The first clear true mini-paradigms are suppletive verbs. Until the end of the analysed period suppletive and irregular verbs constitute the biggest proportion of lemmas and types involved in paradigmatic contrasts. To a big extent, this is a consequence of the comparatively big portion of grammatical verbs in Antonija's productions, which already have been introduced in previous sections (cf. section 4.1., 4.3. and 5.). On the one hand, these forms show a very high degree of opacity and irregularity throughout the whole paradigm. Examples for such forms are *sam* 'be-1s.pres' '*si* 'be-2s.pres'' *je* 'be-3s.pres'. On the other hand, many other forms of suppletive or irregular verbs show morphotactic transparency. E.g. some forms of *ići* 'go': *idem* (1s.pres), *ideš* (2s.pres), *ide* (3s.pres) *idemo* (1p.pres/imp). The latter verb appears very often in contrastive contexts. Within every month it constitutes mini-paradigms and appears in almost all of the categories the child has shown until the end of the analysed period. In using contrastively the "erroneous" form *hoćem* instead of irregular *hoću* the child demonstrates that she has identified form and meaning relations of particular suffixes and that she can use at least some creatively (cf. section 7.). All other form oppositions appear almost exclusively with lexical verbs of the most homogeneous classes, primarily 4/a but also 3/1. Verb forms belonging to these classes increase in number after every month of life. Finally, at the age of 2;0 Antonija shows 5 verb lemmas from class 4/a and 3/1/a which have two- and three form oppositions.

Categories involved in form oppositions are predominantly indicative singular forms and 1p. indicative or imperative. To a smaller extent, 2s. imperatives, infinitives and (from the age of 1;10) also forms of participle feminine singular are involved in paradigm formation. Categories involving both bases (infinitive and present) appear first with verbs of the most homogeneous class (4/a) (see section 4.4.).

(12) a. 1;9   *dati, -am*   (4/a):   *dati* 'give, inf.' – *daj* 'give-2s.imp'
   b. 2;0   *pjevati, -am* (4/a): *pjevaj* 'sing-2s.imp' – *pjevati* 'sing-inf' – *pjevala* 'sing-part.fem.sg'
   c. 1;10 *kupiti, -im* (3/1/a): *kupi* 'buy-2s.imp' – *kupila* 'buy-part.fem.sg'

Until the end of the analysed period Antonija did not produce form contrasts which show class-specific alternation of the base.

6.2. Quantitative analysis

The following table 14 presents the quantitative distribution of mini-paradigms. Numbers of two-member and true mini-paradigms (MPs) per month are given. Suppletive lemmas are given in separate columns.[23]

In addition to various other factors depending on the recording situation, the number of attested form contrasts in one session depends also on the amount of produced lemmas which for their parts depend on sample size. In order to achieve better comparability, especially between particular sessions and between different corpora, numbers of two-member and true mini-paradigms are set into relation to the total amount of produced lemmas. The resulting value P(lem) with its corresponding percentages is listed in table 14.[24]

Table 14. Mini-paradigms and paradigm value

| Age | 2-Member MPs | | True-MPs | | %P(lem) | Lemmas |
	-suppl.	+suppl.	-suppl.	+suppl.		total
1;6	0	0	0	0		
1;7	0	0	0	0		
1;9	4	0	0	2	21	28
1;10	7	3	2	1	33	40
1;11	9	3	0	1	42	31
2;0	4	1	3	4	36	33

258 *Antigone Katičić*

Table 14 shows that Antonija's production of paradigmatic contrasts continuously increases with 1;9 and reaches a peak at 1;11. Two-member mini-paradigms dominate sessions at 1;10 and 1,11. True mini-paradigms exceed two form oppositions at 2;0. This distribution is confirmed by absolute numbers and also when these numbers are set in relation to the produced lemmas per month.

7. Morphological substitutions
7.1. Category substitution

Category-substitution is the most frequent type of substitution that can be observed in Antonija's data. The child produces verbs in their basic form, which corresponds to the 3s.pres.ind in the target language and appears to have default character. This type of substitution (omission of markers) is typical for the premorphological period (1;6–1;7). Examples are given below.

(13) a. 1;6.15 *(h)oću* 'want-1s.pres' > *(h)oće* 'want-3s.pres'
      b. 1;7.2   *gledam* (?) 'look-1s.pres' > *g(l)eda* 'look-3s.pres'[25]
      c. 1;7.2   *čitaj*! 'read-2s.imp' > *čita*! 'read-3s.pres'
      d. 1;7.27 *vidim (ja)* 'see-1s.pres(I)' > *vidi ja* 'see-3s.pres.I'

After the premorphological phase, only three instances can be classified as category substitution, e.g. at 1;10

(14) bude   ja   tebi   kupija [: kupila]
      AUX-3S   I   you-DAT   buy-PART.FEM.SG
      kotojadice [:čokoladice].
      chocolate-GEN.SG.DIM
      'I am going to buy you chocolate.'

7.2. Analogy and class shift

After omitting the 1s.pres-suffix (1;6.15–1;7.27) in the verb *htjeti* 'want' Antonija starts marking the 1s.pres in analogy to all other verbs with the suffix *-(e)m*. From now on she produces repeatedly the form *hoćem* (see section 4.3.). Furthermore, at 1;10.30 the first 3p.pres forms appear with verbs from class 3/1/a which require in the target language the change of the thematic vowel -*i* and the addition of the suffix -*e*. E.g. inf., 1s.pres and 3p.pres forms of the verb 'to carry' are respectively: *nositi, nosim, nose*. When Antonija uses such verbs in 3p she adds by analogy the suffix -*ju* to the base and treats them thereby like verbs belonging to more transparent classes, such as *gledati* 'look-inf' – *gledam* 'look-1s.pres' – *gledaju* 'look-3p.pres'.[26] Examples are given below.

(15) a. *ljube* > **(l)jubiju*   'kiss/love-3p.pres'
     b. *rade* > **radiju*   'work-3p.pres'

These analogical formations have been described also in other studies (cf. Kovačević, Jelaska, and Brozović 1998 and Anđel et al. 2000) and are typical for Croatian children in general. Class shifts are rare in Antonija's data. In the analysed period, four instances in total were found (see section 4.4.). The term "class shift" refers to classes according to the adult system. This shows the child's preference for certain inflectional patterns, but this does not imply that she has already established all respective classes in her morphological system. All cases which were identified as class shifts involve verbs from classes, where the base forms in infinitive and present are not the same and which are thus much more opaque than verbs which have the same base throughout the whole paradigm.

(16)[27] a. 1;6.15 *pisati: pišem*   *piše* > **pisa*   2/2/a > 4/a
                                          'write-3S.PRES'
        b. 1;10   *kucnuti: kucnem*   *kucnuti* > **kuciti* 2/1/A/a > 3/1/a
                                          'knock-INF.PFV'
        c. 1;11.25 *nazvati: nazovem*   *nazovi* > **nazvaj*   2/2/c > 4/a
                                          'call-2S.IMP'
        d. 2;0.2   *okrenuti: okrenem*   *okrenuti* > **ok(r)eniti* 2/1/A/a >
                                          'turn-INF.PFV'   3/1/a

8. Conclusion

According to the observations mentioned in the previous sections we assume that after a period (1;6–1;7) of rote-learnt and context bound use of verbs at 1;9 the child has already began to identify morphological characteristics of her target language and that she therefore has entered the protomorphological phase. Since we have no documentation of Antonija's productions for almost two months, it is not possible to clearly detect, when and how the transition has taken place.

At 1;9, a change in the quality of the verbal system in general and of verb morphology in particular has taken place. Analogy errors (*hoću* > *hoćem*), frequent and correct marking of subject-verb agreement in contrast to the very few instances of agreement errors, syntactic development, the use of more and different verbal categories and finally, the emergence of mini-paradigms indicate that the child has become morphologically active.[28] In the following months there appear additional indications which show that Antonija is identifying inflectional patterns of her target language. More categories are used recurrently, new analogical substitutions and class shifts emerge and the number of lemmas which appear in contrasting forms grows rapidly. In all analysed sessions, though especially in the beginning of the protomorphological period, mini-paradigms appear with suppletive and irregular verbs, which generally indicates that in producing form contrasts morphosemantic relations are primary for the child. But, there are also form contrasts in morphotactically transparent true mini-paradigms of suppletive verbs which are thus suitable for detection of form and meaning correlation of specific inflectional elements.

Taking the above mentioned factors into consideration, we assume that, at the latest at 1;10, Antonija has discovered the first and most transparent inflectional relations of her target language and that she became morphologically creative, although the third true and not suppletive mini-paradigm was not attested before the age of 2;0.

Regarding verb use in quantitative terms, the emergence of mini-paradigms coincides with an increase in verb production (tokens) and a syntactic spurt, but according to percentages, there is no rapid verb spurt (lemmas and types) accompanying morphological development.

The earliest category to appear is 3s.pres.ind and 2s.imp. Both categories correspond to the least marked base form (root and thematic vowel) of the paradigm in lexical verbs. But, for the 2s.imp, this holds only for one verb class. In indicative mood verbs in 1s are more marked forms. They also emerge early, but are very rare.[29] The more marked 2s.ind – which is strongly represented in the input – appears later and is comparatively rare. The preference for the base form shows up also in category substitutions. The latter are characteristic for Antonija's early sessions, where she is assumed to be in the premorphological phase.

Clear oppositions in person (synthetic) and tense marking (for all non-present tenses analytic) appear for the first time in the same recording-session (1;9.15). Due of lack of data after 1;7 it is not possible to definitely find out whether both categories appear at the same time or whether one category appears before the other. The relatively early emergence of analytic tense forms is in line with a general (morpho-)syntactic developmental spurt at 1;9. The fact that comparatively many categories are realised through analytic constructions in the target language presumably induces their early use.

Antonija marks the category of person distinctively before number. In addition to semantic markedness, this could be due to the fact that both categories are distinctively marked in the target language.

As regards classes, Antonija shows on the one hand many and contrastively used suppletive and irregular verbs. Because of their grammatical function, they are also high-token-frequency verbs in the target language. Nevertheless, Antonija's strong tendency of using grammatical verbs is remarkable, especially in the earliest sessions. Possible reasons for this will have to be looked for in future work including also syntactic analysis. Moreover it will be of interest, whether this characteristic is child- or also language-specific.

With lexical verbs, on the other hand, the child shows a clear preference for homogeneity and transparency. The most productive, frequent and thus transparent classes in the target language (4/a and 3/1/a) are also the most frequent classes in Antonija's lexical-verb productions in general, and in particular also in paradigm formation. The child's preference for transparent and homogeneous patterns is also shown by analogical substitutions and class shifts. Finally, oppositions involving morphologically more complex relations (e.g. base alternations) were attested in the input, whereas in Antonija's productions they did not appear until the end of the analysed period.

Appendix

Table A1. Two-member mini-paradigms

Age	Lemma	Forms	Category	Class	English
1;9	htjeti, clitic	ću	1S PRES	isolated	want
	AUX-FUT I	ćeš	2S PRES		fut.I aux.
	dati	daj	2S IMP	4/a	give
		dati	INF		

Table A1. continued

Age	Lemma	Forms	Category	Class	English
	nemati	nemam	1S PRES	4/a	not have
		nema	3S PRES		
	htjeti	(h)oću /hoćem*	1S PRES	isolated	want
		(h)oćeš	2S PRES		
1;10	htjeti, clitic AUX-FUT I	ću ćeš	1S PRES 2S PRES	isolated	want fut.I aux.
	biti, pfv. AUX-FUT II	budem bude	1S PRES 3S PRES	suppletive	be fut.II aux.
	ne htjeti MOD / AUX-FUT I	neću neće	1S PRES 3S PRES	isolated	not want
	biti, clitic COP/AUX-PERF	sam je	1S PRES 3S PRES	suppletive	be
	ne biti COP/AUX-PERF	nisam nije	1S PRES 3S PRES	suppletive	not be
	dati	daj dala	2S IMP PART FEM SG	4/a	give
	imati	imaš ima	2S PRES 3S PRES	4/a	have
	nemati	nemam nema	1S PRES 3S PRES	4/a	not have
	kupiti	kupi kupila	2S IMP PART FEM SG	3/1/a	buy
	plakati	plakati plakala	INF PART FEM SG	2/2/a	cry
1;11	htjeti, clitic AUX-FUT I	ću će	1S PRES 3S PRES	isolated	want
	ne htjeti MOD / AUX-FUT I	neću neće	1S PRES 3S PRES	isolated	not want
	biti, pfv. AUX-FUT II	budeš bude	2S PRES 3S PRES	suppletive	be
	biti, clit. COP/AUX-PEF	sam si	1S PRES 2S PRES	suppletive	be

Table A1. continued

Age	Lemma	Forms	Category	Class	English
	gledati	gledati	INF	4/a	look
		gle	2S IMP (colloquial)	irregular	
	imati	imam	1S PRES	4/a	have
		imaš	2S PRES		
	kašljati	kašljaš (*)	2S PRES	2/2/b>4a	cough
		kašlja (*)	3S PRES	(ZKD)	
	morati	moram	1S PRES	4/a	must
		moraš	2S PRES		
	pitati	pitala	PART FEM SG	4/a	ask
		pitaj	2S IMP		
	znati	znam	1S PRES	4/a	know
		znaš	2S PRES		
	doći	doći	INF	suppletive	come
		došla	PART FEM SG		
	moći	mogu	1S PRES	isolated	be able
		možeš	2S PRES		
2;0	morati	moram	1S PRES	4/a	must
		moraš	2S PRES		
	ići	idemo	1P PRES/IMP	suppletive	go
		ide	3S PRES		
	moći	mogu	1S PRES	isolated	be able
		možeš	2S PRES		
	čuti	čujem	1S PRES	1/2/a	hear
		čuješ	2S PRES		
	snimiti	snimi	2S IMP	3/1/a	record
		snimila	PART FEM SG		

Notes

* This research was funded by the Austrian Science Fund (FWF P 13371-SPR). It was made possible by the cooperation of two projects at the Commission for Linguistics of the Austrian Academy of Sciences "First Language Acquisition of Austrian German" (headed by Chris Schaner-Wolles) and "Pre- and Protomorphology in Language Acquisition" (headed by Wolfgang U. Dressler). Thanks are due to Dagmar Bittner, Wolfgang U. Dressler, Natalia Gagarina and Marianne Kilani-Schoch for reading and commenting on draft versions of this paper. I would also like to thank Carmen Aguirre, Christine Czinglar, Sabine Klampfer, Katharina Köhler and Chris Schaner-Wolles for useful discussions and comments. Of course, all errors are mine.

1. Standard (written) Croatian shows furthermore the following categories: imperfect (synthetic), aorist (synthetic), optative, past participle agent and adverbial participles. In aorist and imperfect aspect is expressed inflectionally.
2. There is also 3. person in imperative mood, but it has no distinct inflectional form. It is formed by the particle *nek* and the indicative present forms.
3. In ZKD auxiliary clitic forms are also used: *bum* (1s), *buš* (2s), *bu* (3s), *bumo* (1p), *bute* (2p), *buju* (3p).
4. Traditional classifications can, among others, be found in: Babić et al. (1991) and Barić et al. (1997). A contrastive presentation of the Croatian inflectional classes in terms of Natural Morphology is presented in Dressler, Dziubalska-Kołaczyk, and Katičić (1996).
5. The material presented here has been collected and transcribed by Draženka Blaži, the mother of the child, in the framework of the project "Psycholinguistic Aspects of the Acquisition of the Croatian Language", Department of Speech and Language Pathology (University of Zagreb). Thanks are due to Melita Kovačević and her colleagues, who supplied me with the material.
6. To qualify as an utterance, a production had to include at least one meaningful unit corresponding to a Croatian word in form and meaning.
7. In cases where repeated utterances were interpreted as appropriate reactions also in regard to adult communication, they were not excluded from the analysis. This holds especially for elliptic affirmations or denials with verbs, mostly copulas or auxiliaries.
8. Primarily Antonija's communication with her mother has been recorded. Sporadically also her father and grandmother participated in certain sessions.
9. Specifications shall be interpreted as follows: Number of session: the respective lemma in infinitive: pres.1s. 'English translation': class: uttered forms (category).
10. Aspectual pairs (involving different suffixation), e.g. *baciti*, pfv. – *bacati*, ipfv. 'throw', also perfective and imperfective forms of the verb *biti* 'be' as copula or auxiliary verbs are treated as forms from two different lemmas. Furthermore, clitic and strong forms of the auxiliary verbs *htjeti* 'want' and *biti* 'be' were considered as different lemmas. Negated verbs were considered as different lemmas in regard to their affirmative counterpart only in cases of verbs with special negated forms: i.e. *imam – nemam, hoću-neću* and *jesam-nisam*. Paradigmatic oppositions of verbs regarding prefixes were not found in the analysed period. Antonija used, all in all, 9 prefixed verbs. Except for one case none of these stems showed up with another prefix.

11. In all following tables numbers in brackets represent subsets of numbers without brackets given in the same cell (i.e. figures in and without brackets must not be added).
12. Erroneous forms, i.e. forms which do not exist in the target language, were counted as types. Such types are generally rare: in absolute figures there are 7 types of 7 lemmas formed by analogy, class shift and the production of the root form *bac* 'throw' (see section 7.).
13. In these figures full analytic forms are counted as two verbs, i.e. they were counted as 2 items for each group.
14. The slight decrease seems not to reflect any qualitative change in the child's lexicon, it appears to be due to differences in the recording situations.
15. Also according to analyses which do not take *-a-* as a thematic vowel, but as part of the person/number suffix (e.g. Babić et al. 1991), the 3s represents the least marked form.
16. In the first analysed recording (AB6) the negated 3s form of the copula (*nije*) appears to be used also as a form of negation in general.
17. Besides *gle* there is also the reduced *ček* instead of *čekaj* 'wait!' used in colloquial speech very often in reduplicated form (*ček-ček!*), as in Antonija.
18. Sometimes it is hard to decide whether the child refers to herself in the 3s., as Antonija and also many other children do in this age, or whether she skips the 1s. agreement marker. But there are also instances, where the pronominal subject is overt while the realised verb does not agree in number and person, e.g. *ja p(r)ima* 'I grasp, 3s' (see section 5.).
19. Note that in the same session Antonija produces the full target form, (base plus final *-j*) of a phonologically similar verb, which belongs to the same class: *čekaj!* 'wait, imp'.
20. For similar findings in another Croatian child see Anđel et al. (2000).
21. Column "AUX" shows the amount of lemmas and tokens of auxiliary verbs. These figures include verbs which appear alone and also those which are part of full analytic constructions. Numbers for the corresponding infinite verb forms are given in column "+INF" and "+PART".
22. The three listed tokens marked with an asterisk are erroneous only according to Standard Croatian, but they correspond to the target language. In colloquial speech many verbs belonging to this class (2/2/b) are inflected as verbs belonging to class 4/a, e.g. *kašljati, -em* > *kašljati, -am* 'cough' (cf. section 1.2.).
23. Note that suppletion refers to the paradigm of the respective lemma in the target language and not in all cases to the forms produced by the child.
24. We follow the proposal of Klampfer (2000), who primarily had the idea to apply the term "P(lem)" and the corresponding procedure.
25. Phonologically similar contexts indicate that the child at that time was able to produce final *-m*.

26. Corresponding forms like *hoćem* and *govoriju* sometimes appear also in ZKD. Nevertheless, Antonija's mother confirmed my impression that these forms were not used in the family and by the social surrounding the child was confronted with, and that they were constructed by the child herself.
27. Specifications shall be interpreted as follows: age, lemma in infinitive: lemma 1s.pres., target form > realised form and target class > realised class.
28. Additional evidence from Antonija's development in the nominal system will be provided in future analyses.
29. Anđel et al. (2000) found a similar order of emergence in their contrastive study of the acquisition of Croatian, French and Austrian German.

References

Anđel, Maja, Sabine Klampfer, Marianne Kilani-Schoch, Wolfgang U. Dressler, and Melita Kovačević
    2000   Acquisition of verbs in Croatian, French and Austrian German – an outline of a comparative analysis. *Suvremena Lingvistika* 49/50: 5–25.

Babić, Stjepan, Dalibor Brozović, Milan Moguš, Slavko Pavešić, Ivo Škarić, and Stjepko Težak
    1991   *Povjesni pregeld, glasovi i oblici hrvatskoga književnog jezika.* [Historical Survey, Sounds and Forms of the Croatian Literary Language.] Zagreb: HAZU i Globus.

Barić, Eugenia, Mijo Lončarić, Dragica Malić, Slavko Pavešić, Mirko Peti, Vesna Zečević, and Marija Znika
    1997   *Hrvatska gramatika.* [Croatian Grammar.] Zagreb: Školska knjiga.

Bittner, Dagmar, Wolfgang U. Dressler, and Marianne Kilani-Schoch (eds.)
    2000   *First Verbs: On the Way to Mini-paradigms.* (ZAS Papers in Linguistics 18.) Berlin: Zentrum für Allgemeine Sprachwissenschaft, Typologie und Universalienforschung (ZAS).

Dressler, Wolfgang U. and Annemarie Karpf
    1995   The theoretical relevance of pre- and protomorphology in language acquisition. *Yearbook of Morphology* 1994: 99–122.

Dressler, Wolfgang U., Katarzyna Dziubalska-Kołaczyk, and Antigona Katičić
    1996   A contrastive analysis of verbal inflection classes in Polish and Croatian. *Suvremena Lingvistika* 22: 127–138.

Katičić, Antigone
1997   Zum Erstspracherwerb des Kroatischen: Morphologische und syntaktische Aspekte beim Erwerb des Verbalsystems. M.A. thesis, Department of Linguistics, University of Vienna.

Kilani-Schoch, Marianne, and Wolfgang U. Dressler
2000   The emergence of inflectional paradigms in two French corpora as an illustration of general problems of pre- and protomorphology. Manuscript, extended version of poster presentation at the 9th International Morphology Meeting, Vienna, February 2000.

Klampfer, Sabine
2000   Early verb development in one Austrian child. In: Dagmar Bittner, Wolfgang U. Dressler, and Marianne Kilani-Schoch (eds.) *First Verbs: On the Way to Mini-paradigms*, 7–20. (ZAS Papers in Linguistics 18.) Berlin: Zentrum für Allgemeine Sprachwissenschaft, Typologie und Universalienforschung (ZAS).

Kovačević, Melita, Zrinka Jelaska, and Blaženka Brozović
1998   Comparing lexical and grammatical development in morphologically different languages. In: Ayhan Aksu Koç, Eser Erguvanli Taylan, Ayşe Sumru Özsoy, and Aylin Küntay (eds.), *Perspectives on Language Acquistion: Selected Papers from the VIIth International Congress for the Study of Child Language (July 14–19 1996)*, 368–383. Istanbul: Boğaziçi University Printhouse.

MacWhinney, Brian
1978   *The Acquisition of Morphophonology*. Chicago: University of Chicago Press.

MacWhinney, Brian
2000   *The CHILDES Project: Tools for Analyzing Talk*. Mahwah, New Jersey: Lawrence Erlbaum.

Magner, Thomas F.
1966   *A Zagreb Kajkavian Dialect*. (The Pennsylvania State University Studies 18.) University Park: Pennsylvania State University Press.

Šojat, Antun
1979   O zagrebačkom kajkavskom govoru. [On the Zagreb kajkavian idiom.] *Rasprave Zavoda za jezik Institutua za filologiju i folkloristiku* 4/5: 119–123.

Early verb inflection in French: An investigation of two corpora[*]

Marianne Kilani-Schoch

0. Introduction

This paper deals with early verb development (e.g., person, tense) until the emergence of verb-paradigms in two French-speaking children.

I will show the parallelism between the two children in the gradual building of paradigms, despite considerable differences in the rate of development. Individual differences on the other hand will bring me to distinguish some early patterning in the premorphological rote-learnt forms of one of the children's data.

1. Description of verbs in the target language

Grammatical categories of the French verb are person (1, 2, 3), number (S, P), tense, mood (Indicative and Imperative in early child language) and voice. However, in the spoken language, depending on the inflectional class (see below), these categories may not be expressed by suffixes, and verbal forms may be distinguished only by proclitic markers (*je, tu, il, elle, ils, elles, on parle* /parl/ 'I, you, he, she, we speak'[1]) and by auxiliaries (see below). In other words, the 2P is the only plural form having a verb suffix (e.g. *parl-ez*) and in the productive microclass 1 (mc.1) of macroclass I (and in some microclasses, and paradigms of the unproductive macroclass II[2]) it is often the only distinct plural form:

Table 1. Person and number marking in the Present Indicative and Imperative, Macroclass I, mc.1, parler 'speak'[3]

	Present Indicative		Imperative	
	Singular	Plural	Singular	Plural
1.	*parle* /parl/	(*parlons* /parl-õ/)		*parlons* /parl-õ/
2.	*parles* /parl/	*parlez* /parl-e/	*parle* /parl/	*parlez* /parl-e/
3.	*parle* /parl/	*parlent* /parl/		

Homophonic forms in the categories used by the children in pre- and protomorphology are:

a) Pres.1S, Pres.2S, Pres.3S, Pres.3P, Imp.2S: /parl/
b) Inf parler, PP parlé: /parle/ (Pres.2P and Imp.2P parlez).

Non-finite categories (in child language) are Infinitive and PP. Infinitive is the citation form in French and is used in periphrastic constructions such as Compound Future and modal ones. Non-finite PP is part of Compound Past (see below).

Within the category tense, spoken French has 4 compound forms (Compound Past, Compound Future, and Pluperfect, Past Future, both not expected in early child language), and two synthetic forms less frequent in the input and rare in early child language: Imperfect (*parl-ais*)[4] and Simple Future (*parl(e)-ra*). The Simple Past (*parl-a*) is used only in fairy tales.

Compound Past is auxiliary *avoir* 'have'/*être* 'be'+PP, *elle a parlé* 'she has spoken':

Table 2. Compound Past

	Singular		Plural	
	AUX	PP	AUX	PP
1.	*ai* /e/	*parlé* /parle/	(*avons* /avõ/)	*parlé* /parle/
2.	*as* /a/		*avez* /ave/	
3.	*a* /a/		*ont* /õ/	

Compound Future is semi-auxiliary *aller* 'go' + Inf: *il va parler* 'he will speak':

Table 3. Compound Future

	Singular		Plural	
	AUX	INF	semiAUX	INF
1.	*vais* /ve/	*parler* /parle/	(*allons* /alõ/)	*parler* /parle/
2.	*vas* /va/		*allez* /ale/	
3.	*va* /va/		*vont* /võ/	

Isolated paradigms and unproductive classes of macroclass II have amplified bases and, depending on the inflectional class, vowel change, e.g.

Table 4. Examples of macroclass II

mc.11	INF:	*partir* /partir/	'leave'	S:	*part* /par/	3P:	*partent* /part/	PP:	*parti* /parti/
mc.19		*mordre* /mɔrdr/	'bite'		*mord* /mɔr/		*mordent* /mɔrd/		*mordu* /mɔrdy/
mc.13		*venir* /vənir/	'come'		*vient* /vjẽ/		*viennent* /vjen/		*venu* /vəny/
mc.17		*recevoir* /rəsəvwar/	'be-come'		*reçoit* /rəswa/		*reçoivent* /rəswav/		*reçu* /rəsy/
				1P:	*recevons* /rəsəvõ/				

2. Data description

My study is based on the corpora of two children from Lausanne (Switzerland): Sophie (SOP) (1;6.14–3;8.09, 60 recordings, 30 hours) and Emma (EMM) (1;4.13–2;11.3, 40 recordings, 19 hours).[5] This study focuses on the data until the beginning of protomorphology (see below), i.e. until 2;0 in SOP's corpus (2978 utterances[6]), and 1;8 in EMM's corpus (1079 utterances).[7] For the sake of comparison, however, some of the tables contain data of Emma until 2;0 (2684 utterances) and SOP 2;1. Transcription and coding have been done according to CHILDES and quantitative analyses according to CLAN programs.[8]

SOP can be characterized as following a prosodic (formulaic strategy in Peters and Menn 1993: 745; cf. also Peters 1997: 159; Bates, Dale, and Thal 1995) rather than a segmental strategy: she makes massive phonological substitutions and a long and varied use of fillers (which disappear between 2;6 and 3;0).

EMM, an early talker (MLU of 2.4 already at 1;7 and of 3.3 at 1;10), is rather a segmental child (cf. Peters and Menn 1993) but favours also the imitative strategy (cf. several examples of rote-learned sequences in which she seems to play with her words and transform them in successive steps).

The phases of pre- and protomorphology correspond to the following time periods of the corpora:

	SOP	EMM
Premorphology:	1;6.14–1;10.4	1;4.13–1;7.27
Protomorphology:	1;11.19–2;1.18[9]	1;8.10–1;10.29

In SOP's corpus, protomorphology is demarcated by a syntactic spurt: 2-word utterances with verb reach almost 50% of the utterances with verb. There is also a first advance in article use and hence in the development of the noun phrase. First subject pronouns appear (cf. Kilani-Schoch and Dressler 2000, 2001).

In EMM's corpus protomorphology starts when articles (74% of prenominal contexts) and subject pronouns become frequent and fillers mostly preverbal. Syntax develops as well with first 3-complement utterances, dislocated and cleft sentences.

3. Emergence of verb-forms

3.1. Quantitative data

Verb increase is strong at 1;11.7 in SOP's corpus and at 1;7 in EMM's corpus, i.e. at the turning-point between pre- and protomorphology (see 2 and tables 5a and 5b).

Table 5a. SOP: % of verb lemmas, types & tokens in relation to analyzed utterances[10]

age	utterances	utt. with verb	utt. with verb%	lemmas	lemmas %	types	tokens	tokens %
1;6	109	9	8.2	3	2.8	3	9	8.2
1;7	225	17	7.5	8	3.6	8	17	7.5
1;8	245	19	7.5	10	4	10	19	7.5
1;9	606	95	15.7	27	4.4	33	95	15.7
1;10	555	86	15.5	31	5.6	34	87	15.7
1;11.7 PROTO	176	39	22.1	16	9.1	16	39	22.1
1;11 end	592	129	21.8	37	6.2	45	129	21.8
2;0	470	143	30.4	49	10.4	63	143	30.4
2;1	674	198	29.4	52	7.1	63	199	29.5

French 273

Table 5b. EMM: % of verb lemmas, types & tokens in relation to analyzed utterances

age	utterances	utt. with verb	utt. with verb %	lemmas	lemmas %	types	tokens	tokens %
1;4	136	9	7	5	3.7	5	9	7
1;5	287	71	24.7	21	7.3	24	72	25
1;6	186	15	8	10	5.4	11	15	8
1;7	133	53	39.8	21	15.8	24	53	39.8
(1;7 rec. only)	(103)	53	39.8	(16)	(15.5)	(17)	53	39.8
PROTO								
1;8	337	119	35.3	35	10.4	49	122	36
1;9	371	153	41	45	12.1	52	153	41
1;10	631	263	41.7	54	8.5	84	273	43
1;11	348	160	46	49	14.1	71	164	47
2;0	255	79	31	30	11.8	41	86	34

Categories used before the beginning of protomorphology (i.e. SOP 1;6–1;11.7, 266 verb tokens, EMM 1;4–1;7, 149 tokens) are Present Indicative Singular, Imperative, Infinitive,[11] Past Participle, and lately Compound Past, plus for EMM isolated occurrence of Compound Future and Imperfect.[12]

Table 6. SOP: Emergence of verb categories (lemmas/tokens) until protomorphology[13,14]

age	Pres.Ind.S[15]	IMP	INF	PP	Compound Past	Compound Fut.	Pres. Passive
1;6	2/6						
1;7	3/7		2/3	1/2			
1;8	5/10	1/4	2/4	1/1			
1;9	18/47	3/4	8/23	2/11			
1;10	12/22	4/8	8/15	6/19	2/2		
1;11.7	6/11	1/3	5/16	3/3	2/2		
PROTO							
1;11 end	19/52	2/5	11/24	6/9	6/21		
2;0	24/56	5/17	14/37	7/13	9/13	1/1	2/2

Table 7a. EMM: Emergence of synthetic verb categories (lemmas/tokens) before protomorphology

age	Pres.Ind.S	Pres.3P	IMP	INF	PP	Imperfect	Simple Past	Simple Fut.
1;4	?1/1		1/1	2/4	?1/3			
1;5	7/14		4/12	13/32	3/10			
1;6	6/7			3/3	1/3			
1;7	10/20		4/6	11/17	1/4	1/1		
PROTO								
1;8	18/51	1/1	4/11	16/28	4/8	1/1	1/2	
1;9	16/55+ 1/1 Pres.1S	2/7	3/19	20/50	6/9	1/1		1/1

Table 7b. EMM: Emergence of periphrastic verb categories (lemmas/tokens) before protomorphology

age	Compound Fut.	Compound Past	Pres.Passive
1;4			
1;5			1/3
1;6			
1;7	1/1	1/1	
PROTO			
1;8	2/2	6/9 (1 token = 1S)	1/1
1;9	3/3	5/6	

Table 8. Summary of verb categories before protomorphology (ambiguities excluded)

	SOP			EMM		
	lemmas	tokens	%	lemmas	tokens	%
Pres.Ind.S	32	103	46.2	16	42	29.4
Infinitive	18	61	27.4	22	56	39.2
Imperative	6	19	8.5	5	19	13.3
Past Participle	9	36	16.1	4	20	14
Compound Past	3	4	1.8	1	1	0.7
Periphr. Passive	2	2	0.9	1	3	2
Comp.Future				1	1	0.7
Imperfect				1	1	0.7
Total	51	223		37	143	

The verb categories occurring before protomorphology are quite similar in both children. However, the two children differ strikingly as far as the number of Pres.Ind.S vs. infinitive forms is concerned: whereas SOP has a preference for Pres.Ind.S forms over infinitives, EMM has the opposite preference for infinitives over Pres.Ind.S forms. Put differently, EMM seems to have a preference for morphological forms while SOP seems to rather prefer root-forms (cf. 3.2.). The comparison between all morphological forms (Inf + all PP, included PP of periphrastic verb-forms) and all root-forms (Pres.Ind + Imp) does not contradict this finding: SOP has still more root-forms (54.7%) and EMM more morphological forms (57.3%).

At the onset of protomorphology, verb categories in EMM's language are more numerous and varied than in SOP's language at the same age. This underlies the different rates of development of the two children. In EMM's corpus, plural verb forms occur from 1;8 on,[16] Present 1S from 1;9, Imperfect from 1;11. Notice in addition an isolated occurrence of Simple Past (1;8) and one of Simple Future (1;9).

No formal, class shift or agreement error occur yet in the corpus of EMM (cf. 5.). In SOP's corpus there are 3 possible number agreement errors at 1;8 and 1;9. More important in her corpus are the ambiguities between AUX (*avoir*, *être*) of, e.g., Compound Past, semi-AUX (*avoir*, as in *avoir peur* 'be afraid') and fillers (43 tokens vs. only 6 in EMM's corpus in premorphology): in SOP's corpus Pres.S forms of *avoir* and *être* are difficult to identify due to the massive use of fillers (e.g. /a, ə, e/ *peur* 'is afraid', /a, ə, ɛ/ *beau* for *est beau* 'is beautiful', /a, ə, ɛ/ *là/dur* 'is there/hard', /apabe/ for Comp.Past *est tombé* 'has fallen' or PP *tombé* 'fallen', /atate/ for Comp.Past *a sauté* 'has jumped' or PP *sauté* 'jumped').

3.2. Distinctions among rote-learnt forms

First verb-forms of the French corpora can be divided into 3 major types (plus intermediate forms):

a) verb-forms corresponding to roots, i.e. without any inflection, e.g.
    SOP   1;6 Pres.3S *dort* 'sleeps', Pres.3S *pleut* 'rains'
    EMM 1;5 Imp.2S *donne* 'give',   1;6 Pres.3S *aime* 'likes'.

b) Inflected verb-forms (not before 1;8 in SOP), e.g.
    SOP   1;8 Inf *donner* 'give', PP *cassé* 'broken';
    EMM 1;4 Inf *sortir* 'go out',   1;5 PP *parti* 'gone';

c) frozen/formulaic forms, i.e., in terminological difference to e.g. Pine and Lieven (1993), a subset of rote-learnt, contextually/situationally bound, morphologically non-distinctive forms. A frozen form frequently occurs in one single pattern, but the constituent verb never in any other pattern; the contextual meaning of this pattern may not be clearly linked to the lexical meaning of the verb, especially if it is idiomatic, especially regulative, phatic, e.g. French *ça marche* 'I agree', German *passt* 'fits', which can be simply substituted by 'ok, fine'. A frozen-form candidate is unlikely to be frozen, if the constituent verb emerges earlier as single verb than the frozen-form candidate, but there are exceptions: English *to go* as a main verb may emerge earlier than the adult amalgam *gonna*. Moreover, a frozen form generally constitutes a single-element utterance: if it combines with other elements, it is on a way of "defrozeness". In our corpora a frozen form is used repeatedly and is not limited to isolated examples (cf. SOP *ça marche* 'it works' not a likely candidate for frozen form). We distinguish:

i. amalgams which are always frozen forms, i.e. adult multiword combinations treated as one unanalyzed word by the child, thus morphosemantically and morphotactically opaque (even fused), e.g. SOP and EMM /alɛla/ and variants for *il/elle est là* 'he/she is there', /tɛjɛ/ and variants for *ça y est*; SOP /ewawa/ and variants for *on va voir* 'we will see', SOP *à boire* 'I want to drink';

ii. regulative or phatic forms corresponding to a single verb-form or to a verb-form plus proclitic: SOP *attends* 'wait', EMM *tu sais* 'you know', EMM *ça va* 'it's ok'. Such forms correspond to adult automatic speech and could be substituted easily by a pragmatically synonymous form of very different structure, e.g. *attends!* → *une minute! tu sais* → *eh!* (?), *ça va* → *ok*[17];

iii. imitated forms, i.e. repetitions of the adult target in the next turn.

The difference between a), b) and c) is gradual. Segmentation is probably the most important difference between frozen forms and other verb-forms. Whereas root-forms and inflected forms have been segmented from the rest of the phonological word, frozen forms represent generally a whole utterance or turn and may be memorized as such. But basically these first verb productions are all rote-learnt (cf. MacWhinney 1978) and lexically-based (Tomasello 1992; Akhtar and Tomasello 1997; Lieven 1998; Tomasello and Brooks 1999): in the first 2 months of recording (before 1;8 SOP and 1;6 EMM), all verbs have one single form and later on at most 2 forms (see below), i.e. they are invariable and unanalysed.

Things may be further refined however. We have, indeed, noticed already some pattern in the repartition of verb-categories among the two children (table 8), i.e. SOP's preference for root-forms opposed to EMM's preference for inflected forms.

Moreover, whereas nothing relevant seems to be found in root-forms and frozen forms, another pattern emerges from inflected forms. Several measures show that EMM has a strong preference for macroclass I types (and tokens) of infinitive (see table 9):[18]

Table 9. Bare infinitives

	SOP 1;8–1;11.7				EMM 1;4–1;7			
	lemmas	%	tokens	%	lemmas	%	tokens	%
macroclass I	10	56	29	48	19	83	30	65
macroclass II	8	44	31	52	4	17	16	35

The difference between Sophie and Emma's infinitives does not appear in the input: first macroclass types are preferred in Emma (65% vs. 35%) and Sophie's input (60% vs. 40%). The opposite preference holds for tokens but the proportions are less similar in the two inputs: whereas Sophie's input clearly favours tokens of macroclass II (69% vs. 31%), Emma's input has an almost equal proportion of the two classes. It appears that several tokens are repetitions of the child's production and that, when putting them aside, there is a majority of tokens of macroclass II (51% vs. 47%) (the percentages of Sophie's input almost do not change with the same deduction: 70% vs. 30%). Finite forms of macroclass II are also dominant.

Table 10. Percentages of infinitives in the input

	SOP input		EMM input	
	lemmas	tokens	lemmas	tokens
macroclass I	60	31	65	47
macroclass II	40	69	35	51

The preference for macroclass I types and tokens of infinitives in Emma's corpus is confirmed by the examination of the first 50 lemmas produced by the children: of the 14 infinitives occurring in Sophie's corpus, 7 (50%) belong to macroclass I and 7 to macroclass II, i.e. there is no apparent selectivity with regard to the inflectional classes; in the corpus of Emma, 13 of the 16 infinitives produced belong to macroclass I (81%).

The same result obtains again with all types of inflected forms (PP, Compound Past, Infinitive, Compound Future) of the first 50 lemmas:

SOP: 54% of lemmas of macroclass I – 46% of others
EMM: 70% of of lemmas of macroclass I – 30% of others.

EMM appears thus to be more of a morphotactic child than SOP. This difference fits with the pattern of verb-categories mentioned above (3.1.) and with morphosemantic aspects (see Kilani-Schoch and Dressler 2002). With such morphologically conditioned selection, EMM's premorphological phase can be said to show a greater variety of patterns than SOP's premorphological phase, i.e. there is more (pre)morphology in the former.

4. Emergence of mini-paradigms
4.1. Criteria

How do children start to form paradigms at all, and what evidence do we have ? Since the occurrence of more than one verb form of a verb does not constitute in itself evidence for paradigm formation (Cf. Tomasello 1992; Behrens 1999), methodological prerequisites for assessing morphological relatedness between distinct verb forms of the same lemma in the data are necessary (cf. Allen 1996). We propose five criteria for establishing the onset of a paradigm, i.e. spontaneous production (not imitative), spontaneous production (not formulaic), articulatory accuracy, use in contrasting contexts, recurrence (of the lemma) (cf. Kilani-Schoch 2000; Kilani-Schoch and Dressler 2002), e.g., in SOP:

(1) 1;11.19
chercher 'look for' : /a ʃeʃe/ for *chercher* /ʃɛrʃe/
FILLER INF INF
(with Pres.Ind meaning)
and *a cherche* /ʃɛrʃ/
FILLER PRES.IND.S
'(I) look for'

Inf and Pres.Ind.S seem to be optional variants, whereas in (2) the forms represent a true mini-paradigm:

(2) 2;0.22
mettre 'put' : *i met* /mɛ/ *tatalon* for *je   mets   pantalon*
                                            PRO   PRES.IND.S   N
                                            'I put trousers on',

and   *a mis* /ami/ *do*   for   *a mis   de   l'eau*
                                        COMP.PAST 3S   ART   N
                                        'has put some water'

and   *a mettre a papo*   for   *mettre   le   chapeau*
                                        INF   ART   N
                                        'put the hat on'.

Compare also in the corpus of EMM:

(3) 1;7.27
appuyer 'press': *apini*[19] *[///] apie [/] apie [/] apie a Papa [///] apie Papa [///] apier Papa* (sequence)

                                 for   *appuie   appuyer*
                                        IMP.2S   INF
                                        'press'

with a true mini-paradigm:

(4) 1;8.10
mettre 'put': *on   le   <u>met</u>   là*
                  PRO   PRO   PRES.IND.S   ADV
                  'we put it there',

and   /fa/ <u>*mett(re)*</u>   for   *va/veux   mettre*
                                          AUX/MOD   INF
                                          'will put /wants to put',

and   *t'   <u>as mis</u>   où ?*
           PRO   COMP.PAST   ADV
           'where did you put'.

All three forms have to appear within at least one month, i.e. either in the same month or within a distance of maximally one month.

Hence we define the first "true", but still very incomplete, thus minimal, paradigms as non-isolated sets of minimally three accurate and distinct inflectional forms of the same verbal lexeme produced spontaneously in contrasting contexts.

This leads to an analysis of the development of paradigms as a gradual process with different building steps.

4.2. Mini-paradigms: Steps of development

First two forms of a verb-lemma appear at 1;8 for SOP, at 1;5 for EMM. First mini-paradigms have been considered to occur not earlier than three months later, i.e. at the end of 2;0 for SOP, and at 1;8 for EMM. In the meantime several mini-paradigm candidates (pairs or triplex of verb-forms) occur:

SOP (1;8–2;0.22): 16 lemmas
Unclear: 9, context-bound: 8, isolated: 4, imitations: 3, formulaic: 2[20]

EMM (1;5–1;8.10): 7 lemmas
Unclear: 4, isolated: 2, context-bound: 2, imitations: 2, formulaic: 1/2.[21]

On the basis of the criteria mentioned above, we distinguish three steps in the emergence of paradigms.

4.2.1. Step A

A very first step consists in approximations of different verb-forms of verb types, e.g.

SOP (1;8–1;9/1;10)
(5) 1;7.26 *laver* 'wash' /awa/ for *?lave* /lav/
                                         ?PRES.IND:S
                                         'wash',
     1;9.13   /œve/   for *laver* /lave/
                                         ?INF

EMM (1;5–1;6)
(6) 1;5.3 *donner* 'give' /tate/ for *?donner* /dɔne/
                                          ?INF
                                    and *donne* /dɔn/
                                          IMP

In this first step the forms are also rather isolated and do not recur before at least two months. This preliminary step is followed by a second pre-paradigm step.

4.2.2. Step B

The different verb forms of lemmas which occur in this second step before the first mini-paradigms, are either isolated forms, imitated forms, formulaic forms, context-bound forms or optional variants connected by some irregular (not rule-governed) morphotactic similarity, e.g.

SOP (1;9–2;0)
(7)　2;0.10　*essayer* 'try':　*Maman　essaie* /ɛsɛ/
　　　　　　　　　　　N　　　　IMP
　　　　　　　　　　　'Mum try',
　　　　next utt.:　　*non　là,　Maman　essayer* /ɛsɛje/
　　　　　　　　　　　NEG　ADV　N　　　　INF
　　　　　　　　　　　'Mum try'.

EMM (1;7–1;8), e.g. (3) above.

4.2.3. Step C

After a slow extension of verb forms for some verb lemmas, first true mini-paradigms appear. A time interval and a sufficient number of "preparadigms", i.e. verb-specific inflected forms, seem thus to be needed by the children before they can recognize the morphological principle of related form and meaning (plus distinctivity) and can actively use formal marking of verb inflection. On the basis of the criteria presented above, we can conclude that there is no mini-paradigm before the occurrence of 3 forms of a verb.[22] In the two corpora, the first evidence for a true mini-paradigm is given by the occurrence of a macroclass II verb with three contrasting forms along with other two-member paradigms in the same month:[23]

SOP (2;0.22)
(8)　*mettre* 'put':
　　　met /mɛ/　　–　*mett(re)* /mɛt/　　–　*a mis* /a mi/
　　　PRES.IND.3S　　INF　　　　　　　　　COMP.PAST 3S

(9) *partir* 'leave':
 est parti /ε parti/ — *part* /par/
 COMP.PAST 3S   PRES.IND.3S

(10) *mordre* 'bite':
 mord /mɔr/ — *a mordu* /a mɔrdy/
 PRES.IND.3S   COMP.PAST 3S

(11) *sortir* 'go out':
 sort /sɔr/ — *sortir* /sɔrtir/
 PRES.IND.3S   INF

(12) *boire* 'drink':
 boit /bwa/ — *a bu* /a by/
 PRES.IND.3S   COMP.PAST 3S

The following mini-paradigm candidates do not match at least one of the criteria: *cacher* (unclear) 'look for', *casser* 'break' (imitated), *chercher* 'look for' (unclear and context-bound), *essayer* 'try' (optional variants), *laver* 'wash' (unclear), *regarder* 'look' (context-bound), *sauter* 'spring' (unclear), *tomber* 'fall' (unclear), *venir* 'come' (context-bound), *voir* 'see' (frozen), *s'asseoir* 'sit down' (unclear).

EMM (1;8.10)

(13) *mettre* 'put':
 mets /mε/ — *mettre* /mεt/ — *as mis* /a mi/
 PRES.IND.3S   INF   COMP.PAST 3S

(14) *manger* 'eat':
 mange /mɑ̃ʒ/ — *manger* /mɑ̃ʒe/
 PRES.IND.3S   INF

(15) *sortir* 'go out':
 sortir /sɔrtir/ — *a sorti* /a sɔrti/
 INF   COMP.PAST 3S

(16) *s'asseoir* 'sit down':
 (s')asseoir /aswar/ — *s'est assis* /sε asi/
 INF   COMP.PAST 3S

vs. *donner* 'give' (optional variants), *marcher* 'walk' (formulaic), *casser* 'break' (unclear), *attacher* 'bind' (unclear and imitated), *appuyer* 'press' (unclear/sequence), *partir* (sequence) 'leave'.

In both children the first mini-paradigm with three contrasting forms coincides with the beginning of protomorphology. Moreover, in both children it is the verb *mettre* (cf. Guillaume 1927; Martinot 1998; cf. Noccetti for Italian, this volume). Frequency of *mettre* in the input does not account for this finding: indeed the results of verb (lemma) frequency in SOP and EMM's inputs rank *mettre* respectively in the seventh and fifth position only:[24]

input SOP: *être, faire,* AUX|*avoir, aller,* AUX|*aller, vouloir, mettre*
input EMM: *être, faire,* AUX|*avoir,* AUX|*aller, mettre, aller, vouloir.*

In addition to structural reasons (*mettre* is more "regular" than the other verbs with high frequency), semantic and pragmatic factors must be considered: *mettre* is a "light" verb which indicates only the moving of an object by an agent without specifying manner and location and it is an important verb in situations of play. In addition this finding can be attributed to the characteristics of the input language (system-adequacy). The first conjugation class – the most frequent and the only productive verb type in French – has more homophony in the categories used by the little child than the other verbs. Hence the child has first more difficulty in forming 3-member paradigms with distinct members of the macroclass I than with members of macroclass II.

Table 11a. New mini-paradigms in SOP's corpus

SOP	new mini-paradigms (2-members or more) per total of lemmas /month	%	3-member mini-paradigms	number of mini-paradigms /month
2;0	5/49	10.2	1	5
2;1	9/52	19.1	4	14
2;2	11–12/60	20	4	23
2;3	14/56	25	8	23
2;4	14/80	17.5	9	25

Table 11b. New mini-paradigms in EMM's corpus

EMM				
1;8	8/35	20	1	8
1;9	6/45	13.3	1	10
1;10	14/54	25.9	6	18
1;11	6/49	12.2	3	13
2;0	3/30	10	2	13

5. Morphological substitutions
5.1. Root infinitives

By far the most frequent morphological substitutions in the period considered and in the whole corpora are root-infinitives (see also other languages of this volume: Dutch: Gillis, German: Bittner, English: Gülzow, Finnish: Laalo and Russian: Gagarina) :

SOP 1;6–1;11: 76/374 verb-forms (20%), 1;6–2;0: 113/512 (22%),
Input: infinitives represent 17% of all verb-forms,
EMM 1;4–1;7: 49 /122 verb-forms (40%), 1;4–1;8: 73/245 (30%),
Input: 21%.

Root infinitives may result from omission of the auxiliary or modal verb, e.g. 0Aux/0Mod + Inf (root infinitives):

SOP
(17) 1;9 /atetir əwã/ for *(il) veut sortir (l')éléphant*
(FILLER) MOD INF N
'the elefant wants to go out',

(18) 1;11 *là Papa gicler* for *là Papa va gicler*
ADV N INF ADV AUX INF
'Daddy will squirt with water'

or – less frequently – occur instead of a finite form, e.g.

SOP
(19) 1;9.13 /açaçe/ = for *(je) cherche* /ʒə ʃɛrʃ/
chercher (PRO) PRES.IND.S
INF '(I) am looking for',

EMM
(20) 1;8 *faire bobo là* for *ça fait bobo là*
INF N ADV PRO PRES.IND.S ADV
'(it) is hurting there'.

Root infinitives however are more of a syntactic than of a morphological type of production (cf. Phillips 1995): among other factors they may be attributed to the saliency of the infinitive in syntactic structures such as modal structures (see Gillis this volume; Wijnen, Kempen, and Gillis 2001) and to the ambiguity of the preverbal position (several clitic options appear before an infinitive, e.g., semi-auxiliary *va*, prepositions *à*, *de*, which cannot be predicted by the form of the immediately following verb). In languages such as French and German, the homophony of infinitive with PP and plural forms also favours their occurrence.

5.2. Analogical formations

All examples of analogical formations or overgeneralizations occur significantly after the first mini-paradigms (cf. 6.). For lack of space we will consider class shift only.[25]

SOP: between 2;2.0 and 2;7.18: 5 types/10 tokens + ?1
EMM: between 1;9 and 2;9: 2 types/5 tokens.

Class shifts are mainly overgeneralizations of first macroclass infinitive, e.g.

SOP and EMM
(21) 2;2.0 *metter* for *mettre*
INF
'put'[26]

SOP
(22) 2;2.22 *descender* for *descendre*
INF
'go down'

SOP
(23) 2;5.3 *pompirer* for *remplir*
INF
'fill'

EMM
(24) 1;10 *sorter* for *sortir*
INF
'go out'

SOP
(25) 2;5.27   *a voulé*   for   *a voulu*
                                          COMP.PAST 3S
                                          'wanted'

(26) 2;6.25   *a vé*   for   *a vu*
                                          COMP.PAST 3S
                                          'has seen'

i.e. overgeneralizations based on the productive class. But there are also overgeneralizations within macroclass II, e.g.

SOP (2;7.18) and EMM (2;4.15)
(27)   *tiendre* /tjẽdr/   for   *tenir* /tənir/
                                          INF

SOP
(29) 2;2.13 *a prendu* /a prãdy/ for   *a pris* /a pri/
                                          COMP.PAST 3S
                                          'has held'

i.e. not based on a productive model. The latter must be analysed as rime analogies based on phonological and prosodic similarities. The child has related verb forms of isolated paradigms (Inf *tenir* 'hold' and *prendre* 'take') to sets of whole paradigm riming verbs, i.e. to verbs having the same phonological form except the initial sequence, e.g. *rendre, (en)tendre, descendre, (dé)fendre, vendre, pendre*. The verb *prendre* is an isolated paradigm of this set, but it rimes with its members in a great part of the paradigm (not in Pres.Plural, Imperfect and Past Participle). What seems most important here is the rime in the base form (Pres.S) *prend* and in the base derived Inf *prendre*. The childish Comp.Past *a prendu*, based on the rime between *rend* and *prend*, is derived by a minor rule coresponding to the proportional analogy: *rend: prend = rendu: x*. The overgeneralization *tiendre* is based on a rime with the set of verbs *peindre, teindre, atteindre, éteindre, plaindre, craindre*. In the adult language the base forms with stressed nasal vowels rime: *tient* /tjẽ/ rimes with *teint* /tẽ/, *éteint* /etẽ/, *peint* /pẽ/. The riming part of the paradigm is however more limited than in the case of *prendre* since it applies only in the Pres.S and in the Simple Future (*tiendrai, peindrai*). The proportional analogy seems to be: *éteint: tient = éteindre: x*.

These examples demonstrate that no inflectional imperialism (cf. Slobin 1985: 1216) occurs in my corpora.

6. Conclusion
6.1. Early verb development and pre- and protomorphology

First, in premorphology, the emergence of verbs is lexical (steps 1 and 2). Premorphology is the phase in which no system of grammatical morphology has dissociated from a general cognitive system. Morphological operations are extragrammatical ones or rote-learnt precursors of later grammatical rules (cf. Dressler and Karpf 1995; Dressler 1997; Dziubalska-Kołaczyk 1997; Kilani-Schoch and Dressler 2001).

In protomorphology the system of morphological grammar and of its subsystems starts to develop without reaching the status of modules (components) or submodules (subcomponents). The paradigm formation process starts to emerge: at the beginning it is limited to some lemmas (overlap of steps 2 and 3), and there is no across-the-board generalization. However it soon develops into an increasing number of new mini-paradigms.

This development will lead to morphological productivity in modularized morphology[27] (cf. Kilani-Schoch et al. 1997; Kilani-Schoch and Dressler 2001).

The identification, during protomorphology, of morphosemantic oppositions and the establishment of mini-paradigms seems to be the precondition for identifying analogical relationships and for extending them in terms of proportional analogies. Creative morphological patterns, e.g., overgeneralizations, indeed follow two months later (from 2;2 on in SOP's corpus, from 1;10 on in EMM's corpus).

These observations, together with EMM's morphotactic selectivity which seems to imply that some general grouping of verbs has been already made by the child, indicate that some generalization has taken place, i.e. in protomorphology the children have started to understand the morphological principle of relating forms and meanings in regular ways.

I thus rather adopt an intermediate position with regard to the lexically specific vs. verb-general account of verb emergence (cf. Tomasello 1992; Akhtar and Tomasello 1997; Lieven 1998; Tomasello and Brooks 1999; Behrens 1999) and see a similar pattern of gradual and progressive (inflectional) development as observed by Allen (1998); Ninio (1999); and

Mueller Gathercole, Sebastián, and Soto (1999), up to a point where a qualitative change takes place.

6.2. Typological characteristics

A first general property of French which is weakly inflecting and approaches the isolating type is that many verb-forms do not involve any morphological operation. With regard to this criterion one may expect that

a) non-inflected (verbal root) forms, i.e. Pres.Ind.S or Imp, should appear first and earlier than inflected categories. This prediction is born out for SOP's data where inflected forms occur at 1;8 only, but not in the case of EMM. As said above, EMM favours inflected forms which are used from the very beginning. Individual differences hence go beyond typological adequacy;
a') inflected forms such as plural forms should emerge later than in non-isolating languages, e.g. in stronger inflecting languages (cf. Kilani-Schoch et al. 1997, cf. another Romance language of the volume, i.e. Spanish: Aguirre);
a") periphrastic Past and Future should emerge before their synthetic competitors. This is amply documented by any study on acquisition of French;
b) nouns and verbs emerge simultaneously, particularly that earliest verb forms emerge as early as first nouns (but individual strategies put a strong limitation to this prediction, cf. Braunwald 1995). In other words, French morphology should not stimulate children to acquire nouns or verbs earlier than the other category. Indeed this expectation is born out in my data;
c) the non-differenciation of singular and plural forms (in macroclass I) should ease reference to plural subjects. However instances of plural meaning (i.e. contextual meaning) of verb forms in this early stage are almost inexistent;
d) tense distinctions emerge before person and number distinctions. This holds true for my data where the categories involved in the first mini-paradigms are Ind.Pres.S, Infinitive and Compound Past (see tables 6 and 7) (cf. Aguirre this volume). As far as tense is concerned, however, considering that early Past Participle and Compound Past are mostly used with telic lemmata (Vendler 1967) (e.g. *casser* 'break', *fermer* 'close', *tomber* 'fall', *partir* 'leave', *finir* 'end'), this first distinction

between finite verb-forms (let alone Imp) could be rather characterized in terms of aspect rather than in terms of tense (but cf. Shirai and Andersen 1995). It seems nevertheless that both children extend Compound Past to activity (SOP: 2;2.13 *a léché* 'licked', EMM 1;8.24 *a pleuré* 'cried') and stative verbs (SOP: 1;11.29 and EMM 1;8.10 *t' as vu* 'you have seen') before they introduce first person distinction, i.e. the distinction between first and third person (Pres.1S = SOP 2;5, EMM 1;9) in suppletive verbs; Comp.Fut. – Present distinction is frequent at 2;4 in SOP, at 1;10 in EMM; as to number distinction, Pres.3P is frequent later than first non-present tenses and 1S (in addition to 3S): SOP at 2;7, EMM at 2;2.

More system-specific but still typologically adequate is, e.g., the homophony between Inf and PP in the productive macroclass I. From this homophony one could make the hypotheses that:

e) Inf and PP would emerge earlier and with higher frequency than in languages not having this homophony (cf. Kilani-Schoch et al. 1997; but cf. Aguirre this volume); but see the individual difference between SOP and EMM (table 8);
f) periphrastic verb-forms should emerge earlier than in isolating languages and others not having this homophony (cf. Kilani-Schoch et al. 1997);
g) there should be analogical PP forms based on Inf (less probably vice versa, because Inf is less marked than PP) in unproductive microclasses and isolated paradigms. However there is only one instance in the corpus of SOP: 2;5 PQP *avait mettre* for *avait mis* 'has put';[28]
h) since in French the productive macroclass I has also the highest lemma frequency and is the default class, it is easily predictable that morphological substitutions occur exclusively in unproductive microclasses and isolated paradigms; my data are in accordance with this prediction (see 5.2.);
i) since french aspectual distinctions are not encoded separately from tense and are tied to the opposition between periphrastic and synthetic tense, aspectual distinctions obviously depend on the mastery of the respective tense subsystem, i.e. the opposition between imparfait (Imperfect as in Latin and in the other Romance languages) and passé composé (Compound Past).

Notes

* I would like to thank W.U. Dressler, D. Bittner, S. Klampfer and C. Aguirre for their many helpful comments and suggestions. I am grateful to Sophie and Emma's parents for their collaboration in collecting the data and checking the transcriptions. Finally my thanks go to Philippe Carrard for checking my English.
1. *On parle* instead of *nous parlons*.
2. On French inflectional classes, see Dressler and Kilani-Schoch to appear.
3. Verbs of mc. 2,3,4 (types *semer, céder, payer*) are not yet relevant for the early data dealt with here.
4. Which corresponds to imperfective aspect opposed to perfective aspect of Compound Past.
5. The data of Emma are more limited than the data of Sophie. Emma was recorded generally only twice a month and some of the recordings are very short (e.g. 1;6, 1;7, 2;0; at 1;7 diary notes are used to complement the recordings). This diversity in the data of Emma is probably responsible for the greater heterogeneity of some of the findings on her language development.
6. To qualify as an utterance, a production has to include at least one meaningful unit resembling a French word in form and meaning.
7. This corresponds roughly to the first 50 verb lemmas.
8. Thanks are due to Steven Gillis for introduction to CLAN, to Marc Xicoira for technical help and to the University of Lausanne for financial support.
9. There is a transition phase between pre- and protomorphology in SOP's corpus.
10. Frozen forms (and fillers) are excluded.
11. These 3 categories are the most important categories in spoken French and several verbs have no other forms used (Blanche-Benveniste and Adam 1999).
12. In imitation.
13. In all tables direct imitations are included: in my corpora (and especially in EMM's corpus), a verb form may alternatively appear as spontaneous or imitated without any apparent systematicity such as, e.g. imitated form first. Imitations thus deserve a specific study.
14. Compound Past and Compound Future forms are counted as single verb-forms of these categories.
15. SOP and EMM (one isolated example in EMM's corpus at 1;9 however) do not have yet person distinction but recall that in French conjugation only suppletive verbs mark first person distinctly from 2./3. person, cf. 1.
16. Notice however that they are not productive before 2;2: the corpus shows either formulaic plural verb forms (*partez* 'go', *attendez* 'wait') or the Present 3P form of *être* 'be' *sont* 'are' and other verb forms with family resemblance (*font* 'do', *ont* 'have').

17. As mentioned by Blanche-Benveniste and Adam (1999: 90), it is sometimes difficult to distinguish between a phatic and a plain use of verb forms.
18. Finite forms in general do not display the same distribution: in both corpora tokens or lemmas of macroclass I are dominant. Recall however that Pres.Ind.S (and 3P in macroclass I and in some verbs of macroclass II) has no inflectional marking and corresponds to the simple base.
19. *apini* may be a blend of *finir*, Comp.Past 3S *a fini* /a fini/ 'ended' and of Imp.S *appuie* 'press'.
20. The numbers correspond to verb-lemmas. There is overlapping of criteria for several verbs.
21. All numbers are tokens.
22. Cf. in a different context and for a different purpose Pine and Lieven (1993: 558): three instances of a construction are needed for qualifying as constructed.
23. On the parallel establishment of recurrent morphosemantic oppositions, see Kilani-Schoch and Dressler 2002.
24. In the GARS's corpus of spoken French (cf. Blanche-Benveniste and Adam 1999: 101), *mettre* is not among the most frequent verbs either (less than 1000 occurrences) but is morphologically differentiated (21 categories used).
25. Category shifts are rare (around 5 per child) and not clearly of an analogical nature. My formulae of proportional analogy takes the most similar verbs as model but the actual model may be also another verb or an abstract pattern (minor rule).
26. A similar example is mentioned by Clark (1985: 703).
27. Modularized morphology contains the nucleus of mature morphological grammar. Subsystems of verb and noun inflection are distinguished.
28. The analogical Inf *metter* 'put' also occurs in the same recording session.

References

Akhtar, Nameera, and Michael Tomasello
    1997   Young children's productivity with word order and verb morphology. *Developmental Psychology* 33: 952–965.

Allen, Shanley
    1996   Assessing productivity in acquisition data from polysynthetic languages: An Inuktitut example. Paper presented at the 7th International Congress for the Study of Child Language, Istanbul, July 1996.

Allen, Shanley
1998   Categories within the verb category: Learning the causative in Inuktitut. *Linguistics* 36: 633–677.

Bates, Elizabeth, Philip S. Dale, and Donna Thal
1995   Individual differences and their implications for theories of language development. In: Paul Fletcher, and Brian MacWhinney (eds.), *The Handbook of Child Language*, 96–151. Oxford: Blackwell.

Behrens, Heike
1999   Was macht Verben zu einer besonderen Kategorie im Spracherwerb? In: Jörg Meibauer, and Monika Rothweiler (eds.), *Das Lexikon im Spracherwerb*, 32–50. Tübingen: Francke.

Blanche-Benveniste, Claire, and Jean-Pierre Adam
1999   La conjugaison des verbes: Virtuelle, attestée, défective. *Recherches sur le français parlé* 15: 87–112.

Braunwald, Susan R.
1995   Differences in the acquisition of early verbs: Evidence from diary data from sisters. In: Michael Tomasello, and William E. Merriman (eds.), *Beyond Names for Things*, 81–111. Hillsdale, New Jersey: Lawrence Erlbaum.

Clark, Eve V.
1985   The acquisition of Romance, with special reference to French. In: Dan I. Slobin (ed.), *The Crosslinguistic Study of Language Acquisition*. Vol. 1, 687–782. Hillsdale, New Jersey: Lawrence Erlbaum.

Dressler, Wolfgang U. (ed.)
1997   *Studies in Pre- and Protomorphology*. Wien: Verlag der Österreichischen Akademie der Wissenschaften.

Dressler, Wolfgang U., and Annemarie Karpf
1995   The theoretical relevance of pre- and protomorphology in language acquisition. *Yearbook of Morphology* 1994: 99–122.

Dressler, Wolfgang U., and Marianne Kilani-Schoch
to appear   Hierarchy and the classification of French verbs. In Ruth Brend, Thomas N. Headland, and Mary Ruth Wise (eds.), *Language and Life. Essays in Memory of K. Pike*. Arlington: SIL.

Dziubalska-Kołaczyk, Katarzyna (ed.)
1997　　*Pre- and Protomorphology in Language Acquisition.* (Papers and Studies in Contrastive Linguistics 33.) Poznań: Adam Mickiewicz University.

Guillaume, Paul
1927　　Le développement des éléments formels dans le langage de l'enfant. *Journal de Psychologie* 24: 203–229.

Kilani-Schoch, Marianne
2000　　Early verb development in two French-speaking children. In: Dagmar Bittner, Wolfgang U. Dressler, and Marianne Kilani-Schoch (eds.), *First Verbs: On the Way to Mini-Paradigms,* 79–98. (ZAS Papers in Linguistics 18.) Berlin: Zentrum für Allgemeine Sprachwissenschaft, Typologie und Universalienforschung (ZAS).

Kilani-Schoch, Marianne, Anna De Marco, Anastasia Christofidou, Maria Vassilakou, Ralph Vollmann, and Wolfgang U. Dressler
1997　　On the demarcation of phases in early morphology acquisition in four languages. In: Katarzyna Dziubalska-Kołaczyk (ed.), *Pre- and Protomorphology in Language Acquisition,* 15–32. (Papers and Studies in Contrastive Linguistics 33.) Poznań: Adam Mickiewicz University.

Kilani-Schoch, Marianne, and Wolfgang U. Dressler
2000　　Are fillers as precursors of morphemes relevant for morphological theory? In: Wolfgang U. Dressler, Oskar E. Pfeiffer, Markus Pöchtrager, and John Rennison (eds.), *Morphological Analysis in Comparison,* 89–111. Amsterdam: John Benjamins.

Kilani-Schoch, Marianne and Wolfgang U. Dressler
2001　　Filler+Infinitive and Pre-&Protomorphology demarcation in a French acquisition corpus. *Journal of Psycholinguistic Research* 30 (6): 653–685.

Kilani-Schoch, Marianne, and Wolfgang U. Dressler
2002　　The emergence of inflectional paradigms in two French corpora: An illustration of general problems of pre- and protomorphology. In: Maria D. Voeikova, and Wolfgang U. Dressler (eds.), *Pre- and Protomorphology: Early Phases of Morphological Development in Nouns and Verbs,* 45–59. München: Lincom.

Lieven, Elena. V. M. (ed.)
1998   *Developing a Verb Category: Cross-linguistic Perspectives. Linguistics* 36, 4. Berlin: Mouton de Gruyter.

MacWhinney, Brian
1978   *The Acquisition of Morphonology.* (Monographs of the Society for Research in Child Development 43, 1/2.) Chicago: University of Chicago Press.

Martinot, Claire
1998   Développement de la construction argumentale de trois verbes essentiels. *Langue française* 118: 61–83.

Mueller Gathercole, Virginia C., Eugenia Sebastián, and Pilar Soto
1999   The early acquisition of Spanish verbal morphology: Across-the-board or piece-meal knowledge? *International Journal of Bilingualism* 3: 133–182.

Ninio, Anat
1999   Model learning in syntactic developement: Intransitive verbs. *International Journal of Bilingualism* 3: 111–132.

Peters, Ann M.
1997   Language typology, prosody and the acquisition of grammatical morphemes. In: Dan I. Slobin (ed.), *The Crosslinguistic Study of Language Acquisition.* Vol. 5, 135–197. Mahwah, New Jersey: Lawrence Erlbaum.

Peters, Ann M., and Lise Menn
1993   False starts and filler syllables: Ways to learn grammatical morphemes. *Language* 69: 742–777.

Phillips, Colin
1995   Syntax at age 2: Crosslinguistic differences. *MIT Working Papers in Linguistics* 26: 325–382.

Pine, Julian M., and Elena V. M. Lieven
1993   Reanalysing rote-learned phrases: Individual differences in the transition to multi-word speech. *Journal of Child Language* 20: 551–571.

Shirai, Yasuhiro, and Roger W. Andersen
1995   The acquisition of tense-aspect morphology: A prototype account. *Language* 71: 743–762.

Slobin, Dan I.
   1985   Crosslinguistic evidence for the language-making capacity. In Dan I. Slobin (ed.), *The Crosslinguistic Study of Language Acquisition.* Vol. 2, 1157–1256. Hillsdale, New Jersey: Lawrence Erlbaum.

Tomasello, Michael
   1992   *First Verbs: A Case Study of Early Grammatical Development.* Cambridge: Cambridge University Press.

Tomasello, Michael, and Patricia Brooks
   1999   Early syntactic development: a construction grammar approach. In: Martyn Barrett (ed.), *The Development of Language*, 161–191. Hove: Psychology Press.

Vendler, Zeno
   1967   *Linguistics in Philosophy.* Ithaca: Cornell University Press.

Wijnen, Frank, Masja Kempen, and Steven Gillis
   2001   Root infinitives in Dutch early child language: An effect of input. *Journal of Child Language* 28: 629–660.

Emergence of verb paradigms in one Austrian child[*]

Sabine Klampfer

0. Introduction

The purpose of this paper is to trace the early development of verb morphology in one Austrian child. The paper will focus on the emergence and development of verb paradigms and on its relation to the transition from pre- to protomorphology (Dressler and Karpf 1995; Dressler 1997a). We will argue that the development of verb paradigms constitutes a gradual process which in our data can best be described by three main building steps: a first step (premorphology), where no form oppositions occur, a second step (onset of protomorphology), where first form oppositions emerge, and a third step (protomorphology), which is characterized by a clear increase of verb paradigms. We will analyze the stepwise expansion of verb form types, verb categories and inflectional class distinctions occurring in form oppositions and confront these findings with input frequencies. Furthermore, we will relate the development of verb morphology at the transition from pre- to protomorphology to morphological changes observed in other subdomains (especially nouns) and investigate interdependencies between early lexical and morphological development.

1. (Austrian) German verbal system

German is a weakly inflecting language with moderately rich verb morphology. Austrian German is even weaker inflecting than Standard High German.

1.1. Grammatical categories

German verbs encode the grammatical categories of person, number, tense, mood, and voice. There exists no grammatical verbal category of aspect in German.

Person (1st, 2nd, 3rd) and number (sg, pl) are expressed fusionally by verbal suffixes (and by subject pronouns which are obligatory unless there is ellipsis, or if the noun renders a 3rd person pronoun superfluous). Table 1 gives an overview of the suffixes used in the present indicative and in the imperative. Parentheses and slashes indicate possible alternations in colloquial Austrian German.

Within the category tense, spoken Austrian German distinguishes between present, future, perfect, and pluperfect. In contrast to Northern German varieties, the synthetic preterite is unproductive in spoken Austrian German (except for the verb *sein* 'to be'). The present is formed synthetically. Perfect, pluperfect and future tense are expressed by periphrastic constructions, i.e. by combination of Aux (*haben* 'to have', *sein* 'to be') + PP (e.g. *er hat gespielt* 'he played / has played') and Aux (*werden* 'to become') + INF (e.g. *er wird spielen* 'he will play') respectively.

Table 1. Person and number marking in the present indicative and imperative: the weak German verb *spielen* 'to play'

	PRES. INDICATIVE		IMPERATIVE	
	Sg.	Pl.	Sg.	Pl.
1st Person	spiel-(e)	spiel-(e)n[1]		spiel-(e)n wir! / spiel-ma!
2nd Person	spiel-st	spiel-t / -ts	spiel-∅!	spiel-t! /-ts!
3rd Person	spiel-t	spiel-(e)n		

Within the category mood, spoken Austrian German distinguishes between indicative, imperative and conditional (= conjunctive II), the last one being formed analytically in Standard Austrian German (e.g. *ich würde spielen* 'I would play'), and synthetically in some Austrian dialects (e.g. [i ʃpy:lat]). Passive voice is expressed by the construction Aux (*werden* 'to become' for the event passive and *sein* 'to be' for the stative passive) + PP (e.g. *es wird gespielt* 'it is played').

1.2. Inflectional classes and productivity

Following A. Bittner (1996), Dressler (to appear) proposes a subdivision of the German verb – according to different patterns of stem vowel change (Umlaut [U], Ablaut [A]) and weak vs. strong inflectional properties of category symbolization – into 15 different inflectional microclasses. This classification established for the adult language appears however to be too detailed for the study of child language. For example, in spoken Austrian German, children are hardly ever exposed to preterite forms (except for the verb *sein* 'to be' and for fairytales) and therefore children before the age of 3;0 are rather unlikely to make distinctions between microclasses which differ by the use of Ablaut in the preterite. Collapsing microclass distinctions which are of little relevance for small Austrian children, German verbs may thus be grouped into the following classes (cf. Dressler and Klampfer 2000; Klampfer 2000); the forms given are Inf., 3.Sg. Pres.Ind., 1.Pl. Pres.Ind., 2.Sg. Imp., PP:

Class 1: weak verbs
    e.g. *spielen* 'to play': *er spielt, wir spielen, spiel!, gespielt*
Class 1': weak verbs (+A)
    e.g. *brennen* 'to burn': *es brennt, wir brennen, brenn!, gebrannt*

Class 2: strong verbs (+A)
    e.g. *bleiben* 'to stay': *er bleibt, wir bleiben, bleib!, geblieben*

Class 3: strong verbs (+1U)
    e.g. *schlafen* 'to sleep': *er schläft, wir schlafen, schlaf!, geschlafen*
Class 3': strong verbs (-U)
    e.g. *kommen* 'to come': *er kommt, wir kommen, komm!, gekommen*

Class 4: strong verbs (+2U)
    e.g. *lesen* 'to read': *er liest, wir lesen, lies!, gelesen*

Class 5: strong verbs (+2U, +A)
    e.g. *brechen* 'to break': *er bricht, wir brechen, brich!, gebrochen*

Modals: e.g. *können* 'can': 1.Sg.Pres.Ind. *ich kann, er kann, wir können, gekonnt*

Auxiliaries / suppletive auxiliaries as main verbs: *sein* 'to be', *haben* 'to have', *werden* 'to become'
    e.g. *sein* 'to be': 1.Sg.Pres.Ind. *ich bin, er ist, wir sind, gewesen*

Suppletives: e.g. *gehen* 'to go': *er geht, wir gehen, geh!, gegangen*

Class 1 consists of German weak verbs. Class 1 (e.g. *spielen* 'to play') is the only productive verb class and has also the highest lemma frequency (Dressler 1997b). Subclass 1' (e.g. *brennen* 'to burn') is formed by unproductive weak verbs taking Ablaut in the PP. Classes 2–5 consist of German strong verbs.[2] Verbs of class 2 (e.g. *bleiben* 'to stay') take Ablaut in the PP. Class 3 (e.g. *schlafen* 'to sleep') is represented by verbs displaying a stem vowel change in the 2. and 3. Sg. Pres.Ind. In colloquial speech this Umlaut may be levelled. Verbs of subclass 3' (e.g. *kommen* 'to come') never take Umlaut. In class 4 (e.g. *lesen* 'to read'), Umlaut is used in the 2.Sg. Imp. as well. Class 5 verbs (e.g. *brechen* 'to break') take both Umlaut and Ablaut.

Despite different details in their paradigms, modal verbs (e.g. *können* 'can') share several morphosyntactic and semantic properties and thus are grouped together for the purpose of this paper. Auxiliaries and suppletive auxiliaries as main verbs are put together for the same reason. Suppletive main verbs (e.g. *gehen* 'to go') will be analyzed separately.

1.3. Other important characteristics

Another important characteristic of German verbs are separable stressed prefixes such as *weg* 'away' in the verb *weggehen* 'to go away'. In matrix clauses of the present indicative and in the imperative, they get separated from the base (e.g. *er geht weg* 'he goes away', *geh weg!* 'go away!'). Although German verb prefixes may be used to distinguish between *Aktionsarten* (e.g. durative *essen* 'to eat' vs. non-durative *aufessen* 'to eat up', prefixed verb forms usually bear different lexical meanings and thus will be treated as different verb lemmas.

2. The data
2.1. General data description

The present study is based on longitudinal spontaneous speech data of one Austrian boy, Jan. Jan is the second child of an Austrian couple living in Vienna. He was (and is still being) audiorecorded at home, in interaction with his mother. Recording situations vary between free play, everyday situations (e.g. eating, washing) and picture book sessions. Up to the age of 3 years, Jan was recorded 4 times a month for 1 hour, from 3 years onwards recordings are taken twice a month for 1 hour. The data are transcribed and morphologically coded according to the norms of the international child language database CHILDES (MacWhinney 2000).[3] For quantitative analyses of the data, the CLAN programs of CHILDES are used.

2.2. Data analyzed for this contribution

This study focusses on the very early period of Jan's verb development, i.e. from the beginning of recording (1;3), until the occurrence of several three-member verb paradigms per month (2;0), see table 2. For the following analyses, recording sessions within one month of age will be grouped together.

Table 2. Jan's longitudinal corpus: characteristics of analyzed sessions from 1;3 to 2;0

session	age	duration	productions	analyzed utterances[4]
jan01	1;3.30	45 min.	302	182
jan02	1;4.27	30 min.	231	132
jan03	1;5.24	30 min.	193	120
jan04	1;6.10	30 min.	234	165
jan05	1;7.3	30 min.	210	158
jan06	1;8.3	60 min.	435	335
jan07	1;8.12	60 min.	392	295
jan08	1;8.19	60 min.	348	259
jan09	1;8.26	60 min.	390	288
jan10	1;9.8	60 min.	424	306
jan11	1;9.15	60 min.	453	333
jan12	1;9.23	60 min.	426	294
jan13	1;9.30	60 min.	437	337
jan14	1;10.6	60 min.	640	501
jan15	1;10.13	60 min.	456	353
jan16	1;10.26	60 min.	180	144
jan17	1;11.2	60 min.	414	380
jan18	1;11.8	60 min	230	168
jan19	1;11.16	60 min.	392	336
jan20	1;11.24	60 min.	474	422
jan21	2;0.0	60 min.	524	452
jan22	2;0.11	60 min.	602	523
jan23	2;0.21	60 min.	502	424
jan24	2;0.29	60 min.	467	369

2.3. Learning strategy and demarcation of phases

Jan is an early talker – his onset of speech can be dated around 1;3. His approach to language can be characterized as 'word-oriented' (Peters and Menn 1993: 745), i.e. he initially focusses on single words rather than on multisyllabic chunks of speech. Furthermore, imitative learning plays an important role in Jan's early acquisition phase (Tomasello 2000).

Jan's transition from pre- to protomorphology can be described by several, successive developmental steps observed in the period from age 1;8 – 2;0. This suggests rather a continuous and gradual developmental progression than a sudden, discontinuous change.

As can be seen in figure 1, the onset of protomorphology (1;8), is characterized by a first increase in the overall lexical diversity in the child's language (measure D^5, cf. Richards and Malvern 1999). Here, D was computed for all major word classes (nouns, verbs, adjectives and function words)[6] simultaneously.

Figure 1. Development of lexical diversity (measure D)

A closer look at the D value shows that this first increase is mainly due to increase of D in nouns (see also Klampfer 2001). At 1;8, noun compound formation emerges (e.g. compound *Feuer(wehr)auto* 'fire(brigade)-car', simplex *Auto* 'car', *Feuer* 'fire') and shows a considerable increase already from 1;9 onwards. This suggests that the child starts to detect morphology via compound formation. At the same time, the first oppositions of sg. vs. pl. nouns (*Auto – Auto-s* 'car', *U-Bahn – U-Bahn-en* 'underground', *Pferd – Pferd-e* 'horse') and within verbs, first two-member mini-paradigms appear – but both are low in frequency.

Age 1;9 – 1;10 is characterized by an increase of D in verbs. At 1;10, verb production increases (see section 3). At the same time a first slight increase in MLU is observed (see figure 2).[7]

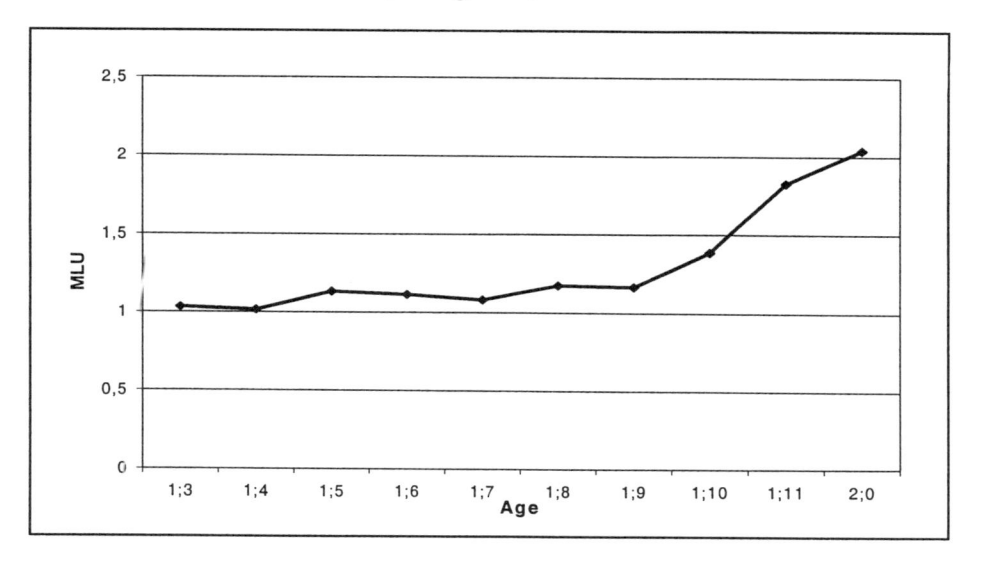

Figure 2. Development of MLU

In nouns, first analogical formations occur: pl. **Jeep-en* (< *Jeep-s* 'jeeps'), pl. **Zug-en* (< *Züge* 'trains'), compound **Lasterwagen* (< *Laster* 'truck', *Lastwagen* 'truck', lit. 'freight car') – proving that the child has started to creatively use noun morphology (Allen 1996).

Age 1;11 – 2;0 is characterized by a developmental spurt of function words (Klampfer 2001). Within verbs, first periphrastic tense constructions emerge and verb paradigms increase (see sections 4, 5). At 2;0, first analogical formations in verbs are observed: PP **runter(ge)gebt* (< *runtergegeben*) 'given down', PP **(ge)blast* (< *geblasen*) 'blown'. This discrepancy between first analogical formation in nouns vs. verbs suggests an asynchrony in the development of noun vs. verb morphology.

3. Emergence of verbs

Verbs start to emerge with Jan at the age of 1;4. Table 3 gives an overview of the number of utterances with verbs per month of age. As can be seen in figure 3, utterances with verbs start to slightly increase at 1;6, from 1;10 onwards, a clear increase of verb production can be observed. At 2;0, nearly half of all analyzed utterances contain at least one verb.

Table 3. Number of utterances with verbs with respect to the number of analyzed utterances

age	utterances with verbs	analyzed utterances	utt. with verbs / analyzed utt.
1;4	9	132	7%
1;5	10	120	8%
1;6	31	165	19%
1;7	19	158	12%
1;8	247	1177	21%
1;9	274	1270	22%
1;10	301	998	30%
1;11	560	1306	43%
2;0	746	1768	42%

Figure 3. Utterances with verbs

The number of verb lemmas and verb tokens and the respective type (= lemma) / token ratio per month of age is given in table 4. Furthermore, value D for verbs was calculated for four different age periods.[8] As shown in figure 4, lexical diversity of verbs shows a clear increase in the third age period (1;9 – 1;10).

Table 4. Number of verb lemmas and tokens, type (=lemma) / token ratio, value D (optimum average)

age	lemmas	tokens	TTR	D (optimum average)
1;4	4	9	0,444	4,87
1;5	5	10	0,5	
1;6	8	31	0,258	
1;7	11	19	0,579	12,61
1;8	44	247	0,178	
1;9	72	274	0,263	35,35
1;10	83	308	0,269	
1;11	108	593	0,182	25,8
2;0	150	824	0,182	

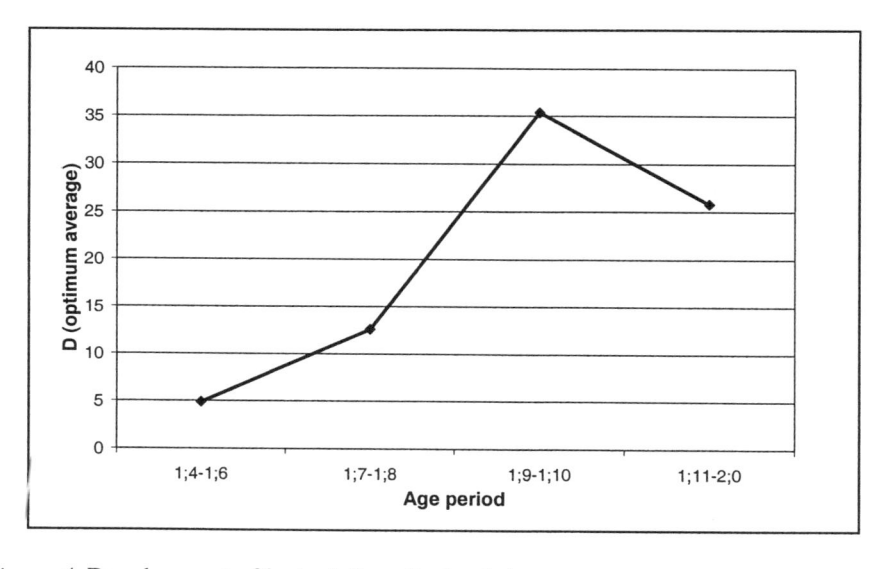

Figure 4. Development of lexical diversity (verbs)

4. Emergence of verb categories

Table 5a shows the order of emergence and absolute frequency (types/tokens) of verb categories in Jan's data. Note that this and also the following analyses are based on function, i.e. homophonous forms such as the *-t* form *spiel-t* 'play' which may either be interpreted as 3.Sg. Pres. Ind., 2.Pl. Pres. Ind. or as a PP without prefix *ge-* have been disambiguated with respect to the situational context. Thus, the form *spiel-t* occurring in a present context has been categorized as either 3.Sg. or 2.Pl. Pres. Ind., whereas when occurring in a perfective context, it has been categorized as an incorrect PP (omission of the prefix *ge-*).[9] Unclear cases have been classified as ambiguous (see table 5b).

As can be seen in table 5a, the first verb category to emerge in Jan's data are infinitives (1;4 *habm (= haben)* 'have', *etten (= essen)* 'eat', *kuten (= kuscheln)* 'snuggle'), followed by a few (mostly frozen) instances of 3.Sg. Pres. Ind. (1;5 *lacht* 'laughs', *daise (= da ist er/es)* 'there he/it is', *wos (= wo ist)* 'where is', *spasst (= es passt)* 'OK'). At 1;7, past participles emerge (e.g. 1;7 *zu(ge)gangen* 'closed', 1;8 *weh(ge)tan* 'hurt', *(ger)iss(e)n* 'torn', *rein(ges)teckt* 'put into').[10] From 1;7 to 1;10, single examples of 1.+2.Sg., 1.+3.Pl. Pres. Ind., 2.Sg.+1.Pl. Imp. are attested – but all of them can be characterized as frozen.

From 1;10 to 1;11, a switch from non-finite towards finite forms is taking place: whereas before 1;11, infinitives are clearly most frequent in token frequency, from 1;11 onwards, 3.Sg. Pres. Ind. and Inf. have roughly the same token frequency. In the same month an expansion in the use of verb categories can be observed: first non-frozen occurrences of 1.Sg. Pres. Ind. (e.g. *darf ich?* 'may I?'), 2.Sg. Pres. Ind. (e.g. *kannst* '(you) can'), 3.Pl. Pres.Ind. *(fahr(e)n Autos* 'drive cars') and 2.Sg. Imp. (e.g. *komm!* 'come!') are attested. Furthermore, compound past (Aux+PP: *weh(ge)tan hat* 'has hurt') starts to emerge. At 2;0, first unambiguous examples of 1.Pl. Pres. Ind. (e.g. *fahr(e)n wir* 'we drive'), 1.Pl. Imp. *(gebma weg!* 'let's give away!' and 3.Sg. Pret. *(war das* 'this was') are attested. First examples of future (Aux+Inf: *wird sein* 'will be') and passive (Aux+PP: *ab(ge)broch(e)n wer(de)n* 'get broken') appear in Jan's data.

The distribution of incorrect and ambiguous verb forms with regard to verb categories (best guess analysis) is given in table 5b. Incorrect forms fall into the target categories 3.Sg. Pres. Ind., Inf., PP and Aux+PP (for a more detailed error analysis see section 6).

Table 5a. Emergence of verb categories (types/tokens). Frozen forms are indicated by parentheses. Colloquial verb types are marked with c. Incorrect and ambigous forms are listed seperately (see table 5b).

Age	Pres.Ind.					Imp.		Pret.	Inf.	PP	Aux + Inf.	Aux + PP	Total
	1.Sg.	2.Sg.	3.Sg.	1.Pl.	3.PL.	2.Sg.	1.Pl.	3.Sg.					
1;4									3/3				3/3
1;5			1/1 (2/3)						2/3				3/4 (2/3)
1;6			1/1 (1/5)						5/20				6/21 (1/5)
1;7			(1/1)			(1/1)			6/9	1/5c			7/14 (2/2)
1;8		(1/1)	5/10 (3/33)			(1/2)			29/147 (1/2)	2/6, 3/12c			39/175 (6/38)
1;9	(1/2)		1/1,1/1c (6/24)			(1/2)	(1/1)		47/154 (1/1)	4/9, 4/22c			57/184 (10/30)
1;10	(1/4)		8/16 (6/24)	(1/1)	(1/1)	(3/5)			48/158	4/13, 3/10c			63/197 (12/35)
1;11	6/10 (1/8)	3/3 (4/7)	11/200 (9/42)	1/1 (1/1)		2/21 (1/1)			66/200	3/19, 6/10c	1/1 + 1/1c		100/466 (16/59)
2;0	9/21	8/12 (1/3)	45/301, 3/4 2/3c		3/4	5/19 (1/2)	2/2	1/1	97/318	8/20, 6/10c	4/5 + 4/5	2/3 + 2/3c	201/731 (2/5)

Most ambiguous forms are observed in the category of infinitives – this is due to the homophony of Inf. with 1. and 3.Pl. Pres. Ind. In terms of relative token frequency, there is an increase of Inf. ambiguities from 1;8 to 1;9 (1;8: 4,5% = 11/247 tokens, 1;9: 14,6% = 40/274 tokens) showing that the child's use of *-(e)n* forms in potential 1. or 3. Pl. contexts has become more frequent. At 2;0, Inf. ambiguities are again below 5% (4,2% = 35/824 tokens) – this results from the increasing overt realization of plural subject pronouns which allows the disambiguation of formerly ambiguous *-(e)n* forms.

Table 5b. Distribution of incorrect and ambiguous verb types and tokens with regard to verb categories

Age	Pres. Ind. 3.Sg.	Pret. 3.Sg.	Inf.	PP	Aux + PP	Total
1;4						
incorrect			2/5			2/5
ambiguous			1/1			1/1
1;5						
incorrect			1/3			1/3
ambiguous						
1;6						
incorrect	1/2		2/2			3/4
ambiguous	1/1					1/1
1;7						
incorrect			1/1			1/1
ambiguous	1/1		1/1			2/2
1;8						
incorrect	1/1		2/7	4/13		7/21
ambiguous			8/11	2/2		10/13
1;9						
incorrect	1/1		4/4	4/7		9/12
ambiguous	1/1		15/40	3/4		19/45
1;10						
incorrect	3/4		5/9	10/21		18/34
ambiguous	5/10		11/32			16/42
1;11						
incorrect			2/2	6/12	1/1 + 1/1	9/16
ambiguous	5/8	1/1	17/43			23/52
2;0						
incorrect			1/1	14/24	1/2 + 1/2	17/29
ambiguous	8/20	1/1	19/35	2/3		30/59

5. Emergence of verb paradigms

One important evidence for the fact that a child is starting to detect verb morphology, is the emergence of verb paradigms (Bittner, Dressler, and Kilani-Schoch 2000; Kilani-Schoch and Dressler 2002). With Jan, three main building steps in the early development of verb paradigms have been identified.

5.1. Step 1 (1;4 – 1;7)

During step 1, no form oppositions between different verb types occur in Jan's data. The only form alternations observed consist between *-(e)n*, *-e* (presumably phonological approximations of *-(e)n*) and incorrect stem forms. All of them have been attributed to the target category of infinitives (best guess analysis):

(1)   1;4   Inf.   *trinken* 'drink'   :   *tinke, ginke, minke, tink, gink*
        1;5   Inf.   *bauen* 'build'   :   *bauen, baue*
        1;6   Inf.   *drücken* 'press' :   *gickn, dückn, gücken, dück, dicken*
        1;7   Inf.   *haben* 'have'   :   *haben, hab*

5.2. Step 2 (1;8 – 1;10)

The onset of step 2 is characterized by the appearance of oppositions of two different verb types. Most of them are however imitated, formulaic or used in non-contrastive contexts and thus do not fulfill the criteria established for the formation of mini-paradigms (see Introduction to this volume), e.g.

(2)   1;8 *reissen*   'tear': Inf. *(r)eiss(e)n* – PP *(ger)iss(e)n* (no contrastive context, both refer to a torn page in a book)
        1;8 *drehen*   'turn': Inf. *d(r)eh(e)n* – 3.Sg. Pres. Ind. *d(r)eht* (no contrastive context, both refer to the turning audio-tape)
        1;8 *gehen*   'go': Inf. *geh(e)n* – 3.Sg. Pres. Ind. *geht's* ? (formulaic: 'does it work?') – 3.Sg. Pres. Ind. *geht s(ch)wer* (formulaic: 'difficult')

Form oppositions fulfilling the mini-paradigm criteria are rare in this period. They consist of oppositions between Inf. and PP and are reduced to form oppositions between *-(e)n* and *-t* forms, e.g. *machen* 'make': Inf. *mach(e)n* – PP *g(e)macht*, *malen* 'paint': Inf. *mal(e)n* – PP *(ge)malt*, *runterrutschen* 'slide down': Inf. *runterruts(che)n* – PP *runter(ge)ruts(ch)t*. In step 2, no class-distinctive form use can be observed: all mini-paradigms belong to the most productive and transparent inflectional class 1 – with the only exception of suppletive *haben* 'have', but also here only the equally morphotactically transparent forms Inf. *haben* – PP *(ge)habt* are attested.

At the end of step 2 (1;10), the first true mini-paradigm appears. It consists of verb forms of the class 1 verb *machen* 'to make': Inf. *mach(e)n* – PP *gemacht* – 3.Sg. Pres. Ind. *macht*.[11] It is interesting to note here that form oppositions of the verb *machen* are used relatively often by Jan's mother in child-directed speech. As can be seen in table 6, the lemma *machen* is ranked in the fourth position of the five most frequent three-member paradigms in Jan's input. Most frequent are form oppositions with the verbs *sein*, *haben* and *können*.[12]

Table 6. Five most frequent 3-member paradigms in Jan's input

frequency ranking	lemma	infl. class	translation	form	category	tokens	tokens total
1.	sein	suppl	be	ist	Pres. Ind. 3.Sg.	3221	3707
				sind	Pres. Ind. 1. + 3.Pl.	291	
				bist	Pres. Ind. 2.Sg.	195	
2.	haben	suppl	have	hat	Pres. Ind. 3.Sg.	462	1107
				hast	Pres. Ind. 2.Sg.	387	
				haben	Inf., Pres. Ind. 1. + 3.Pl.	258	
3.	können	mod	can	kann	Pres. Ind. 1. + 3.Sg.	530	866
				kannst	Pres. Ind. 2.Sg.	256	
				können	Inf., Pres. Ind. 1. + 3.Pl.	80	
4.	machen	class 1	make	macht	Pres. Ind. 3.Sg.	217	436
				machen	Inf., Pres. Ind. 1. + 3.Pl.	141	
				machst	Pres. Ind. 2.Sg.	78	
5.	müssen	mod	must	muss	Pres. Ind. 1.+ 3.Sg.	188	351
				musst	Pres. Ind. 2.Sg.	103	
				müssen	Inf., Pres. Ind. 1. + 3.Pl.	60	

5.3. Step 3 (1;11 – 2;0)

The beginning of step 3 (1;11) is characterized by a clear increase in the production of verb paradigms (see figure 5).

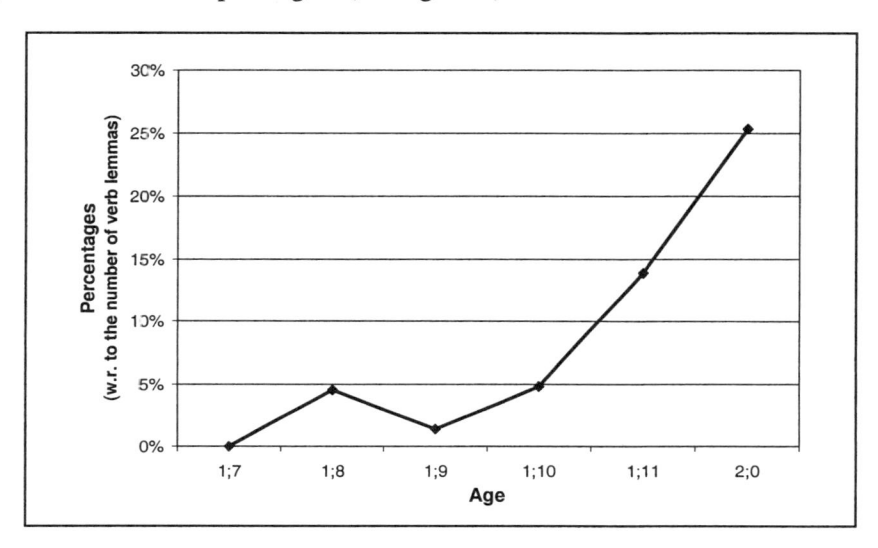

Figure 5. Emergence and development of verb paradigms

Form oppositions are extended towards 1.Sg., 2.Sg. Ind., 2.Sg. Imp., 1. or 3. Pret, e.g. *haben* 'have': Inf. *hab(e)n* – 1.Sg. Pres. Ind. *hab*, 2.Sg. Pres. Ind. *hast*, *schauen* 'look': Inf. *schau(e)n* – 2.Sg. Imp. *schau!*, *wollen* 'want': 1. & 3.Sg. Pres. Ind. *will* – 1. & 3.Sg. Pret. *wollte*. This category extension goes hand in hand with the emergence of the respective subject pronouns, which allow the disambiguation of formerly ambiguous homophonous verb forms. In the same month, class-distinctive form use starts, namely with the use of Ablaut in the PP (class 2 *schreiben* 'write': Inf. *s(ch)reib(e)n* – PP *(ge)s(ch)rieb(e)n*) and of Umlaut in the 3.Sg. Pres. Ind. (class 3 *schlafen* 'sleep': Inf. *s(ch)laf(e)n* – 3.Sg. Pres. Ind. *s(ch)läft*).

At 2;0, one fourth of Jan's verb lemmas occur in at least two different forms fulfilling the mini-paradigm criteria. As a result of overt realization of plural subject pronouns, form oppositions are extended towards plural forms, i.e. 1.Pl., 3.Pl. Pres. Ind. and 1.Pl. Imp.: *fahren* 'drive': 3.Sg. Pres. Ind. *fährt* – 1.Pl. Pres. Ind. *fahr(e)n wir*, *schauen* 'look': 2.Sg. Imp. *schau!* – 1.Pl. Imp. *schauma!* Now, verbs of all five inflectional classes occur in form oppositions.

5.4. Summary: frequency of mini-paradigms

Table 7 summarizes the number of mini-paradigms observed in Jan's data analyzed for this paper. (A full list of all 2-member and true mini-paradigms is given in the appendix).

Table 7. Frequency of mini-paradigms (1;8 – 2;0)
(Mini-paradigms belonging to the class of suppletives are listed in parentheses)

age	2-member mini-paradigms	true mini-paradigms	total	total / number of verb lemmas
1;8	2	0	2	5%
1;9	1	0	1	1%
1;10	2 (1)	1	4	5%
1;11	10 (3)	1 (1)	15	14%
2;0	27 (5)	3 (3)	38	25%

6. Form errors

Within the period from age 1;4 to 1;7 (see table 5b), form errors mainly consist of verb forms ending in schwa – presumably phonological approximations of infinitive forms, e.g. 1;4 *tinke (← trinken)* 'drink'. Other form errors in this very early phase are incorrect stem forms (e.g. 1;4 *tink*) – most of them have been attributed to the target category infinitive (best guess analysis).

From 1;8 onwards, omissions of the prefix *ge-* in past participles become the most frequent form errors in Jan's data, e.g. 1;8 *peat (← gesperrt)* 'shut', *issn (← gerissen)* 'torn', *reinteckt (← reingesteckt)* 'put into', *umfalln (← umgefalln)* 'fallen over', see also table 5b. Errors of this type are characteristic of German-speaking children (Elsen 1991; Behrens 1992, 1993; Vollmann et al. 1997; Lindner 1998; Klampfer 2000).

First analogical formations are observed with past participles and occur at 2;0, i.e. at the end of the observed period: PP **runter(ge)gebt* (← *runtergegeben*) 'given down', PP **(ge)blast* (← *geblasen*) 'blown'. Both examples are characterized by a class shift towards the only productive verb class 1.

7. Conclusion

This study examined very early phases in the acquisition of verb morphology in one Austrian child. Focus was laid on the emergence and early development of verb paradigms and on its relation to the transition from pre- to protomorphology.

As has been shown, Jan's transition from pre- to protomorphology can be characterized by several, successive developmental steps beginning with age 1;8. In contrast to noun morphology which shows a considerable developmental progression already in the first three months of protomorphology, verb morphology is still reduced in this period – suggesting an asynchrony between the development of morphology in nouns vs. verbs.

Three main building steps in the early development of verb paradigms have been identified in Jan's data: In premorphology (step 1, age 1;4 – 1;7), Jan's production of verb forms is limited to infinitive forms and a few occurrences of 3.Sg. Pres. Ind. and PP. No form oppositions occur in this stage. Beginning with the onset of protomorphology (step 2, age 1;8 – 1;10), first oppositions of two different verb forms appear. Most of them are either imitated, formulaic or used in non-contrastive contexts. Occurrence of form oppositions which fulfill the mini-paradigm criteria, is rare and is limited to oppositions between -(e)n and -t forms in the productive class of weak verbs. Three months after the onset of protomorphology (step 3, age 1;11 – 2;0), there is a clear increase of verb paradigms. It is preceded by an increase of lexical diversity in verbs at 1;9 – 1;10 and an increase in verb production at 1;10, which suggests a close relationship between lexical and morphological development (cf. Marchman and Bates 1994; Bates, Dale, and Thal 1995; Bates and Goodman 1999). During step 3, form oppositions are extended to other form types and verb classes. First analogies are attested, which proves that the child has started to creatively use verb morphology. These observations fit the assumption that – in addition to a critical mass of verb lexicon and verb form types – a certain amount of form oppositions may be needed by the child in order to detect morphological operations and to generalize over them.

Appendix

Jan's 2-member and true mini-paradigms (1;8 – 2;0)

age	lemma	infl. class	translation	form	category
1;8	machen	class 1	make	mach(e)n	Inf
				g(e)macht	PP
	reinstecken	class 1	put into	eingecken	Inf
				rein(ges)teckt	PP
1;9	machen	class 1	make	mach(e)n	Inf
				g(e)macht	PP
1;10	malen	class 1	paint	mal(e)n	Inf
				(ge)malt	PP
	runterrut-schen	class 1	slide down	runterruts(che)n	Inf
				runter(ge)ruts(ch)t	PP
	machen	class 1	make	mach(e)n	Inf
				gemacht	PP
				macht	Pres. Ind. 3.Sg.
	haben	suppl	have	haben	Inf
				(ge)habt	PP
1;11	aufdrehen	class 1	turn on	aufdreh(e)n	Inf
				auf(ge)dreht	PP
	drehen	class 1	turn	dreh(e)n	Inf^Pres.Ind. 1.Pl.
				dreht	Pres. Ind. 3.Sg.
	machen	class 1	make	mach(e)n	Inf
				macht	Pres. Ind. 3.Sg.
	niedersetzen	class 1	sit down	niedersetz(e)n	Inf
				niedersetzt	Pres. Ind. 3.Sg.
	sagen	class 1	say	sag(e)n	Inf
				sagt	Pres. Ind. 3.Sg.
	schauen	class 1	look	s(ch)au(e)n	Inf
				s(ch)au !	Imp. 2.Sg.
	spielen	class 1	play	(s)piel(e)n	Inf^Pres. Ind. 1.Pl.
				(ges)pielt	PP
	schreiben	class 2	write	s(ch)reib(e)n	Inf
				s(ch)reib	Pres. Ind. 1.Sg.
				(ge)s(ch)rieb(e)n	PP
	schlafen	class 3	sleep	s(ch)laf(e)n	Inf^Pres.Ind. 1.Pl.
				s(ch)läft	Pres. Ind. 3.Sg.

Appendix. continued

age	lemma	infl. class	translation	form	category
	können	mod	can	kann	Pres. Ind. 3.Sg.
				kannst	Pres. Ind. 2.Sg.
	wollen	mod	want	will	Pres. Ind. 1.^3.Sg.
				wollte	Pret. 1.^3.Sg.
	essen	suppl	eat	ess(e)n	Inf
				isst	Pres. Ind. 3.Sg.
	gehen	suppl	go	geh(e)n	Inf
				geht	Pres. Ind. 3.Sg.
	sein	suppl	be	is(t)	Pres. Ind. 3.Sg.
				bin	Pres. Ind. 1.Sg.
	haben	suppl	have	hab(e)n	Inf
				hab	Pres.Ind. 1.Sg.
				hast	Pres. Ind. 2.Sg.
				hat	Pres. Ind. 3.Sg.
2;0	aufsetzen	class 1	put on	aufsetz(e)n	Inf
				auf(ge)setzt	PP
	aufsperren	class 1	unlock	aufsperr(e)n	Inf
				aufg(e)sperrt	PP
	drehen	class 1	turn	dreh(e)n	Inf
				dreht	Pres. Ind. 3.Sg.
	drücken	class 1	press	drück(e)n	Inf
				(ge)drückt	PP
	klopfen	class 1	knock	klopf(e)n	Inf
				klopft	Pres. Ind. 3.Sg.
	kuscheln	class 1	snuggle	kus(che)ln	Inf
				kus(che)lt	Pres. Ind. 3.Sg.
	picken	class 1	stick	pick(e)n	Inf^Pres. Ind. 1.^3.Pl.
				pickt	Pres. Ind. 3.Sg.
	putzen	class 1	clean	putz(e)n	Inf
				putzt	Pres. Ind. 3.Sg.
	runterrut-schen	class 1	slide down	runterruts(che)n	Inf
				runter(ge)ruts(ch)t	PP
	schauen	class 1	look	s(ch)au!	Imp. 2.Sg.
				s(ch)auma!	Imp. 1.Pl.
	stellen	class 1	put	stell(e)n	Inf
				(ge)stellt	PP

Appendix. continued

age	lemma	infl. class	translation	form	category
	suchen	class 1	look for	such(e)n	Inf^Pres. Ind. 1.Pl.
				such	Pres. Ind. 1.Sg.
	umkippen	class 1	tip over	umkipp(e)n	Inf
				kippt um	Pres. Ind. 3.Sg.
	zeigen	class 1	show	zeig(e)n	Inf
				zeig	Pres. Ind. 1.Sg.
	zumachen	class 1	close	zumachen	Inf
				zu(ge)macht	PP
	machen	class 1	make	mach(e)n	Inf, Pres. Ind. 1.Pl.
				machst	Pres. Ind. 2.Sg.
				macht	Pres. Ind. 3.Sg., PP
	niedersetzen	class 1	sit down	niedersetz(e)n	Inf
				nieder(ge)setzt	PP
				setz dich nieder!	Imp. 2.Sg.
	schmeissen	class 2	throw	s(ch)meiss(e)n	Inf
				s(ch)meisst	Pres. Ind. 2.^3.Sg.
	aussteigen	class 2	get off	aussteig(e)n	Inf
				aus(ge)stieg(e)n	PP
	bleiben	class 2	stay	bleib(e)n	Inf
				bleibt	Pres. Ind. 3.Sg.
				(ge)blieb(e)n	PP
	schlafen	class 3 > 3' (c)	sleep	s(ch)laf(e)n	Inf
				s(ch)laft	Pres. Ind. 3.Sg.
	fahren	class 3	go / drive	fahr(e)n	Inf, Pres. Ind. 1.+3.Pl.
				fährt	Pres. Ind. 3.Sg.
	hinauffahren	class 3	go / drive up	h(i)nauffahr(e)n	Inf
				h(i)nauffährt	Pres. Ind. 3.Sg.
	runtergeben	class 4	give down / remove	runtergeb(e)n	Inf
				runter(ge)gebt	PP*
	sehen	class 4	see	seh(e)n	Inf
				sieht	Pres. Ind. 3.Sg.
	weggeben	class 4	give away	weggeb(e)n	Inf, Imp. 1.Pl.
				gib weg!	Imp. 2.Sg.
	helfen	class 5	help	helf(e)n	Inf
				hilft	Pres. Ind. 3.Sg.

Appendix. continued

age	lemma	infl. class	translation	form	category
	können	mod	can	kann	Pres. Ind. 1. + 3.Sg.
					Pres. Ind 1.^3.Sg.
				kannst	Pres. Ind. 2.Sg.
	sollen	mod	shall	soll	Pres. Ind. 1. + 3.Sg.
					Pres. Ind 1.^3.Sg.
				sollst	Pres. Ind. 2.Sg.
	wollen	mod	want	will	Pres. Ind. 3.Sg.
					Pres. Ind. 1.^3.Sg.
				wollte	Pret. 1.^3.Sg.
	essen	suppl	eat	ess(e)n	Inf
				isst	Pres. Ind. 3.Sg.
	sitzen	suppl	sit	sitz(e)n	Inf
				sitzt	Pres. Ind. 3.Sg.
	stehen	suppl	stand	steh(e)n	Inf
				steht	Pres. Ind. 3.Sg.
	werden	suppl	become	wer(de)n	Pres. Ind. 1. + 3.Pl.
				wird	Pres. Ind. 3.Sg.
	kommen	suppl	come	kommen	Inf
				komm!	Imp. 2.Sg.
	haben	suppl	have	hab(e)n	Inf, Pres. Ind. 1.Pl.
					Inf.^Pres. Ind. 3.Pl.
				hab	Pres.Ind. 1.Sg.
				hast	Pres. Ind. 2.Sg.
				hat	Pres. Ind. 3.Sg.
	sein	suppl	be	sein	Inf
				bin	Pres. Ind. 1.Sg.
				bist	Pres. Ind. 2.Sg.
				is(t)	Pres. Ind. 3.Sg.
				sind	Pres. Ind. 3.Pl.
				war	Pret. 3.Sg.
	tun	suppl	do	tu	Pres. Ind. 1.Sg.
				tut	Pres. Ind. 3.Sg.
				(ge)tan	PP

Notes

*   Written by Sabine Klampfer after discussion with Wolfgang U. Dressler. We would like to thank Carmen Aguirre, Dagmar Bittner, Christine Czinglar, Antigone Katičić, Katharina Köhler, Marianne Kilani-Schoch and Chris Schaner-Wolles for their valuable comments on an earlier version of this paper. Special thanks go to Katharina Korecky-Kröll for her excellent job in collecting and transcribing the Jan corpus. The present study is supported by the *Fonds zur Förderung der wissenschaftlichen Forschung* (Project number P13681-SPR) and by the Austrian Academy of Sciences.
1. In cases in which verb forms of the 1.Pl. are directly followed by the colloquial subject pronoun *ma*, the alternations observed in the imperative hold also for the indicative.
2. In contrast to weak verbs, German strong verbs take the suffix *-en* in the PP (e.g. class 1 *ge-spiel-t* 'played' vs. class 3 *ge-schlaf-en* 'slept'.
3. Data are collected and transcribed by Katharina Korecky-Kröll (and double-checked by Sabine Klampfer). Sabine Klampfer is responsible for the automatic morphological coding of the data (using CLAN's MOR utility) and for the creation of the full-form lexicon GER.LEX which is used for this purpose. Thanks are due to Steven Gillis for introduction to MOR-coding.
4. To qualify as an utterance, a production had to include at least one meaningful unit resembling a German word in form and meaning. Babbling, vocalizations and completely incomprehensible strings were not considered utterances. Citations (e.g. nursery rhymes and songs) and direct imitations were excluded from the analysis. Pure yes/no answers were not excluded.
5. D is a new measure of lexical diversity developed by Brian Richards and David Malvern (University of Reading) and recently also available within the CLAN-package (VOCD, cf. MacWhinney 2000). D is comparable to Type-Token Ratio (TTR), but is independent of sample size; it is calculated by fitting empirical data to the theoretical curve of TTR plotted against token size. Note that the value D obtained in figure 1 corresponds to the ratio word types (=lemmas) / word tokens.
6. The class of nouns consists of common and proper nouns. Within verbs, prefixed verbs have been considered as different verb lemmas (i.e. as not identical with the respective simplex verbs). Function words include pronouns, determiners, prepositions, conjunctions and auxiliaries.
7. For MLU, repetitions and retracings have been excluded.
8. Data had to be grouped into age periods, because in the early recordings, too few verb tokens were available for allowing random sampling without replacement and thus computation of D per month of age.
9. This classification is justified by two formal arguments (cf. Behrens 1992): First, omission of *ge-* is also observed in verb classes which take Ablaut in the

PP (e.g. Inf. *reissen* – PP *(ger)iss(e)n* 'torn') – which indicates that these forms are intended as PP. Second, omission of *ge-* also occurs within the compound past construction (e.g. *hab ich zu(ge)macht* 'I have closed'). An alternative approach (as discussed by Bittner this volume) would be to assume one unified meaning associated with the -t form.
10. Note that the prefix *ge-* may be omitted in low-style colloquial Austrian German before occlusives (ex. *gebracht* 'brought' → *bracht*). Examples of this type have been analyzed as correct and have been marked by (c) in table 5a.
11. For a similar observation with another Austrian child (Katharina), see Klampfer (2000).
12. For input token frequency we have analyzed all child-directed utterances of Jan's mother in the Jan corpus from 1;3 – 2;0, yielding the total sum of 15587 verb tokens.

References

Allen, Shanley
    1996   Assessing productivity in acquisition data from polysynthetic languages: An Inuktitut example. Paper presented at the 7th International Congress for the Study of Child Language, Istanbul, July 1996.

Bates, Elizabeth, Philip S. Dale, and Donna Thal
    1995   Individual differences and their implications for theories of language development. In: Paul Fletcher, and Brian MacWhinney (eds.), *The Handbook of Child Language,* 96–151. Oxford: Blackwell.

Bates, Elizabeth, and Judith C. Goodman
    1999   On the emergence of grammar from the lexicon. In: Brian MacWhinney (ed.), *The Emergence of Language*, 29–79. Mahwah, New Jersey: Lawrence Erlbaum.

Behrens, Heike
    1992   Early encoding of temporal reference in German. In: Eve V. Clark (ed.), *Proceedings of the Twenty-fourth Annual Child Language Research Forum*, 60-71. Stanford, CA: CSLI.

Behrens, Heike
    1993   Temporal reference in German child language: Form and function of early verb use. Ph.D. thesis, Universiteit van Amsterdam.

Bittner, Andreas
1996 *Starke "schwache" und schwache "starke" Verben.* Tübingen: Gunter Narr.

Bittner, Dagmar, Wolfgang U. Dressler, and Marianne Kilani-Schoch (eds.)
2000 *First Verbs: On the Way to Mini-Paradigms.* (ZAS Papers in Linguistics 18.) Berlin: Zentrum für Allgemeine Sprachwissenschaft, Typologie und Universalienforschung (ZAS).

Dressler, Wolfgang U.
1997a Introduction. In: Katarzyna Dziubalska-Kołaczyk (ed.), *Pre- and Protomorphology in Language Acquisition*, 7–14. (Papers and Studies in Contrastive Linguistics 33.) Poznań: Adam Mickiewicz University.

Dressler, Wolfgang U.
1997b On productivity and potentiality in inflectional morphology. *CLASNET Working Papers (Montréal)* 7: 3–22.

Dressler, Wolfgang U.
to appear A sketch of dynamic morphology of German verb inflection. Manuscript. For Festschrift Hans Basbøll.

Dressler, Wolfgang U., and Annemarie Karpf
1995 The theoretical relevance of pre- and protomorphology in language acquisition. *Yearbook of Morphology* 1994: 99–122.

Dressler, Wolfgang U., and Sabine Klampfer
2000 On the emergence of inflectional classes – the case of Austrian German (with a typological perspective). Paper presented at the Max-Planck-Institute for Evolutionary Anthropology, Leipzig, February 2000.

Elsen, Hilke
1991 *Erstspracherwerb: Der Erwerb des deutschen Lautsystems.* Wiesbaden: DUV.

Kilani-Schoch, Marianne, and Wolfgang U. Dressler
2002 The emergence of verb paradigms in two French corpora as an illustration of general problems of pre- and protomorphology. In: Maria D. Voeikova, and Wolfgang U. Dressler (eds.), *Pre- and Protomorphology: Early Phases of Morphological Development in Nouns and Verbs*, 45–59. München: Lincom.

Klampfer, Sabine
2000 Early verb development in one Austrian child. In: Bittner et al. (eds.) 2000, 7–20.

Klampfer, Sabine
2001 Early lexicon acquisition from a morphological perspective: Austrian children's developmental changes from pre- to protomorphology. In: Sophie Kern (ed.), *Early Lexicon Acquisition: Normal and Pathological Development*, CD ROM. Lyon: Université Lumière Lyon 2.

Lindner, Katrin
1998 Overgeneralization revisited: The case of German past participles. In: Ray Fabri, Albert Ortmann, and Teresa Parodi (eds.), *Models of Inflection*, 152–174. Tübingen: Niemeyer.

MacWhinney, Brian
2000 *The CHILDES Project: Tools for Analyzing Talk*. Vol. I: Transcription, Format and Programs. Mahwah, New Jersey: Lawrence Erlbaum.

Marchman, Virginia A., and Elizabeth Bates
1994 Continuity in lexical and morphological development: A test of the critical mass hypothesis. *Journal of Child Language* 21: 339–366.

Peters, Ann M., and Lise Menn
1993 False starts and filler syllables: Ways to learn grammatical morphemes. *Language* 69 (4): 742–777.

Richards, Brian, and David Malvern
1999 The application of a new measure of lexical diversity to preschool children. Paper presented at the 8th International Congress for the Study of Child Language, San Sebastian, July 1999.

Tomasello, Michael
2000 Do young children have adult syntactic competence? *Cognition* 74: 209–253.

Vollmann, Ralf, Maria Sedlak, Brigitta Müller, and Maria Vassilakou
1997 Early verb inflection and noun plural formation in four Austrian children. In: Katarzyna Dziubalska-Kołaczyk (ed.), *Pre- and Protomorphology in Language Acquisition*, 59–78. (Papers and Studies in Contrastive Linguistics 33.) Poznań: Adam Mickiewicz University.

Early verb development in Finnish: A preliminary approach to miniparadigms[*]

Klaus Laalo

0. Introduction

This paper presents a preliminary investigation of the early acquisition of verb inflection in Finnish. The analysis of the first miniparadigms concentrates on one girl (called Tuulikki).

1. Verb inflection in spoken Finnish

The Finnish verb categories which emerge early in the speech of children are (cf. Toivainen 1980):

a) person (+ voice)
- active (unmarked): 3 persons in singular and in plural (total 6)
- "passive" = the indefinite 4th person without person distinctions (the forms of this so-called personal passive are also used in spoken Finnish – and in child language – in the function of the 1st person plural)

b) tense
- present (unmarked)
- preterite (past): *i*-suffix in Standard Finnish, e.g. present *nukkuu* 'is sleeping' vs. past *nukkui* 'slept', present *antaa* 'gives' vs. past *antoi* 'gave'; in colloquial speech also stem alternation without suffix = shortening or change of the final stem vowel, e.g. present *antaa* vs. past *anto*, present *nukkuu* vs. past *nukku*; in spoken Finnish the 3rd person singular of contracted verbs -si > -s (e.g. *haukkasi* > *haukkas*), and the *s* originally belonging to the stem is now a tense marker

c) mood
- indicative (unmarked)
- imperative
- conditional (isi-suffix)

d) infinitives
- 1st infinitive (TA-suffix)
- 3rd infinitive (mA-suffix + case endings: illative -Vn, inessive -ssA etc.)
- 2nd infinitive (not in the investigated data)
e) participles
- active and passive past participles (obligatory in analytic constructions, e.g. in past tense negation)

There are two important analytic constructions:

- NEGATION CONSTRUCTION: Finnish has a negation verb (stem e-, in imperative stem äl-). This verb is inflected and the main verb is in the negation form (which is identical with the 2S imperative, e.g. *minä en nuku* 'I don't sleep', *sinä et nuku* 'you don't sleep', *hän ei nuku* 'he doesn't sleep', *me emme nuku* 'we don't sleep' etc.).
- COMPOUND PAST ("perfect tense") = AUX *olla* 'to be' + the past participle of the main verb.

In the acquisition of Finnish, the long analytic constructions are at first shortened to their key parts: the negation construction is realized by the negation verb alone (at the beginning in the 3S form *ei*) and the compound past is realized by the participle of the main verb.

All these verb categories are productive. The morphologically most simple forms, 3S indicative and 2S imperative, can be regarded as the basic forms of the verb (cf. Toivainen 1980: 44).

There are four verb classes which Finnish-speaking children use relatively early:

A. Verbs with a vowel stem that ends in a short vowel (e.g. *istua* 'to sit' : *istu!* 'sit!', *sanoa* 'to say' : *sano!* 'say!'; the A is the suffix of the infinitive, the "!" signals the 2S imperative); this is the most common type of Finnish verbs and still fairly productive.

Present
indicative   SG   PL
1. person   *istu-n* *istu-mme* ~ *istutaan*[1]
2. person   *istu-t* *istu-tte*
3. person   *istu-u* *istu-vat*

Past tense (preterite) stem: *istui-* (*istuin, istuit, istui* etc. but in colloquial speech the 3S is *istu*);
1ˢᵗ infinitive: *istua*;
Passive: *istutaan* (present) : *istuttiin* (past).

B. Monosyllabic verbs with a vowel stem that ends in two vowels (e.g. *syödä* 'to eat' : *syö!* 'eat!', *juoda* 'to drink' : *juo!* 'drink!', *viedä* 'to take away' : *vie!* 'take away!'); the past tense in this class is exceptional because of the vowel change (not simply suffixation), cf. *syön* 'I eat': *söin* 'I ate', *juon* 'I drink' : *join* 'I drank'; this class is unproductive

Present
indicative   SG   PL
1. person   *vie-n*   *vie-mme* ~ *viedään*²
2. person   *vie-t*   *vie-tte*
3. person   *vie*   *vie-vät*

Past tense (preterite) stem: *vei-* (*vein, veit, vei* etc.);
1ˢᵗ infinitive: *viedä*;
Passive: *viedään* (present) : *vietiin* (past).

C. Contracted verbs; these verbs have both a vowel stem, which ends in at least two vowels, and a consonant stem (e.g. *hyppää* 'jumps' : *hyppää!* 'jump!' (2S imperative) : *hypät+kää* 'jump! (2P imperative)'; this verb class is very productive

Present
indicative   SG   PL
1. person   *hyppää-n*   *hyppää-mme* ~ *hypätään* ("pseudopassive")
2. person   *hyppää-t*   *hyppää-tte*
3. person   *hyppää*   *hyppää-vät*

Past tense (preterite) stem: *hyppäsi-* (*hyppäsin, hyppäsit, hyppäsi* etc.);
1ˢᵗ infinitive: *hypätä*;
Passive: *hypätään* (present) : *hypättiin* (past).

D. Other verbs with both a vowel and a consonant stem: the vowel stem ends in a short *e* preceded by a dental consonant, the consonant stem ends in this dental consonant and the stem-final *e* is dropped, e.g. *tule-e* 'comes' : *tule!* 'come!' (2S imperative) : *tul+kaa* 'come! (2P imperative)' : *tul+lut* 'has come', *mene-e* 'goes' : *mene!* 'go!' : *men+kää* 'go! (2P imperative)' : *men+nyt* 'has gone'; this class is only marginally productive (there are some new derivatives belonging to this class).

Present
indicative SG   PL
1. person   *tule-n* *tule-mme* ~ *tullaan*[3]
2. person   *tule-t* *tule-tte*
3. person   *tule-e* *tule-vat*

Past tense (preterite) stem: *tuli-* (*tulin, tulit, tuli* etc.);

1st infinitive: *tulla* (consonant stem);

Passive (consonant stem): *tullaan* (present) : *tultiin* (past).

2. Data description

This study is mainly based on the speech of Tuulikki (girl, born in June 1991). Some observations from Tuomas (boy, born in May 1997) are also presented. There is diary data from both children from the onset of speech and monthly recordings. The earliest recordings of Tuulikki (1;7 – 1;11), which have been systematically transcribed and morphologically coded, cover the period of the first miniparadigms. The following recordings from Tuulikki's speech have been used in the analysis:

Table 1. Recordings from the speech of Tuulikki

Age	appr. duration	analysed child utterances
1;7	90 minutes	212
1;8	90 minutes	304
1;9	30 minutes	219
1;10	30 minutes	76
1;11	60 minutes	309
2;1	60 minutes	136

Some truncated forms occur, notably in the first recordings, and it is not possible to identify the morphological category of these shortened verb forms with certainty (e.g. *katte*, cf. the verb stem *kastele-* 'to water, to moisten'). Sometimes it is not even evident whether the form is a verb or not (e.g. *mita, mitta*, cf. the verb *mitata* : *mittaa* 'to measure : measures' and the noun *mitta* 'the measure'). These unclear forms have been excluded from the analysis. The analysed verb forms of Tuulikki are presented in Table 2 below.

Table 2. Emergence of verb forms and categories (F: = formulaic expressions; I: = imitated forms)

MORPHOLO-GIC CATE-GORIES	DIARY (number of verb lemmas)				RECORDINGS (verb lemmas/tokens)					
	1;3	1;4	1;5	1;6	1;7	1;8	1;9	1;10	1;11	2;1
2S imperative	2	1	3	2	3/5	8/12	1/1	3/5	2/2	2/2
3S indicat. pres.	–	2	11	20	30/54	38/99	22/51	18/54	29/117	19/65
3S ind. past	–	–	(F:1)	(F:2)	5/6	6/9	10/20	2/4	13/39	6/7
1S ind. present	–	–	–	1	–	–	1/1	–	7/12	6/8
1S ind. past	–	–	–	–	–	–	–	–	1/1	2/2
2S ind. present	–	–	–	–	–	–	–	1/1	–	1/1
passive present	–	(F:1)	–	–	(I:2/3)	2/5	2/3	4/5	12/18	8/14
passive past	–	–	–	–	–	–	2/2	–	4/6	2/2
3rd infin. illative	–	–	–	(F:1)	–	1/2	1/1	1/4	4/5	1/2
1st infinitive	–	–	–	–	–	1/1	–	–	7/9	5/8
PASTPT passive	–	–	–	–	–	–	–	–	1/1	1/1
PASTPT active	–	–	–	–	–	–	–	–	4/7	2/2
3S conditional	–	–	–	–	–	–	–	–	–	1/1
3rd infin. inessive	–	–	–	–	–	–	–	1/1	–	–
negat. active (3S)	–	–	–	–	1/1	1/12	2/21	1/2	6/12	2/2
negation passive	–	–	–	–	–	–	–	–	1/1	1/1
2P ind. present	–	–	–	–	–	–	–	–	–	1/1

3. Precursors of verbs

Among the very first word-forms used by Tuulikki and Tuomas there were some which expressed actions, events and processes before adult-like verbs:

a) The adverb *pois* 'away' (also in truncated form: *po, poo* etc.) was used by both Tuulikki (from the age of 1;4 onwards) and Tuomas (from the age of 1;3 onwards) much in the same way as the English verb particle *away* (cf. partially the German prefix *weg*). Presumably, *pois* (or the truncated variant of it) is favoured by small children because it is short and has only one form, whereas the verb is more demanding: it is inflected in different forms and it is longer (e.g. *mene ~ mennä(än) pois* 'go ~ let's go away').

b) Certain case forms of nouns in expressions consisting of a single word-form:

b1) objects, especially mass nouns in partitive instead of their governing verbs: *vettä ~ tettä* 'water' in the meaning 'give me some water (to drink)', *pullaa, puuroa ~ puuvoo* etc. in the meaning 'give me some buns, porridge (to eat)';

b2) adverbs: The dynamic local cases, especially the illative, seem to be an alternative to certain verb forms in early child speech, c.f. *kotiin* '(let's go) home' and *syliin* '(I want to come) into someone's lap' (morphologically *kotiin* = koti 'home' + the illative suffix *-in*, and *syliin = syli +* the illative suffix *-in*). These illative forms are used much like the early illative forms of the 3rd infinitive, e.g. *syömään* 'come ~ let's go and eat' (consisting of the verb stem *syö-*, 3rd infinitive suffix *-mA-* and illative suffix *-än*) or such early pseudopassives as *mennään* 'let's go' or. These two verb forms and the illative forms of nouns also have the same type of final suffixes: vowel lengthening + *n*.

c) Early reduplicative expressions, also attested from other Finnish children (e.g. Kauppinen 1981: 18): *anna-anna-anna-anna ~ mam-mam-mam-mam ~ nam-nam-nam-nam* 'give (something to eat/drink, used often in combination with a pointing gesture)'. Some more idiosyncratic ones: Tuulikki's *ihhaa ihhaa* (< shortened from the nursery rhyme "ihhahhaa, ihhahhaa, hepo hirnahtaa", used when riding with a toy horse or – by the child – even when seeing a picture of a horse). The form *anna* is the 2S imperative of the verb *antaa* 'to give', the other reduplicative expressions are built on onomatopoiea; both *nam* 'yum yum' and *ihahaa* (imitating the whinny of the horse) can occur also alone in Standard Finnish, but *mam* is not an established interjection in (adult) Finnish.

d) Onomatopoiea, both reduplicative (cf. point c above) and others, e.g. *miau* imitating the purring of the cat, *surrur* and *prr* imitating the sounds of different machines. These onomatopoiea are iconic in the sense that they refer directly to their referents; they are also indexical in the sense that they refer specifically to the sound produced by their referents. At the age of 1;5 Tuulikki often used the sound-imitating reduplicative formation *kipi kipi* when she was herself pattering (cf. the Finnish verb *kipittää* 'to patter, to scamper'); she also said *kopu kopu kopu* when she heard a neighbour using a hammer (cf. the verb *koputtaa* 'to tap'). The formation *kipi kipi* is also used in adult Finnish as an onomatopoeic reduplicative particle, and the other may be based on it (but cf. also the adult reduplicative interjection *kop kop* 'tap tap').

4. Emergence of verbs and verb categories
4.1. Two basic verb forms

The 2S imperative and the 3S indicative forms are the first verb forms used by Finnish-speaking children (Toivainen 1980: 33, 44). They can be regarded as basic forms of the verbs because they are morphologically basic (short and simple) and are used as building bricks for more complicated forms to be acquired later. They are also basic from the categorical view: the 3S indicative is semantically the most neutral verb form and it has high frequency; the 2S imperative can be regarded as a basic verb form for the child in the instrumental use of language. These two forms are used pragmatically in an accurate way from the very beginning: the imperatives in requests and the indicatives in declarative sentences when speaking about ongoing action.

In spoken Finnish, the initial consonant of the word following an 2S imperative form can appear as an additional marker of the imperative, e.g. *annas se minulle* 'give it to me' (cf. Toivainen 1997: 109), but small children usually omit this final segment, and the vowel stem alone is then used to represent the imperative, e.g. *anna* 'give', *sano* 'say', *tule* 'come'. The opposition between this 2S imperative and the 3S indicative is then based on vowel quantity: the 3S indicative is in the present tense formed by lengthening the short stem-final vowel, e.g. *istuu* 'is sitting', *sanoo* 'says', *tulee* 'comes'. The long final vowel remains unchanged, as in the monosyllabic verbs (e.g. *vie* 'takes', *syö* 'is eating') and in contracted verbs (e.g. *hyppää* 'jumps'). In monosyllabic verbs and in contracted verbs there is thus no formal opposition between 2S imperative and 3S indicative until the child begins to use the final segment in the imperative, but then there is an opposition, e.g. *avaa laatikot* 'opens the boxes' vs. *avaal laatikot!* 'open the boxes!'). Nevertheless, imperatives and indicatives can in most cases be identified on pragmatic grounds.

In contrast to many other languages, the infinitives are used relatively late in Finnish child language. The reasons for this may be that the Finnish infinitives are morphologically complex and that there are several infinitives, two of which have several case forms.

4.2. Other verb forms

The third verb form to be used by many Finnish-speaking children is the 3S preterite (past tense) (Toivainen 1980: 66–69, 162). The very first (formulaic) preterite forms may be such as *tippu* 'fell' (used when for example food or toys have fallen on the floor) or *loppu* 'end(ed)' (used typically when the food has all been eaten up). Soon, different preterite forms are used accurately when speaking about actions and events that happened before the present time. There is a clear contrast between present and past, in some instances even in successive utterances, e.g. Tuulikki 1;8 *äiti hakee* 'Mother is fetching' (a book) vs. *äiti haki* 'Mother fetched' (when the mother had brought the book).

Also, the negation construction emerges fairly early in the formulaic expression *ei ole ~ ei oo* 'is not'. Other verbs were used only much later (Tuulikki 1;9 *ei mahdu* /ei mahu/ 'does not fit').

The early occurrences of other verb forms are mostly isolated and rare but used in a correct way, typically in connection with daily routines: Tuulikki 1;4 the passive present form *mennään* 'let's go', 1;6 the 3rd infinitive illative *syömään* 'come to eat' (morphologically syö-mä-än = eat-3rdinfinitive illative) and the 1S form *kuulen* 'I hear' (cf. 5.1.); Tuomas 1;6 the passive present form *pestään* /pettää/ 'let's wash', 1;7 the 1st infinitive *pestä* /pettä/ 'to wash' and the passive past participle *pesty* /petty/ 'has been washed' in connection with washing routines.

4.3. Diary data: Tuulikki, girl

Diary data is presented as background information and analysed as supplementary material for two reasons: because many verbs were already used by Tuulikki before the first recordings and because some verb forms which were accurately used by her during a certain month are missing from the recordings of that month, often due to the topic and speech situation.

The basic forms of the Finnish verbs, imperative singular 2nd and indicative singular 3rd, are short and simple and they are used as building bricks for other forms to be acquired later. These were also the first verb forms used by Tuulikki. Some isolated forms from other categories were also used by her rather early (passive, the 1st and the 3rd infinitive, negation verb, participles) but the third form to be used productively was the 3S preterite (past tense). Certain forms were shortened because of the strong trochaic tendency in Tuulikki's speech, e.g. 1;5 *kävelee* 'is walking' > *käme*.

The very first verb form used by Tuulikki was 0;10 *kato* (phonetically: *ato*) 'look', which is the 2S imperative of the verb *katsoa* 'to look'. This form was one of her very first words and was based on the adult imperative *kato*, but at first it was an isolated form which Tuulikki used together with a pointing gesture and perhaps rather a predecessor of verb forms than an actual imperative. Later on, it became a member of the verb paradigm *katto-* (*katso-*) 'to look'. The subsequent early imperatives were 1;3 *avaa* 'open' and 1;4 *anna* 'give'. From these two, especially *avaa* was used by Tuulikki in a semantically flexible way: besides the adult meaning 'open' it was used in such meanings as 'skin this fruit', 'wind this toy', 'turn the page', 'construct' and 'take to pieces'. This kind of overextension is typical for early child language (cf. Barrett 1995; Clark 1993: 33–36).

Even if the semantics of these early forms was somewhat vague, considered from the pragmatic perspective these forms were imperatives used correctly, and they were clearly based on the adult imperatives. They were the child's first expressions of action.

From the age 1;4 onwards, Tuulikki started to use 3S present tense indicatives. The number of new verb lemmas used in the 3S present indicative grew rapidly: at the age of 1;4 the first two appeared but at the age of 1;5 there were 11 and at the age of 1;6 even 20 verb lemmas used in the 3S present indicative.

The number of imperatives grew steadily but rather slowly: after the first three mentioned above there were three new 2S imperatives at the age of 1;5. One of these, *ota* 'take' was the first 2S imperative form contrasting with a 3S indicative form, so in the diary data the first two-member mini-paradigm of Tuulikki was 1;5 *ota* 'take' : *ottaa* 'takes'.

At the age of 1;6 Tuulikki had about 40 verb lemmas. From most verbs she used either the 2S imperative or the 3S indicative form. The early representatives of these forms were

(1) 2S.Imp forms: 0;10 *kato* /ato/ 'look'
　　　　　　　　 1;3 *avaa* 'open'
　　　　　　　　 1;4 *anna* 'give'

	1;5	*pane* /mane/	'put'
	1;5	*ota*	'take'
	1;5	*pese*	'wash'

(2) 3S.Ind forms:
	1;4	*hyppii*	'is jumping'
	1;4	*vetää*	'is pulling'
	1;5	*istuu* /ittuu/	'is sitting'
	1;5	*kävelee* /käme/	'is walking'
	1;5	*nukkuu*	'is sleeping'
	1;5	*ottaa*	'is taking'
	1;5	*pakkaa*	'is packing'
	1;5	*piirtää* /piivtää/	'is drawing'
	1;5	*pitää*	'must' (modal)
	1;5	*potkii* /pokkii/	'is kicking'
	1;5	*tanssii* /ta(a)ssii/	'is dancing'

At the age of 1;4 – 1;6 Tuulikki also used some isolated forms from other verb categories:

(3)
	1;4	*mennään*	'let's go'	(passive present)
	1;5	*tippu*	'fell'	(a frozen past indicative 3S)
	1;6	*kiitti*	'thanks'	(a frozen past indicative 3S)
	1;6	*loppu* /boppu/	'end' ~ 'ended'	(possibly a frozen past indicative 3S)
	1;6	*syömään*	'come and eat'	(illative of the 3rd infinitive)

The first past tense form contrasting with the present tense form of the same verb was used by Tuulikki at the age of 1;7 when she was playing with her toy animals and said: *puskee* /pukkee/ 'butts' : *puski* /pukki/ 'butted'.

4.4. Tuomas, boy: Preliminary comparison (diary data)

As in the case of Tuulikki, so also in the case of Tuomas the first verb forms to emerge were the two basic forms. The very first verb form used by Tuomas was the 2S imperative *anna!* 'give!'. The following two were *pelaa* /peeaa/ 'play! ~ plays' and *avaa* 'open! ~ opens'. These two are forms of contracted verbs and they are ambiguous: they may represent both

2S imperatives and 3S indicatives, and they seemed to be used by Tuomas in both functions.

At the age of 1;3 Tuomas started to use verb forms that were unambiguously 3S indicatives, namely *kiikkuu* 'is swinging' and *nukkuu* /kukkuu ~ gukkuu/ 'is sleeping'.

The first (formulaic) 3S past tense form was used by Tuomas at the age of 1;4, namely *tippu(i)* /pippu/ 'fell' (cf. Tuulikki 1;5). At the same age he also used the form *loppu* /poppu/, which can be either the 3S past tense indicative of the verb *loppua* 'to end' or the nominative singular of the noun *loppu* 'the end'.

The first two-member miniparadigms of Tuomas were two oppositions of 3S indicative and 2S imperative at the age of 1;7, namely *auttaa* /attaa/ 'helps' : *auta* /autta/ 'help!' and *istuu* /ittuu ~ ihtuu/ 'is sitting' : *istu* /ittu/ 'sit!'. The first opposition of present and past emerged also at the same age: *kaatuu* /kattuu/ 'is falling' : *kaatu(i)* /kaatu ~ kattu/ 'fell'.

At the age of 1;8 the morphological opposition of active and passive (actually pseudopassive used in the function of 1P) emerged, e.g. *istuu* 'is sitting' : *istuttiin* 'we were sitting' (passive past) and *meni* 'went' : *mennään* 'let's go' (passive present). At 1;8 Tuomas also had the first three-member miniparadigm, namely *kato* 'look!' : *kattoo* 'is looking' : *katottiin* 'we were looking' (passive used in the function of 1P); some other verbs were occasionally used in 3 – 4 forms but these forms were not really established yet. The opposition of present and past was used in many verbs (e.g. *hyppää* 'jumps' : *hyppäs* ~ *hyppi* 'jumped', *kääntyy* 'is turning' : *käänty* 'turned', *lähtee* 'goes' : *lähti* 'went'). There were also some analogical past tense forms such as *autti* 'helped' from the verb *auttaa* 'to help' (cf. the standard past tense form *auttoi*) and contaminations, e.g. *ajee* 'is driving' = *ajaa* 'is driving' + *ajelee* 'is driving' (frequentatively; *-ele-* is a derivative element used to form frequentative verbs).

5. Emergence of miniparadigms

The miniparadigms are established following the criteria proposed by Kilani-Schoch and Dressler (2000): spontaneous production (neither imitative nor formulaic), articulatory accuracy in the suffix elements, contrasting contexts (not strictly context-bound), recurrence (cf. also Kilani-Schoch, this volume). Since the transcripts are relatively short and abundant diary data is available, diary data is used as supplementary material in evaluating whether certain verb forms and inflectional categories were established in the speech of Tuulikki at a certain age.

5.1. The first contrasting verb-forms of Tuulikki

The first oppositions of verb forms to emerge in Tuulikki's speech were oppositions of the two basic verb forms, the 2S imperative and the 3S indicative. This opposition was manifest early in many verbs belonging to class A:

(4) 1;5 *ota* 'take!'   : *ottaa* 'takes'   (diary)
    1;7 *nosta* /notta/ 'lift!' : *nostaa* /nottaa/ 'lifts'   (diary)
    1;7 *katso* /kato/ 'look!'   : *katsoo* /kattoo/ 'is looking' (record.)
    1;8 *nouda* /noula/ 'fetch!' : *noutaa* 'fetches'   (record.)
    1;8 *tule* ~ *tuu* 'come!'   : *tulee* 'is coming'   (diary + record.)

In the contracted verbs (e.g. Tuulikki 1;3 *avaa*, 1;5 *pakkaa*, 1;6 *hörppää, pelaa, nojaa*) there is no overt morphological difference between the two basic forms before the children start to use the final segment (gemination of the following consonant ~ glottal stop) of the imperative (after that the opposition is: indicative -VV vs. imperative -VV'); the inflectional category of the occurrences can nevertheless often be inferred from the context.

The opposition of 3S indicative present and preterite was also soon in frequent use and at the age of 1;7 Tuulikki had many two-member mini-paradigms consisting of the 3S present and past tense forms:

(5) *heittää* 'throws'   : *heitti*   'threw'   (record.)
    kaatuu   'falls'   : *kaatu*   'fell'   (record.)
    laittaa 'puts'   : **laitti* 'put'(SF *laittoi*) (record.)
    nukkuu   'is sleeping' : *nukku*   'slept'   (record.)
    on   'is'   : *oli*   'was'   (diary)
    peittää 'covers'   : *peitti*   'covered'   (diary)
    puskee   'butts'   : *puski*   'butted'   (diary)
    riisuu   'strips'   : *riisu*   'stripped'   (record.)
    vie   'takes away'   : *vei*   'took away'   (diary)

The opposition of 3S indicative present and preterite was even more frequently used at the age of 1;8:

(6) | antaa | 'gives' | : | anto | 'gave' | (diary) |
| --- | --- | --- | --- | --- | --- |
| hakee | 'fetches' | : | haki | 'fetched' | (diary) |
| keittää | 'is cooking' | : | keitti | 'cooked' | (diary) |
| kerää | 'is collecting' | : | *keri (= keräsi) 'collected' | | (diary) |
| laittaa | 'puts' | : | laitto | 'put' | (diary + record.) |
| loppuu | 'ends' | : | loppu | 'ended' | (diary) |
| lähtee | 'goes away' | : | lähti | 'went away' | (diary) |
| menee | 'goes' | : | meni | 'went' | (diary) |
| muistaa | 'remembers' | : | muisti | 'remembered' | (record.) |
| on | 'is' | : | oli | 'was' | (diary) |
| ottaa | 'takes' | : | otti | 'took' | (diary) |
| pesee | 'washes' | : | pesi | 'washed' | (record.) |
| pitää | 'holds' | : | piti | 'holded' | (diary) |
| putoo | 'is falling' | : | *puto ~ putos 'fell' | | (diary) |
| saa | 'gets' | : | sai | 'got' | (diary) |
| sanoo | 'says' | : | sano | 'said' | (diary) |
| syö | 'is eating' | : | söi ~ *syöi 'ate' | | (diary) |
| syöttää | 'feeds' | : | syötti | 'feeded' | (diary) |
| tulee | 'is coming' | : | tuli | 'came' | (diary) |
| vaihtaa | 'changes' | : | vaihto | 'changed' (-ht->-tt-) | (diary) |
| vetää | 'pulls' | : | veti | 'pulled' | (diary) |
| vie | 'takes away' | : | *viei (= vei) 'took away' | | (diary) |

In the recorded material there are just a few 2S imperative forms. Nevertheless, in the recording 1;7.28 there is also one imperative (kato 'look') which contrasts with the 3S indicative form of the same verb, namely kattoo 'is looking' (the Standard Finnish stem katso- 'to look' is in colloquial Finnish phonetically modified to kat(t)o-).

The next verb categories to emerge were passive, negation, 1S and the infinitives, particularly the 1st infinitive and the illative of the 3rd infinitive. These will be examined in detail in section 5.2., but some preliminary comments are presented already now.

The first (formulaic) passive form used by Tuulikki was 1;4 mennään 'let's go'. In the recordings made at the age of 1;7 there are also some shortened passive forms, but these are either imitated and truncated (in 1;7.28: laite < laitetaan 'let's put') or belong to a rhyme (in 1;7.23: saadaan kaloja 'we will get some fish'). In spoken Finnish, the 1P forms have mostly been replaced by the passive forms.

The first negation form was used by Tuulikki in the verb olla 'to be, to exist' at the age of 1;7: on 'is' : ei oo 'is not' (colloquial variant of the negation, Standard Finnish *ei ole*). Together with the preterite these two forms established a three-member suppletive paradigm *on* 'is' : *oli* 'was' : *ei oo* 'is not'. At the age of 1;8 negation also occurred in the following oppositions: *autti* 'helped' (an analogical form, normally *auttoi* 'helped') vs. *ei isi auta* 'Father shall not help' (negation used in a modal context) and *putoo* 'is falling' : *ei pulo* 'does/did not fall' (truncated form of the main verb).

The first verb in 1S present indicative registered from Tuulikki's speech was 1;6 *kuulen* 'I hear'. This form was used by Tuulikki as an appropriate answer to the question *kuuletko?* 'do you hear' (the noise of the refrigerator). At the age of 1;8 Tuulikki used two variants of her playful ultimatum: *muuten suutun ~ muuten suuttuu* 'otherwise I will get angry ~ otherwise gets angry'. This seems to be the first candidate for the formal (but not yet semantic) opposition of 1S and 3S indicative. In general, the different persons af active emerged rather slowly: 1S was used more frequently first at 1;11. The 2S and 2P were used only in a few isolated forms in the recorded material.

The verb *nukkua* 'to sleep' was used by Tuulikki frequently in the 3S form. At the age of 1;8 she also tried to use the illative of the 3rd infinitive (*nukku+ma+an*), but because of the trochaic tendency she shortened the form: *ei vielä nukku* 'not yet sleep-', *ihan vielä nukku* 'quite yet sleep-' and *pankkii nukkuu* 'on the balcony to sleep' (the last form seems to represent the colloquial variant of the illative of the 3rd infinitive, *nukku+un*, where the *ma*-suffix of the 3rd infinitive is dropped). At this age Tuulikki also used the colloquial preterite *nukku*.

5.2. The first three-member miniparadigms of Tuulikki

At the age of 1;7 Tuulikki started to use three-member miniparadigms. One of these was suppletive: Tuulikki used from the verb *olla* 'to be, to exist' the 3S present indicative *on* 'is', the colloquial variant of the negation form *ei oo* 'is not' and the 3S preterite *oli* 'was'.

Another candidate for a three-member miniparadigm at the age of 1;7 was the verb *laittaa* 'to put'. From this verb, Tuulikki used the 3S *laittaa* 'puts', the analogical preterite *laitti* (= laittoi) 'put' and (in an answer to a question, recorded session 1;7:28) the shortened passive form *laite* (= laitetaan) 'let's put'. Here the passive suffix itself is dropped but the passive is nevertheless signalled by the change of the final stem vowel from *a* to *e* (*laita-* > *laite*). All these forms appear in the recording 1;7. The trochaic phase of Tuulikki explains why the trisyllabic *laitetaan* 'let's put' was shortened; nevertheless, the shortened form *laite* was used as an adequate answer to the question *laitetaanko* ...? 'shall we put...?'.

At the age of 1;8 Tuulikki had several three-member miniparadigms. One type of miniparadigms consisted of the three early verb forms: 2S imperative, 3S present indicative and 3S preterite. These forms were used from two verbs: *anna* 'give!' (diary + rec.) : *antaa* 'is giving' (diary) : *anto(i)* 'gave' (diary) and *tule* ~ *tu(u)* 'come!' (diary) : *tulee* 'is coming' (diary + rec.) : *tuli* 'came' (diary).

These two paradigms are fairly transparent, although in the first one there are certain stem alternations: grade alternation (*nt* : *nn*) and the alternation *a* ~ *o* in the final stem vowel. From the second verb, the passive preterite was also used: *tultiin* 'we came'. The passive is based on the consonant stem, which makes it less transparent.

Another type of miniparadigms consisted of 3S active (present and preterite, both frequently registered) and passive in the function of 1P (the passive present *mennään* was attested already at the age of 1;4, now also passive preterite and negation): *menee* 'goes' (diary + rec.) : *meni* 'went' (diary) : *mennään* 'let's go' (diary) : *mentiin* 'we went' (diary) : *ei mennä* 'we shall not go' (diary). Tuulikki also used the 2S imperative from this verb, but there is only one occurrence in the diary data. The paradigm is fairly transparent, although the passive forms are based on the consonant stem.

A third type of miniparadigms included the negation form. The suppletive paradigm of the verb *olla* 'to be, to exist' was already mentioned: *on* 'is', *ei oo* 'is not' and *oli* 'was'. The corresponding forms were also used from the verb *ottaa* 'to take', but the negation form *ei ota* 'does not take' was used only during the last day of the age month 1;8 and only in the context of eating. These forms (3S present and preterite + negation) were furthermore used from the verb *saada* 'to get; may', but the negation form belonged to the modal use of this verb (*ei saa* 'must not') and the two other forms to the meaning 'to get' (3S present *saa* 'gets' and preterite *sai* 'got'). One further candidate for this group of miniparadigms is *pudota* 'to fall' with the forms *putoo* 'is falling', *ei pulo* 'does/did not fall' : *puto(s)* 'fell', but the forms of this contracted verb were both truncated and influenced by analogy. These are not complete three-member miniparadigms but nevertheless they show that the 3S negation form is becoming productive.

Within the first miniparadigms, one special case was the verb *syödä* 'to eat'. At the age of 1;8 Tuulikki used many forms of this verb, at least the following nine: *syö* (3S present indicative, diary + rec.) 'is eating', *syö!* (2S imperative, diary), *söi* ~ **syöi* (3S preterite, both regular and analogical, diary) 'ate', *syömään* (illative of the 3rd infinitive, diary) 'go eating', *syödään* (the present tense of the pseudopassive used in the function of 1P, diary + rec.) 'let's eat', *syötiin* (preterite of passive, diary) 'was eaten', *syönyt* (past participle of active, e.g. *syönyp paljon* 'has eaten much', diary) 'has eaten', *syöty* (past participle of passive, e.g. *syöty kaikki* 'all has been eaten up', diary) 'has been eaten', *syödä* /tyälä/ (1st infinitive, e.g. *tyälä puuvoo* 'to eat porridge', diary + rec.). Some of these nine forms have been registered only once or twice, but the following ones were used frequently and were registered at least three times: *syö*, *söi* ~ *syöi* (both variants), and *syödään*.

In sum: at the age of 1;8 Tuulikki had at least the following true miniparadigms:

1. *anna* 'give!' (2S imperative) : *antaa* 'is giving' (3S indicative) : *anto(i)* 'gave' (3S preterite)

2. *tule* ~ *tu(u)* 'come!' (2S imperative) : *tulee* 'is coming' (3S indicative) : *tuli* 'came' (3S preterite)

3. *menee* 'goes' (3S indicative) : *meni* 'went' (3S preterite) : *mennään* 'let's go' (passive present in the function of 1P): *mentiin* 'we went' (passive past in the function of 1P) : *ei mennä* 'we shall not go' (passive negation form used in the function of 1P)

4. *on* 'is' (3S indicative) : *ei oo* 'is not' (colloquial 3S negation form) : *oli* 'was' (3S preterite)

5. *syö* 'is eating' (3S indicative) : *söi* ~ *syöi* (both variants) 'ate' (3S preterite) : *syödään* 'let's eat' (passive present in the function of 1P); this is the only one that can be established on recordings alone

Further candidates for three-member miniparadigms at the age of 1;8 are *saada* (both modal use and the meaning 'to get') and *pudota* 'to fall'.

The recordings 1;9 and 1;10 are short but they both include a few three-member miniparadigms, e.g. 1;9 *on* 'is' : *oli* 'was' : *ollaan* 'we are' : *oltiin* 'we were' (passive in the function of 1P), *menee* 'goes' : *mennään* 'let's go' : *mentiin* 'we went' (passive in the function of 1P); 1;10 *tulee* 'comes' : *tule!* 'come!' : *tullaan* 'we are coming' (= passive in the function of 1P), *syö* 'is eating' : *syömään* 'come to eat' : *syödään* 'let's eat' (= passive in the function of 1P). The number of the true miniparadigms is increased by using diary data: the suppletive verb *olla* 'to be, to exist' was also used at the age of 1;10 and the miniparadigms used at 1;8 were all used at 1;9 and 1;10 as well.

In the recording 1;11 the following verbs have at least three different inflectional forms: *haluta* 'to want', *laskea* 'to release, to let off', *mennä* 'to go', *olla* 'to be, to exist', *ottaa* 'to take', *panna* 'to put', *tulla* 'to come'.

Unfortunately there is no recording from the age of 2;0.

In transcript 2;1 there are several miniparadigms of as many as 4 and more members. The following verbs have three or more different inflectional forms: *haluta* 'to want', *lukea* 'to read', *mennä* 'to go', *nukkua* 'to sleep', *olla* 'to be', *panna* 'to put', *saada* 'to get, to receive; may', *syödä* 'to eat'.

The number of the first three-member miniparadigms in Tuulikki's corpus (especially recordings; only recordings considered at 1;9 – 2;1) is presented in Table 3:

Table 3. Three-member paradigms used by Tuulikki at 1;7 – 2;1

Age	Number of miniparadigms: non-suppletive	suppletive: *olla* 'to be'	special: further candidates
1;7	–	1	1 (including a shortened "passive" form)
1;8	1 + 3 (rec. + diary)	1	2 (almost miniparadigms)
1;9	1 + 3 (rec. + diary)	1	
1;10	2 + 2 (rec. + diary)	1	
1;11	6 (only rec.)	1	
2;1	7 (only rec.)	1	

The verbs used in the early miniparadigms belong to the verb classes A, B (*syödä* 'to eat') and D; the contracted verbs (class C) were shifted to the class A (cf. section 6.).

5.3. The first contrasting verb-forms of Tuomas

The first verb of Tuomas occurring both in the present tense and in the preterite was 1;4 (and onwards) *tippu* 'fell down' vs. 1;6 *tippuu* 'is falling down' (when porridge was continuously dropping from the spoon onto the tablecloth). Interestingly enough, the past tense form of this verb emerged first. In other verbs the present tense emerged first (e.g. 1;7 *lähtee* 'goes' vs. 1;8 *lähti* 'went', 1;7 *hyppää* 'jumps' vs. 1;8 *hyppäs* 'jumped') or at the same time as the past tense (e.g. 1;7 *kaatuu* 'is falling' vs. *kaatu* 'fell' and 1;8 *auttaa* 'helps' vs. *autti* 'helped').

Another early contrast was the opposition of 2S imperative and 3S indicative, e.g. 1;7 *kato* 'look!' (formulaic, used often with a pointing gesture) vs. *kattoo* 'is looking'.

On the basis of diary data, the first miniparadigm of Tuomas with at least three members was 1;7 *kato* 'look!' : *kattoo* 'is looking' : *katottiin* 'was looked' (passive preterite) : *kattomaan* 'to look' (illative of the 3rd infinitive). Another candidate for an early miniparadigm consisted of forms based on the consonant stem: 1;7 *pestään* 'let's wash' : *pestä* 'to wash' : *pesty* 'has been washed'. These three forms were used frequently by Tuomas but they were rote-learned and used only in connection with the washing routines. Moreover, the passive past participle *pesty* was the only representative of this inflectional category and should thus not be counted as such an inflectional form that could be a real paradigm member in this phase. This formula could be interpreted as an announcement such as 'ready with the washing' or 'washing done'.

5.4. Miniparadigms and the emergence of categories

The morphological categories that occurred in the first true miniparadigms of Tuulikki were the same that also in general emerged early (cf. Toivainen 1980): 2S imperative, 3S indicative present and preterite, passive (in the function of 1P) and the 3S negation form. The morphological contrasts in the first true miniparadigms were the following:

(7)   a. 3S imperative 2S vs. 3S indicative
         1;7   *kato*   'look!'   :   *kattoo* 'is looking at'

    b. 3S indicative present vs. preterite
         1;7   *heittää*   'throws'   :   *heitti*   'threw'
         1;7   *kaatuu*   'falls'   :   *kaatu*   'fell'
         1;7   *laittaa*   'puts'   :   **laitti*   'put' (= *laittoi*)
         1;7   *nukkuu*   'is sleeping' :   *nukku*   'slept'

    c. 3S indicative affirmative vs. negative
         1;8   *on*   'is'   : *ei ole ~ ei oo*   'is not'
         1;11 *haluaa ~ haluu* 'wants' : *ei haluu*   'does not want'

1;11   *mahtuu*   'fits'   : *ei mahdu* /mahu/ 'does not fit'

d. 3S active vs. passive (in the function of 1P)
   1;8   menee 'goes' : mennään 'let's go' (also: 'we are going'))
   1;8   syö   'eats' : syödään 'let's eat' (also: 'we are eating')

e. passive (in the function of 1P) present vs. past
   1;9   *mennään* 'let's go' : *mentiin* 'we went'
   1;9   *ollaan* 'we are'   : *oltiin*   'we were'

In the speech of Tuomas, the first contrasts were very similar to those attested from the speech of Tuulikki (all the examples in 8 below are from the age of 1;7):

(8)   2S imperative vs. 3S indicative, e.g.
       kato   'look!'   :   *kattoo*   'is looking at'
       3S indicative present vs. preterite, e.g.
       tippuu 'is falling down' : *tippu*   'fell down'
       3S active vs. passive (in the function of 1P), e.g.
       menee   'goes'   :   *mennään*   'let's go'
       finite forms vs. 3rd infinitive illative, e.g.
       nukkuu 'is sleeping' : *nukkumaan* 'to sleep'

6. Analogical formations

6.1. The formation of the preterite (past tense): Class shifts

Most of the early analogical verb forms in Tuulikki's speech were past tense (preterite) forms. There is in principle only one preterite suffix in Finnish, namely *-i*. But because of the morphophonological interplay between this *i*-suffix and different stem-final phonemes, there are actually three preterite types in Standard Finnish: the past tense stem of the verb can end in

a)   *-i*   e.g. 3S *istuu* 'is sitting' : *istui* 'sat' (verb class A), *tulee* 'comes' : *tuli* 'came' (class D); 1S *istun* 'I sit' : *istuin* 'I sat', 2S *tulet* 'you come' : *tulit* 'you came';

b)   *-si* e.g. 3S present *hyppää* 'jumps' vs. past *hyppäsi* 'jumped' (verb class C); the *si*-preterite is originally used only in contracted verbs but it has expanded to other verb classes in some Finnish dialects and it often also expands in child language (presumably due to greater saliency);

c) *-oi* (in certain A-class verbs with a stem-final *a*, where the stem-final *a > o* before the *i*-suffix), e.g. 3S *antaa* 'gives' : *antoi* 'gave'; in spoken Finnish, these preterites often lose their final *i* and variants such as *anto* are thus also used. This class is supported by *o*-stems having the *i*-suffix, e.g. *sano-* 'to say' : *sanoi* 'said'.

In colloquial Finnish there is still a fourth type: the labial final vowel of the 3S present is shortened in the preterite, e.g. *istuu* 'is sitting' : *istu* 'sat' (Standard Finnish *istui*), *sanoo* 'says' : *sano* 'said' (SF *sanoi*).

The first types to emerge in child language are, in addition to the colloquial one, especially the *i*-type and the *si*-type (cf. Lieko 1994: 82). These two productive types also often expand beyond the limits of their normal use. The child usually starts from either the *i*- or the *si*-preterites but later, when the child acquires other preterite types, these new types may also expand beyond their normal use; this holds to some degree also for the *oi*-type.

Tuulikki started her past tense formation from colloquial vowel shortening (*tippuu* 'is falling' vs. *tippu* 'fell') and the *i*-type; she used analogical preterite forms from the age of 1;8 on, especially in contracted verbs and in monosyllabic verbs. The first (formulaic) past tense forms used by Tuulikki were 1;5 *tippu* 'fell' and 1;6 *loppu* /poppu/ 'ended'.

From the age of 1;7 onwards, Tuulikki used preterites formed by the *i*-suffix, e.g. *heitti* 'threw' (cf. *heittää* 'throws'). The first analogical preterite *sati* (from the verb *sataa* 'to rain', standard preterite *satoi* 'it was raining') was followed by an immediate self-correction: 1;7 *lunta sati / sato* 'it was snowing'. At the age of 1;8 the *i*-type of preterite was also used by Tuulikki in the contracted verbs. It is possible that the inflectional classes were still not acquired and the child assumes more or less the same inflection for all verbs. Another possibility is analogical levelling. For example, the verb *kerätä* 'collect' was not inflected as a contracted verb but as a verb of the class A:

(9) *kerää* 'is collecting' : *keri* 'collected' (pro *keräsi* 'collected')

The inflection model is constituted by the A-class verbs ending in *-ää* in the present tense:

(10) *heittää* 'throws' : *heitti* 'threw'
vetää 'pulls' : *veti* 'pulled'

Similar forms of contracted verbs were also used later, for example 1;9 *kiipee* : *kiipi* (instead of *kiipesi* 'climbed'; in this verb ending in *-ee* the inflectional model is constituted by such A-class verbs as *lukee* 'is reading' : *luki* 'read', *tulee* 'comes' : *tuli* 'came'). Another example: 1;10 *harjaa* : *harjo* (instead of *harjasi* 'brushed'; here the model is *antaa* 'gives' : *anto(i)*'gave').

The link between these two inflections – the A-class with only minor (if any) stem alternations and the C-class consisting of contracted verbs with rather complex stem alternations – is probably the 3S present tense, which has a similar shape in both verb classes: word-final long vowel (cf. the 3S forms mentioned above: *kerää* – *heittää*, *vetää*; *kiipee* – *lukee*, *kylpee*; *harjaa* – *antaa*, *auttaa*). The other inflectional forms are rather different, but the differences are partially levelled out in early child language by the use of analogical forms when the respective forms of contracted verbs have not yet emerged.

Tuulikki also used the *i*-type preterite instead of the *oi*-type, e.g. *laittaa* : *laitti* (instead of *laittoi* 'put'). The tendency to replace the relatively rare *oi*-type (e.g. *laittaa* : *laittoi*) with the very frequent *i*-type (e.g. *nostaa* 'lifts' : *nosti* 'lifted', *ottaa* 'takes' : *otti* 'took') where the *i*-suffix causes the deletion of the stem-final vowel, is a common phenomenon both in child language and in certain spoken variants of Finnish (e.g. dialects).

At the age of 1;11 Tuulikki started to use *s(i)*-preterites in contracted verbs, e.g. *putoo* ~ *putoaa* 'is falling' : *putos* (< *putosi*) 'fell down', *pelkää* 'is afraid of' : *pelkäs* (< *pelkäsi*) 'was afraid of', *tykkää* 'likes' : *tykkäs* (< *tykkäsi*) 'liked', *haluu* ~ *haluaa* 'wants' : *halus* (< *halusi*) 'wanted'. This new preterite type (schematically: 3S present -VV, preterite -Vsi) expanded to other verbs than the contracted ones, e.g. 1;11 *hakes* 'fetched' (instead of *haki*, cf. 3S present tense *hakee*), *lennäs* 'flew' (instead of *lensi*, stem of the present is *lentä-* ~ *lennä-*), 2;0 *auttasin* 'I helped' (instead of *autoin*, cf. 3S present tense *auttaa*), *hakes* 'fetched', *nauras* 'laughed' (instead of *nauroi*, cf. 3S present tense *nauraa*). This analogical expansion was soon weakened, but interestingly enough, in one group of verbs it remained and flourished: in the *i*-stems, in which the opposition of present and preterite has no overt marking in the 1st and 2nd person (both SG and PL) in Standard Finnish (cf. *leikin* 'I play' vs. *leikin* 'I played', *leikimme* 'we are playing' vs. *leikimme* 'we were playing'). Here the analogical expansion of the *si*-preterite provides the opportunity to mark the preterite forms with the *si*-element. This possibility was utilized by Tuulikki, e.g. 2;3 *leikkisin* 'I played', *poimisin* 'I picked up' (Standard Finnish *poimin*, identical with the present tense *poimin*), 2;5 *tönisin* 'I jostled' (Standard Finnish *tönin*, identical with the present tense *tönin*), *yskisin* 'I coughed' (Standard Finnish *yskin*, identical with the present tense *yskin*). This is a good example of constructional iconicity. Similar expansion of the *si*-preterite also appears in certain adult spoken variants of Finnish (e.g. in the SW dialects) and in Estonian.

In the same way as Tuulikki, so also Tuomas started from the *i*-type and expanded it to certain *oi*-preterites, e.g. 1;8 *ajaa* 'is driving' : *aji* (instead of *ajoi* 'drove') and *auttaa* 'helps' : *autti* (instead of *auttoi* 'helped'). A little later, Tuomas began to use the *s*-type in contracted verbs (1;9 *avaa* 'opens' : *avas* 'opened', *piippaa* 'is beeping' : *piippas* 'beeped', *toppaa* 'stops' : *toppas* 'stopped') and favoured it in expense of other types, both of the *oi*-type (1;9 *auttaa* 'helps' : *auttas* instead of *auttoi* 'helped', *laittaa* 'puts' : *laittas* instead of *laittoi* 'put'), and of the *i*-type (1;9 *ylttää* 'reaches' : *ylttäs* instead of *yltti* 'reached' and *itkee* 'is crying' : *itkes* instead of *itki* 'cried').

In the class of monosyllabic verbs, the preterite is formed by diphthong change (present *syö* 'is eating' : preterite *söi* 'ate', present *vie* 'takes away' : preterite *vei* etc.) or the formation of a diphthong from a long vowel (e.g. *saa* 'gets' : *sai* 'got'). This type of preterites usually emerges first in child language (e.g. Tuulikki 1;7 *söi*, *vei*) and it is an example of rote learning of frequent forms in the beginning of the acquisition process. Later on many Finnish-speaking children produce more transparent (= without changes in the stem) analogical preterite forms like *syö+i* 'söi', *vie+i* 'vei' despite of their articulatory difficulties (triphthongs instead of diphthongs), e.g. Tuulikki 1;8 *syöi*, *viei*. These analogical forms evidence that the child is actively processing morphological elements.

6.2. Other early types of analogies: Class shifts

Typical early analogies in verb inflection are the expansion of the alternation between short final vowel in 2S imperative and long final vowel in 3S indicative to verbs which do not have this alternation in the standard language. This alternation of the A-class verbs (e.g. *ota* 'take!' : *ottaa* 'takes', *kato* 'look!' : *kattoo* 'looks', *tule* 'come!' : *tulee* 'comes') is easily expanded by children to the contracted verbs, e.g. Tuulikki 1;10 2S imperative *leika* 'cut!' (instead of *leikkaa*, cf. the 3S indicative *leikkaa*), 1;11 2S neg. imperative *älä napa* 'don't take!' (instead of *älä nappaa*, cf. the 3S indicative *nappaa*).

The first analogical forms are an indication of the child's own active processing of the elements of language. The very first isolated analogies of Tuulikki were observed at the age of 1;7 (*sati instead of *satoi*), more systematic analogies were frequent at the age of 1;8. Thus the age of 1;8 can be regarded as the onset of the protomorphological period.

7. Syntactic development: Some preliminary observations

The one-word stage of Tuulikki continued till the age of 1;5. At 1;5 Tuulikki used mostly 1- and 2-word utterances but at the end of 1;5 she produced some isolated 3-word utterances, e.g.

(11) *kukka   kakka   mane*   (= forms used by Tuulikki;
                                          the illative suffix is missing)
     sukka   jalkaan   pane   (= Standard Finnish)
     the sock foot(-ILLATIVE) put
     'put the sock on the foot (illative, literally: in the foot)'

At the age of 1;6 Tuulikki combined the subject and the predicate verb with an adverbial, e.g. when playing a jigsaw puzzle she said

(12) *talo   tähän   sopii* /topii/
     the house here (illative)   fits
     'the house fits in here'

The case marking of the adverbial was sometimes defective. In the following example, the illative suffix from *kuppi+in* 'into the cup' is missing:

(13) *kaataa   isi   kuppi*
     is pouring father   cup
     'Father is pouring (tea) into the cup'

Nominal suffix elements were often dropped still at the age of 1;7, especially in longer utterances, e.g. *Puppe nuukkii* (= *nuuhkii*) *kissa* (= *kissaa*) 'Puppe (= a dog) sniffs the cat' (no object marking) and *hakee Tuuti Leego pali* (= *palikan*) 'fetches Tuuti (= Tuulikki) the Lego brick' (last word truncated, both the derivation element -*kka* and the accusative suffix -*n* are missing). In both sentences there is no morphological marking of the object but both the subject and the object are well specified by the word order.

At the age of 1;8 Tuulikki used some 4-word utterances, e.g. *vesimuki(n) mukaan tarttee Tuuti* 'the water mug along needs Tuuti', *kantaa Tuuti hatun tinne* (= sinne) 'carries Tuuti the hat over there'. The marking of the object was accurate, and this made it possible for Tuulikki to use exceptional word order (OVS and VSO instead of the usual SVO of Finnish). At this age she started to use the morphological resources of the language more effectively, and this was also reflected in her use of verb forms.

8. Conclusion: From first verb forms to verbal inflection

Finnish-speaking children start their use of verbs from the two basic forms, the 2S imperative (e.g. *kato* 'look!', *anna* 'give!') and the 3S present indicative. Typically, only one or the other is used from a given verb, but a few combinations (two-member miniparadigms) of these basic forms are also used early. This is easier to verify with diary data (cf. 4.3), because imperatives are not frequently used in the recordings. These two verb forms have very little if any morphological marking (depending on the verb class) and they are thus typical to premorphology: rote learned base forms which are mapped to certain situational contexts.

These two morphological categories of verbs also emerge early in many other languages, for example in German (Klampfer 2000), in Lithuanian (Wojcik, this volume), in Croatian (Katičić, this volume) and in English (Gülzow, this volume); the English *ing*-form corresponds in many cases to the Finnish 3S present tense form. But the infinitives emerge only later in Finnish. In many other languages the infinitive of the verb is used quite early by the children, yet these early infinitives may also be "root infinitives" used in the function of other verb forms (see e.g. Gülzow, this volume for English).

It is interesting to note that – apparently for pragmatic reasons – the 2S imperatives of certain verbs are used by small children acquiring quite different languages. For example, the first verb form used by Tuulikki was the 2S imperative *(k)ato* 'look!'; the 2S imperative of the verb meaning 'look' is also one of the early (frozen) verb forms used by an Austrian girl (Klampfer 2000). In a similar way, one of the earliest verb forms of

Tuulikki and the very first of Tuomas was the 2S imperative *anna* 'give!', which has about the same pragmatic content as the early amalgam *b(r)auchich* 'I need' used by the Austrian girl Katharina (Klampfer 2000).

In what order are the inflectional suffixes typically acquired in Finnish child language? In his study based on the recorded material of 25 Finnish-speaking children aged 1 – 3 years, Toivainen (1980: 33, 44, 160–163) defined the following serial order of the first suffix elements (the order is based by the age of the median child in his material; the verb categories are given in italics): *basic forms of verbs* (= 2S imperative and 3S indicative), partitive, *past tense (preterite), neg. construction*, adessive (adverbs), illative, inessive and allative (adverbs), *1st person singular*, adessive, plural -*i*-, genitive (attribute), *passive*, inessive, accusative, allative, *perfect 3rd singular, 3rd inf. illative*, plural -*t*. As can be seen, the verb suffixes and the nominal suffixes were acquired in a fairly balanced way, almost by turns.

The basic forms of Finnish nouns are nominative and partitive singular. Partitive is the first form to be used from uncountables (Toivainen 1980: 125; Laalo 1999: 363). A third early case form is the illative, the first local case form to be used by Finnish-speaking children. The first illatives are often used in an adverb-like manner (e.g. *kotiin* 'home', cf. nominative *koti*, *syliin* 'into the lap', cf. nominative *syli*). At the very beginning, children may use some rote-learned partitive and illative forms instead of verbs (cf. section 3. under b)).

Active morphological processing of nouns typically starts from the formation of genitive-accusatives which constrast clearly with nominatives. Active morphological processing of verbs often starts from the formation of past tense at about the same age. For example, Tuulikki started to produce both past tense forms and genitive-accusatives at 1;7, Tuomas at 1;8. Both nominal and verbal inflection thus start at about the same age.

The paradigm formation in verbs seems to begin with the production of 3S past tense forms; these contrast with 3S present tense forms of the same verbs. The early two-member miniparadigms of imperatives and indicatives (cf. 4.3 and 4.4) may also be based at least partly on morphological processing, but they may consist of two separate rote-learned forms as well.

The tempus domain is thus differentiated quite early, even before the productive use of 1S present tense forms (cf. Toivainen 1980: 162). This is quite different from e.g. German (Bittner, this volume; Klampfer 2000). The 3S past tense form is used relatively early not only in Finnish but also in e.g. Yucatec Maya (Pfeiler, this volume) and Lithuanian (Wojcik, this volume).

Other verb forms used relatively early are the pseudopassives (present and past) in the function of 1P, the negation verb (3S *ei* 'does not') and the most frequent infinitive forms (the 1st infinitive and the illative of the 3rd infinitive). Passive forms in the function of 1P are at first used in formulaic expressions (e.g. *mennään* 'let's go!') but they soon become productive and are used in different forms, e.g. Tuulikki 1;8 *mennään* 'let's go' (passive present) : *mentiin* 'we went' (passive past) : *ei mennä* 'we shall not go' (passive neg.).

The first infinitive form to be used by Finnish-speaking children is typically the illative of the 3rd infinitive (Toivainen 1980: 163). In the recordings of Tuulikki, the illative of the 3rd infinitive was first (at 1;6) used in the expression *syömään* 'come to eat ~ let's go and eat' and at 1;8 in the expression *nukkumaan* 'let's go to sleep'. The inessive of the 3rd infinitive appeared only once in the recording 1;11. The 1st infinitive appeared once in the recording 1;8 (*syödä* /syälä/ 'to eat') and thereafter not until at 1;11.

The suffix *A* is used in Standard Finnish both in verbs (1st infinitive) and nominals (partitive case). Some children start the active production of *A*-partitives at the same time as the production of *A*-infinitives. For example, Tuulikki used assimilated and contracted (= 2-syllabic) partitives still at 1;8 (e.g. *ovee* < *ovea*, *puuvoo* < *puuroa*). When she started to produce 3-syllabic *A*-partitives at 1;9 (e.g. *apua* 'help', *nakkia* 'some sausage', *namia* 'some yum-yum', *peukkua* 'thumb [object]'), she also started to produce *A*-infinitives at the same age (e.g. *nukkua* 'to sleep', *töniä* 'to jostle'; diary data).

Tuulikki started the active processing of morphological elements (genitive-accusatives of nouns and past tense forms of verbs) at the age of 1;7, Tuomas at 1;8. This start in both nominal and verbal inflection precedes protomorphology; the first three-member miniparadigm (suppletive) emerged at the same age. The first analogical forms and a number of non-suppletive miniparadigms emerged at the age of 1;8. This can be regarded as the onset of the protomorphological phase.

Notes

* I would like to thank Wolfgang U. Dressler, Dagmar Bittner and Marianne Kilani-Schoch for their insightful comments. I am also grateful to Virginia Mattila for checking my English.
1. The latter form, "passive", is used in spoken Finnish.
2. The latter form is the "pseudopassive" used in the function of 1P.
3. This "passive" form is based on the consonant stem.

References

Barrett, Martyn
    1995   Early lexical development. In: Paul Fletcher, and Brian MacWhinney (eds.), *The Handbook of Child Language*, 362–392. Oxford: Blackwell.

Clark, Eve V.
    1993   *The Lexicon in Acquisition.* Cambridge: Cambridge University Press.

Kauppinen, Anneli
    1981   Varhaiskieli ja yksisanavaihe [Protolanguage and the one-word stage]. *Publications de l'association Finlandaise de linguistique appliquee* 31: 15–28. Jyväskylä.

Kilani-Schoch, Marianne, and Wolfgang U. Dressler
    2000   The emergence of verb paradigms in two French corpora as an illustration of general problems of pre- and protomorphology. Poster presented at the 9th International Morphology Meeting, Vienna, February 2000.

Klampfer, Sabine
    2000   Early verb development in one Austrian child. In: Dagmar Bittner, Wolfgang U. Dressler, and Marianne Kilani-Schoch (eds.), *First Verbs: On the Way to Mini-Paradigms*, 7–20. (ZAS Papers in Linguistics 18.) Berlin: Zentrum für Allgemeine Sprachwissenschaft, Typologie und Universalienforschung (ZAS).

Laalo, Klaus
    1999   Ensisanoista ja esimorfologiasta varhaismorfologiaan: lapsen sijajärjestelmän ja verbintaivutuksen alkuvaiheita. *Virittäjä* 1999: 354–377. Helsinki: Kotikielen Seura. [An English summary "From

the first words and premorphology to protomorphology" is available at http://www.helsinki.fi/jarj/kks/vir99laalo.html.].

Lieko, Anneli
    1994   Lapsen kielen morfofonologiaa: indikatiivin imperfektin muodostus. [Child language morphophonology: Acquisition of the past tense forms in Finnish.] *Suomen logopedis-foniatrinen aikakauslehti* 14: 81–89. Helsinki.

Toivainen, Jorma
    1980   *Inflectional Affixes Used by Finnish-Speaking Children Aged 1–3 years*. Helsinki: Suomalaisen Kirjallisuuden Seura. (The Finnish Literature Society.)

Toivainen, Jorma
    1997   The Acquisition of Finnish. In: Dan I. Slobin (ed.), *The Crosslinguistic Study of Language Acquisition*. Vol. IV, 87–182. Mahwah, New Jersey: Lawrence Erlbaum.

Acquisition of verb morphology in Italian: A case study*

Sabrina Noccetti

0. Introduction

In this paper, I trace the development of the Italian verb system in an Italian child during eight months of recordings. The aim of the paper is to show how the child detects verb morphology and how he begins to acquire the morphological system of the adult language. I will give special attention to the features which characterise the transition from pre- to protomorphology, in order to show the most significant changes in the child's linguistic behaviour with regard to verb morphology.

Italian verb morphology has received special attention by research on early operativeness of principles of Universal Grammar and, in particular, on the possibility that the theory of parameters (together with assumptions on the initial values of parameters) could allow an explanation for some developmental characteristics such as the Null-Subject option (Hyams 1986).

Other models of language development have been proposed to confront the validity of the parameter setting model. For example, Pizzuto and Caselli (1992, 1993) examine the acquisition of several Italian grammatical morphemes. They observe that Italian children acquire verb grammatical morphemes only after some months from their emergence and that some morphemes have not reached the point of mastery (i.e. 90% use in obligatory contexts) by the end of the study. According to Pizzuto and Caselli, the time lag between the emergence and the acquisition of morphemes and the individual differences observed among children cannot be accounted for by the nativist parameter-setting theory. The authors find that token frequency, perceptual salience, distributional factors and cognitive abilities play a fundamental role in morphological development.

More recently, within the connectionist framework, the acquisition of Italian verb morphology has been the focus of Orsolini and Marslen-

Wilson (1997), Orsolini, Fanari, and Bowles (1998) studies. Their works are aimed at testing if the dual mechanism model (Pinker 1991; Pinker and Prince 1994) is a valid account for dissociative behaviour in the mental representation of inflectional morphology. In line with the predictions made in Bybee (1995), these studies propose that morphological learnability and generalisability are determined either by the effects of type and token frequency and by the surface phonological characteristics and properties of inflected forms. They also claim that these characteristics affect both regular and irregular inflection. Thus, Orsolini and Marslen-Wilson (1997) and Orsolini, Fanari, and Bowles (1998) criticise the claims of the dual mechanism model that: a) only rule-generated inflections are productive, insensitive to type-token frequency and generalisable; b) irregular inflections are not productive, sensitive to type-token frequency; c) generalisability of irregular inflection depends on lexical constraints and phonological characteristics of the words.

Despite the fact that the findings on Italian morphological development are compatible with the data here analysed, an accurate comparison between previous researches and this one is not possible because: 1) they focus on the acquisition of either irregular past tenses and past participles (Orsolini, Fanari, and Bowles 1998) or simple forms of definite verbs, excluding non-finite verb forms and compound forms (Pizzuto and Caselli 1992, 1993). This contribution, instead, traces the development of verb morphology from the onset of the first verbs to the first verb paradigms; 2) they lack an explicit comparison between input data and child speech, while here two samples of adult speech are employed for comparison with child speech: child-directed speech and the regional variety of adult speech; 3) Pizzuto and Caselli (1992) use a different methodology for evaluating the acquisition of morphemes and their productivity, i.e. when the morpheme is correctly used in 90% of obligatory context and when it appears with two different verbs, e.g. *apri!* 'open' and *vieni!* 'come'. Here the acquisition of verb morphology is instead related to the emergence of paradigmatic contrast (see section 5). 4) Orsolini, Fanari, and Bowles (1998) use an elicitation task with 23 older subjects, i.e. from four to six-year-old children, while this is a longitudinal study of one two-year-old child.

This contribution is in line with the studies that claim the importance of type and token frequency for the emergence of verb forms. It is here claimed that 1) the child initially operates pattern selection on the basis of input frequency; 2) the first verb forms more bound to be acquired in early stages are the most transparent, iconic and showing biuniqueness (Dressler et al. 1987; Dressler and Karpf 1995; Dressler and Thornton 1991); 3) the transition from a phase where the items are rote-learned to a phase characterised by morphological activity is marked by a conspicuous increase of word types and tokens in the child's lexicon.

1. Inflection of Italian verbs and tense frequency in adult speech (AS)[1] and child directed speech (CDS)

The grammatical categories of the Italian verb are person (1, 2, 3), number (sg, pl), tense (present, future, imperfect, simple and compound past, two pluperfects), non-finite verb forms (infinitive, past participle, gerund), mood (indicative, imperative),[2] and voice (active, analytic passive). The verb obligatorily carries the features of person, number, tense, mood and aspect (see table 1) because the pronoun subject is optional.

The Italian verb paradigms follow different patterns that partially depend on the inflectional classes to which they belong (see table 2).

Table 1. Person/number inflection of verbs in *-are, -ere, -ire* (*parl-are* 'to speak', *prend-ere* 'to take', *dorm-ire* 'to sleep', *fin-ire* 'to end')

Present indicative			
1s	*parl-o, prend-o, dorm-o*	1p	*parl-iamo, prend-iamo, dorm-iamo*
2s	*parl-i, prend-i, dorm-i*	2p	*parl-a-te, prend-e-te, dorm-i-te*
3s	*parl-a, prend-e, dorm-e*	3p	*parl-a-no, prend-o-no, dorm-o-no*
1s	*finis(k)-o*	1p	*fin-iamo*
2s	*fini(š)-i*	2p	*fin-i-te*
3s	*fini(š)-e*	3p	*finis(k)-ono*
Imperative			
2s	*parl-a, prend-i, dorm-i*	2p	*parl-a-te, prend-e-te, dorm-i-te*
2s	*fini(š)-i*	2p	*fin-i-te*

The description of the Italian inflectional classes of the verbs used here follows the classification by Dressler and Thornton (1991) (see also Tonelli, Dressler, and Bonifacio 1997; Tonelli et al. 1998) which distinguishes two macroclasses (see table 2) – the former including all verbs in *-are*, characterised by the thematic vowel *-a*, the latter comprising verbs in

-ere, *-ére* and *-ire*, distinguished by the thematic default vowel *-i* (Dressler and Thornton 1991).

The first macroclass in *-a-re* shows the most homogeneous paradigm. It includes the productive default microclass verbs which follow the pattern of *parl-a-re* 'to speak' (see table 1), and a few other verbs with suppletive marked paradigms and with asyllabic roots which show isolated paradigms (see table 2). The unique microclass of the first macroclass in *-a-re* is morphotactically the most transparent, together with the microclass A.1a (type *sent-i-re* 'to hear') of the second macroclass.

The other microclasses of the second macroclass are opaque, and all are unproductive, with the exception of the A.2 microclass, with the amplified stem *-is(k)*, used in the formation of parasynthetic verbs such as *immilanesisco* 'to become like a citizen of Milan'. The A2 microclass attracts verbs which do not have this type of extension in the standard, e.g. *apparisco* ← *appaio* 'I appear', *eseguisco* ← *eseguo* 'I execute' (Rohlfs 1968; Dressler and Thornton 1991), is quite frequent (see inventory by Moretti and Orvieto 1983 in Serianni 1988) and is stable because it does not have a complementary class (Dressler and Thornton 1991). Despite the frequency and slight productivity, the A2 microclass (type *finire* 'to end') is less transparent than the first macroclass because of the morphonological rule of palatalisation which applies in the 2s and 3s of the present indicative and in the 2s of the imperative, i.e. *fini(š)i, fini(š)e* and *fini(š)i!* (Dressler 1985a, 1985b). Thus, A2 microclass verbs show a non-homogeneous paradigm in the verb forms relevant in early phases and are opaque morphotactically because the inflectional suffixes attach to the extension *-is(k)* and not to the stem as in the other microclasses (Tonelli, Dressler, and Bonifacio 1997). A2 verbs are therefore expected to be acquired later than 1st macroclass verbs (type *parlare*).

Both classes A and B include verbs with many irregular, suppletive and isolated paradigms, such as A.1b, B.1b etc. (table 2). These microclasses, which include few verbs, the most numerous being the classes of verbs B.2b and B.2c, have non-homogeneous paradigms, a conflictual formation of some simple pasts and past participles (Rohlfs 1968; Serianni 1988) and are less transparent and less natural than the first macroclass verbs.

The tense system in Italian has present tense paradigms with fewer irregularities, i.e. they are morphotactically more transparent than the past tenses, with the exception of the 2nd macroclass A2 verbs (type *finis(k)o, fini(š)i*), and show superstable markers for the first and second person singular (*-o, -i*), the first and second plural (*-iamo, -te*) (see table 1). The present is expected to be widely used in child speech as a deictic tense because this makes it suitable to the hic et nunc of adult-child interactions, where the moment of speech coincides with the moment of action. However, this tense also shows a non-deictic use whenever it is used to refer to actions which can occur at any time in the future and the past and which do not have a precise temporal reference, i.e. scientific assertion, instructions, comments on a text (Bertinetto 1986, 1991). It is an autonomous tense and must not be linked textually to other tenses and reference points (Lo Cascio 1982) and our samples of CDS and AS (table 21) confirm that it is the most used tense with more than 50% of form tokens.

Table 2. Verb macroclasses in Italian[3]

Macroclass I thematic vowel -a-	Macroclass II thematic default vowel –i–			
-are	A: *-ire*		B.1: *-ére*	B.2: *-ere*
	A.1a	A.2	B.1a	B.2a
parlare (*parl-o, ai, ato*)	*sent-ire* (*sent-o, ii, ito*)	*fin-ire* (*fin-isco, ii, ito*)	*tem-ére* (*tem-o, etti, uto*)	*cred-ere* (*cred-o, etti, uto*)
suppletive/isolated	A.1b		B.1b	B.2b
fare (*faccio, feci, fatto*)	*aprire* (*apr-o, ii, aperto*)		*tacere* (*taccio, tacqui, taciuto*)	*decidere* (*decido, decisi, deciso*)
	A.1c		B.1c	B.2c
andare (*vado, andai, andato*)	*salire* (*salgo, salii, salito*)		*tenere* (*tengo, tenni tenuto*)	*piangere* (*piango, piansi, pianto*)
asyllabic root	A.1d		B.1d	B.2d
dare, stare (*d-o, detti, dato*) (*st-o, stetti, stato*)	*venire* (*vengo, venni, venuto*)		*vedere* (*vedo, vidi, visto*)	*concedere* (*concedo, concessi, esso*)
	+isolated paradigms		+isolated paradigms	

The past tenses are five: simple past, compound past, imperfect, two pluperfects (Plpf I and Plpf II).

The simple past and the past participle show many irregularities or subregularities, since many verbs have strong past forms and opaque paradigms. The imperfect instead is expressed via quite transparent suffixes, although it implies more complex sequences of events and must be anchored temporally (Lo Cascio 1982).

In our data the imperfect, the compound past and, to a smaller extent, the past participle turn out to be fairly frequent, while the simple past shows low frequency in CDS and AS (table 21).

The past participle and compound past express actions which have been accomplished and, according to many studies on the acquisition of aspect, are acquired early in childhood (Antinucci and Miller 1976; Bronckart and Sinclair 1973; Aguirre 2002).

Morphology in the Tuscan variety has some differences from the standard. In the present tense there are some simplifications of the paradigms. The 1p is seldom marked by the suffix *-iamo*, but (almost) always coincides with the impersonal form *si parl-a* 'one speaks'. The choice of this form in the compound past, which implies the use of the auxiliary 'to be' instead of 'to have', can generate problems in the selection of the auxiliary, e.g. 1p *s'è/abbiamo parlato* '(we) are/have spoken'. Another difference occurs in the 3p suffix of the indicative present tense of the 2nd macroclass verbs which is substituted with that of the 1st macroclass verbs in *-are*, i.e. instead of *dorm-o-no* 'they sleep' it is possible, and frequent, to hear *dorm-a-no* on the pattern of *parl-a-no* 'they speak'.

In this paper, I will analyse the corpus of the child's production using the percentages of table 21 to evaluate how frequency in input can affect child speech.

2. Description of the Data

The present analysis covers an age range of 2;0.10 – 2;7. Camillo, the Italian child recorded, is the second child of a middle class Italian (Tuscan) family. His caretakers speak Standard Italian, alternating it with some elements of the Tuscan language variety.[4] The child can be considered a late speaker and was still in the premorphological period at the beginning of the data collection.

On the basis of the child's acquisition of morphology, the data have been divided into three different periods:

Premorphology :	2;0 – 2;3
Transition period:	2;4
Protomorphology:	2;5 – 2;7[5]

Recordings took place at Camillo's home, in the presence of his mother, the interviewer, and sometimes his brother and grandmother.[6] The recordings show a great deal of variation in length and in the number of utterances analysed, since they depend on the child's willingness to speak (see table 3).

Table 3. Length of recordings, number of utterances analysed, and word-tokens

Age	Length of rec. in minutes	No. of Utt.	No. of Utt. with verbs	W-tokens
2;0	23	82	3	91
2;1	58	265	2	295
2;2	51	177	9	284
2;3	53	181	7	217
2;4	20	138	6	220
2;5	50	270	15	538
2;6	25	138	29	219
2;7	30	360	88	1050

3. Premorphology (2;0 – 2;3)

3.1. Predecessors of verbs in predicative function

When the recording started and throughout the premorphological period, Camillo's data show few verb lemmas (from 1% to 9% of word tokens) and a bias for noun lemmas (34 – 40%) (Noccetti 2002). This early preference for nouns has already been observed crosslinguistically and is supposed to depend on pragmatic and discourse factors which focus on the importance of objects in adult-child interaction as well as on the importance of labelling in child-directed speech (Tomasello and Merriman 1995). Although some authors disagree with this view (Gopnik and Choi 1995), labelling is very frequent during the early recordings of Camillo. Almost all nouns are uttered in ostensive contexts by the child's caretakers, while verbs are mainly uttered in non-ostensive contexts to draw the child's attention to objects and persons. From this, we can deduce that the child is not given many contexts for producing verbs.

In this linguistic context, some extragrammatical predecessors of verbs are still used by the child to express an action together with very few lexical verbs which have very likely been learned by rote. Although prosodic fillers are documented in place of articles and prepositions, they do not replace verbs, with the exception of a schwa replacing the auxiliary verb of a non-spontaneous compound past.

There are instead some onomatopoeic words – *tah!*, *pah!*, *ah ah ah!* – which are used in the place of lexical verbs such as 'to beat, strike, mash'. Whenever the child uses extragrammatical devices to describe an action, he accompanies the onomatopoeic words with gestures.

In these early recordings, Camillo uses few relation words encoding actions and relations between people and objects, such as prepositions and adverbs, which are used in the target language with verbs of movement/ state, e.g. *sopra* 'on' in *salire/montare sopra* 'to climb on', *dentro* 'inside' in *essere dentro* 'to be inside'.

More often the child uses nouns, which would occupy the direct and indirect object position in the adult language, e.g.

(1) MOT: *cosa fa Scar?*
what does Scar?
'what does Scar do?'
CAM: *l(e)one.*
lion.
'lion.'
MOT: *picchia il leon in testa.*
beats the lion on head.
'he beats the lion on its head.'

The child is in the one-word-utterance period and still shows many phonological lenition processes such as monophthongisation, cluster and syllable reductions (Noccetti 2002) which serve him to make the segments easier to pronounce (Stampe 1979; Donegan and Stampe 1979).

3.2. The emergence of verb forms

Camillo's early verbs show all the characteristics of rote-learned and frozen forms, as defined in Kilani-Schoch (this volume), i.e. they show contextually bound morphologically non-distinctive forms, uttered in familiar idiosyncratic linguistic contexts. The contexts in which these early verbs occur are essentially of two types: a) those referring to objects and events present at the time of speech, i.e. hic et nunc events and b) others referring to the non-immediate present, to past events or to 'family-bound' situations, which are meaningless outside the family context since they refer to personal experiences.

The verbs in type (a) contexts, which are spontaneous, are in the present and the imperative, while those in type (b) contexts, where the child is likely to produce non-spontaneous language, are in the past participles and even in the imperfect *si vergognava* '(he) was shy' (excluded from table 4, but included in table 5 (*)).[7] Whenever a verb is uttered, it is used without arguments, e.g.

(2) *chiappo*
     catch
     'I catch'

Table 4. Analysed utterances, verb lemmas, types, tokens, new lemmas, types%, tokens % (of utterances)

Age	Utterances	Lemmas	Types	Tokens	New Lemmas	Types%	Tokens%
2;0	82	3	3	3	3	3.60	3.60
2;1	265	2	2	2	1	0.75	0.75
2;2	177	7	7	9	5	3.90	5.10
2;3	181	4	5	7	4	2.76	3.90

Almost all the spontaneous verbs found in the first recordings are uttered in type (a) contexts *vieni!* 'come!', *chiappo* '(I) catch', *corre* '(he) runs'. Other verb forms, produced in non-spontaneous language, include past participles, i.e. *perso* 'lost', *rotto* 'broken', *parlato* 'spoken'. Amalgams and phatic forms as well as root reduplications have not been documented. Some of these early verbs also have suffixes which do not have adult morphological functions as they lack verb-subject agreement, e.g.

(3) BRO: *cosa fanno i   bisonti?*
           what   do   the buffaloes?
           'what do the buffaloes do?'
     CAM: **corre*.
           run-3s-present-indicative.
           'it runs'.

Up to 2;3, verbs are in the corpus with only one form of their paradigm, i.e. in the early period of observation each single verb is produced only in one person, one tense, one mood (see table 6): the verb *correre* 'to run', for example, is only used in the 3s present indicative *corre*, while *chiappare* 'to catch' is only used in the 1s *chiappo*; *venire* 'to come' only in the 2s imperative *vieni!*, and *rompere* 'to break' only in the past participle *rotto*.

In this period of time, which covers four months of recordings, the first tenses emerging are the present, 1s and 3s, the past participle (singular) and the 2s of the imperative. The data also show the 3p present form of *andare* 'to go' → *vanno*, which is an isolated verb with a suppletive paradigm only occurring in the plural in one recording of the premorphological phase with 1 token. At the end of premorphology and in the transition to protomorphology (see also table 9) the data record the emergence of the first two compound past forms, one type in its plural form, i.e. *sono (scap)pati* 'they have run away', and the other in its singular form, i.e. *è rotta* 'it is broken'. These early compound pasts with the auxiliary *essere* show the same construction of 'copula + adjectives' and express a perfective semantic meaning in these contexts.

Table 5. Types and tokens of tenses in CS

Age	Present		Imperative		Infinitive	Past Partic.	Imperfect		Compound Past	
	sg	pl	sg	pl			sg	pl	sg	pl
2;0	2/2	1/1	–	–	–	–	–	–	–	–
2;1	1/1	–	1/1	–	–	–	–	–	–	–
2;2	5/7	–	1/1	–	–	1/1	*1/1	–	–	–
2;3	3/4	–	1/1	–	–	–	–	–	–	1/2

The child mainly uses the 1s of the present to ask questions (4) and the 3s and 3p to describe ongoing actions (5):

(4)   *alzo?*   '(may) I lift (it)?'

(5)   *(l'uccellino) cammina*   '(the bird) is walking'

and the past participle to refer to an accomplished action with a perfective meaning, e.g. *rotta* 'broken'. The imperative forms are used without any significant difference from the target language and emerge in their unmarked form, i.e. the 2s.

Table 6. The emergence of paradigms: the number of lemmas showing opposition

Age	No. of lemmas with an opposition	No. of types occurring in opposition	Lemmas	Tokens
2;0	–	–	3	3
2;1	–	–	2	2
2;2	–	–	7	9
2;3	1	2	4	7

In this first premorphological period, there are no verb paradigms. These appear at 2;3 with a two-term paradigm of the verb *cascare* 'to fall', which belongs to the most transparent productive macroclass of verbs in *-are* (type *parlare*). These first oppositions occur when verb and word types and tokens still show low percentages (see tables 5 and 4), i.e. before the first lexical spurt at 2;5 (see table 3). The first miniparadigm opposes the category of person, i.e. the 1s and 3s, without any tense distinction, e.g.

(6) INV: *ci   sali   sull'altalena?*
         There you sit   on the swing?
         'do you sit on swings?'
    CAM: *no, casco.*
         no, fall down.
         'no, I fall down'.

vs.

(7) INV: *me lo   (il pallone) tiri?*
         To me it   (the ball) you throw?
         'will you throw it (the ball) to me?'
    CAM: *casca   casca.*   (pushing the ball with his hands)
         falls   falls.
         'it falls, falls'.   (it is about to fall? / it is falling?)

There are doubts if this can be regarded as a true miniparadigm (Kilani-Schoch this volume) because the 1s form is uttered in 'family-bound' contexts and may be regarded as a delayed repetition. For this reason, I postponed the beginning of the transition period to 2;4.

4. The transition period: From pre- to protomorphology (2;4)

This month of recordings can be considered a transition period between pre- and protomorphology because it has some features in common with both the preceding and the following period.

Camillo is more talkative during the recording sessions of this month of transition (see table 17), and he shows a slightly higher number of verb types and tokens, i.e. 6.52% and 13% respectively vs. 3.9% and 5.1%, in the highest peaks of the premorphological period (compare table 7 with table 4). The increasing number of verbs anticipates the spurt of the protomorphological phase, but nouns are still more frequent than verbs (24% vs. 6%) and the quantitative analysis of word types and tokens does not reveal a significant change with respect to premorphology.

Table 7. Analysed utterances, verb lemmas, types, tokens, new lemmas, types%, tokens % (of utterances)

Age	Utterances	Lemmas	Types	Tokens	New Lemmas	Types%	Tokens%
2;4	138	9	11	18	5	6.52	13.04

This transition period is characterised by the first arguments which start to appear in sentences with the function of direct objects, i.e. Camillo transits from one-word utterances to two-word utterances, although the latter are only 14% of the analysed utterances (of which only 6.6% show verb+object, subject+verb).

The child has suppressed some but not all the phonological processes of the early recordings. He still has depalatalisation processes of fricatives, palato-alveolars and affricates but no more stopping processes and monophthongisations. The syllable reductions of plurisyllabic words is also meaningful. Camillo shows his preference for disyllabic words with trochaic pattern by a) reducing clusters to syllables of the type CV: *te* ← *tre*; b) deleting atonic syllables of multisyllabic words in both pretonic position: *melle* ← *caramelle* 'candies', and post-tonic position: *minno* ← *mignolo* 'little finger'.

However, the child seems to start morphological activity, as it is shown by diminutives co-occurring with their simplicia and by few fillers, now replacing grammatical words, i.e. articles and auxiliary verbs, e.g. (8). The child also has a paradigm of the 1st macroclass verb *levare* 'remove', where the 1s contrasts with the 3s, i.e. *lev-o* vs. *lev-a*. This two-member miniparadigm is spontaneous, has articulatory accuracy, is used in contrasting contexts and represents a good candidate for true miniparadigms of the next period.

In this month, Camillo also produces one two-term paradigm of the 2nd macroclass B2 verb *rompere* 'break', i.e. present tense *romp-e* vs. filler plus past participle /ə/ *rotta* (table 7, see (8)). These verbs are uttered within the same context while the child is observing the tape of a cassette which is about to break. The present tense is produced while Camillo is observing this event and is in clear contrast to the past participle uttered as a comment of what has just happened a moment before, e.g.

(8) CAM: *rompe, rompe.*
 breaks, breaks.
 'it breaks'.
 MOT: *uh s'è rotta.*
 oh has broken.
 'oh, it has broken'.
 CAM: *ə rotta ta ta ta.*
 'ə broken tah tah tah!'

According to the criteria established to identify true miniparadigms (Kilani-Schoch this volume; Kilani-Schoch and Dressler 2002), this two-term paradigm does not fulfill the criteria. The verb *rompe*, pronounced as *loppe*, lacks articulatory accuracy. Moreover, the past participle is imitative and, even if the criterion of recurrence must be regarded as a strong criterion (Bittner this volume; Klampfer 2000) the miniparadigm is isolated in the data and reappears at 2;7, i.e. only three months later.

Table 8. Emergence of paradigms: number of lemmas showing opposition

Age	No. of lemmas with an opposition	No. of types occurring in opposition	Lemmas	Tokens
2;4	2	4	9	18

Table 9. Types and tokens of tenses in CS

| Age | Present | | Imperative | | Infinitive | Past Part. | Compound Past | |
	sg	pl	sg	pl			sg	pl
2;4	7/12	–	3/5	–	–	1/1	–	–

The criteria here adopted to identify the transition between pre- and protomorphology are marked by seven linguistic changes in the data:

1) the child utters some two-word sentences, either verb-object or subject-verb sentences;
2) he starts to suppress some phonological processes, i.e. stopping processes and monophthongisations;
3) the number of verb types slightly increases and the child uses some new verb lemmas;
4) some morphological operations appear, i.e. diminutive formations;
5) different verbs of the same macroclass or microclass are present with different forms of their paradigm (I will discuss this in section 6.2.);
6) the emergence of at least one good candidate for true miniparadigm whose morphosemantic and morphotactic transparency favour the detection of morphological suffixes;
7) the opposition between past participle (or compound past) with present tense.

The miniparadigm with the opposition in ostensive context of present and past participle, also marking the transition period in Sophie's corpus (Kilani-Schoch this volume), makes explicit the aspectual distinction between accomplished and imminent actions. This posits the premises for the acquisition of other aspectual and temporal differences of the following recordings.

5. Emergence of miniparadigms
5.1. Premorphology

In premorphology the data of Camillo show one single two-member miniparadigm:

Table 10. Miniparadigms in premorphology

Age	2 members	3 members
2;0 – 2;2	–	–
2;3	1 (*casco/casca* 'I fall/it fall's')	–

Table 11. Verb use in premorphology[8]

Age	Lemmas	Unclear	Context-bound	Isolated	Imitations	Formulaic
2;0	3	1	1	1	–	–
2;1	5	–	2	2	2	1
2;2	10	–	8	2	3	–
2;3	6	1	2	1	2	1

In premorphology only the contrasts between 1s *-o* vs. 3s *-a* of *chiapp-o* 'I catch' vs. *cammin-a* 'he walks' and the one between the 3s of B2e (type *corr-ere*) *corr-e* 'he runs' and 1st macroclass verbs (type *parl-are*) *port-a* 'he brings' can be regarded as precursors of miniparadigms. These forms appear before 2;3, when the first two-member miniparadigm is recorded.

5.2. Transition to protomorphology

There are two miniparadigms at 2;4: *rompe – rotta* 'he breaks – broken', *leva – levo* 'he removes – I remove'.

Table 12. Miniparadigms in transition to protomorphology

Age	2 members	3 members
2;4	2	–

Table 13. Verb use in transition to protomorphology

Age	Lemmas	Unclear	Context-bound	Isolated	Imitations	Formulaic
2;4	14	1	8	4	5	–

Other candidates for miniparadigms are 1st macroclass verbs which occur in one single type: 1s present indicative *pettin-o* 'I comb', *casc-o* 'I fall down' vs. 2s *chiapp-i* 'you catch' vs. 3s *indor-a* 'it gilds', *torn-a* 'he comes back' vs. 2s imperative *aspett-a!* 'wait' vs past participle *parl-ato* 'spoken' vs. 3s imperfect *port-a-va* 'he brought' vs. infinitive *vendemmi-are* 'to collect grapes'.

Some of these verbs are non-spontaneous, others are isolated forms but they show the variety of forms the child produces and it is not improper to imagine that they have an impact on the child's representations, in particular, on the acquisition of person distinction on verbs.

5.3. Protomorphology

Table 14. Miniparadigms in protomorphology

Age	2 members	3/4 members
2;5	1	–
2;6	1	–
2;7	8	5

Table 15. Verb use in protomorphology

Age	Lemmas	Imitations	Formulaic[9]
2;5	21	2	1
2;6	21	1	1
2;7	47	3	–

In addition to the true miniparadigms (discussed in section 7), some candidates for further distinctions among verb microclasses appear in the data. At 2;5, 2s imperative of B1 microclass vs. 1st macroclass verbs: *prend-i* 'take' vs. *tir-a* 'throw'; at 2;6 – 2;7, past participles of 1st macroclass verbs vs. A2 verbs (type *finire*): *divent-a-to* 'become' vs. *cap-i-to* 'understood', *fer-i-to* 'wounded', *fin-i-to* 'ended'.

6. Protomorphology (2;5 – 2;7)

Protomorphology is characterised by a lexical spurt, two-word utterances (at least) and an increase in the morphological operations of diminutivisation and plural marking. The number of verb types, tokens and lemmas also increases (see table 16). If one compares the ages of 2;2 and 2;5, shown in table 17, one can see that the child has a higher and steadily increasing number of word tokens and utterances.

From the age of 2;5 onwards, the number of verb lemmas increases in a crescendo that reaches 44 lemmas at 2;7. A comparison between the column of types and lemmas in table 16 in fact shows that verb lemmas are used in more than one form of their paradigm, i.e. there is a number of different types for verb lemmas.

Table 16. Analysed utterances, verb lemmas, types, tokens, new lemmas, types%, tokens % (of utterances)

Age	Utterances	Lemmas	Types	Tokens	New Lemmas	Types%	Tokens%
2;5	270	19	22	43	15	8.14	15.90
2;6	138	20	22	30	9	15.94	21.70
2;7	360	44	68	131	25	12.22	36.40

Almost all the miniparadigms in these recordings are still two-term paradigms, which are mainly produced at 2;7. They show an opposition between the categories of person and number (9), finite vs. non-finite verb forms (10), and tenses and mood (11):

(9) – 1s vs. 3s: *guardo – guarda* '(I) look, (he) looks', *gioco – gioca* '(I) play, (he) plays'; *volo – vola* '(I) fly, (he) flies'
 – 2s vs. 3s: *vai – va* '(you) go, (he) goes'
 – 2/3s vs. 3p: *è – sono* 'is, are', *fai – fanno* 'you/they do'

(10) – imperative vs. present indicative vs. infinitive: *guarda! – guardo – guardare* 'look!, (I) look, to look'
 – present indicative vs. past participle: *prendo – preso* '(I) take, taken', *rompo – rotto* '(I) break, broken'
 – present vs. infinitive: *pesca – pescare* '(he) fishes, to fish'
 – infinitive vs. past participle/compound past: *finire – finito* 'to finish, finished', *tagliare – ho tagliata* 'to cut, cut'

(11) – present vs. imperative: *mette – metto – metti!* '(he) puts, (I) put, put!'
 – present vs. compound past: *fai – fanno – ha fatto* '(you) do, (they) do, (he) has done'

Table 17. The emergence of paradigms: the number of lemmas showing opposition

Age	No. of lemmas with an opposition	No. of types occurring in opposition	Lemmas	Tokens
2;5	3	6	19	43
2;6	2	4	20	30
2;7	13	37	40	131

If we compare protomorphology to premorphology, quantitative and qualitative differences emerge. This second period is characterised by a) an increasing number of word and verb lemmas and tokens and b) by a great variety of verb patterns, i.e. Camillo has a richer vocabulary where verbs belonging to different macroclasses appear. He can contrast 1st productive macroclass past participles *lasci-ato, tagli-ato*, (suppletive) *fatto, and-ato*, with 2nd macroclass verbs, some of which belong to the A2 microclass, e.g. *fin-ito* (see also section 6.3.), while others belong to the opaque B2 microclasses, e.g. *rotto* from *rompere* and *preso* from *prendere*. He starts detecting some morphological suffixes of the present tense (1s and 3s) of verbs belonging to the 1st macroclass, e.g. (3s) *parl-a, vol-a, pesc-a, gioc-a* vs. 2nd macroclass *mett-e, dorm-e* and imperative (2s), e.g. 1st macroclass *parl-a, guard-a, parl-a!* vs. 2nd macroclass *mett-i, prend-i, sent-i, vien-i* – the latter belonging to different microclasses.

At 2;7, 13 verb lemmas have more than one type. The data record the first three-term paradigms of the suppletive verb *fare* 'do', i.e. *fai – fanno – fatto*, which is a transitional verb between the 1st and the 2nd macroclass and is one of the most frequent verbs both in CS (13 types / 57 tokens in the whole corpus) and in CDS (380 tokens), and the 2nd macroclass B2 verb *mettere* 'put' *mette – metti – metto* (as Sophie in Kilani-Schoch this volume), also quite frequent in the input language (83 tokens).

In these recordings the child makes his first analogical errors in the formation of the imperative of the 1st macroclass verbs **guard-i!* ← *guardare* and **alz-i!* ← *alzare* since he takes the suffix of the imperative of the 2nd macroclass verbs, e.g. *vien-i, prend-i* ← *venire, prendere* and of the superstable indicative. These two erroneous forms show that the child still has a strong preference for a biunique relationship between form and function and the suffix *-i* becomes a superstable marker for the 2s, a frequent generalisation among Italian children (see Tonelli, Dressler, and Bonifacio 1997; Tonelli et.al. 1998).

Table 18. Types and tokens of tenses in CS

Age	Present		Imperative		Infinitive	Past Participle	Compound Past	
	sg	pl	sg	pl	–	–	sg	pl
2;5	14/34	1/1	3/3	–	1/1	1/2	2/2	–
2;6	10/16	6/8	–	–	5/5	1/1	–	–
2;7	29/61	2/4	15/38	–	5/7	11/13	6/8	–

When comparing pre- to protomorphology, data show that the child starts to detect the morphology of the two verb macroclasses (see table 2), even though he prefers 1st macroclass verbs, which are the most numerous in CDS (see table 19).

Table 19. Verb macroclasses in CDS and CS whole corpus

		Lemmas	Types	Tokens
-are	CDS	190	659	2215
	CS	85	169	431
-ere (B2)	CDS	53	195	1214
	CS	23	46	209
-ére (B1)	CDS	15	106	646
	CS	9	23	98
-ire (A1)	CDS	11	37	159
	CS	4	11	20
-ire (A2)	CDS	11	23	41
	CS	2	6	11
(Isolated)	CDS	7	62	441
	CS	4	21	51

The lexical spurt documented at 2;7 during the protomorphological period coincides with the emergence of three-term paradigms and the increasing number of two-term paradigms, whose emergence is instead documented since 2;3. The lexical spurt shows a variety of verb patterns which induces the child to organise input data into miniparadigms. These reflect preferences for the least marked devices and the most frequent items in CDS.

7. CS and CDS: A comparison

CS is characterised, especially in the earliest recordings, by a strong dependence on the input language. From a comparison between CDS and CS it emerges that:

1) CS sample shows a preference for the most natural, unmarked verb microclass *-are* (see table 19), and the most frequent verbs among the irregular paradigms (see table 20).

2) The frequency in input of these microclasses is reflected in the order in which paradigms emerge in CS. The verbs which show a high number

370 *Sabrina Noccetti*

of types and tokens, in fact, are more likely to occur in different contexts facilitating semantic bootstrapping and are, therefore, the first to emerge in CS and the first to show some forms of their paradigms. The first two-term paradigm belongs to the 1st macroclass, which has 2215 tokens in CDS. The second and third two-term paradigms belong to the class in *-ere*, which is the second most frequent macroclass with 1214 tokens (see table 19):

a) *-are*: 1st macroclass (*cascare* 'to fall')   – at 2;3,
b) *-ere*: 2nd m. B2 (*rompere* 'to break')   – at 2;4,
c) *-ere*: 2nd m. B1 suppletive (*essere* 'to be') – at 2;5.

3) Lemmas of verbs in *-ére* are quite infrequent both in CDS and CS, but the number of tokens is high in CDS with 167 tokens of the suppletive verb *avere* 'to have', 146 of *vedere* 'to see', 138 of *sapere* 'to know', 90 of *volere* 'want', 34 of *dovere* 'must', 22 of *potere* 'can'. These verbs follow irregular opaque paradigms and are good candidates to be learned by rote; moreover, their meaning is 'abstract' and is not as 'salient' as the verb *rompere* 'to break'.[10] Here the 'saliency of one verb meaning' can be understood by looking at the ongoing action expressed by the verb, i.e. if an object falls, the change of state/position of the object is a relevant fact. Mental and modal verbs, by contrast, are not perceptively salient and do not belong to the early phases of acquisition.

4) A1 and A2 verbs are also infrequent both in CDS and CS. The first two-term paradigm of A1 verbs emerges at 2;7, whilst paradigms of A2 verbs are not produced in these earliest recordings.

Table 20. Comparison between the most frequent verb tokens in CDS and CS

	CDS	Token	Token %	CS Types/Tokens	Token %
1)	*essere* 'be'	857	18.1	6/119	14.5
2)	*fare* 'do'	380	8.05	13/57	6.9
3)	*dire* 'say'	304	6.4	12/31	3.8
4)	*andare* 'go'	267	5.6	10/51	6.2
5)	*avere* 'have'	167	3.5	3/31	3.7
6)	*guardare* 'look'	149	3.1	5/26	3.1
7)	*vedere* 'see'	146	3.09	8/15	1.8
8)	*mettere* 'put'	83	1.7	5/11	1.3
9)	*parlare* 'talk'	76	1.6	5/24	2.9
10)	*dare* 'give'	62	1.3	5/30	3.6
11)	*rompere* 'break'	35	0.7	5/11	1.3

Frequency and naturalness in the input language also determine tense choice in CS. As emerges from table 21 below the present is the most frequent tense in CDS, AS, and CS, with more than half of the tokens.

The first difference which emerges is the lower number of imperative tokens in AS, while they make up 20% of the tokens in CDS. This mood, which is considered the unmarked term among the other directives (Palmer 1986), shows an unmarked paradigm (exception: verbs in -*is(k)*). It is considered neutral from a temporal point of view and an autonomous form, which is very likely to occur in CDS as it is employed not only to give orders but also to capture the attention of the addressee with perceptive verbs in phatic expressions, i.e. *guarda* 'look', *vedi* 'see', *ascolta/senti* 'listen'. This difference is connected with the percentages of infinitives in the two samples. In fact, AS has more infinitives than CDS presumably because the preferred pattern for suggestions and orders in adult-adult interaction is that of a modal verb followed by the infinitive, while the imperative would be considered impolite in many contexts, even though it is more suitable to adult-child interaction.

Table 21. Percentages of the use of verb categories in CS, CDS, and AS

Verb categories	CDS	AS	CS
Present	53.02	54.89	61.58
Imperative	20.59	2.69	17.19
Compound Past	9.11	10.01	7.80
Infinitive	7.86	13.13	5.48
Imperfect	5.04	7.31	3.41
Past Participle	0.57	0.96	4.14

The imperative, which has a high token percentage, the compound past, the infinitive and the imperfect have fewer tokens in CS than in CDS, which are likely to be balanced by a higher percentage of present tenses and past participles. The past participle, which is hardly uttered in CDS or AS, makes up 4.14% of tokens in CS due to the omission of auxiliary verbs (i.e. the past participle must be counted as compound pasts lacking the auxiliary verb).

The imperfect, which shows a higher number of tokens in AS than in CDS, confirms that it is less suitable to adult-child interaction, since its reference points are not deictic and involve a more elaborate syntax.

8. Conclusions

During the premorphological period Camillo does not show morphological patterns. Nouns are dominant and the earliest verbs are learned by rote and coexist together with some extramorphological words used in place of verbs. In this period, characterised by holophrases and child-specific phonological processes, there are no errors in paradigm formation and the child is input-dependent. Rote-learned forms show one verb type in the data and are linked to the same (extra) linguistic contexts. For instance, the verb *chiappo* 'I catch' is used to refer to the same event and elicited by the same question.

Some of the features of the early period also characterise the transition to protomorphology, but in this period some important linguistic changes have been observed: a) the transition from holophrases to two-word utterances, which allow a clearer investigation on subject-verb, object-verb agreement (in the case of past participles, for instance); b) better articulatory accuracy; c) presence of one (even two-member) miniparadigms and candidates for true miniparadigms with morphotactic and morphosemantic transparency, which help to detect grammatical morphemes. The presence of one miniparadigm, i.e. spontaneous, articulatorily accurate and used in contrasting context, can be meaningful in a data base which consists of two recording sessions a month (Klampfer 2000); d) the contrastive use of past participle/ past tense and present tense in the same context. This latter criterion has been adopted because it introduces the child to a tense distinction between verb forms. This does not mean that at the time of the emergence of this opposition the child has already related the two verb forms to one another, and that he already uses the past participle to refer to past events, but that he accumulates forms for further learning (Bittner this volume) on the semantic base.

In transition to protomorphology the spontaneous miniparadigm *leva – levo* only opposes the category of person, i.e. 1s vs. 3s, and can be related to the tendency to establish biunique relationship one-form one-meaning, observed in these early data in the functions of different tenses as well as in verb inflection – i.e. every verb in premorphology and almost all the verbs in the transition period are only inflected in one form of their paradigm.

It seems that the changes in the period of transition are a prelude to the linguistic development of the next phase, although comparative studies with other Italian children are needed to determine what is general and what is idiosyncratic.

During protomorphology the child starts to detect morphology and builds the first patterns: miniparadigms increase in number and the opposition is extended to tense and mood. The paradigms belong to different microclasses and are made up of three and four terms. Only after the emergence of the first paradigms and the verb spurt the child makes his first overgeneralisation of patterns, which shows that he is creating his verb system and trying to organise the verb material with the forms that have already been acquired by analogy.

The emergence of morphology is guided by naturalness principles which favour the least marked patterns: present tense, indicative, singular, 1/3rd person, 2s imperative.

The last period analysed shows more paradigms with a greater variety of patterns. The data do not exhibit many analogical forms, but Camillo utters many irregular and (in the input) frequent compound pasts and past participles, which favour the oppositions of different verb microclasses.

In protomorphology the child starts to develop the system of morphological grammar and is guided by language-specific characteristics and naturalness principles, which favour morphotactic and morphosemantic transparency. However, the child speech is also composed of the most frequent items in input which sometimes coincide with the most natural within the language system, but are certainly determined by pragmatic factors.

Notes

*   I would like to thank Dagmar Bittner, Wolfgang U. Dressler and Marianne Kilani-Schoch for their useful comments on earlier versions of this paper.
1. The adult speech sample I refer to is a long recording session of one interaction among Camillo's caretakers. This sample is a non-guided recording, where the caretakers deal with many topics. It was collected in order to show the differences between the speech addressed to the child (CDS) and the linguistic variety and style used when the adults of Camillo's family were talking to each other.
2. The subjunctive, conditional and other tenses which are not present in CS data have been excluded from this analysis.

3. The verb patterns in this table are far from complete (especially B1 and B2), and are meant to show the two macroclasses and some of the most representative microclasses.
4. It is commonly believed that the simple past is not used in northern Italy, where it has totally disappeared in certain dialects. The distinction between the two tenses is maintained instead in the Tuscan region, where our data have been collected, and in the south of Italy, (for details see Bertinetto 1991; Bertinetto and Squartini 1996; Lepschy and Lepschy 1992).
5. Camillo has been recorded for one and a half year, i.e. from 2;0 to 3;6, but the other data where not relevant for the present analysis on the emergence of paradigms (Noccetti 2002).
6. The author of this paper, who also transcribed and coded the data in CHAT format (MacWhinney 2000), was helped by the child's mother whenever difficulties were encountered.
7. In table 4 only spontaneous verbs are included, and this verb form is a delayed repetition, which cannot be considered a form anticipating the imperfect tense.
8. The number of lemmas does not correspond to the one shown in tables 4, 8, 11 because imitations are also included. Several verbs fulfil different criteria and there is a consequent overlapping.
9. The verbs produced in this period do not match the previous definitions any longer, i.e. there are no isolated, unclear, context-bound forms.
10. Of course, this and other verbs can be justified in the data on the basis of their pragmatic function in adult-child interaction.

References

Aguirre, Carmen
    2002   The acquisition of tense and aspect morphology: A key for semantic interpretation. In: Maria D. Voeikova, and Wolfgang U. Dressler (eds.), *Pre- and Protomorphology: Early Phases of Morphological Development in Nouns and Verbs*, 163-176. München: Lincom.

Antinucci, Francesco, and Ruth Miller
    1976   How children talk about what happened. *Journal of Child Language* 3: 167–189.

Bertinetto, Pier Marco
    1986   *Tempo, aspetto e azione nel verbo italiano: Il sistema dell'indicativo*. Firenze: Accademia della Crusca.

Bertinetto, Pier Marco
1991   Il verbo. In: Lorenzo Renzi, and Giampaolo Salvi (eds.), *Grande grammatica italiana di consultazione*. Vol. 2, 13–161. Bologna: Il Mulino.

Bertinetto, Pier Marco, and Mario Squartini
1996   La distribuzione del perfetto semplice e del perfetto composto nelle diverse varietà di italiano. *Romance Philology* 49: 383–419.

Bronckart, Jean Paul, and Hermina Sinclair
1973   Time, tense and aspect. *Cognition* 2: 107–130.

Bybee, Joan
1995   Regular morpholgy and the lexicon. *Language and Cognitive Processes* 10: 425–455.

Donegan, Patricia, and David Stampe
1979   The study of natural phonology. In: David Dinnsen (ed.), *Current Approaches to Phonological Theory*, 126–173. Bloomington: Indiana University Press.

Dressler, Wolfgang U.
1985a   *Morphonology: The Dynamics of Derivation*. Ann Arbor: Karoma Publishers.

Dressler, Wolfgang U.
1985b   Sur le statut de la suppléance dans la morphologie naturelle. *Langages* 78: 41–56.

Dressler, Wolfgang U., and Annemarie Karpf
1995   The theoretical relevance of pre- and protomorphology in language acquisition. *Yearbook of Morphology* 1994: 99–122.

Dressler, Wolfgang U., Willi Mayerthaler, Oswald Panagl, and Wolfgang U. Wurzel
1987   *Leitmotifs in Natural Morphology*. Amsterdam: John Benjamins.

Dressler, Wolfgang U., and Anna M. Thornton
1991   Doppie basi e binarismo nella morfologia italiana. *Rivista di Linguistica* 3: 3–22.

Gopnik, Alison, and Soonja Choi
1995   Names, relational words, and cognitive development in English and Korean speaker: Nouns are not always learned before verbs.

In: Michael Tomasello (ed.), *Beyond Names for Things*, 63–80. Hillsdale, New Jersey: Lawrence Erlbaum.

Hyams, Nina
1986 *Language Acquisition and the Theory of Parameters*. Dordrecht, Holland: Reidel.

Kilani-Schoch, Marianne, and Wolfgang U. Dressler
2002 The emergence of verb paradigms in two French corpora as an illustration of general problems of pre- and protomorphology. In: Maria D. Voeikova, and Wolfgang U. Dressler (eds.), *Pre- and Protomorphology: Early Phases of Morphological Development in Nouns and Verbs*, 45–51. München: Lincom.

Klampfer, Sabine
2000 Early verb development in one Austrian child. In: Dagmar Bittner, Wolfgang U. Dressler, and Marianne Kilani-Schoch (eds.), *First Verbs: On the Way to Miniparadigms*, 7–20. (ZAS Papers in Linguistics 18.) Berlin: Zentrum für Allgemeine Sprachwissenschaft, Typologie und Universalienforschung (ZAS).

Lepschy, Anna Laura, and Giulio Lepschy
1992 I tempi del passato. *Linguistica* 32: 75–88.

Lo Cascio, Vincenzo
1982 Temporal deixis and anaphor in sentence and text: Finding a reference time. *Journal of Italian Linguistics* 7: 31–70.

MacWhinney, Brian
2000 *The CHILDES Project: Tools for Analyzing Talk*. Mahwah, New Jersey: Lawrence Erlbaum.

Noccetti, Sabrina
2002 *Pre- and Protomorphology in Language Acquisition: An Italian Case Study*. Pisa: Edizioni Plus, Università di Pisa.

Orsolini, Margherita, Rachele Fanari, and Hugo Bowles
1998 Acquiring regular and irregular inflection in a language with verb classes. *Language and Cognitive Processes* 13: 425–464.

Orsolini, Margherita, and William Marslen-Wilson
1997 Universals in morphological representation: Evidence from Italian. *Language and Cognitive Processes* 12: 1–47.

Palmer, Frank R.
    1986   *Mood and Modality.* Cambridge: CambridgeUniversity Press.

Pinker, Steven
    1991   Rules of language. *Science* 253: 530–535.

Pinker, Steven, and Alan Prince
    1994   Regular and irregular morphology and the psychological status of rules of grammar. In: Susan D. Lima, Roberta L. Corrigan, and Gregory K. Iverson (eds.), *The Reality of Linguistic Rules*, 321–351. Amsterdam: John Benjamins.

Pizzuto, Elena, and Maria Cristina Caselli
    1992   The acquisition of Italian morphology: Implications for models of language development. *Journal of Child Language* 19: 491–557.

Pizzuto, Elena, and Maria Cristina Caselli
    1993   L'acquisizione della morfologia flessiva nel linguaggio spontaneo: Evidenza per modelli innatisti o cognitivisti. In: Emanuela Cresti, and Massimo Moneglia (eds.), *Ricerche sull'acquisizione dell'Italiano*, 165–187. Roma: Bulzoni.

Rohlfs, Gerhard
    1968   *Grammatica storica della lingua italiana e dei suoi dialetti. Morfologia.* Torino: Einaudi.

Serianni, Luca
    1988   *Grammatica italiana. Italiano comune e lingua letteraria. Suoni, forme e costrutti.* Torino: UTET.

Stampe, David
    1979   *A Dissertation on Natural Phonology.* New York: Garland.

Tomasello, Michael, and William E. Merriman
    1995   *Beyond Names for Things.* Hillsdale, New Jersey: Lawrence Erlbaum.

Tonelli, Livia, Wolfgang U. Dressler, and Serena Bonifacio
    1997   L'acquisizione delle classi verbali dell'italiano: Studio di un caso. *Mondo Ladino* 21: 505–512.

Tonelli, Livia, Anna De Marco, Ralf Vollmann, and Wolfgang U. Dressler
    1998   Le prime fasi dell'acquisizione della morfologia: Un confronto tra l'italiano e il tedesco. In: Patrizia Cordin, Maria Iliescu, and

Heidi Siller-Runggaldier (eds.), *Parallela 6. Italiano e tedesco a contatto e confronto. Atti dell'incontro italo-austriaco dei linguisti*, 281–301. Trento: Università di Trento.

Early acquisition of the verbal complex in Yucatec Maya*

Barbara Pfeiler

0. Introduction

The purpose of this study is to show the processes and strategies employed by one Yucatecan child, Sandi, in the acquisition of verb morphology leading to the building of three-member inflectional paradigms. Data presented here were gathered during a period of eight months, from Sandi's age of 1;9 to 2;4. We will trace her acquisition of the verbal complex by describing the emergence of particular verbs, specific patterns of status inflection and the use of person-marking inflectional and derivational morphology. We will identify early errors, such as the overgeneralized use of an imperative suffix, the omission of obligatory person-markers and auxiliaries, and the analogic extension of an incorrect form. This study is based on the analysis of the early verb inflection in Yucatec Maya (Pfeiler and Martín Briceño 1997).

1. Verb and person classification in Yucatec

Yucatec Maya is a head-marking language: the verbal complex can function on its own as a complete sentential proposition (Lucy 1994: 627).

Verbs are distinguished into classes of transitive and intransitive verbs according to their argument marking properties. "Intransitive verbs are inflected by cross-reference marking for their S-argument, [and] transitive verbs are inflected by cross-reference marking for their A-argument and their O-argument" (Bohnemeyer 1998: 155–156). In the verb complex, person, mood, and aspect are represented by sets of inflectional affixes.

Person markers are expressed through bound pronominal indices on the verb. There are two sets of markers, Set-A and Set-B.

380 *Barbara Pfeiler*

Table 1. Person markers

Person	Set-A clitics (ergative)		Set-B suffixes (absolutive)	
	Singular	Plural	Singular	Plural
1st	iN(w)	iN(w) ...-o'on	-en	-o'on
2nd	a(w)	a (w) ...-e'ex	-ech	-e'ex
3rd	u(y)/y	u(y)/y ...-o'ob	-Ø /-ih[1]	-o'ob

The morphological structure of the inflected verb in Yucatec Maya can be described in three different schemas: one for transitive verbs, one for intransitive verbs inflected for incompletive status, and one for intransitive verbs inflected for the completive and subjunctive status. The subject person of transitive verbs is marked by a set-A clitic interposed between the auxiliary and the verb stem and the intransitive subject by a set-A clitic or set-B suffix according to the aspect. The object person is marked by a set-B suffix on the verb stem, optionally followed by a subject plural marker. There are no morphological case markers on nouns or modifiers.

Transitive and intransitive verbs are inflected with specific status suffixes (see table 2). Yucatec aspect and mood markers which appear in the analyzed corpus are set out in the following table:

Table 2. Partial description of Yucatec status inflection according to verb classes (Bohnemeyer 1998: 221). (Sandi's usage of status forms is marked in italics)

		Incompletive	Completive	Subjunctive	Imperative
Intransitive	Active	-Ø	-nah	-nak	-nen
	Inactive	-Vl	-Ø	-Vk	*-en*
	Positional	*-tal*	-lah	-l(ah)ak	-(l)en
Transitive	Active voice	*-ik*	-ah	-Ø / -eh[2]	-eh

These status suffixes are linked with auxiliary elements, which themselves are divisible into three classes: underlying intransitive verbs, adverbs and particles. The completive status for transitive verbs, marked by the suffix *-ah*, only allows the auxiliary *t-*[3], while the incompletive status, with the suffix *-ik*, occurs with many auxiliaries. In Sandi's data the following auxiliaries linked with incompletive status are found: the progressive *táan* 'ongoing, be...ing', the incompletive *k-*, the terminative *ts'o'ok* 'conclude, result', the obligative *yaan* 'must, have to', the desiderative *taak*, and the assurative future *he'el ..-e'* 'surely, indeed'. Although both completive and incompletive status suffixes are found in the data, only one token of the suffix *-ah* is linked correctly with the auxiliary *t-* in Sandi's corpus. In addition, among the auxiliary elements which are linked with the subjunctive status, the first auxiliary used by Sandi in a correct form is the temporal modifier *sáan* (recent past), followed by *uuch* (remote past).

The most frequent suffixes of status inflection in our data are the following:

Table 3. Sandi's favorite status markers

TRANSITIVE VERBS (active voice)	INTRANSITIVE VERBS
-eh imperative /subjunctive	*-Vk*[4] subjunctive
-ik incompletive	*-Vl* incompletive
-ah completive	*-Ø-ih*[5] completive, B.3S

In Yucatec most intransitive roots can be derived into transitive stems, and most transitive roots produce derived intransitive stems. Each valency alternation is explicitly marked.

In the present data two derivational patterns from intransitive to transitive are registered, expressed by two different suffixes for argument extension: the suffix *-s* encodes the introduction of a causer, and the suffix *-t* encodes the introduction of an affected object (cf. Krämer and Wunderlich 1999: 460). In Sandi's corpus the following examples are found: the intransitive verb *lúub* 'fall' appears with incompletive (*-ul*), completive (*-ih*) and subjunctive (*-uk*) status suffixes, and in the causative form *lu'ubs-* 'make fall' with the imperative suffix *-eh*. The intransitive verbs *báaxal* 'play' and *hanal* 'eat' are also used in the derived transitive forms, both in the imperative status. Examples are: *han-en* 'eat!' and *haant-eh* 'eat it!' which will be discussed later. Valence changing derivation from transitive to intransitive is represented by antipassive forms.[6]

Three kinds of participles can be derived from verbal stems: (1) participles ending in *-a(h)-a'an (-an)*, (2) participles ending in *-Vl*, and (3) participles involving full or partial reduplication of the verb stem (Bricker, Po'ot Yah, and Dzul de Po'ot 1998: 372–373). The participle ending in *-a(h)-a'an (-an)*, which can be derived from root transitives, intransitives and positionals, is the most frequent in Sandi's analyzed data.

2. Data description

The data analyzed in the present study represent the age range of 1;9.27 to 2;4.4, covering 15 recordings (see table 4) as part of a three-year longitudinal study. Sandi's family lives in the rural community of Yalcobá, in the eastern part of the state of Yucatán, about 150km from Mérida, the state capital. Sandi was selected because she is the first born child of a monolingual family, which were the criteria for this study.

Table 4. Corpus used for the analysis of Sandi's verb development

Number of recordings	Age	Time of recordings (in minutes)	Number of analyzable utterances
2	1;9.27 and 1;9.29	120	207
2	1;10.17 and 1;10.24	120	214
2	1;11.9 and 1;11.14	90	686
3	2;0.6 /2;0.21/2;0.27	120	251
2	2;1.3 and 2;1.26	90	289
2	2;2.2 and 2;2.27	90	320
1	2;3.8	60	240
1	2;4.4	45	111

In the corpus, the utterances with verbs were selected and classified according to the criteria of: number of lemmas, types and tokens.

Table 5. Total number of analyzable utterances, verb lemmas, types and tokens; percentage of tokens in relation to the total number of child utterances per month

Age	Analyzable utterances	Utterances with verbs +imitation	–imitation	Verb lemmas/ new lemmas	Types	Tokens	Tokens %
1;9	207	59	53	15	19	63	30,4
1;10	214	77	74	18/8	21	75	35,0
1;11	686	226	209	37/13	46	218	31,8
2;0	251	111	101	38/8	46	119	47,4
2;1	289	152	124	36/11	49	150	51,9
2;2	320	156	149	46/10	76	161	50,3
2;3	240	141	138	36/11	59	186	77,5
2;4	111	64	62	18/7	27	65	58,6
Total	2318	986	910	244/68	343	1037	44,7

Table 5 shows the quantitative development of verb usage by Sandi. From age 2;0 on verb tokens represent around 50% of the total number of utterances. The very frequent use of verbs at age 2;3 is due to the recording session in which Sandi's mother did the recording while playing with her daughter. The reduced number of utterances at age 2;4 can be accounted for by the reduced number and time of the analyzed recording.

3. Development of verb categories

Table 6. Sandi's verb categories (types/tokens)

Verb suffix (grammatical categories)	1;9	1;10	1;11	2;0	2;1	2;2	2;3	2;4
-eh (TRANS:SUBJV/IMP)	10/27	11/61	19/79	18/59	17/106	21/87	14/58	5/6
-Ø (INTR:INCOMPL; TRANS:SUBJV/IMP)	7/21	6/14	11/26	13/28	22/40	18/18	9/37	2/4
-Ø-ih (INTR:B.3.SG., COMPL)	1/11	4/11	5/8	3/4	2/3	4/7	2/2	1/1
-tal (INTR/ POSITIONAL: INCOMPL)	1/5	1/2	–	2/7	1/1	1/1	–	1/1
-Vl (INTR:INCOMPL)	–	1/2	3/8	3/9	7/11	6/7	2/5	–
-ik (TRANS:INCOMPL)	–	–	1/1	2/2	6/6	8/19	3/6	3/5
-Vk (INTR:SUBJV)	–	–	–	1/3	2/7	2/2	–	–
-mah (TRANS:PERF)	–	–	1/1	1/1	1/1	–	–	–
-a(h)-a'an (INTR/TRANS:PART; INTR:PERF)	–	–	1/1	–	–	2/2 1/1	3/3	–
-ah (TRANS:COMPL)	–	–	–	–	1/1	3/4	3/3	1/1
-en (INTR:IMP)	–	–	–	–	1/1	1/1	–	1/2
-o'ob (B.3.PL.,COMPL, INTR:SUBJ TRANS:OBJ)	– –	– –	1/1 –	– –	– –	1/2 1/1	– –	1/1 –
-ech (B.2.SG. TRANS:OBJ INTR:SUBJ)	– –	– –	– –	– –	– –	– –	2/3 –	– 1/2
-ak/-lak (INTR:SUBJV)	–	–	–	–	–	–	4/5	–
-en (B.1.SG., COMPL, INTR:SUBJ)	–	–	–	–	–	–	2/3	–

Table 6 (above) showed the overall development of Sandi's verb categories. The data were presented as number of types/number of tokens of utterances of each verbal suffix, by age. The data from table 6 will be referred to throughout the remainder of this paper.

3.1. First verb forms in the premorphological phase

Adapting Dressler and Karpf's model of Pre- and Protomorphology (1995) to the Yucatec data we may determine age 1;10 as the end of the premorphological phase. At age 1;9 and 1;10, according to table 6, Sandi's verb forms are dominated by the suffix -*eh* (21 types of 88 tokens), and by bare roots (-Ø) (13/35). Both forms are used as imperatives, but some of the unmarked root/stem forms also occur as desiderative illocutions. Verbal expressions composed of bare roots may be hard to distinguish from verb roots used as nouns. In Mayan languages, many roots appear both as nouns and as verb stems. In our data this is the case with *chu'uch* 'suckle/breast', *hanal* 'eat/food', *chi'* 'bite/mouth', *báaxal* 'play/toy', *xóok* 'read/count', and *pax* 'play/music'.

Among the status suffixes, as we see in table 6 (row 3), the suffix sequence -Ø-*ih* expresses the completive aspect of set B third person singular. This sequence occurs with intransitive verbs *bin* 'go', *lúub-* 'fall', *máan* 'pass by' and the antipassive form *xuup* 'use up'. The fact that Sandi uses these verbs exclusively inflected for B.3S COMPL suggests that these are memorized as a lexical whole.

Two types of formal errors are found in the premorphological phase:

1.) The use of the suffix -*eh* with intransitive verbs: This suffix corresponds to the subjunctive/imperative status of transitive verbs, but Sandi also uses this suffix in intransitive verbs instead of -*en*. This error had been considered a categorical underspecification between transitive and intransitive verbs (Pfeiler and Martín Briceño 1997), but phonological similarities between both suffixes are rather to be supposed. Examples of Sandi's usage are: **éem-eh* ← *éem-en* 'descend!'; **ok-eh* ← *ok-en* 'enter!'; **koteh* ← *koten* 'come!'[7]; **wa'al-eh* ← *wa'al-en* 'stand up!' and **méek'-eh* ← *méek'-en* 'hug me'. The same error appears with the following common phonologically reduced morphological combination: **táat-eh* ← *ts'ah-ten* ← *ts'ah ti' teen* 'give (it to) me'.

2.) The use of the incompletive status *-tal* with the positional intransitive verb *kul-* 'sit down' but with imperative meaning. Until age 2;4, two different forms are still used alternately to express imperative, namely **ku(l)tal* and the correct form *kul-len* 'sit down!'.

The first lemma occuring with different forms within the same verb class during the period of 1;9 and 1;10 are: *mach* 'grasp', *wach'* 'untie', *ok* 'enter', and *wa'al* 'stand up', presented in table 7. Another highly frequent verb used in this age range is *méek'* 'hug'; because of its importance, it will be discussed in detail in the body of the paper.

Table 7. First forms to emerge at age 1;9 and 1;10

LEMMA	TRANSITIVE VERB (Imperative)	LEMMA	INTRANSITIVE VERB (Imperative)
mach 'grasp'	*mach 'grasp' (=mach N) mach-eh 'grasp it!'	ok 'enter'	*ok ~ *ok-eh 'enter!' (=ok-en)
wach' 'open'	*wach' 'untie' (=wach' N) wach'-eh 'untie it!'	wa'al 'stand up'	*wa'al ~ *wa'al-eh 'stand up!' (=wa'al-en)

The first forms to emerge are the bare root and the root inflected with suffix *-eh,* as demonstrated in table 7. The alternating use of transitive roots with and without the suffix *-eh* could be taken as evidence that the child has started to detect morphology, because with transitive verbs the syntax determines the paradigmatic alternation of the suffixes *-eh* and *-ih* and the zero-marking. Nevertheless both forms are used by Sandi solely with an imperative meaning. This alternating use could therefore be interpreted as a precursor of the child's construction of mini-paradigms. The first mini-paradigm of two members within the same verb class occurs at 1;10 but still with errors.

(1) *ok* 'enter': *ok-ih* 'he entered' **ok-eh* 'enter!' (=*ok-en*) 1;10

The child first uses the intransitive root *ok* 'enter', with the intention of completive meaning, using the completive status marker in third person *-ih* as a "frozen" form. The verb also appears with the suffix **-eh* in the imperative meaning. The correct imperative form of this verb would be *ok-en.*

At age 1;10 the verb *báaxal* 'play' is inflected with status markers of the intransitive and transitive classes:

Table 8. First forms based on both verb classes

AGE	LEMMA	TRANSITIVE/INTRANSITIVE VERB FORMS
1;10	báaxal 'play'	báaxt-eh (TRANS:IMP) 'play it!'
		m(a') u báaxal-Ø (NEG A.3Sg. INTRANS:INCOMPL) 'he doesn't play'

The intransitive verb *báaxal* is used also in an analytic form with a relational noun, as in: *báax-Ø y-éetel* (INTRANS:IMP POSS3 REL N) 'play with him!'.

Comparing now the use of suffixes to the use of prefixes, including especially the person marking affixes that cross reference core arguments, only the third person singular of Set-A is registered at age 1;10: *t-u* (= *táan*, progressive aspect marker, and the Set-A of 3S *u* = *tu(n)*).

In conclusion, we can state that during the premorphological phase of verb development in Sandi's speech, the unmarked and prototypical characteristics of the verb/noun roots in Yucatec Maya, as well as the isolated and less marked characteristics of the imperative mood, are both present in this phase, confirming the predictions of Natural Morphology.

3.2. Transition phase from pre- to protomorphology

Referring once again to table 6, we see that at age 1;11 the morphological activity in Sandi's speech is increasing and new categories are found, such as the incompletive status for transitive verbs (*-ik*), the perfect status suffix (*-mah*) and the participle (*-a(h)-a'an*) with transitive verbs, and the third person plural of Set-B (*-o'ob*), which appears as subject for the first time. Also new is the hortative form of the irregular verb *bin: ko'ox* 'let's go', which in this case is followed by the verb 'play'. Inflected verbs with the suffix *-eh* and bare roots still dominate, as well as the incorrect use of the imperative form in intransitive verbs such as **kul-eh* 'sit down!', or **ok-eh* 'enter!'.

One of the first morphological combinations in Sandi's production is the form *méek'-ech* 'hug you' which she uses for *méek'-en* 'hug me' (Pfeiler and Martín Briceño 1997: 120) imitating the form of one of the most frequent utterances of Sandi's parents shown in the following example:

(2) MOT: *Ko'oten   kah   in   méek'-t-Ø-ech.*
come:IMP   AUX   A.1S   hug-TR-SUBJV-B.2S
'Come (here) for me to hug you.'

A new kind of error appears at this age, an analogical extension of *méek'-ech* 'hug you'. Now Sandi uses **éem-ech* in alternation with **éem-eh* instead of the correct form *éem-en* in imperative or desiderative expressions of 'put me down!'

At age 1;11 two mini-paradigms of two members are found; one is constructed with transparent types of forms, the other from a suppletive verb. These are the following:

Table 9. The first 2-member mini-paradigms

AGE	LEMMA	TRANSITIVE VERB	LEMMA	SUPPLETIVE VERB
1;11	*k'al* 'close'	*k'al-eh* (IMP) 'close it!' *k'al-a'an* (PART) 'closed'	*bin* 'go'	*(h)bin-o'ob* (COMPL- B.3P) 'they went' *xi'ik-o'ob* (SUBJV-B.3P) *(ka xi' ik-o'ob)* 'be gone!'

Due to the irregularity of the verb *'bin'* it is possible that both forms are memorized. At age 2;0.27, the first three-member mini-paradigm is found. This is the case with the frequent transitive verb *mach* 'grasp', as shown below in table 10. It should be noted that in the case of *mach-ik*, the correct incompletive status suffix is used, but the obligatory aspect and person markers are still missing.

Table 10. The first 3-member mini-paradigm

AGE	LEMMA	TRANSITIVE VERB
2;0.27	*mach* 'grasp'	**mach* (=*mach* N) ~ *mach-eh* (IMP) 'grasp it!' *mach-mah* (PERF) 'he has grasped it' (= *u mach-mah*)[8] *mach-ik* (INCOMPL) 'he grasps it' (= *k-u mach-ik*)

At around the same age, two new mini-paradigms of two members are found, as shown in table 11. One of them is formed with the transitive verb *haant* 'eat' marked with the imperative and incompletive status suffixes; the other is formed with the intransitive inactive verb *lúub* 'fall', marked with the completive and the perfect status suffixes. However, in incompletive constructions, here and in table 10 above, Sandi omits the obligatory auxiliaries *k-* or *táan* and also the Set-A pronouns.

Table 11. New 2-member mini-paradigms at age 2;0

LEMMA	TRANSITIVE VERB	LEMMA	INTRANSITIVE VERB
haant 'eat it'	*haant-eh* (IMP) 'eat it!' *haant-ik* (INCOMPL) 'he eats it' (= *k-u haant-ik*)	*lúub* 'fall'	(*h*) *lúub-ih* (COMPL-B.3S) 'he fell' *lúub-a(h)-a'an* (PART) 'fallen'

Bare roots still appear with the imperative or desiderative meaning. Furthermore, the data until 2;0 contains only two person Set-A clitics and two auxiliaries correctly used with transitive verbs. With respect to intransitive verbs the completive aspect of the third person singular clause finally (the suffix *-ih*) still dominates.

Also appearing at the age of 1;11 is the first distinction of person, in the formation of the transitive verbs *ts'ah* 'give' and its combination with independent pronouns: *ts'ah-(ti') teen* 'give (it to) me!' and *ts'ah-ti' (leti')* 'give (it to) him/her!'.

3.3. Verb categories and inflection in protomorphology

In the numbers for age 2;1 in table 6, we see increased frequency of verbal inflection, especially in the use of incompletive status suffixes of transitive and intransitive verbs. Some new lemmas are expressed, generally as root forms first and subsequently as the root form with the suffix *-eh*, both with imperative meaning. Two examples of transitive verbs are *cha'* 'untie' and *oks* 'insert'. The frequent intransitive verb *lúub* 'fall', which previously was used only in completive form, begins to appear with the incompletive status (*-ul*) and the subjunctive suffix (*-uk*). The verb *méek'* 'hug' still is used both correctly and incorrectly with a variety of person suffixes, all of them with the imperative or desiderative meaning of 'hug me': **méek'-ech* 'hug you', **méek'-eh* 'hug him/her', and the root form **méek'* 'hug'. Not until age 2;1 does Sandi begin to use the completive status *-ah* with the transitive verb *pul* 'throw', with the corresponding meaning of 'threw', but still without the obligatory auxiliary *t-* and the person marker. At the same time, one token of the incompletive auxiliary *k-* appears.

In contrast, the temporal modifier *sáan* (recent past, linked with the subjunctive status) appears often with the intransitive verbs *lúub* 'fall', and *wen* 'sleep', correctly linked with the appropriate subjunctive status marker, forming *lúub-uk*, *wen-ek*. Even the frequency of the ergative person markers of Set-A is increasing, especially the first and third persons singular, *in* and *u* respectively.

From age 2;1 on, the number of bare roots steadily decreases (in relation to the total number of verb tokens) as shown in table 6.

At age 2;2 six lemmas are found in mini-paradigms of two members; four of them appear with omissions or show a third analytical form composed of an auxiliary. Representative examples are shown in table 12 below.

Table 12. New 2-member mini-paradigms at age 2;2

AGE	LEMMA	TRANSITIVE VERB
2;2	*man* 'buy'	*man-eh* (IMP) 'buy it!'
		man-a(h)-a'an (PART) 'bought'
2;2	*k'ax* 'tie up'	*k'ax-eh* (IMP) 'tie it up!'
		k'ax-a(h)-a'an (PART) 'tied up'
		Analytical form: *koten k'ax N* (AUX *k'ax* N) 'come tie it up'
2;2	*púust* 'brush clean'	**púust (= púust N) ~ púust-eh* (IMP) 'brush it clean!'
		púust-a(h)-a'an (PART) 'clean brushed'

The participle is used with various lemmas, and the incompletive status suffix *-ik* is used with increasing frequency. The suffix *-eh* continues to play an important role. One new intransitive, inchoative verb (*lu'unt-* 'get dirty'), used incorrectly with the suffix *-eh*, is found in Sandi's corpus at age 2;2.

A second suppletive verb appears in a mini-paradigm of two members, this is *taal* 'come', as shown in (3).

(3) *koten* (IMP) 'come!' (2;2)
     taal (INCOMPL) 'he is coming' (= t(áan) u taal)

The development of two-member mini-paradigm formation over the entire period analyzed is shown in table 13:

As shown in table 13, there are more two-member mini-paradigm formations with transitive than with intransitive verbs. This fact can be explained by examining the input data, where transitives are used more frequently than intransitives. Furthermore, intransitive verbs are used above all in declarative utterances, while the transitive verbs in this corpus are used in utterances with imperative, interrogative and declarative meaning.

Table 13. Increase of 2-member mini-paradigms

AGE	TRANSITIVE VERBS	INTRANSITIVE VERBS	SUPPLETIVE VERBS
1;9	1	–	–
1;10	1	1	–
1;11	1	–	1
2;0	1	1	1
2;1	2	1	–
2;2	5	1	1
2;3	2	–	–
2;4	2	–	1
Total	15	4	4

The process of two-member mini-paradigms acquisition can be observed clearly in the status suffixes. First, only bare roots and the suffix *-eh* are used, with imperative or desiderative meaning and without categorical specification. Second, the imperative and the participle are marked and semantically differentiated. Concurrent with the increasing number of verb types (table 5) there is also an increase of paradigm formation at age 2;2. Extensions in the building of paradigms can be traced in five lemmas throughout the corpus: transitive verbs *il*, *méek'(t)* and *púust*, and intransitive verbs *bin* and *lúub*. These lemmas occur in nearly every recording in the corpus.

3.4. The building of three-member mini-paradigms

In the following examples we can observe three-member mini-paradigms in both verb classes, but with person and aspect omissions:

Table 14. The building of 3-member mini-paradigms with transitive verbs

AGE	LEMMA	TRANSITIVE VERB
2;2	*pul* 'throw'	*pul-eh* (IMP) 'throw it!' *pul-ah* (COMPL) 'I threw it' (= *t-in pul-ah*) *pul-ik* (INCOMPL) 'he throws it' (= *k-u pul-ik*)
	haant- 'eat it'	*haant-eh* (IMP) 'eat it!' *haant-ah* (COMPL) 'I ate it' (= *t-in haant-ah*) *haant teech* (IMP) 'eat it (you)!'
2;3	*méek'* 'hug'	*táas in méek'(-t)-eh* 'bring it A.1S *méek'*:SUBJV.' 'bring it so I can hug it' *méek'-eh míis* (IMP) 'hug the cat!' (= *méek'(-t) le míis-o'*) *man méek'-ah* (NEG A.2S COMPL) 'you didn't hug it' (= *ma' t-a méek'(t)-ah*) *la' in meek'(t)-a'an* (DEICT A1Sg. PART) 'here is my embraced'
2;4	*púust* 'brush clean'	*púust-(l)e iik-o'* (IMP DET N) 'brush it clean from the chili!' (= *púus-t le íik-o'*) *púust u-iik-il* (IMP POSS N) 'brush it clean from the chili!' *púust-(eh)-o'ob* (IMP B.3P/OBJ) 'brush them clean!'

Imperative *-eh* and completive *-ah* are the status suffixes most frequently used to build three-member mini-paradigms of transitive verbs. Next in frequency is the participle (*-a'an*) (see table 12), followed by the incompletive *-ik* and the suffix of third person plural *-o'ob* (Set-B object). Up until 2;2, the most frequent suffixes ocurring with intransitive verbs are *-ih*, the completive B.3S, and the participle *-a(h)-a'an*. At 2;3 the forms used for positional verbs are the incompletive suffix *-tal*, the subjunctive *-Vk,* and the imperative *-en,* as shown in table 15.

Table 15. The building of 3-member mini-paradigms with an intransitive positional verb

AGE	LEMMA	INTRANSITIVE POSITIONAL VERB
2;2	*kul* 'sit down'	*kul-tal* (INCOMPL) 'he is sitting down' (= *t(áan)-u kul-tal*) *kul-ak* (SUBJV) 'he might sit down' (= *ka'ah kul-ak-Ø*) *kul-en* (IMP) 'sit down!'

The first three-member mini-paradigm constructed with both transitive and intransitive verb classes is formed with the root *han* 'eat' at age 2;3, as shown in table 16.

Table 16. A 3-member mini-paradigm constructed with both verb classes

AGE	LEMMA	INTRANSITIVE POSITIONAL VERB
2;3	han 'eat'	haant-eh (TRANS: IMP) 'eat it!' haant-ah (TRANS: COMPL) 'he ate it' (= *t-u haant-ah*) han-en (INTRANS:IMP) 'eat!'

Paradigms based on the suppletive verbs *bin* 'go' and *taal* 'come' are shown below:

Table 17. The building of a 3-member mini-paradigm with irregular intransitive verbs

AGE	LEMMA	SUPPLETIVE VERBS
2;2	bin 'go'	(h)bin-Ø-ih (COMPL-B.3S) 'he went' ko'ox (HORT) 'let's go' bin (INCOMPL) 'I'm going' (= *t(áan)-in bin*)
2;3	bin 'go'	bin-a(h)-a'an (PERF) 'he has gone' *t-*u bin-Ø-ih (COMPL-B.3S) 'he went' (= *(h)bin-ih*) memorized utterance: *tu'ux k-a bin* (INCOMPL) 'where are you going?'

It should be noted that in all paradigms, suffixes are acquired before prefixes, such as Set-A pronouns and aspect auxiliaries, which for certain verb complexes are obligatory.

The first error-free three-member mini-paradigm is based on the intransitive inactive verb *lúub* 'fall' but with the omission of the aspect auxiliary *sáan*.

Table 18. The first error-free 3-member mini-paradigm with an intransitive verb

AGE	LEMMA	INTRANSITIVE INACTIVE VERB
2;2	lúub- 'fall'	(h)lúub-Ø-ih (COMPL-B.3S) 'he fell' (h)lúub-Ø-o'ob (COMPL-B.3P) 'they fell' lúub-uk-(Ø) SUBJV-B.3S) 'they fell a while ago' (= *sáan lúub-uk-Ø*)

At age 2;4 this intransitive and very frequent verb 'fall' also appears with the participle *-a(h)-a'an,* 'fallen', and inflected for subjunctive status, with negative imperative meaning.

(4) lúub-   'fall'
     lúub-a(h)-a'an (PART)   'fallen'   (2;4)
     lúub-uk-ech (SUBJV B.2S)   'don't fall' (= bik lúub-uk-ech!)

Regarding the use of set-A pronouns, there is constant use of first and third persons from age 2;1 on. This is shown in table 19 below.

Table 19. Set-A person markers in Sandi's corpus (lemmas/Set-A clitics)

Set-A pronouns	1;10	1;11	2;0	2;1	2;2	2;3	2;4
iN(w) (1S)	–	1/1	–	2/2	1/1	6/11	–
a(w) (2S)	–	–	–	–	–	2/2	2/2
u(y)/y (3S)	1/1	–	–	3/3	1/1	4/4	1/3

Sandi uses third person Set-B markers productively from age 1;9 on; but she does not use first and second person Set B markers productively until 2;3, as shown in table 20:

Table 20. Set-B person markers in Sandi's corpus (lemmas/Set-B suffixes)

Set-B suffixes	1;9	1;10	1;11	2;0	2;1	2;2	2;3	2;4
-en (1S)	–	–	–	–	–	–	2/3(subj)	–
-ech (2S)	–	–	–	–	–	–	2/3(obj)	1/2(subj)
-Ø-ih (3S)	1/11	4/11	5/8	3/4	2/3	4/7	2/2	1/1
-o'ob (3P) subj.	–	–	1/1	–	–	1/2	–	1/1
-o'ob (3P) obj.						1/1		

The development of aspect auxiliary usage parallels the acquisition of Set A person markers.

Table 21. Acquisition of auxiliaries in Sandi's corpus (continued at page 394)

Auxiliaries of aspect/mood/ temporal modifiers	1;10	1;11	2;0	2;1	2;2	2;3	2;4
Progressive (táan)	1	–	–	–	–	1	–
Completive (t-)	–	1	–	–	–	2	–
Incompletive (k-)	–	–	–	1	–	1	4
Assurative future (he'(el)...-e')	–	–	–	1	–	–	2
Subjunctive (ka'ah)	–	–	–	2	–	–	–
Desiderative (taak)	–	–	–	1	–	–	–
Obligative (yaan)	–	–	–	–	–	1	–

Table 21. continued

Auxiliaries of aspect/mood/ temporal modifiers	1;10	1;11	2;0	2;1	2;2	2;3	2;4
Terminative (*ts'o'ok*)	–	–	–	1	–	–	–
Recent past (*sáan*)	–	–	–	4	–	–	–
Remote past (*uuch*)	–	–	–	–	–	1	–

The fact that the corpus shows the acquisition of set-A pronouns to be parallel to the acquisition of auxiliaries could confirm Lehmann's (1992) argument, namely that the auxiliaries attract the subject markers and are independent elements, rather than prefixes or clitics on the verb. Some examples in Sandi's corpus of age 2;2 are the following:

(5) *táan* (PROG) + *in* (A.1S) = *tin, táan* (PROG) + *u* (A.3S) = *tun*
     ts'o'ok (TERM) + *u* (A.3S) = *ts'u*

Many compound verb complexes are formed with the hortative form *ko'ox* 'let's go', for example: *ko'ox báaxal* 'let's play!'; *ko'ox xok-eh* !'let's read it'; *ko'ox chuk-eh!* 'let's catch it'. Among the subject Set-A pronouns the third person is the most frequent.

Referring to Set-B suffixes, table 6 shows us that third person singular ocurring as subject in clause-final position *-Ø-ih* and in relation with the completive aspect is present from age of 1;9 on, while the plural form *-o'ob* is used more with subject than object meaning. The use of second person singular *-ech* is found first in the incorrect frozen forms *méek'-*ech* with the intended meaning 'hug me' and *éem-*ech* 'let (put) me down', and in combination with the independent pronoun. These forms encode 2S mostly as an object, while first person singular *-en* occurs in the role of subject.

4. Conclusion

We have been examining utterances produced by the child Sandi, whose spontaneous speech was recorded and studied starting at age 1;9. The data show that from this age on there is a constant increase of the spontaneous and productive use of verbs. In most recordings, almost 50% of the total analyzable utterances consist of verbs. There was no verb/word spurt which could be related to the emergence of mini-paradigms.

The first verb suffix to emerge in Sandi's speech was the imperative/subjunctive suffix of transitive verbs, followed by many other status markers in both verb classes.

The period of age 1;9 and 1;10 was defined as the premorphological phase because of the presence of the frozen form *méek'-ech* and memorized inflected verb forms which are at the same time the precursors of the first mini-paradigms.

At age 1;11, we observe strong morphological activity in new verb forms and meanings, which are characteristic of a transition phase. The first three-member mini-paradigms are formed with the suppletive verb *bin* 'go' on the one hand and the verb forms of *mach* 'grasp' on the other. At age 2;1, two-member mini-paradigms increase, there are more and more inflected forms, and the imperative begins to distinguish correctly between both the clause-final (*-eh*) and non-clause-final (*-Ø*) forms. However, in almost all recordings, the imperative suffix of transitive verbs (*-eh*) is used in place of the intransitive suffix *-en*. This error persists in most of the analyzed corpus of Sandi's speech.

In the protomorphological phase (2;1 to 2;4) different two- and three-member mini-paradigms of transitive and intransitive verbs are formed. The new categories involved are: the incompletive status of transitives *-ik*, the subjunctive of inactive intransitives *-Vk* and positionals *-ak*, the completive status of transitive verbs *-ah* and the participle *-a(h)-a'an* of transitive and intransitive verbs.

Among the status markers, the incompletive of transitive and intransitive verbs is increasingly found at 2;1. The completive status appears throughout the analyzed period[9] predominantly with intransitive verbs in the third person singular, while with transitive verbs it begins to appear only at the end of the observed period.

Table 22 shows that the most frequent *-Ø* form, which corresponds to the subjunctive status of transitive verbs in non-clause-final position, is used by Sandi in almost all cases with an imperative meaning; sometimes the bare root is used in the correct position and sometimes not. In the entire corpus, the most frequent formal errors are found in the context of the imperative status of intransitive verbs. In table 22 the overall use of the suffix *-eh* is shown, with intransitive verbs and with transitive verbs non-clause-finally. From age 2;1 on, the use of transitive bare roots with imperative meaning decreases in frequency; at the same time, the use of bare roots followed by an object (non-clause-finally) becomes increasingly more frequent. This indicates that the child is becoming aware of the correct usage of the imperative in transitive verbs.

Table 22. The correct and incorrect (*) use of imperative/subjunctive suffix -∅ ~ -eh in transitive verbs

Verb suffix (gramm. categories)	1;9	1;10	1;11	2;0	2;1	2;2	2;3	2;4
-*∅ (TRANS:IMP clause-final)	6/20	5/13	7/17	8/10	11/20	8/9	–	1/3
-∅ (TRANS:IMP non-clause-final)	–	–	2/8	1/2	8/11	6/6	4/9	6/8
-eh (TRANS:SUBJV/ IMP clause final)	10/27	11/61	19/79	18/59	17/106	21/87	14/58	5/6
-*eh (TRANS:IMP non-clause-final)							2/5	
-*eh (INTRANS:IMP)	3/4	3/13	3/7	2/3	1/1	2/2	2/3	1/4

Among the total verb lemmas of the analyzed corpus (244), 30 belong to the intransitive verb class. Most intransitive verbs involved in the formation of mini-paradigms are inactive intransitives, such as *éem* 'descend', *ok* 'enter', *lúub* 'fall', *wen* 'sleep', as well as *máan* 'pass by' and *bin* 'go'; or are positional verbs, such as *kul* 'sit down' and *wa'al* 'stand up'. The relatively frequent use of completive aspect with inactive intransitive verbs (-∅) could be epiphenomenal of the semantics of the specific verbs and their aspect-marking patterns. All intransitive verbs in the analyzed corpus are inherently completive verbs; with these predicates, -∅ in fact marks completive aspect.

With respect to cross-reference marking of verbal core arguments, at age 2;1 Sandi begins to produce Set-A pronouns, and from age 2;2 on, the data show a slow development of absolutives or Set-B suffixes for first and second persons occurring as subjects.

The acquisition of status and person markers of the Yucatec verb complex which are listed in order of frequency of occurrences within each stage, are summarized in table 23 below.

Evidence of mini-paradigms with derivational forms is found in the occurrence of the applicative suffix -*t* with the verbs: *haan-t* 'eat it', *púus-t* 'brush clean', and with the verbalized noun of *lu'um* 'earth' as *lu'un-t* 'make dirty'.

Table 23. Acquisition of status and person markers in Sandi's corpus

Age	New forms (categories of transitive verbs)	New forms (categories of intransitive verbs)
PREMORPHOLOGY 1;9–1;10	Ø~-eh (SUBJV/IMP)	-*Ø ~ -*eh (IMP); -Ø-ih (B3S COMP) -tal (INCOMPL)
TRANSITIONAL PHASE (new forms with low frequency) 1;11–2;0	-a(h)-a'an (PART) -mah (PERF) -ik (INCOMPL) in (A.1S)	-o'ob (B.3P (Subj) -Vk (SUBJV) -Vl (INCOMPL) -a(h)-a'an (PART)
PROTOMORPHOLOGY 2;1–2;4	-ik (INCOMPL) -ah (COMPL) in (Set-A.1S) -a (Set-A.2S -u (Set-A.3S) -ech (Set-B/OBJ) (AUX)	-Vk (SUBJV) -Vl (INCOMPL) -en (Set B.1S) -ech (Set B.2S) POSITIONALS: -tal (INCOMPL) -en (IMP) -ak (SUBJV)

As has been seen over the length of the study, the child's speech development behaviour progressed from minimal morphological activity at age 1;9 to a phase of great creative activity at 2;1 to 2;4. Starting from a stage characterized by the management of forms principally memorized, she moved into a period of applying incipient morphological rules. Many of the errors of underspecification of verb forms in the premorphological phase, as well as the frozen form *méek'-ech* and its analogical form *éem-ech,* show us the process in which Sandi selects and rejects certain ways of constructing verbal mini-paradigms. By the end of the observed period, it is clear that Sandi's speech is moving in the direction of modular morphology, as seen in the reduced number of uninflected forms and in the increasing frequency and diversification of Sandi's verb inflections. Intransitive inactive verbs are first marked with the completive and subjunctive status linked correctly with Set-B person markers. Obviously the child has begun to abandon forms such as the underspecified imperative forms *-eh* and *-en*. Subject and object markers scarcely appear in the protomorphological phase but become fundamental in the following months, given their relationship with the transitive and intransitive natures of the verbs. Of equal importance, the auxiliaries which are slowly emerging along with the ergative clitics will determine the expression of mood and aspect.

Notes

* I would like to thank Loretta O'Connor, Roberto Zavala, and Jürgen Bohnemeyer for critical reading of an earlier draft of this manuscript.
1. The suffix -*ih* only appears clause-finally.
2. The suffix -*eh* only appears clause-finally.
3. "There is only one auxiliary that occurs with intransitive verbs in the perfect, namely *h*, (alternating with Ø), similarly to the transitive verbs, which allow only *t*- in the perfect." (Krämer and Wunderlich 1999: 444).
4. Many Yucatec suffixes have vowel harmony with the preceding vowel; these are shown with V.
5. "B.3.SG -ih occurs exclusively with intransitive verbs where it has been reanalysed from an older marker of completive status." (Bohnemeyer 1998: 159)
6. "A transitive verb [also] becomes intransitive by means of antipassive...which is realized by vowel lenghthening combined with low tone." (Krämer and Wunderlich 1999: 458).
7. *Koten* is a suppletive form of the verb *taal* (come).
8. Person and aspect marking missing from Sandi's utterances, but clear in the context of the conversation, is restored in the glosses throughout the paper.
9. According to the data on Quiché acquisition, the use of the aspect markers was in constant increase with little variation. The order of acquisition, independent of the three subjects, is the following: the completive aspect, the progressive of intransitive verbs and the intransitive volitives of the verbs 'go' and 'come'. (Pye 1992: 254–255).

References

Bohnemeyer, Jürgen
    1998   Time relations in discourse: Evidence from a comparative approach to Yukatek Maya. Doctoral dissertation, Katholieke Universiteit Brabant, Tilburg.

Bricker, Victoria R., Eleuterio Po'ot Yah, and Ofelia Dzul de Po'ot
    1998   *A Dictionary of the Maya Language as Spoken in Hocabá, Yucatán*. Salt Lake City: The University of Utah Press.

Dressler, Wolfgang U., and Annemarie Karpf
1995   The theoretical relevance of pre- and protomorphology in Language acquisition. *Yearbook of Morphology* 1994: 99–122.

Krämer, Martin, and Dietrich Wunderlich
1999   Transitivity alternations in Yucatec, and the correlation between aspect and argument roles. *Linguistics* 37: 431–479.

Lehmann, Christian
1992   The genesis of auxiliaries in Yucatec Maya. In: André Crouchetière et al. (eds.), *Endangered Languages/Les Langues menacées, Actes du XVe Congrès International des Linguistes.* Vol. 2, 313–316. Quebec: Université Laval.

Lucy, John
1994   The role of semantic value in lexical comparison: Motion and position roots in Yucatec Maya. *Linguistics* 32: 623–656.

Pfeiler, Barbara, and Enrique Martín Briceño
1997   Early verb inflection in Yucatec Maya. In: Katarzyna Dziubalska-Kołaczyk (ed.), *Pre- and Protomorphology in Language Acquisition*, 117–125. (Papers and Studies in Contrastive Linguistics 33.) Poznań: Adam Mickiewicz University.

Pye, Cliff
1992   The acquisition of K'iche' Maya. In: Dan I. Slobin (ed.), *The Crosslinguistic Study of Language Acquisition.* Vol. 3, 221–308. Hillsdale, New Jersey: Lawrence Erlbaum.

Early verb inflection in Lithuanian

Paweł Wójcik

1. Adult oral verb inflection in Lithuanian

Lithuanian is a highly inflected synthetic language belonging to the Baltic branch of Indo-European languages. The only other living language belonging to this group is Latvian.[1] Baltic is closely related to Slavic.

1.1. The Lithuanian verb system[2]

The inflectional system of the Lithuanian verb is based on tense/mood distinctions: There are three moods (indicative, conditional, imperative) and three synthetic tenses (present, past, future[3]). Verbs are inflected for three persons and two numbers. Nominal/pronominal reference is optional. There is no number distinction in the 3rd person, and, except for participles, no gender distinction in verbs.

The markers of categories are fusional endings; in some verbs, tense is additionally marked by means of morphophonemic alternations in the stem.

Aspectual distinctions (imperfective vs. perfective and habitual in the past) are introduced by means of prefixes and suffixes. However, there are no systematic oppositions between perfective and imperfective forms, as there are in the case of the Slavic languages, so that aspect is considered a semi-grammatical category in Lithuanian.

Non-finite categories are represented by the Infinitive and a large set of participles (declinable and indeclinable, marked for tense and voice).

1.2. Inflection

In Lithuanian there are three main conjugations in the present and two conjugations in the past tense (for examples of inflectional paradigms see table A1 in the appendix). The future tense and the marked moods (imperative, conditional) are derived from the Infinitive stem. Thus, normally, the three basic forms one has to know in order to construct the whole paradigm are: the Infinitive, the 3rd person present, and the 3rd person past. Traditionally, verbs are assigned to a conjugation class according to their stem suffix. This stem suffix is most transparent in the 3rd person forms, which consist of bare stems. In the present tense, verbs with the stem suffix *-a* form the 1st conjugation, verbs with the stem suffix *-i* – the 2nd conjugation, and verbs with *-o* – the 3rd conjugation.

In the two conjugations of the past tense, verbs with the stem suffix *-o* (as in the 3rd conjugation in the present tense) form the first (A) conjugation, and verbs with the stem suffix *-ė* – the second (B) conjugation. Verbs belonging to the 1st or the the 3rd conjugation in the present may belong to either conjugation, A or B, in the past. All verbs belonging to the 2nd conjugation in the present have the stem suffix *-o* in the past.

One can thus distinguish five major conjugational classes in Lithuanian (cf. Wójcik and Smoczyńska 1997): 1A, e.g. *supti, supa, supo* 'swing'; 1B, e.g. *kelti, kelia, kėlė* 'lift, pick up'; 2A, e.g. *turėti, turi, turėjo* '1. have, 2. must'; 3A, e.g. *žinoti, žino, žinojo* 'know'; 3B, e.g. *daryti, daro, darė* '1. do, 2. make'.

Verb inflection is, in general, strikingly regular. The endings are superstable markers (cf. Dressler 1995) – they are the same across all synthetic tenses and in the imperative plural: 1sg *-u*, 2sg *-i*; 1pl *-m(e)*; 2pl *-t(e)*.

In some verbs belonging to the 2nd conjugation (*mylėti* 'love'), the forms of the 2sg and the 3rd person are homophonous in the present tense. In others (e.g. *turėti*) – the 2sg and 3rd person forms are differentiated by stress.

1.3. Verb structure

According to their stem structure, Lithuanian verbs are divided into three classes: (i) primary verbs with the structural pattern *root-ending*[4] in all basic forms (*sup-ti*; *sup-a, sup-o*); they may belong to conjugation 1A or 1B; (ii) secondary verbs with the structure *root+suffix-ending* (*aug+in-ti, aug+in-a, aug+in-o* 'to grow sb. or sth.'); these belong to conjugation 1A; and (iii) mixed type verbs (*dar+y-ti, dar-o, dar-ė*; *žin+o-ti, žin-o, žin+oj-o*) which may belong to conjugation 2A, 3A or 3B.

Morphophonemic modifications in primary verbs (consonant infixes and suffixes, quantitative alternations, qualitative gradations) are quite frequent.

As mentioned above, prefixation is one of the devices used to mark aspectual distinctions in Lithuanian. Moreover, prefixes often convey spatial relations (e.g. *dėti* – 'put': *pa-dėti* – 'put down'; *su-dėti* – 'put together'; *į-dėti* – 'put into'); sometimes they also modify lexical meaning (e.g. *pa-dėti* – 'help').

Verbs are negated by means of the prefix *ne-* (also *nebe-* 'no more'). Reflexivity is marked with a mobile affix *s(i)* which takes final position in simplex verbs and moves to the position directly before the root when a verb is prefixed or/and negated, e.g. *supa-si* 'is swinging', *ne-si-supa* 'is not swinging'.

In the case of reflexive forms, the use of a prefix influences the inflection. When reflexive verbs are not prefixed (i.e. when the reflexive affix is at the end of the word), the 1sg and 2sg markers of the 1st and 2nd conjugation of the present tense, as well as the 1sg and 2sg markers of the future tense, change from *-u* and *-i* to *-uo-* and *-ie-* respectively: pres.1sg *sup-u* – rfl. *sup-uo-si*, fut.1sg *sup-s-iu* : rfl. *sup-s-iuo-s*. In the plural of all moods and conjugations the markers have the long vowel *ė*: pres.1sg *sup+a-m(e)* – rfl. *sup+a-mė-s*.

2. The database
2.1. General data description

The source of the data used in this paper are recordings of conversations with a Lithuanian girl, Rūta. Rūta lives in Vilnius and is the only child in the family. Both parents speak standard Lithuanian without dialectal influences. The recordings were taken on a free basis without a fixed schedule, then transcribed by the mother of the child, double-checked and coded in accordance with CHILDES by the author of the paper. At the moment of writing this contribution the data taken between 1;7–2;5 have been fully processed. Over this period about 34.5 hours of recordings were collected.

Table 1. Rūta's data processed

Age	Duration	Productions (Rūta / input)	Verb tokens (Rūta / input)
1;7	35 min.	293 / 383	42 / 304
1;8	1h 5 min.	1018 / 1448	119 / 1156
1;9	3h 45 min	2635 / 3120	416 / 2504
1;10	4h 15 min.	2735 / 2978	897 / 2603
1;11	2h 40 min.	1590 / 1466	925 / 1196
2;0	3 h 15 min.	1796 / 2008	871 / 1553

Table 1. continued

Age	Duration	Productions (Rūta / input)	Verb tokens (Rūta / input)
2;1	3 h 20 min.	1776 / 1410	1291 / 1348
2;2	3 h 45 min.	1861 / 1644	1355 / 1633
2;3	3 h 45 min.	2011 / 1789	1372 / 1716
2;4	3 h 35 min.	2065 / 1467	1303 / 1292
2;5	3 h 10 min.	1809 / 1469	1074 / 1428
Total	34h 20 min	19589 / 19182	9665 / 16733

2.2. Data portion analysed for this contribution

The data portion studied in this paper covers the period from 1;7 till 1;10 when Rūta begins the protomorphological stage of linguistic development. Over that period about 9.5 hours of recordings were taken during which the girl produced 6491 utterances.[5]

The numbers in the third column of table 2. show the number of days in the course of which the recordings were taken. It can easily be seen that both the duration of the data portions and the number of sessions differed for particular months. This fact should be borne in mind especially when analysing the results of calculations given in absolute numbers.

Table 2. Rūta's data used in the paper

Age	Duration	No. of Sessions	Utterances
1;7	35 min.	5	283
1;8	1h 5 min.	15	959
1;9	3h 45 min	19	2576
1;10	4h 15 min.	24	2673
Total	9h 40 min	73	6491

2.3. Verbs singled out for the analysis

Two different kinds of methodological approaches in selecting verbs for analysis were adopted in this paper. In the sections 3–4 and 6, where the process of verb acquisition in general is discussed, we excluded from the analysis: (i) amorphous baby talk forms, onomatopoeia etc., (ii) verbs which could not be clearly identified even if their form and/or syntactic position attested that they might be predicates, and (iii) citations, nursery rhymes, songs etc. Verb forms which occurred in directly preceding utterances of adults (e.g. forms used in answer to yes/no questions, also non-reversals) are not excluded. It seems impossible to judge in advance which of them might have been imitated and which were creative uses. In section 5., on the emergence of paradigms, a few additional restrictions are made.

3. The emergence of verb categories in Rūta[6]

At the age of 1;7 the only categories recorded in the girl's speech were present tense and imperative 2sg (see table A1 in the appendix). In the following month Rūta started using infinitives. At 1;9 past and future tense as well as the first participles emerged. At this time a verb spurt could be observed. Conditionals were first recorded at 1;10; however, they were used very rarely and almost exclusively in the form of 3rd person.

As far as the category of person is concerned, 3rd person and 1sg forms could be found in the first portion of the data studied. 2sg forms were recorded at 1;8 but all of them were non-reversals occurring in answers to yes/no questions. The first correct instance of 2sg was found at 1;10 but it should be emphasised that only at 2;1 the ratio of non-reversals decreased significantly (from 67% at 2;0 to 3% at 2;1). A 1pl form was used already at 1;8 (in a hortative expression) and the number of 1pl increased in the course of the following months. 2pl verbs were rare in the whole corpus.

Most frequent were 3rd person verbs which were commonly used in self-reference and in addressing the interlocutor. As shown in table 3, most of the 3rd person forms referred to non-plural subjects. The conversations were child-oriented, so 1sg forms were more numerous in the girl's utterances than 2sg forms.

Table 3. The number of the 3rd person forms used in singular and plural contexts in Rūta's utterances

	1;7	1;8	1;9	1;10	1;11	2;0	2;1	2;2	2;3	2;4	2;5	Total	(%)
3sg	21	63	198	439	503	437	535	533	567	502	395	4193	94,5
3pl	0	6	10	1	12	17	34	66	43	28	27	244	5,5
Total	21	69	208	440	515	454	569	599	610	530	422	4437	4437

4. Development of the verbal lexicon
4.1. Predecessors of verbs

In the first months of the data one can find a number of onomatopoeias and words belonging to the common Lithuanian baby-talk lexicon (BT)[7] used in predicative function, e.g.: *bū* 'go (by a vehicle)', *puški-puški* 'BT – wash, have a bath'; *popa* 'BT – hurts', *tepu-tepu* 'BT walk'; *babak!* 'BT fall'. Moreover, Rūta used a large number of other BT words and onomatopoeias whose function is not clear (they might also be used in nominal function), e.g. *kar-kar* 'BT 1. to fly; 2. a bird', *niam-niam* 'BT 1. eat; 2. food'; *au-au* '1. bark; 2. dog'; *miau-miau* '1. meow; 2. cat' etc.

BT verbs and onomatopoeias were still present in Rūta's speech at 2;5, e.g. *padarysiu pyp* 'lit. I will do *beep*' when about to press a computer's button.

4.2. Verb production

When studying the development of the lexicon and the problems connected with the emergence of inflection in Lithuanian, one has to be aware of the role of prefixation. In Lithuanian, as mentioned above, prefixes modify the lexical and/or aspectual meaning of verbs. For a long time, however, Rūta tended to omit them or replace them with fillers (section 6.1). Therefore, when the situation is not completely clear, it is often difficult or even impossible to establish beyond doubt what the verb the child wanted to use exactly was.

What is even more important, in the data studied prefixation did not affect inflection – the non-prefixed reflexive forms referred to in section 1.3. were very rare in the parents' speech and practically did not occur in the girl's utterances. Thus, when dealing with the development of the lexicon and the acquisition of paradigms, in addition to the notion of lemma, the term *identical root with the same stem formations*[8] (further on abbreviated to ISF and written in CAPITALS) will be used. An ISF is defined as an abstract representation of a group of verbs sharing a common root and differing only by the presence or absence of prefixes and/or the reflexive marker. For instance, the lemmas: *mokyti* 'teach', *mokyti-s* 'learn', *pa-mokyti* 'teach for a certain period of time' represent the ISF 'MOKYTI'.

Table 4 presents the development of Rūta's active vocabulary. The calculations were done cumulatively, i.e. new items were added to those found in the earlier portions of the corpus. It can easily be seen that between 1;7 and 2;5 Rūta's lexicon developed considerably. The relatively most rapid growth of the girl's vocabulary took place till 1;11, but later on the number of new ISF and lemmas increased considerably.

Table 4. The number of ISF's and lemmas in Rūta's utterances

	1;7	1;8	1;9	1;10	1;11	2;0	2;1	2;2	2;3	2;4	2;5
ISF	8	26	70	116	144	165	188	213	239	254	267
LEMMA	8	27	91	167	223	275	327	380	440	482	513

A very important point of time in the development of Rūta's lexicon was the age of 1;9, when an expansion of derivational processes took place – the difference between the number of ISF's and the number of lemmas became conspicuous for the first time. In the following months the difference gradually became more salient. Their ratio is represented in figure 1, where the results of calculations of the data coming from particular sessions recorded during the four months in question are given.[9]

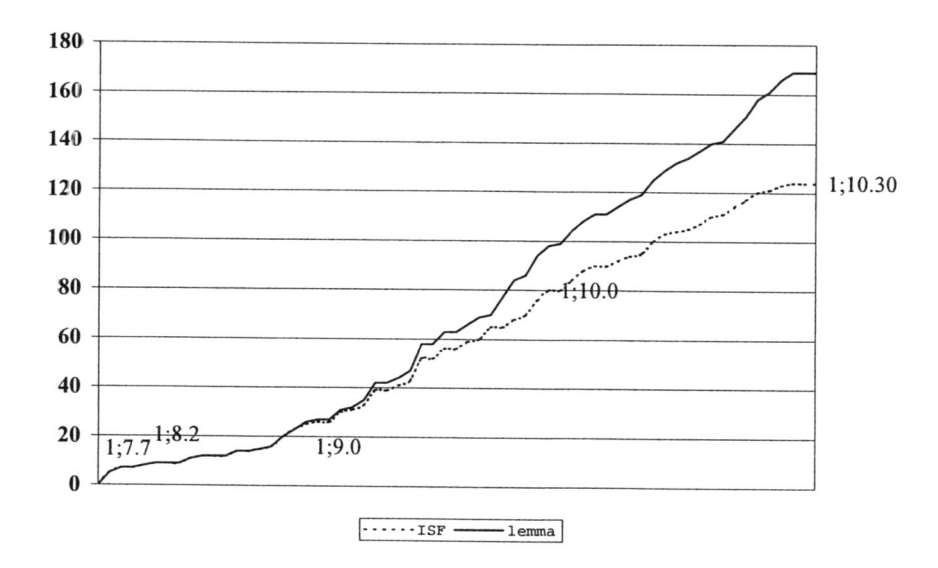

Figure 1. The number of verb ISF's and lemmas in Rūta's utterances

The end of 1;8 and the beginning of 1;9 was the point when a verb spurt could be observed. However, one has to bear in mind that at 1;9 twice the amount of data was collected when compared to the preceding month. On the other hand, the relative frequency of utterances containing a verb (last column of table 5) did not change considerably. Only at 1;10 the amount of utterances with verbs reached one-third of all utterances.

Table 5. The development of Rūta's verbal lexicon till the onset of protomorphology[10]

Age	ISF	Lemmas	Verb token	Utterances	V/Utterance
1;7	8 (8)	8 (8)	42	283	14,8
1;8	23 (26)	24 (27)	118	959	12,3
1;9	68 (70)	87 (91)	419	2576	16,2
1;10	97 (116)	131 (167)	897	2673	33,5

5. The development of paradigms
5.1. Method

When studying the emergence of inflectional paradigms we excluded from the analysis[11] the verb forms occurring in such contexts for which it might be suggested that they were not produced fully spontaneously or that they were modelled in some way on directly preceding adults' utterances. Therefore, the 3rd person verbs used in answers to yes/no questions were excluded, even though such a way of answering questions is a common phenomenon in colloquial Lithuanian. All non-reversals which occurred in analogical contexts were left out of consideration as well. However, the 1sg forms used in answer to yes/no questions asked in 2sg were analysed, since their correct use attested that the girl had mastered the category actively.

The assumption was made that if a verb form was used spontaneously at some age, it should be considered acquired when analysing the later portions of the data and recording another form of the same lemma. Thus, when constructing the list of paradigms given below, the search was done cumulatively.

5.2. Paradigms at 1;7

ISF 8; lemmas 8; verb tokens 42; utterances 283
categories: Present: 1sg, 3rd
             Imperative: 2sg

In the first portion of the data collected at this age (1;7.7) no instances of verb forms were recorded. However, during the following sessions the first instance of a two-member paradigm was recorded:

MOKĖTI 1A 'can-dynamic':
(*ne*)*moku* (7 tokens)
        pres.1sg (the first item at 1;7.14)
        in answer to a yes/no question containing a pres.2sg form;
moka (2 tokens)
        pres.3
        one fully spontaneous (1;7.18) and one classified as modelled; most of other pres.3 forms were used correctly in answer to yes/no questions.

The most frequent verb *miega* 'sleep:pres.3' (15 tokens) was used also in answer to wh-questions.

5.3. Paradigms at 1;8

ISF 23 (26); lemmas 24 (27); tokens 118; utterances 959
categories: Present: 1sg, *2sg, 3rd, 1pl
             Future: *2sg (1 item)
             Imperative: 2sg
             Infinitive

At 1;8 no instances of mini-paradigms fulfilling the criteria mentioned under 5. were found. An unclear instance was MYLĖTI 'love' used erroneously in pres.3 form *mylia* 'love' in answer to a question asked in 2sg. Another form of the paradigm was *myliu* pres.1sg.

5.4. Paradigms at 1;9

ISF 68 (70); lemmas 87 (91); tokens 419; utterances 2576
categories: Present: 1sg, *2sg, 3rd, 1pl

Past: 1sg, *2sg, 3rd
Future: 1sg, *2sg, 3rd
Imperative: 2sg
Infinitive

As mentioned in section 4.2., at 1;9 a verb spurt was observed. In the same month the first 50 verbs were recorded and the first two-member mini-paradigms appeared. Moreover, two three-member mini-paradigms were recorded, one of them (*būti* 'be') suppletive.

5.4.1. Two-member mini-paradigms

1. KALBĖTI 1A 'talk':
    kalba (=*kaba*) pres.3
    kalbėti (=*kabėti*) inf
2. SĖSTI 2A 'sit down':
    sėsk imp.2sg
    sėst inf
3. LAUKTI 1B 'wait':
    laukiu (=*aatiu*) pres.1sg
    palauk imp.2sg
4. NORĖTI 2A 'want':
    noriu (=*noju*) pres.1sg
    (*ne*)*nori* (=*nenionia; nenoja*) pres.3
5. TUPĖTI 2A 'squat':
    tupiu (=*tupu*) pres.1sg
    tupi (=*tipa*) pres.3
6. ŽIŪRĖTI 2A 'watch, look':
    žiūriu (=*ziūju*) pres.1sg
    žiūrėti (=*ziūjėti*) inf
7. EITI 1A 'walk, go':
    neik neg.imp.2sg
    einam (=*eimam*) pres.1pl (hortative)

5.4.2. Three-member mini-paradigms

1. BŪTI 1A 'be':
    yra (=*yja*), NEG: *nėra* (=*nėja*) pres.3
    bus fut.3
    buvo past.3

2. GULĖTI 2A 'lie':
    guliu pres.1sg
    gulėti inf
    guli (=*gulia*) pres.3

5.5. Paradigms at 1;10

ISF 97 (116); lemmas 131 (167); tokens 897; utterances 2673
categories: Present: 1sg, *2sg, 3rd, 1pl
              Past: 1sg, *2sg, 3rd, 1pl
              Future: 1sg, *2sg, 3rd, 1pl
              Conditional: 3rd
              Imperative: 2sg, 1pl
              Infinitive

The age of 1;10 was the point of time when the emergence of new mini-paradigms was particularly spectacular. In the data, one can find a very large amount of new two-member mini-paradigms. Moreover, many new forms of the lemmas already recorded in the earlier portions of the data emerged, which accounts for the rise of new three-and-more-member paradigms. For lack of space only the paradigms with at least three different forms are listed below.

5.5.1. Three-member mini-paradigms

1. GRIŪTI 1A 'fall':
    nenugriūsiu (=*nekakūsiu*) pres.1sg
    nugrius (=*agus*) fut.3
    nugriuvau (=*agavau*) past.3

2. LIPTI 1A 'climb':
   1;9   *lipa* pres.3
   1;10 *lipti* (=*diti*) inf
          lipu pres.1sg

3. LUPTI 1A 'peel':
   1;9   *lupu*
   1;10 *lups* fut.3
          nulupau (=*alupau*) past.1sg

4. MIEGOTI 1A 'sleep':
   1;7   *miega* pres.3
   1;10 *miegos* (=*megos*) fut.3
          miegot (=*magot*) inf

5. TEPTI 1B 'smear':
          patepu (=*atepu*) pres.1sg
          patept (=*atep*) inf
          patepk imp.2sg

6. SĖDĖTI 2B 'sit':
   1;9   *sėdi* pres.3
   1;10 *sėdžiu* (=*sėdu*) pres.1sg
          sėdėk (=*tedėk*) imp.2sg

7. STATYTI 3B 'build; put on':
          statom pres.1pl
          pastatyk (=*patesyk*) imp.2sg
          pastatysiu (=*pastetysiu*) fut.1sg

5.5.2. Larger paradigms

1. DĖTI 1A 'put' – *padėti* '1. ts. PF; 2. help':
          sudedu pres.1sg
          padės fut.3
          padėsiu fut.1sg
          padėk imp.2sg

2. EITI 1A 'walk, go':
   1;9   *neik*
          einam
   1;10 *eini* pres.2sg
          atėjo (=*atejo*) past.3

   ateis fut.3 – *eiti* inf
   eisiu fut.1sg
   eikim (=*eikam, eikim*) imp.2sg
3. VAŽIUOTI 1A 'go (by a vehicle)':
  1;9 *važiuos* (=*teziuos*) fut.3
  1;10 *važiuoja* (=*atioja*) pres.3
    važiuojam (=*aziuojam*) pres.1pl
    važiuosiu (=*vaziuosiu*) fut.1sg
    važiuosim (=*aziuosim*) fut.1pl
4. DUOTI 1B 'give' :
  1;7 *duok*
  1;9 *duoda*
  1;10 *duosi* fut.2sg
    duosiu fut.1sg
    paduotas (?) ptc.pf.pass
    neduodu neg:pres.1sg
5. ŽIŪRĖTI 2B 'watch, look':
  1;9 *žiūriu* (=*ziūju*)
    žiūrėti (=*ziūjėti*)
  1;10 *žiūrėk* (=*ziūjėk*) imp.2sg
    žiūrim (=*ziūjem*) pres.1pl
    žiūri (=*ziūja*) pres.3
6. DARYTI 3B 'do' *padaryti* 't.s. PF.', *uždaryti* 'close', *atidaryti* 'open':
    padaryt (=*padyt*) inf
    uždaryta (=*adedyta*) Ptc.pf.pass
    daro (=*dajo*) past.3
    atidaryk (=*atejėk*) imp.2sg

6. Morphological substitutions

6.1. Fillers

In the data studied, no instance of a whole verb being replaced with a filler was recorded; the occurrence of fillers instead of prefixes as well as of the reflexive affix in prefixed verbs, however, was quite frequent. Two kinds of fillers were involved in verb production:

(i) a neutral vowel *a*; e.g. inf. *a-dėti for *į-dėti* 'put into'; *už-dėti* 'put onto, dress'; *pa-dėti* '1. put; put onto; 2. help'[12],

(ii) reduplication: *de-dėti for pa-dėti.

In the same data portions one can find forms with omitted prefix and with both kinds of fillers alongside correct forms, e.g., at 1;10 the following productions of the perfective verb *nukristi* 'fall' were recorded (adult form in brackets): (i) correct – inf. *nukist, nukist (nukrist)*, past.3 *nukito (nukrito)*; (ii) forms with *a*-filler – **a-kito (nu-krito* or *už-krito)*; (iii) a form with a reduplicated syllable – **ne-ki-kisiu (ne-nu-krisiu)*; (iv) a form with omitted prefix – **ne-Ø-kisiu (ne-nu-krisiu)*.

Reduplicated syllables also replaced the reflexive marker -*si*- in prefixed verbs (cf. 1.3.): fut.1sg **a-ma-mausiu* for *už-si-mausiu* 'put on shoes', past.3 **a-ki-kėlė* for *at-si-kėlė* 'get up'.

6.2. Class shifts

The most conspicuous phenomenon, as far as class shifts are concerned, is that of 2nd conjugation verbs shifting to the 1st conjugation. This could be observed, first of all, in 3rd person forms. The first items of 2nd conjugation verbs were recorded at 1;8. At this age, almost all 3rd person forms took the stem suffix -*a* instead of the expected -*i*, e.g. **noj-a* for *nor-i* 'want'; **sėd-a* for *sėd-i* 'sit'; **gul-ia* for *gul-i* 'lie'; **tup-a* for *tup-i* 'squat' etc. In the following months the relative frequency of errors decreased gradually and it became insignificant after the age of two. However, in the last portions of the processed data isolated instances of shifts still could be spotted (see figure 2.). As mentioned above, the shifts could be found not only within the set of the 3rd person forms. Isolated errors such as 1pl.pres. **ziujam* instead of *žiūrim* 'watch' (1;11) or 1pl.imp. **mamaukiam* instad of *užmaukim* 'put on shoes' were also recorded.

Other kinds of shifts between conjugational classes were sporadic (limited to 2–3 items which often occurred alongside correct forms in the same portions of the data).

The explanation for the occurrence of such shifts should be sought in two factors[13]: First, the 1st conjugation verbs constitute the largest class in Lithuanian. The relative frequency of ISF types in the input and in Rūta's utterances exceeded 70%. 2nd conjugation ISF types were the least numerous: 7% in Rūta and 4.5% in the input, and the relative frequency of the 3rd conjugation IFS was about 18% in both registers. With regard to token frequency the situation was slightly different, as most modal verbs belong to class 2A. Thus, the relative frequency of the 1st and 3rd conjugation ISF tokens was smaller than the frequency of ISF types. The ratio of 2nd conjugation ISF tokens was 15% in Rūta and 14% in the input. Verbs belonging to the 3rd conjugation were not shifted, though. Thus, one may conclude that the relevant factor inducing the shifts was the formal similarity of the 1st and 2nd conjugations.

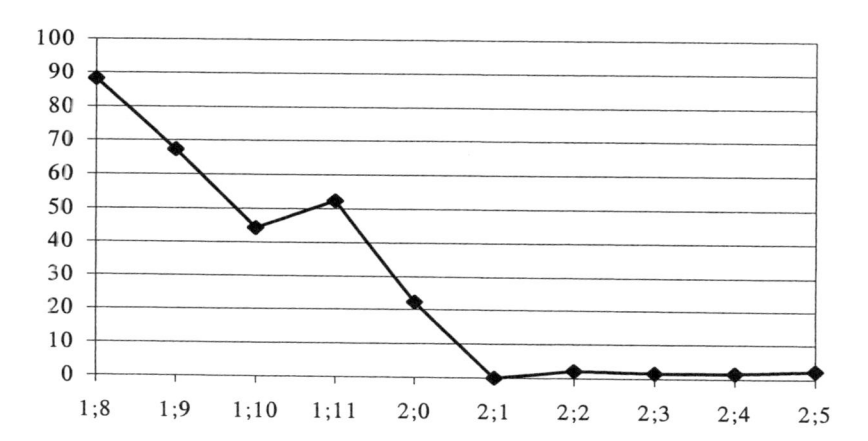

Figure 2. The proportion of shifts from the 2nd conjugation to the 1st conjugation

An additional trigger could be the fact that 2sg and 3rd person forms in the 2nd conjugation have the same endings. The child might have wanted to disambiguate these forms. However, Rūta shifted not only the lemmas in which 2sg and 3rd person are homophonous, but also those in which these categories are differentiated by stress.

Interestingly, in the data studied one can find very few instances of overregularisations involving morphohonemic alternation in primary verbs (all of them after the age of two).

7. Concluding remarks

When analysing the emergence of verb inflection in Lithuanian and comparing it with the development of inflection in other languages, one has to bear in mind that the acquisition of Lithuanian has not been thoroughly studied, and the present contribution is based on the data of one child only. Therefore, one should avoid drawing far-reaching conclusions. One should also take into concern the fact that particular portions of the Lithuanian data differ in their amount which might influence obtained results.

At 1;7 Rūta used very few lexical items. No derivational processes were involved in verb production and the only morphological categories were the present tense and the imperative. Only one two-member mini-paradigm was recorded. In the following month the situation was similar, however the first 2nd conjugation verbs emerged and the process of early pattern selection could be observed: the child shifted the 2nd conjugation verbs to the 1st conjugation, which was a strongly dominant class in the input during the whole period in question.

The age of 1;9 should be considered a point of transition from premorphology to protomorphology. At this time Rūta's active vocabulary expanded and the first prefixed verbs were recorded. Past and present tense emerged and the first two-member mini-paradigms were found. The ratio of utterances containing a verb form was still very small.

At 1;10 the girl was at protomorphological stage. The relative frequency of utterances with verbs increased significantly. A very large number of two-member, as well as the first three-member and larger mini-paradigms were recorded.

Lithuanian is a highly inflected language, therefore one could expect Rūta to become aware of the role of morphology and to apply it earlier than children speaking languages with little morphological marking. This held true for the data studied. By the end of 1;10 almost all categories of the indicative were represented in Rūta's speech. Not all of them, however, were productively and spontaneously used.

As far as the order of acquisition of categories is concerned, one could observe a general tendency in the emergence of unmarked categories before marked ones. The first tense to emerge was the present tense. Past and future forms were used by the girl two months later, and periphrastic constructions with participles (so-called 'compound tenses') did not emerge by the age of 2;6. As for the marked moods, the imperative was frequent in the very first portions of the data, and conditionals were productively used only after the age of two.

Person distinctions emerged before tense distinctions. 3rd person and 1sg forms were recorded already at 1;7. 2sg forms were used relatively early as well, however, till the end of the second year of life most of them were non-reversal errors occurring in answers to yes/no questions.

The first form of plural emerged already at 1;8 and in the following months the number of plurals gradually increased. It has to be marked, however, that during the period under investigation they were used only in modal (mainly hortative) or modelled utterances.

Appendix

Table A1. Inflection of the Lithuanian verb[14]

PRESENT (inflection based on the present stem)

	1 *supti*		2 *turėti*		2 *mylėti*		3 *daryti*	
	singular	plural	singular	plural	singular	plural	singular	plural
1. ps	sup-u	sup+a-m(e)	tur-iu	tur+i-m(e)	myl-iu	myl+i-m(e)	dar+a-u	dar+o-m(e)
2. ps	sup-i	sup+a-t(e)	tur-i	tur+i-t(e)	myl-i	myl+i-t(e)	dar+a-i	dar+o-t(e)
3. ps	sup+a		tur+i		myl+i		dar+o	

PAST (inflection based on the past stem)

	A *supti*		B *daryti*	
	singular	plural	singular	plural
1. ps	sup+a-u	sup+o-m(e)	dar+ia-u	dar+ė-m(e)
2. ps	sup+a-i	sup+o-t(e)	dar+e-i	dar+ė-t(e)
3. ps		sup+o		dar+ė

IMPERATIVE (inflection based on the Infinitive stem: marker -k(i)-)

	supti		*daryti*	
	singular	plural	singular	plural
1. ps		sup-ki-m(e)		dary-ki-m(e)
2. ps	sup-k	sup-ki-t(e)	dary-k	dary-ki-t(e)

FUTURE (inflection based on the Infinitive stem: marker -s(i)-)

	supti		*daryti*	
	singular	plural	singular	plural
1. ps	sup-s-iu	sup-si-m(e)	dary-s-iu	dary-si-m(e)
2. ps	sup-s-i	sup-si-t(e)	dary-s-i	dary-si-t(e)
3. ps	sup-s		dary-s[15]	

Table A2. The distribution of verb forms in Rūta's utterances

	1;7	1;8	1;9	1;10	1;11	2;0	2;1	2;2	2;3	2;4	2;5	TOTAL
PRESENT												
1SG	7	9	40	98	58	88	87	111	145	89	102	834
2SG		3	16	22	4	1	25	56	21	81	58	287
3	21	69	169	286	348	337	363	438	373	325	277	3006
1PL		1	2	6	12	8	16	36	39	55	24	199
2PL						2						2
Total	28	82	227	412	422	436	491	641	578	550	461	4328
PAST												
1SG			3	15	27	28	45	28	18	55	46	265
2SG			3	6	2	2	7	10	11	13	14	68
3			30	57	76	72	113	51	84	126	93	702
1PL				3	9	4	3	16	6	11	16	68
2PL											1	1
Total	0	0	36	81	115	106	168	105	119	205	170	1105
FUTURE												
1SG			2	30	99	68	113	97	80	106	54	649
2SG		1	3	5	1		1	4	3	4	2	24
3			9	101	90	44	91	97	148	75	46	701
1PL				12	17	18	28	28	44	40	11	198
2PL												
Total	0	1	14	148	207	130	233	226	275	225	113	1572
CONDITIONAL												
1SG						1				1		2
2SG										1		1
3				11	1	1	2	13	6	4	7	45
1PL								1				1
2PL												
Total	0	0	0	11	1	2	2	14	6	4	9	49
IMPERATIVE												
2SG	14	28	97	146	103	92	205	176	183	181	177	1402
1PL				5	2			1				8
2PL							1			3		4
Total	14	28	97	151	105	92	206	177	183	184	177	1414
INFINITIVE												
Total			8	37	75	33	57	98	137	129	99	88	761

Table A2. continued

	1;7	1;8	1;9	1;10	1;11	2;0	2;1	2;2	2;3	2;4	2;5	TOTAL
PARTICIPLES												
Total			2	19	40	30	34	11	17	9	19	181
'galima'												
Total			3		2	18	59	44	65	27	37	255
TOKEN	42	119	416	897	924	871	1291	1355	1372	1303	1074	9664

Notes

1. The acquisition of Latvian has been studied by Velta Rūķe-Draviņa (see Rūķe-Draviņa 1982 for references).
2. Authors of contemporary grammars of Lithuanian differ in their opinion as to the number of grammatical categories of the verb and to the way of classifying particular categories. Here, an approach similar to that of Paulauskienė (1979) is taken. For a more detailed description of the Lithuanian verb system see Ambrazas et. al. (1997).
3. Most of Lithuanian grammars include into the system of tenses the fourth synthetic tense – past frequentative (based on the Infinitive stem and denoting habituality). The category did not occur in the data studied.
4. Or *stem – suffix* in the 3rd person.
5. Utterance – a production with at least one identifiable unit.
6. For a more detailed analysis see Wójcik (1998, 2000).
7. See also Wójcik (1994).
8. The term was proposed by Wolfgang U. Dressler during the workshop of Pre- and Protomorphology (Berlin, 2000). In Wójcik (2000) the term "lemma" is used in the meaning of ISF, and the term "lexeme" is used for "lemma".
9. For the sake of lucidity only the dates of the first and last sessions are given.
10. The columns "ISF" and "lemmas" present the numbers of units in particular months and cumulative results (in brackets).
11. In addition to the instances listed in section 2.3.
12. The *a*-filler was also used instead of prepositions.
13. See Wójcik and Smoczyńska (1997); Wójcik (2000).
14. Only the categories which will be discussed in the paper are shown.

References

Ambrazas, Vytautas, Emma Geniusiene, Aleksas Girdenis, Nijole Sliziene, Dalija Tekoriene, Adele Valeckiene, and Elena Valiulyte (eds.)
1997 *Lithuanian Grammar*. Vilnius: Baltos lankos.

Dressler, Wolfgang U.
1995 Inflectional morphology: Theoretical preliminaries. Paper presented at the first Workshop on Pre- and Protomorphology in Language Acquisition, Vienna, February 1995.

Paulauskienė, Aldona
1979 *Gramatinės lietuvių kalbos veiksmažodžio kategorijos* [Grammatical verb categories in the Lithuanian language]. Vilnius: Mokslas.

Rūķe-Draviņa, Velta
1982 *No pieciem mēnešiem līdz pieciem gadiem* [From five months to five years]. Stokholm: The Baltic Scientific Institute in Scandinavia.

Wójcik, Paweł
1994 Some characteristic features of Lithuanian baby talk. *Linguistica Baltica* 3: 71–86.

Wójcik, Paweł
1998 The acquisition of the category of person in the verb by a Lithuanian child. *Linguistica Baltica* 7: 26–38.

Wójcik, Paweł
2000 *The Acquisition of Lithuanian Verb Morphology: A Case Study*. Krakow: Universytet Warszawski.

Wójcik, Paweł, and Magdalena Smoczyńska
1997 Acquisition of Lithuanian verb morphology: A preliminary report. In: Dressler, Wolfgang U. (ed.), *Studies in Pre- and Protomorphology*, 83–100. Wien: Verlag der Österreichischen Akademie der Wissenschaften.

Subject index

analogy, xiv–xxv, 32, 34, 74, 79, 252, 258–260, 286, 313, 337, 344–345, 373
  patterns, xix, 115
  proportional, 286–287
  surface, xxi, 115
bare
  root, 36, 384–386, 388–390, 395
  stem, 175–176, 178, 187–189, 194–195, 402
biuniqueness, xvii, 353
blind alley, viii–ix, xviii, 116
child directed speech, 46, 197, 353
class shift, 157–158, 252, 258–261, 275, 285, 312, 339–344, 414
complexity, xiv, xviii–xix
  grammatical, ix
  morphological, xix, 43
  of verb inflection, 53
  paradigm, xii
  syntactic, xxiii, 60, 138
constructivist model, ix, xvii
connectionist model, xi–xiii, 351
critical mass, vii, xx, 38, 45, 74, 80, 118, 199, 313
demarcation, 137
  criteria, 138, 140
  of phases, 302
  of pre- and protomorphology, xxv, 32, 71, 131, 142, 212
  of preinflectional and inflectional stage, 113
  of stages, 31, 115, 131, 140, 152
developmental spurt, 71, 261, 303
diversity
  in patterns of grammaticization, 90
  inflectional, 135

language-specific, viii
lexical, xx, xxiii, 302, 305, 313
morphological, xxiv, 58, 79
of inflected forms, 135
of utterances, 74
of verb forms, 21–22, 111
of verb types, 64
extragrammatical
  operation, xv, xviii, 115–116, 287
  process, 32
filler, xv, xxii–xxiii, 14, 34, 103, 271–272, 275, 278, 357, 362–363, 406, 413–414
formulaic, 56, 60, 191, 278, 280, 309, 313, 333, 340, 365–366
  child, 57, 98
  expressions, 247, 327, 330, 348
  forms, 68, 95, 150, 191, 242, 276, 281, 330, 333, 335, 342
  learner, 63
  learning, 66
  learning strategy, 76, 271
  utterances, 5
frozen forms, 5–6, 31, 34, 37, 56–57, 95, 98, 276–277, 306, 332, 346, 358, 385, 394–395
grammaticization, 90, 114
holophrase, 90, 98, 372
homophony, xvii–xviii, 3, 21, 283, 285, 289, 308
iconicity, xv, xvii, xxvi, 344
imitation, xxii, 31, 56, 57, 68, 90, 139, 144, 242, 280, 309, 313, 328, 333, 363, 365–366, 382
imitative
  form, 150, 191, 276, 281, 327, 335, 386, 405

422 Subject index

formation, 36
learning, 89, 90, 302
strategy, 271
indexicality, xv
inflectional imperialism, 287
inflectional spurt, 35, 147
infinitive
    bare, 173, 277
    optional, 152
    root, 284–285, 346
innate
    morphology, xiv
    parameters, vii
    learning devices, xii
    linguistic predispositions, xiii
    modules, xiii, xviii
    morphological principles, xiv
input, viii–ix, xiv, xviii, xx, 34, 38,
        45–47, 72, 80, 89, 108, 211, 242,
        261, 352
    category, 89, 97, 239
    change, 91
    characteristics, 199, 283
    dependence, xx, 369, 372
    frequency, xiii, xx, xxii, 9, 21,
        45–48, 74, 91, 196–198, 270,
        283, 297, 310, 352, 356, 368–
        369, 371, 373, 414, 416
    pattern, 34, 47
    property, ix, 49
    structure, 44–45, 48
    verb, 61, 73, 80, 96, 104, 113,
        118, 243, 260, 277, 284, 369,
        390, 403, 415
item-based learning, vii–ix
learnt by rote (see rote-learned)
lexical spurt, 361, 366, 369
MLU (mean length of utterance), 4,
        5, 14, 30, 32, 47, 95, 175, 209,
        271, 303
morphological richness, xvi–xvii,
    xxiv, 135

multi-word utterance, 196
Natural Morphology, xv, xxi, 386
naturalness, ix, 22, 371
    principles, xviii, 373
one-word
    phase, viii
    stage, xxiii, 5, 345
    utterance, 5, 33, 60, 176, 208,
        358, 362
onomatopoeia, xxii, 33, 138–140,
        177, 179, 328, 404, 406
onomatopoeic
    element, 6
    form, 32, 98
    reduplication, xv, xxii, 329
    strategy, 33
    word, 358
overgeneralisation, xviii–xix, xxiii–
        xxv, 15, 20, 22, 39, 74–76, 78,
        80, 106, 133, 138, 153, 158, 205,
        215, 216, 219, 224, 230, 233–
        234, 285–287, 373
overregularisation, 158, 415
parameter-setting, 351
pattern
    extraction, viii, xxi
    recognition, xxiii, xxv
    selection, ix, xviii–xix
poverty
    in inflection, 136
    morphological, xvii
    syntactic 135
precursor
    of grammatical rules, xviii, 115–
        116, 287
    of miniparadigms, xxiv, 61, 68,
        70–71, 145, 254, 365, 385,
        395
    of paradigmatic contrasts, 61
    of verbs, 6, 176–178, 327
    of verbal morphology, 11

Subject index 423

predecessors of verbs, xxii, 33–34, 57, 98, 138, 208, 357, 406
pro-drop, 53, 240
  language, 106, 239, 253
productivity, xii, xxvi, 8–9, 27, 92, 131, 192, 298, 352
  criteria, 108–111, 117
  inflectional, 31–32, 36, 41, 43, 97, 108–111, 241
  morphological, 73, 108, 151, 287
  of constructions, 91
  of inflectional categories, 107
  of inflectional classes, 55, 354
reduplication, xxii, 33, 99, 103, 115–116, 359, 381, 414
reduplicative, ix, 328–329
rote-learned, xviii, xxiv, 8, 10–11, 19–20, 33, 63, 73, 78–79, 81, 115–116, 136, 145, 147, 152, 154–157, 159, 247, 259, 269, 271, 275–276, 287, 340, 346–347, 353, 357–358, 370, 372
rote-learning, vii, xii–xiii, xxii, xxiv, 53, 73, 78–80, 344
rote-learnt (see rote-learned)
saliency, ix, xix, 196–197, 199
self-organization, ix, xv, xviii
self-organizing
  system, 119
  process, xviii
spurt
  in lemmas, 64
  in miniparadigms 14, 20, 22
  of form contrasts, 66
  quantitative, vii
stage model, 92, 210, 224
stage
  developmental, 1, 18, 20, 27, 32–34, 91, 117–118, 131, 136–137
  functional, 113
  inflectional, 113–114

  of transitional morphology, 158
  optional infinitive, 196, 211
  prefunctional, 113–114
  preinflectional, 114
  root-infinitive, xviii
substitution, xxii, xxv, 40
  analogical, 260–261
  category, 251, 258, 260
  error, 39, 41, 44
  lexical, 48
  morphological, 157, 258, 284, 289, 413
  phonological, 271
suppletive, 59–60, 63, 65–66, 68, 244, 252, 256–257, 260, 289, 310, 336–337, 339, 348, 354, 360, 368, 370, 387, 389, 392, 395, 410
syntactic spurt, 260, 272
transition
  non-finite to finite, 225, 229
  period, xxiv, 53, 73–74, 356, 361, 362, 364, 372
  phase, 72, 137, 142, 159, 235, 395, 397
  pre- to protomorphology, 32, 58, 64–67, 73–74, 78–79, 152, 182, 235, 239, 260, 297, 302, 313, 351, 360, 364–365, 372, 386, 416
  preinflectional to inflectional, 114
  stage, 37, 41, 137
transparency, xxvi–xxvii, 199, 244, 261
  conceptual, 211
  morphosemantic, xvi, 256, 372–373
  morphotactic, xv, xviii, 364
  semantic, 198
truncation, xv, 115–116, 189, 194
two-word

construction, 99
sentence, 364
stage, 5
utterance, 4, 60, 362, 366, 372
uniformity, xxvi, 77
universal principles, 77

Universal Grammar, xiv, 115, 351
usage-based model, viii, x–xiii, 89–90, 117
verb spurt, xx, xxiv, 14, 64, 181, 195, 245, 260, 373, 394, 405, 408, 410